Globalization and the Politics of Development in the Middle East

Second Edition

In a new edition of their book on the economic development of the Middle East and North Africa, Clement Moore Henry and Robert Springborg reflect on what has happened to the region's economy since 2001. How have the various countries in the Middle East responded to the challenges of globalization and to the rise of political Islam, and what changes, for better or for worse, have occurred? Utilizing the country categories they applied in the previous book and further elaborating the significance of the structural power of capital and Islamic finance, they demonstrate how over the past decade the monarchies (as exemplified by Jordan, Morocco, and those of the Gulf Cooperation Council) and the conditional democracies (Israel, Turkey, and Lebanon) continue to do better than the military dictatorships or "bullies" (Egypt, Tunisia, and now Iran) and "the bunker states" (Algeria, Iraq, Libya, Sudan, Syria, and Yemen).

CLEMENT MOORE HENRY is Professor of Government at the University of Texas at Austin. His publications include *The Politics of Islamic Finance* (2004), coedited with Rodney Wilson, and *The Mediterranean Debt Crescent: A Comparative Study of Money and Power in Algeria, Egypt, Morocco, Tunisia, and Turkey* (1996); *Images of Development: Egyptian Engineers in Search of Industry* (2nd ed. 1994); and *Politics in North Africa: Algeria, Morocco, Tunisia* (1970).

ROBERT SPRINGBORG is Professor of National Security Affairs at the Naval Postgraduate School. Until August 2008 he held the MBI Al Jaber Chair in Middle East Studies at the School of Oriental and African Studies in London, where he also served as Director of the London Middle East Institute. Professor Springborg's publications include *Politics in the Middle East* (1999), coauthored with James A. Bill, *Mubarak's Egypt: Fragmentation of the Political Order* (1989), and *Family Power and Politics in Egypt* (1982).

The Contemporary Middle East 1

Series editor: Eugene L. Rogan

Books published in **The Contemporary Middle East** series address the major political, economic, and social debates facing the region today. Each title comprises a survey of the available literature against the background of the author's own critical interpretation, which is designed to challenge and encourage independent analysis. While the focus of the series is the Middle East and North Africa, books are presented as aspects of a rounded treatment, which cuts across disciplinary and geographic boundaries. They are intended to initiate debate in the classroom, and to foster understanding amongst professionals and policy-makers.

Books in this Series:

Globalization and the Politics of Development in the Middle East

Second Edition

Clement Moore Henry
University of Texas at Austin

Robert Springborg
Naval Postgraduate School

CAMBRIDGE
UNIVERSITY PRESS

CAMBRIDGE UNIVERSITY PRESS
Cambridge, New York, Melbourne, Madrid, Cape Town, Singapore,
São Paulo, Delhi, Dubai, Tokyo, Mexico City

Cambridge University Press
32 Avenue of the Americas, New York, NY 10013-2473, USA

www.cambridge.org
Information on this title: www.cambridge.org/9780521737449

© Cambridge University Press 2010

First published 2010

Printed in the United States of America

A catalog record for this publication is available from the British Library.

Library of Congress Cataloging in Publication data

Henry, Clement M., 1937–
Globalization and the politics of development in the Middle East / Clement M.
Henry, Robert Springborg. – 2nd ed.
  p.   cm. – (The contemporary Middle East)
ISBN 978-0-521-51939-7 (hardback) – ISBN 978-0-521-73744-9 (pbk.)
1. Middle East – Economic conditions – 1979– 2. Middle East – Politics
and government – 1979– 3. Globalization. I. Springborg, Robert.
II. Title. III. Series.
HC415.15.H463 2010
338.956–dc22   2010026375

ISBN 978-0-521-51939-7 Hardback
ISBN 978-0-521-73744-9 Paperback

Contents

Figures

Tables

Preface to the second edition

Writing a second edition a decade after the first provides ample time to reflect on our original work. By and large it seems to have stood the test of time, even if some assumptions and implied prognoses were off the mark. We overestimated both the magnitude and the consequences of the financial squeeze on the MENA. Excess global liquidity, which caused investors to seek out higher rates of return in emerging markets, combined with substantial increases in hydrocarbon prices, generated financial resources for the region in excess of what we anticipated. Pressures for governments to become more transparent and accountable were correspondingly less. But so, too, did we underestimate the creativity of MENA governments in combining focused governance reforms with persisting authoritarianism, so that they maintained or even enhanced revenue flows without democratizing. We also did not foresee the dramatic emergence within the regional and global economies of the Arab Gulf states and the increased speed and depth of change to their domestic political economies. Iran's collapse into praetorianism was likewise not anticipated. On the other hand, the basic finding of the first edition, which was that the MENA countries can be categorized according to regime types and that those types in turn determine capacities to respond to the threats and opportunities of globalization, has been borne out. Over the past decade the region's worst performers have been the most repressive and the best performers the most democratic, with others similarly arrayed as predicted. So, too, has the claimed relationship between financial sector autonomy and civil society capacity been demonstrated to obtain.

Readers familiar with the previous edition will notice that this one is considerably larger. That is due not just to updating, but to a remarkable increase in available comparative economic and governance data over the past decade, a phenomenon that has paralleled and contributed to economic globalization. We have drawn on this data to evaluate propositions contained in the first edition and to formulate new ones. We have also used it to enrich analyses of specific countries. Discerning readers will notice a substantial increase in tables and figures, which we hope will help both to explicate and to reinforce our arguments that link globalization, regime, and civil society types and capacities with political and economic outcomes.

Instead of imposing a common set of transliteration rules, we have preferred to keep the spellings of proper names as commonly used for the individuals in question.

In the preparation of this edition we have accumulated yet more debts of gratitude. Useful advice and information was provided by Richard Boocock, Graham Boyce, Jason Brownlee, Charles Buderi, Matt Buehler, Christopher Davidson, Mahmoud El-Gamal, Bob Looney, David Lubin, Mahmoud Muhieldin, Robert Parks, Paul Rivlin, M. Saïd Saâdi, Stuart Schaar, John Sfakianakis, Ibrahim Warde, and Eckart Woertz. Our intern, Hela Mehr, helped download data and prepare figures and tables. The United States Institute of Peace supported Clement Henry's brief trips in North Africa in 2007–10, as did a semester leave from the University of Texas at Austin and a supplementary grant from the American Institute for Maghrib Studies. The Naval Postgraduate School provided Robert Springborg with a travel grant and a quarter's leave that facilitated both data gathering and writing. The London Middle East Institute at SOAS kindly hosted him as a Research Fellow in 2009 and 2010. As was the case with the first edition, our spouses, Elizabeth Bouri and Anne-Marie Drosso, both of whom have personal and professional interests in the Middle East, assisted in various ways in the gathering and interpretation of data and in its presentation. We are grateful to all.

Preface and acknowledgments

We were commissioned by the editors of the series in which this volume appears to produce a manuscript on the politics of economic development in the Middle East and North Africa (MENA). In fact we have written a book that seeks to describe and explain the responses of that region to the threats and opportunities posed by economic globalization, the driving force of change not only for these, but for virtually all economies in the developing, not to say developed, world. We have sought to avoid the normative debate over the phenomenon. We have also not speculated on the possible consequences for the MENA of increasing criticism of and resistance to globalization and its standard bearers. We have assumed that at least for the foreseeable future this criticism and resistance are unlikely to fundamentally alter the course or momentum of economic globalization, whatever its consequences for the rhetoric and actions of such standard bearers as the IMF and World Bank.

We are convinced that globalization should be the starting point for understanding economic change in the region. It is the primary thesis against which all countries of the region are struggling to form responses. The widely perceived analogy, at least in the MENA, between today's globalization and yesterday's colonialism provides an analytical framework with which to understand not only the region's response as a whole to 'awlama (the newly coined Arabic term for globalization), but also the strategies employed by individual countries and particular social forces within them. Similar to the colonial dialectic which pitted the region's traditional, radical, and revolutionary nationalists against imperialism, the "globalization dialectic" is now generating three distinct stances contending with what is simultaneously a threat and an opportunity, both politically and economically. Aspiring globalizers contend with reactive moralizers in search of new syntheses that might promote the needed reforms in the name of the authentic Islam.

We have examined the structures of state and civil society that channel the reactions to globalization of different social forces. Particularly vital for civil society is the role of financial systems, the private components of which generate the material resources that sustain civil society. We have, therefore, paid particular attention to those financial systems and the constraints they impose upon political elites while providing them with opportunities to benefit from globalization.

Our investigations suggest a direct correlation between economic performance and the degree of democracy that obtains in any given national political economy in this region. The more open and liberal a polity, the more effective has been its economy in responding to globalization. Additionally encouraging from the perspective of democratization is that the capacity to formulate and execute effective national responses clearly depends not just on the states of the region, but on their respective civil societies as well. Those states that have waged literal or metaphorical wars against their civil societies and the autonomous capital that is both the cause and product of civil society can and sometimes do formulate economic textbook responses to globalization. Those responses, however, are dead letters in the absence of implementation capacity, which only a dynamic civil society appears to be able to provide. On the other hand, those states with comparatively robust civil societies appear to have less autonomy in formulating economic policies, but the greater implementation capacity their civil societies provide more than makes up for policy deficiencies.

Our findings may be read to imply that liberalization and democratization, were they to proceed, would benefit MENA economies. Indeed, they suggest that in the absence of more open, liberal polities, MENA economies are likely to stagnate in comparison to their global competitors. They further suggest that while many responses to globalization are possible, the phenomenon itself will generally support the opening of political economies, even if within a framework of Islamicization. This in turn implies a "win–win" situation, whereby globalization induces political changes that are in turn beneficial for national economic growth. But it may also inspire craftier and more intrusive forms of authoritarianism.

It is worth remembering that, as the eminent MENA economist Charles Issawi once noted, Murphy's Law applies with a vengeance in this region of the world. Bearing that in mind, we will shy away from predicting that globalization will work wonders for the political economies of the region and observe only that the potential for it to do so is there. As we hope the book demonstrates, moreover, there are obstacles aplenty to the realization of the rosy scenario in all the countries of the region, whether they are praetorian republics, monarchies, or democracies.

Finally, our observations reflect a cumulative total of about seven decades of intermittent teaching and fieldwork in the MENA, and we wish to thank our many friends and acquaintances in the region for generously sharing their insights with us over the years. They are too numerous to name and of course bear no responsibility for the conclusions we have drawn in this book. However, Hasan Ersel, Chief Economist of Yapi Kredit Bankası, deserves special mention for his timely responses to email that gave us a better understanding of the Istanbul Stock Exchange. Clement Henry also wishes to thank Abdelmounaim Dilami and Nadia Salah, the publisher and editor-in-chief, respectively, of *L'Economiste*, for their extraordinary hospitality during the summer of 1998 as well as their refreshing insights into Morocco's political economy.

We have also benefited from the advice and constant encouragement of Eugene Rogan and the critical reviews of two anonymous readers for Cambridge University Press. We are grateful, too, for comments from Catherine Boone, Bradford Dillman, Ira Lapidus, and Alan Richards. We are especially indebted to Anne-Marie Drosso, former student of one of us and wife of the other. As a political economist and multilingual author par excellence, her insights and editorial suggestions vastly improved both the content and the style of the book. The other spouse, Elizabeth Bouri, is an information specialist who greatly facilitated our online research efforts with the Arab Social Science Research website (www.assr.org), which she has designed especially for the needs of social scientists.

Our collaboration in drafting and redrafting our manuscript has been exemplary across three continents – Australia, the Middle East, and North America – facilitated by computer support from Macquarie University and the University of Texas at Austin. We particularly wish to thank John Telec, Paul Lyon, and William Bova for their advice and troubleshooting. We also gratefully acknowledge Macquarie's award of a Visiting Research Scholarship to Clement Henry that enabled us to spend a few weeks together in Sydney during July and August of 1999. A special word of thanks is due to an old friend and colleague, Andrew Vincent, director of the Macquarie University Centre for Middle East and North African Studies, for making these weeks so productive and enjoyable. Henry also wishes to acknowledge an earlier grant from the University of Texas at Austin that enabled him to begin drafting some chapters in the spring of 1998 and a grant from the American Institute of Maghrib Studies for fieldwork in Morocco and Tunisia during the summer of 1998. Finally, we thank Sherry Lowrance and Ji-Hyang Jang, doctoral students in political science at the University of Texas, for assembling and checking some of the economic data, and other members of Henry's political economy seminar, especially Sunila Kale, for their editorial help.

Glossary

AKP	Adalet ve Kalkınma Partisi, Justice and Development Party (Turkey)
APICORP	Arabian Petroleum Investments Corporation
Aramco	Arabian-American Oil Company
BAM	Bank Al-Maghrib, Morocco's central bank
bonyads	charitable foundations (Iran), becoming revolutionary business conglomerates after 1979
BDL	Banque du Liban (Lebanon's central bank)
CBRT	Central Bank of the Republic of Turkey
CGEM	Confédération Générale des Entreprises du Maroc
CIM	contract-intensive money (the amount of money held inside a banking system, divided by the total money supply M2)
DRS	Département du Renseignement et Sécurité, Algeria's military security agency
ECU	European Currency Unit, a basket of European currencies, renamed the Euro in 1999
ESCWA	Economic and Social Commission for Western Asia (United Nations)
EU	European Union
FDI	foreign direct investment
FIS	Front Islamique du Salut (Islamic Salvation Front), outlawed Algerian opposition party
GATS	General Agreement on Trade in Services
GATT	General Agreement on Tariffs and Trade
GCC	Gulf Cooperation Council (Bahrain, Kuwait, Oman, Qatar, Saudi Arabia, United Arab Emirates)
GDP	gross domestic product – "the total output of goods and services for final use occurring within the domestic territory of a given country" (World Bank)
GNP	gross national product – GDP "plus any taxes (less subsidies) that are not included in the valuation of

	output plus net receipts of primary income (employee compensation and property income) from nonresident sources" (World Bank)
GOE	Government of Egypt
GTZ	Deutsche Gesellscaft für Technische Zusammenarbeit, official German agency for technical assistance
HDI	Human Development Index
HHI	Herfindahl-Hirschman Index, measuring the degree of concentration of an industry as the sum of the squares of the market shares of its competing firms
IIT index	intra-industry trade index
IMF	International Monetary Fund
infitah	"opening" of the economy to international markets, along lines suggested by Egyptian president Anwar Sadat in 1974
ISCI	Islamic Supreme Council of Iraq
ISE	Istanbul Stock Exchange
ISI	import substitution industrialization
KDP	Kurdish Democratic Party, Iraqi party led by Barzani clan
KFH	Kuwait Finance House
LE	Egyptian pound
M2	measure of the money supply that comprises transferable deposits and currency outside the banking system and time, savings, and foreign currency deposits
makhzan	Moroccan king's household and ruling center
mamlukes	medieval Egyptian military ruling class, recruited from Circassian slaves; the term is also used by Egyptian critics to denote high-ranking officers and security officials in contemporary Egypt and to associate them with medieval practices
MEED	Middle East Economic Digest (London)
MENA	Middle East and North Africa
MNC	multinational corporation
mudir	director, manager
NGO	nongovernment organization
ODA	Official Development Assistance
OECD	Organization for Economic Cooperation and Development
ONA	Omnium Nord-Africain, a Moroccan conglomerate
OPEC	Organization of Petroleum Exporting Countries

PA or PNA	Palestinian Authority or Palestinian National Authority
PJD	Parti de Justice et Développement, Moroccan Islamist party
PKK	Parti Karkerani Kurdistan, Kurdistan Workers' Party
PLO	Palestine Liberation Organization
PUK	Patriotic Union of Kurdistan, Iraqi party headed by Jalal Talebani
S&P	Standard and Poor's, a business information firm that rates countries and enterprises worldwide for their credit-worthiness and financial performance
SABIC	Saudi Arabia Basic Industries Corporation
SAMA	Saudi Arabian Monetary Agency
SOE	state-owned enterprise
Sonatrach	Algerian state oil company, originally the Société Nationale pour la Recherche, la Production, le Transport, la Transformation et la Commercialisation des Hydrocarbures
SSI	State Security Investigations, an Egyptian plainclothes auxiliary police force
TPF	total factor productivity
UNDP	United Nations Development Program
USAID	United States Agency for International Development
USFP	Union Socialiste des Forces Populaires, a Moroccan political party
WTO	World Trade Organization

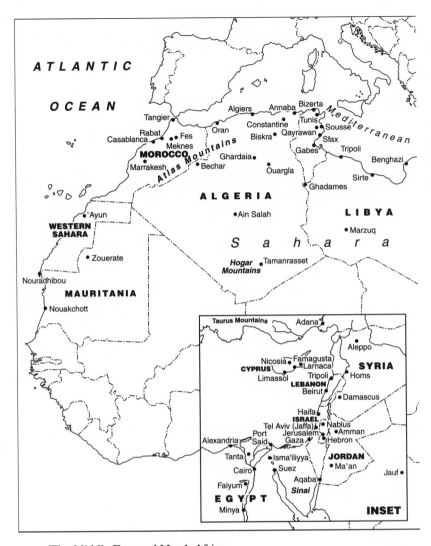

The Middle East and North Africa

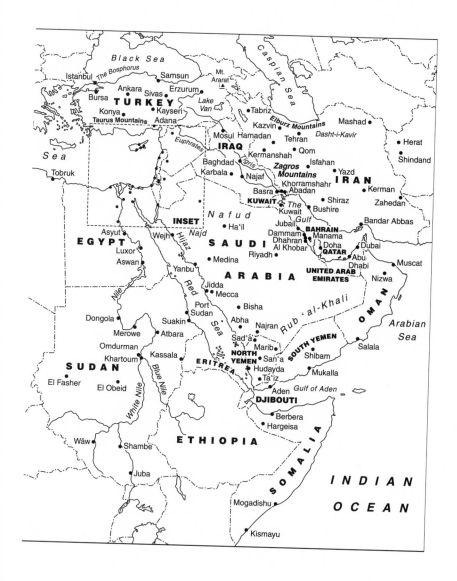

Black Sea

The Bosphorus

Istanbul
Ankara • Samsun
Bursa • Sivas Erzurum • Mt. Ararat
TURKEY • Kayseri Lake Van
Konya • Adana
Taurus Mountains Tabriz

Sea

Tobruk •

EGYPT
Asyut •
Luxor •
Aswan •

SUDAN
El Fasher •
Dongola •
Merowe •
Omdurman •
Khartoum •

Wâw •
Shambe •
Juba •

Caspian Sea

Elburz Mountains
Kazvin • Mashad •
Mosul Hamadan • Tehran Dasht-i-Kavir
IRAQ • • Herat
Kermanshah Qom • Shindand •
Baghdad • Isfahan •
Karbala • Najaf Zagros Yazd • IRAN
Mountains Kerman •
Khorramshahr
Basra • Abadan Shiraz • Zahedan •
KUWAIT The Bushire • Bandar Abbas •
Kuwait
Jubail • Gulf
INSET Najd Dammam BAHRAIN Dubai
N a f u d Dhahran Manama •
Ha'il • Al Khobar QATAR • Muscat •
SAUDI Riyadh • Abu
Medina • UNITED ARAB Dhabi Nizwa •
ARABIA EMIRATES OMAN Arabian
Jidda • Rub 'al-Khali Sea
Mecca •
Port Bisha • Salala •
Sudan Abha • SOUTH YEMEN
Suakin • Najran • Shibam •
Atbara • Sad'a • Marib San'a Mukalla •
Kassala • NORTH • Hudayda
ERITREA YEMEN Ta'iz • Gulf of Aden
DJIBOUTI Aden
Berbera •
Hargeisa •
ETHIOPIA
SOMALIA
INDIAN
Mogadishu • OCEAN
Kismayu •

Nile

Red Sea

Blue Nile

White Nile

Hijaz

Euphrates

Tigris

1   The globalization dialectic

Some readers may have memories of postwar Alexandria and Cairo or will have read Lawrence Durrell's *Alexandria Quartet* – the tales of a cosmopolitan high society. Egypt appeared in the mid-1940s to be as economically developed as war-torn Greece and equally ready to catch up with the rest of Europe. To the north, Turkey was singled out like Greece for special assistance under the Truman Doctrine (March 1947) and seemed virtually a part of Europe. To the west, in "French" Algeria, Algiers was at least as prosperous as the rest of France, and, further west, Casablanca was home to big French industrial interests poised to transform the picturesque Moroccan protectorate into Europe's California. At the eastern end of the Mediterranean, a newly independent and polyglot Lebanon was fast becoming the West's principal commercial gateway to Iran, Iraq, and the Gulf. Riding on the postwar oil boom in those states, Lebanon would become the Middle East's Switzerland in the 1950s and 1960s and apparently exemplify an easy "modernization without revolution" (Salem 1973). Beneath snow-covered mountains, on the unspoiled shores of a clear and relatively unpolluted Mediterranean Sea, Beirut was as pretty as Geneva in those days, at least in the richer parts of the city, and livelier than Calvin's home. Inland, to the east of Lebanon's two mountain ridges, the open Syrian economy boomed with new manufacturing and agricultural development in the 1950s (Sachs and Warner 1995: 34). Morocco and Turkey also grew rapidly during this period because their open economies took advantage of expanding world markets. Of all the new states in the region, however, Iraq had the most promising prospects for balanced development. It was endowed in 1960 with the world's fourth largest proven oil reserves, the most water of any country in the Middle East and North Africa (MENA) including Turkey, some of the richest alluvial soils, a strong British educational system, and a relatively large, skilled workforce. Further east, Iran had three times the population and a diversified economy with oil reserves slightly more plentiful than Iraq's and very substantial natural gas deposits as well (OPEC 2008, Table 9). Captivated by the cash flows, the young shah would dream of making his country into the world's third or fourth mightiest military power.

But over the decades of the Cold War (1946–89), various conflicts within the region dashed any hopes of catching up with Europe. Egypt, Morocco, Syria, and Turkey closed their economies to foreign trade and investment, whereas Greece opened up in 1959 (Sachs and Warner 1995: 79). Consistent with the international model prevailing in the 1960s, most of the MENA states embarked on policies of import substitution industrialization (ISI). Their statist experiments generally resulted in heavier, more bloated bureaucracies than those of other third world countries and more wasteful projects because the financing was so easy. Oil rents or foreign aid – strategic rents of the Cold War – also supported big military complexes and served to inflate their officer corps. When, shocked by the 1982 international debt crisis, the prevailing international consensus changed in the Thatcher-Reagan years to favor market economies and export-oriented development, the MENA states were slower than others to readjust their economic strategies and structures. Shielded directly or indirectly by the region's oil revenues and strategic rents, they took longer than their East Asian or Latin American counterparts to engage in the various forms of structural adjustment advocated by international financial institutions. By the end of the first decade of the twenty-first century, the only countries in the MENA reaching Greek levels of individual prosperity and welfare were little states that had not even existed in the immediate postwar period, Israel and the Greek part of Cyprus. Much of the Arab world was suffering poverty on levels not far removed from those of Sub-Saharan Africa and South Asia.

This book assesses the prospects for reversing these tendencies and accelerating economic development in light of the major regional and international changes currently influencing the region. The end of the Cold War, the new international economic and political order, the increasing attention of Europe to its "Mexico," the occupation of Iraq, the stalled Arab-Israeli peace process, and renewed oil rents coupled with global recession may have major impacts on the region's domestic political economies. All of its regimes are faced with the challenges and opportunities of globalization, yet they also share a defensive legacy ingrained by more than two centuries of interaction with major European powers, joined in the past half-century by the United States. Many Middle Easterners view the globalization of finance and business as a threat to their national, religious, or cultural identities comparable to that of an earlier period of globalization prior to 1914, when the foreign intrusions were associated with European imperialism. The Anglo-American invasion and subsequent occupation of Iraq reinforced this impression.

The dialectics of globalization

The working hypotheses of this book are that politics drives economic development and that the principal obstacles to development in the region have been political rather than economic or cultural in nature. Political rather than economic factors have been the primary cause of the rate and method by which countries of the region have been incorporated into the globalized economy within the framework of the Washington Consensus. Those political factors result from strategies of incumbent elites seeking to retain power – strategies that bear remarkable similarity to those of the "defensive modernizers" of the nineteenth and early twentieth centuries, faced with similar challenges and opportunities of financial globalization prior to 1914. These strategies of "controlled openings" tend to segment the political economy, so that the degree to which various sectors of the economy are globally integrated varies widely. Further differentiation sustains the globalization dialectic, deepening the objective grounds for dividing populations and their elites into globalists and moralists while opening up new opportunities for potential synthesizers.

The drama of globalization is a continuation of the colonial dialectic played out by earlier generations of indigenous elites. Indeed, the most distinctive feature of the MENA region – defined here as the non-European parts of the old Ottoman Empire, plus its respective western, southern, and eastern peripheries in Morocco, Arabia, and Iran – may be not so much Islam – or Arab culture in its heartland – as the tradition of external intervention in the region. As Leon Carl Brown observed,

For roughly the last two centuries the Middle East has been more consistently and more thoroughly ensnarled in great power politics than any other part of the non-Western world. This distinctive political experience continuing from generation to generation has left its mark on Middle Eastern political attitudes and actions. Other parts of the world have been at one time or another more severely buffeted by an imperial power, but no area has remained so unremittingly caught up in multilateral great power politics. (Brown 1984: 3)

In the earlier era of financial globalization lasting until 1914, the encounters tended to produce tensions and fragmentation. The region was too strategically situated to be ignored, yet the Great Powers generally prevented their rivals from definitive conquests while fighting each other for influence, thereby exacerbating internal divisions within the various states or former provinces of the Ottoman Empire. With the discovery of oil in Iran in 1908, then in Bahrain and Iraq in the 1920s and Kuwait and Saudi Arabia in 1938, the region acquired a new strategic importance for international superpowers. During World War I the British coined the term *Middle East* for their Cairo regional command post. Outmaneuvering their French ally's military and diplomatic administrative bureaux of the "Proche Orient" (Near East), they politically and symbolically redefined the region as if to anticipate the world's energy needs. Oil discoveries, coupled with new transport and communications technologies, spread the stakes of Great Power competition out from the Near East to the Middle East, and eventually to North Africa as well. In World War II, Winston Churchill understood the entire region to be Europe's "soft underbelly," and the Allies' campaign to liberate Nazi Europe started in North Africa. The American and British forces converged on Tunisia in 1943, driving Rommel's forces out, before liberating Sicily, Italy, and eventually France.

Outside parties rarely established responsible local government institutions because they were too busy competing with each other for power and influence. In other parts of the world they usually achieved colonial hegemony – the Spanish and Portuguese in Latin America, the British in India and much of North America, and the Dutch in Indonesia. The stakes of conquest were higher in the MENA than elsewhere, however, because it was closer to the European heartland of the Great Powers. And where one power did prevail, the impact on the local society was often more savage than elsewhere, except in the Americas. The French decimated the Muslim populations of Algeria in the mid-nineteenth century, and the Italians followed suit in Libya after World War I. The British protection of harbors along sea-lanes to India was more benign but concerned only a very small fraction of the MENA's population: Aden, Kuwait, Qatar, and other little Trucial States that comprise the United Arab Emirates today. Britain's control over other parts of the region was either transitory (Palestine 1918–48) or veiled in various ways (Egypt 1882–1954, Iraq 1918–58, Iran 1921–53). French rule over Algeria (1830–1962), Tunisia (1881–1956), and Morocco (1912–56) was more durable and transparent, but its control of Lebanon and Syria lasted a bare quarter of a century (1920–46). Italy stayed longer in Libya (1911–43) but was then displaced by the British until 1951. Whether or not the United States crossed the line between technical assistance and veiled control over Saudi Arabia, Aramco, a company registered in Delaware, ran its oil fields until 1990, and the U.S. government helped to establish much of its accompanying state infrastructure (Vitalis 2007).

In short, most of the MENA states were penetrated by a variety of outside parties vying for commercial, cultural, or strategic influence and establishing beach-heads through the various local communities. One widespread effect of these rivalries was to put indigenous business elites at risk. Selective foreign "protection" of local minorities, including grants of foreign citizenship, strengthened them against their local governments and business competitors but ultimately left them vulnerable to retaliation by popular majorities. Another impact was increased sectarianism. Lebanon illustrated how confessional differences, recognized for limited purposes by the Ottoman millet system, were exacerbated by alliances with external powers – the Maronites with the French, the Greek Orthodox with the Russians, the Druze with the British. With the formal freeing of much of the region after World War II, regional powers, including Iran, Israel, and Turkey as well as Arab states, supplemented traditional interventions of the Great Powers vying for influence over their smaller neighbors. The United States, eager to check advances by the Soviet Union, joined the fray and learned to outbid its British and French allies. More external and regional influence peddling and subversion further compounded the divisions of weak states such as Lebanon, the Sudan, and Yemen and provoked others, such as Iraq and Syria, into becoming police states. The rise of transnational Arab and Islamic movements in turn amplified regional and local conflicts.

Whereas colonial rule in the non-Western world usually had a beginning, a long period of insulation from the outside world, and a conclusion, many MENA elites are products of a different legacy. Only the Turks, Algerians, Tunisians, Moroccans, and Israelis can claim to have really won their independence, achieving a degree of national closure, at the expense of either settler or other minorities or, in the case of Israel, the national majority of Palestinians. Others still fear the subversion of foreign powers and interference from their neighbors. Any closure was gained at the expense of local business elites rather than the colonizer. Military coups toppled nominally independent regimes, and then the officers proceeded to restructure their respective political economies. The MENA's special legacy of external intervention has impeded the internal development of public accountability.

Yet just as colonialism gave rise to movements of national liberation assimilating Western forms of political organization to struggle against Western domination, so the dialectics of globalization may integrate countries in the region into the world economy while also emancipating them. To do so in the new context is to assimilate, negate, and through the hard work of negation to supersede the Washington Consensus rooted in Anglo-American capitalism – perhaps by "Islamizing" it. Dialectic here is understood to comprise sets of ideas and attitudes defining elite-mass relationships rather than material forces, though economic interests obviously play a part. In a dialectic of emancipation (modeled after Hegel's master-slave relationship) ideas may – but do not necessarily – gain ever-wider social audiences, achieving what Antonio Gramsci called hegemony (Lustick 1999). In colonial situations, a nationalist elite may mobilize the entire nation, transforming a population defined by colonial borders into a people experiencing civil society.

Schematically the colonial dialectic describes three basic stances (or Hegelian "moments") of a native elite toward the colonizer's political culture. The first stance is that of acceptance associated with efforts to be assimilated into the new elite. But emulating alien values may in turn engender a backlash by those excluded from it. This negative moment of a counter elite asserts its claim to hegemony in the name of indigenous values. Under continued colonial pressure, however, new divisions within this elite may lead to the emergence of an alternative elite that is no longer content to articulate the traditional values of an imagined past. The third moment may more effectively combat the imposition of alien rule by assimilating its positive elements, such as skills and values derived from a Western education, and using them to overcome foreign domination. This deeper assimilation of the colonizer's values plays on the contradictions of colonialism so as to undermine its authority and achieve independence.

Much of the MENA fell under the influence of Western powers without experiencing the full effects of colonial rule. It was in French North Africa that the colonial dialectic was most fully articulated because the colonial presence was more intrusive and protracted than elsewhere. The schema is best illustrated in Tunisia, where French rule lasted long enough to provoke not only emulation and negation but also a nationalist synthesis, yet was not so overpowering that it altogether undermined the authority of any indigenous elite, as in Algeria. Successive generations of educated Tunisians chronologically expressed the logic of the three dialectical moments. Before 1914 aristocratic Young Tunisians emulated French modernity and sought liberal reforms within the system. After World War I a predominantly urban Destour (Constitution) Party rejected the French Protectorate on traditional and legalistic grounds. Then the Neo-Destour, its successor party, with roots in peasant villages, employed modern political methods to organize the entire country against the French occupation. At independence, in 1956, Tunisia had the most deeply rooted nationalist party and trade union federation of any Arab country.

Tunisia was the exception. When, as in much of the Middle East, the "colonial" domination was veiled in technical and military relationships with outside powers, the colonial dialectic could not be completed for lack of a unifying target of opposition or incentive for emancipation. Even in Tunisia, the synthesis led to new tensions and contradictions after independence. Habib Bourguiba's successful movement eventually engendered resistance from social sectors and actors who felt excluded. Once in power, the third generation of nationalists became vulnerable to attack by new generations of rejectionists who could point to the internal contradictions between the incumbent elite's ostensible Western liberal values and the regime's authoritarian practices. But Tunisia's Islamist opposition, progressive by Arab standards, is a legacy of Tunisian modernization: Rashid Ghannoushi can be seen as Bourguiba's "illegitimate offspring" (Zghal 1991: 205). Tunisia's special advantages deserve further scrutiny.

The critical factors for Tunisia's success were the duration of the colonial situation (1881–1956) and the capacity of political elites to forge durable linkages with mass constituencies before independence. Colonial conflict was sufficiently protracted and its education benefits sufficiently extensive to enable a modern educated provincial elite (sons of peasant freeholders) to displace the traditional urban elite of absentee landlords, merchants, and religious figures. The new nationalist elite succeeded in mobilizing broad popular support because the continued French presence offered a convenient focus for mobilization and coalition building. The timing was critical. It took three generations of nationalist struggle for the educated sons of the provincial elite to acquire sufficient weight to displace and absorb the other educated children of the traditional urban elite in the new middle classes (Montety [1940] 1973). Their Moroccan equivalents would not have time to achieve such social and political prominence before independence. Other new middle classes, defined as being not only educated but of predominantly provincial origins outside the old elite strata, did not achieve political hegemony before independence. In the rest of the Middle East and North Africa, only Algeria, Aden, Egypt, Palestine, and Sudan experienced comparable periods of European (or Israeli) colonization. The colonial situation was too veiled in Egypt, however, and too prone to settler violence in Algeria and Palestine for their respective new middle classes to achieve hegemony. If they were to achieve it there or elsewhere in the MENA, it would be after independence and under less auspicious circumstances. In Palestine, however, the Jewish settlers, detached from Europe yet still mostly European, telescoped their nationalism into a third-moment victory over Britain within a generation.

Pervasive Western influence, first exercised through the Ottoman Empire and then more directly by means of mandates from the League of Nations, usually strengthened the hold of urban absentee landowner-merchants over the countryside. Turkey was the prime exception. Ottoman bureaucracy contained them, and an Anatolian third-moment elite then displaced traditional authorities and achieved independence in

1923 through a successful war of national liberation. In most countries, however, the emergent elites benefiting from Western education did not have time to displace the old urban ones before independence: in Syria, Lebanon, and Iraq, the prime "nationalists" and beneficiaries of independence were the urban landowners; in Iraq they included urbanized tribal leaders. Despite a lengthier history of Western intrusion, Egyptian nationalism was also dominated by its landowners until divisions in the Wafd presaged the end of the monarchy in 1952.

Except in the Levant, the colonial powers tended to establish monarchies if they were not already in place. In the Persian Gulf, the British protected ruling families and even imported the Hashemites from Mecca to Jordan and Iraq. The British also disposed of Italy's former colony by uniting Libya under a new monarchy in 1951. Monarchy was usually the sign of a colonial dialectic that had not run its full course. Had the French stayed a generation longer in Morocco, they would doubtless have discredited the venerable Sharifian monarchy by overuse against rising social forces. Instead, they accidentally raised its prestige by exiling the sultan to Madagascar in 1953. Conversely, had the French left Tunis for good during World War II, Moncef Bey might have kept his throne and prevented Bourguiba from founding a republic. The British and subsequently the Americans also strengthened Pahlavi Iran without ever turning it into a formal protectorate. There as elsewhere, the monarchies had trouble coping with the new middle classes nurtured in Western education. Despite his White Revolution, the shah was unable to mobilize support from the countryside to offset them. In Morocco, by contrast, the monarchy came to dominate both the old urban merchants and the new middle classes after independence by manipulating provincial notables to its advantage (Hammoudi 1997; Leveau 1985).

Israel, Tunisia, and Turkey were the only countries where a third-moment elite consolidated itself with independence. Afterwards it would be more difficult for new middle classes, the normal carriers of civil society, to forge durable linkages with other social sectors, whether among peasants, workers, or students. In Iran a genuine revolution was needed to expel the monarchy, but much of the new middle classes then fell victim to the victorious coalition of merchants and religious leaders. Elsewhere they invariably achieved power by plotting within their respective military establishments. Nasser and his Free Officers led the way in Egypt in 1952; after many military coups and countercoups, Hassan Bakr (with Saddam Hussein) and Hafez al-Asad took power in Iraq and Syria in 1968 and 1970, respectively. The officers in turn suppressed civilian politicians and intellectuals who might have deepened their respective civil societies by creating new associations and political spaces. The degree of oppression or liberality of their respective regimes was a function of the potential oppositions they faced. The extent of their economic intervention and financial repression also reflected the strength of their respective merchants and landowners and the degree to which they had coalesced as a class of local capitalists. Thus intervention was heaviest in Egypt, Iraq, Libya, Syria, and Algeria. In fact it is often forgotten that Algeria's more protracted colonial situation had given rise to higher concentrations of Algerian as well as French settler landholdings than in neighboring Morocco. The economic hand of the military was lighter in the Sudan and Yemen, where capitalism was less developed.

The new dialectics of globalization feeds on an unachieved colonial dialectic. Its thesis is the Washington Consensus, shared by "serious" economists irrespective of nationality and vigorously, if selectively, imitated by certain of the local business and political elites as well. It seems hardly coincidental that the countries governed by third-moment elites at independence – Israel, Tunisia, and Turkey – were the quickest to adopt the Washington Consensus. Reform teams of technocrats, supported at least initially by their political leaderships, also made some progress implementing various structural reforms in Algeria, Egypt, Jordan, and Morocco. The Washington Consensus, however, engendered significant backlash in these and other countries. The "globalizers" almost inevitably provoke "moralizers," who seek solutions in cultural authenticity by affirming a religious or ethnic identity, or at least by reaffirming traditional nationalism. Since Libya's Muammar Qaddafi began speaking of a "Third Way" in the 1970s, the siren call of a distinctive, unique, culturally authentic model has gained considerable appeal, and writings on Islamic economics have proliferated.

Much like second-moment responses to colonial situations, however, moralism remains abstract and ineffective unless it can contest the global economy on its own grounds. Most of the "moralizers" seem unable to devise effective alternative economic policies. Moralism takes the form either of Arab nationalism harking back to the command economies of the 1960s or of Islamic revivalism. On the nationalist track, Arab economists have enjoyed only limited success in promoting a free-trade zone as a counterweight to being integrated piecemeal into the international economy (Bolbol 1999). Mainstream Islamism, on the other hand, seems to be more preoccupied with culture than with economics. The moralizers, whether in government or opposed to it, can put globalizers on the defensive, but they rarely promote alternative policies.

Nor do the moralizers have much opportunity to do so. Hesitant moves toward greater political liberalization in the 1980s were sharply reversed in most MENA countries in the 1990s. Tunisia, followed in turn by

Algeria, Egypt, Saudi Arabia, Turkey, and Jordan, severely restricted the Islamist oppositions. There could be little overt, public debate between globalizers and their opponents inside and outside their respective governments, and efforts to incorporate mainstream Islamist oppositions into the political process ceased, except perhaps in Jordan and Morocco. Tunisia perfected the art of running a contemporary police state by claiming to be democratic while preemptively harassing, imprisoning, and routinely torturing its opponents and their families (Beau and Tuquoi 1999).

Indeed, the political conditions prevailing in most Arab states since the American-led liberation of Kuwait – and intensified by America's "war of choice" on Iraq – resemble those of a colonial situation – with the Islamists now playing the role of the erstwhile nationalists. It is an odd reversal of roles, a further unfolding of the colonial dialectic. In colonial situations Islam provided the implicit mobilizing structures of Western-inspired nationalism (articulated in Tunisia, for instance, through the modern Quranic schools), whereas today nationalism acquires an overtly Islamist form. Incumbent rulers, however, are both Muslim and indigenous nationals. They all seek legitimacy as Muslim rulers, even in once "radical" republics such as Syria or Iraq. Most of them therefore feel obliged to tolerate limited public Muslim spaces, such as Friday prayers and *shari'ah* courts, even though the message delivered in those prayers is strictly controlled, as are the judiciaries.

The colonial dialectic, in sum, gave rise to independent states of three different types: praetorian republics (Algeria, Egypt, Iraq, Libya, Palestine, Syria, Sudan, Tunisia, Yemen and, as President Ahmadinejad's re-election in 2009 clarified, Iran), monarchies (Bahrain, Jordan, Kuwait, Morocco, Oman, Qatar, Saudi Arabia, and the United Arab Emirates), and democracies (Israel, Lebanon, and Turkey). The monarchies preserved their traditional elites and international capitalist legacies. The praetorian republics tended to reject theirs in favor of new political economies, although there were significant differences between Algeria and Iraq at one extreme and Egypt and Tunisia at the other. The "bunker" states, such as Algeria and Iraq, rule primarily by coercion – from their metaphorical or, in some cases, actual bunkers – because the state lacks autonomy from social formations. The "bully states," Egypt and Tunisia, insulated by relatively strong administration, are largely autonomous from social forces, whether traditional or modern, although they, too, depend principally on military/security forces. The democracies were more selective in their treatment of local capitalists and landowners. The regimes that left their capitalist legacies intact were technically better able to cope with the new challenges of globalization that have steadily gathered pace since the 1980s; the monarchies of Jordan and Morocco

adapted more quickly to the new world order than the more radical praetorian republics. They were generally better able than these republics to
harness the power of private capital to their political needs. The praetorian republics and democracies varied considerably in their treatment
of earlier generations of agrarian, commercial, and industrial capitalists,
but they are all under some local as well as international pressure to come
to terms with the Washington Consensus.

The Washington Consensus revised

The "Washington Consensus" promoted by the international institutions
and Western donor agencies, albeit in steadily more diluted form as the
decade of the 1990s progressed, used to be a set of ten flexible guidelines for opening up political economies and integrating them into global
markets (Naim 2000). John Williamson, who coined the term, explains
it as "the common core of wisdom embraced by all serious economists."
He leaves open many controversial questions, including even the size of
government and the model of the market economy to be sought, whether
"Anglo-Saxon laissez-faire, the European social market economy, or
Japanese-style responsibility of the corporation to multiple shareholders"
(Williamson 1994: 18). Yet prescriptions that may be standard economics
to academics also carry immediate political implications for power holders. In the 1990s, indeed, the proponents of reform paid increasing attention to its political prerequisites of efficient, responsive, and transparent
institutions (World Bank 1997). The Spence Report, commissioned by
the World Bank in 2008, redefined the Washington Consensus as a diag-
nostic rather than a prescriptive approach to development. Broadly speaking, however, neoliberal economists still agreed on four basic principles,
adding "reasonably good" governance to Williamson's earlier recommendations of maintaining macroeconomic stability, stimulating saving and
investment, and providing market-oriented incentives (Rodrik 2008). All
the more reason, then, that the "rechristened" Washington Consensus
calling for a liberalization and opening up of the domestic economy
spelled imperialism and political as well as economic hardship for many
local policy makers.

In view of the MENA's legacies of foreign intervention, it is hardly surprising that international financial institutions and foreign donors evoke
defensive reactions. IMF observation teams and World Bank missions
are all too reminiscent of the European financiers who helped infor-
mally to colonize much of the region in the nineteenth century. The U.S.
Agency for International Development (USAID) mission in Cairo also
elicits comparisons with the more successful British advisors a century
ago in the ministries of finance and public works. Symptomatically an

States are advised:

1 to reduce the budget deficit to no more than 2 percent of GDP

2 to accord budgetary priority to primary health, education, and infrastructure investments

3 to broaden the tax base, including interest income on assets held abroad, and cut the marginal rates of taxation

4 to liberalize the financial system, at least abolishing preferential interest rates and maintaining a moderately positive real interest rate

5 to adjust the exchange rate to encourage non-traditional exports

6 to liberalize trade, rapidly replacing qualitative restrictions with tariffs and progressively reducing the tariffs to 10 percent (or at most around 20 percent)

7 to remove all barriers to foreign direct investment and enable foreign and domestic firms to compete on equal terms

8 to privatize state enterprises

9 to abolish regulations impeding the entry of new firms or restricting competition and insure that all regulations of a given industry are justified

10 to secure private property rights without excessive costs, for the informal as well as formal sectors.

Figure 1.1 The Ten Commandments of the Washington Consensus
Source: Williamson 1994: 26–8

Egyptian journalist's book about his country's negotiations with the IMF pictures Superman on the cover with a big "IMF" in red letters on his blue uniform (Hilal 1987). Although some Arab governments have officially welcomed 'awlama [globalization], their practices reflect ingrained suspicions of foreign advisors and their prescriptions for reform – "iron and arsenic to all, whatever the illness," as an Egyptian minister once complained (Hilal 1987: 171). The added imperative of "reasonably" good governance only confirmed suspicions that the Washington Consensus was an imperialist plot, especially after the Bush administration toppled Saddam Hussein to bring freedom to Iraq.

The foreign advisors from international financial institutions and the United Nations, however, are hardly supermen (or superwomen, for that matter). Indeed, they must appear to be apolitical lest they offend their hosts or their international board members. They express their "advice" in technical economic policy terms and, even when knowledgeable about the host country's politics, are not usually able to translate the advice into viable political strategies. Any will to change on rational economic grounds also must be reconciled with political rationality and its imperatives for retaining power.

Virtually all of these regimes suffer deficits of legitimacy (Ayubi 1995; Hudson 1977) and buy support through extensive networks of political patronage that permeate their respective economies through the administration, the banking system, and many "private" enterprises. In these patrimonial regimes private property is not secure from the whims of arbitrary rulers. Many regimes have yet to abandon allocation for alternative strategies of political legitimation, and hence must continue to generate rents that accrue to the state. State-society interaction continues to consist of heavy police control coupled with various forms of patronage to keep the police and other administrations loyal. Some of the MENA's regimes carefully mask their repression with information blackouts that further limit their possibilities for economic adjustment. Indeed, their information shyness is becoming a major impediment to attracting capital in global markets. One measure of a regime's political capacity in the twenty-first century is its transparency and openness to new flows of information. On this as on other measures such as the ability to tax their citizens, most MENA regimes display significant limitations. Raising more taxes can stretch a regime's coercive capabilities, and more publicity may embarrass its patronage networks.

Private sectors are also wary of reform. With few exceptions they remain heavily dependent on government favors, tariff protection, and other subsidies. The political relationships with local capital were largely conditioned by struggles against foreign domination, but they were also qualified by the particular variety of capitalism that the foreigners had introduced. These varieties of capitalism deserve some discussion because they condition the structural power (Winters 1994: 431–2) of local capital – an opportunity as well as threat to these regimes in the new era of globalization. Just as the advanced capitalist countries practice their distinct national varieties of capitalism (Berger and Dore 1996), so their colonial offshoots are developing their own trajectories conditioned by the financial systems they inherited. Most of the MENA's business communities are weak, heavily dependent on the state, and hardly about to be agents of political or economic change (Bellin 2000: 175–205) at present, but their various legacies point to future possibilities.

The structural power of capital

The principal challenge of globalization is to tame the powerful force of mobile global capital and to allocate it in constructive ways. Our book focuses on financial systems because they are the critical intermediaries between global capital and states – the brains that allocate scarce capital. The local financial systems filter the structural power of global capital in various ways, depending on their capitalist legacies. The Europeans introduced relatively advanced forms of capitalism into most of the region by the end of the nineteenth century. These consisted of a British model predicated on laissez-faire and an efficient, competitive stock exchange, a German model based on universal banks, and a French model stressing greater state intervention in capital markets. Featuring a weaker private sector more dependent on administrative allocations of credit, the French model did not long survive the departure of its French colonial administrators in Algeria, Syria, or Tunisia and bore little relation to its successor model of state "socialism." Contending British and German models survive, however, where indigenous business classes enjoyed continuity and protection from nationalist revolutions and the confiscation of private property. And the postsocialist bully states of Egypt and Tunisia emulate a French model of sorts to encourage their new captains of industry.

Anglo-American capitalism is characterized by laissez-faire, as Williamson observes (1994: 18), and most basically by open competitive capital markets centered on stock exchanges and bond markets. Commercial banking carries a less significant functional load than in alternative capitalist systems (Zysman 1983). Banks still lend to small and medium enterprises, but they remain subservient to market forces. Retail banks, even in Britain's highly concentrated system, wield little market power because their scope of intervention is limited. Under the impact of financial globalization, the compartmentalization between retail banks and merchant banks has broken down, and new conglomerates are challenging the traditional fragmentation and differentiation of financial markets in the United States as well as in Britain. Financial markets remain highly competitive, however, driven by a multiplicity of actors and, in theory at least, regulated so as to ensure transparency and to prevent insider trading on stock exchanges so far as possible. Walter Bagehot's *Lombard Street* ([1873], 1904) captured its underlying logic of competition and exploration. Britain was constantly seeking new outlets for its massive capital accumulation and hence required a decentralized system that rewarded entrepreneurship. Capital-rich America followed suit. In this model the structural power of capital is exercised through financial markets. This model is subject to periodic booms and busts, of which the Great Recession is the latest manifestation, highlighting the need for ever more complex forms of regulation to tame global finance.

A second model, best articulated by Rudolph Hilferding ([1910], 1981), also stresses relatively autonomous private-sector capitalist activity, but of universal banks, not individual investors. This German model is adapted to situations of capital scarcity. In late nineteenth-century Germany, the largest and most capital-hungry firms, typically in capital-intensive industries such as iron and steel, fell under the control of their creditor banks. The borrowing industries and creditors alike became more concentrated as smaller entities went bankrupt or were acquired by the larger ones, and the banks concentrated and merged to defend themselves against industrial mergers. Finally, an oligopoly of about six large commercial banks based in Berlin at the turn of the century commanded much of German industry. These universal banks, investing heavily in industry, constituted a model that subsequent generations of nationalists in the MENA would try to emulate. In the German model, a small number of bankers scale the commanding heights of the economy and allocate its finance capital. They consult with their government but retain full autonomy and bargaining power. Here structural power works through people rather than markets: a small group of commercial banker/financiers can threaten to withhold loans and investments if the government does not provide an attractive business climate.

The third model is the traditional Napoleonic one of administrative intervention in the French étatiste tradition. Although much of the economy, including the banks, may be privately owned, capital is allocated strategically more by technocrats who supposedly know best than by private financiers. The rationing of capital by state officials also, as in the German model, offers protection to capital-scarce economies. The banks, however, are less autonomous and exercise less control, for that matter, over stock markets. These capital markets are less developed than in the Anglo-American model. The structural power of capital is not as easily ascertained as in either the German model, with its small number of financial conglomerates, or the Anglo-American model, with its efficient market responses to new information. Market forces operate, but they are subject to greater regulation by the technocrats. The best indicators of structural power are the degree of private ownership of the commercial banks and their financial health. Failing banks and ballooning bad loan portfolios (and precursor signs such as chronically low profitability) suggest either that the technocrats have excessively influenced credit allocation or that the banks have not conducted responsible credit analysis. Japan in the 1990s would be an illustration. The structural power of capital is diminished by subsidized credit, but so also is the effectiveness of government to respond to business demands.

The model adopted in a MENA country did not necessarily match that of the politically dominant foreign power. Political domination was usually brief and rarely excluded other foreign capital. French and Belgian enterprises prospered in Egypt under Lord Cromer (1882–1906) more than did British enterprises, and the country remained open to other models as well (Saul 1997). The German model proved attractive to Egyptians, such as Talaat Harb, and other late developers even after Germany was excluded from the region following World War I. Nor did the French, more exclusively rooted in the Maghrib than the British in Egypt, convert all of the local entrepreneurs to their preferred form of capitalism. Moroccan finance looked more "German" than French despite its French and Spanish colonial past. Its French capitalists had themselves adopted the more advanced German universal banking model by 1912, when most of Morocco became a French protectorate. In Tunisia, by contrast, an earlier generation of speculators had projected a traditional form of capitalism similar to that of French Algeria. The French capitalists in Morocco operated through modern German-style universal banks such as Paribas and developed stronger negotiating stances with their colonial government than did their less dynamic counterparts in Algeria or Tunisia, who depended more on the public authorities.

The German model also traveled to Turkey, despite the fact that the Germans were only one of several principal managers of the Ottoman public finances before World War I. The Germans invested more in productive enterprises than did their rivals and offered a more attractive model for postwar Turkish entrepreneurs than did their British or French competitors. Determined to build a Turkish private sector, Mustafa Kemal Atatürk and his top political economist, Celal Bayar, opted for the German model. Subsequently, during the Depression years after 1931, they espoused étatisme but also continued to develop a private sector along German lines (Henry 1996).

Indigenous business communities assimilated the metropolitan models in varying degrees. Many of them consisted of minorities whose ties to foreign powers were distrusted by the nationalist forces that ultimately gained power. Business communities in praetorian regimes experienced sharp turnovers caused by an unstable history of coups and revolutions. In Iraq, for example, families such as the Shalabis promoted under the Ottoman and subsequently British rulers took refuge abroad. Iraq today has virtually no business class, but rather a collection of new people who are personally connected to the ruling factions. Without the security to accumulate capital, there can be no capitalism. Between 1915 and 1922, the Ottomans and then the Turks virtually obliterated Turkey's business minorities. Subsequently, however, a new Turkish business class grew up under Mustafa Kemal to absorb and sustain the German model into the 1980s.

Few of the MENA's business communities display as much continuity as republican Turkey's. Nationalist revolutions in the Arab world did not usually result in as much disruption as in Turkey prior to 1923, but they have had less time than the Turks since independence to recover. And Algeria represented even greater disruption in July 1962 than did Turkey in 1922. An entire French colonial economic, political, technical, and administrative elite departed on vacation rather than face independence, and few ever returned. The transition to independence was more gradual in neighboring Tunisia, but most of the Tunisians who replaced the Europeans owed their new economic fortunes more to their political activity and connections than to any tradition of entrepreneurship. Syria had a strong tradition of entrepreneurship, but by the mid-1960s the old Aleppan and Damascene business families had succumbed to Ba'athist domination, which despite President Hafez al-Asad's cautious "opening" of the economy in the early 1970s was an inheritance he passed to his son Bashar on his death in 2000. Nasser's Free Officers also rid Egypt not only of its European and khedivial business communities, but most native Egyptian capitalists as well, although ten years of state "socialism" (1961–71) did not totally erase the country's capitalist traditions, which reemerged, albeit in substantially modified forms, under Nasser's successors.

The Arab country displaying the most continuous business history is Morocco, where the French presence attracted indigenous Fassi merchant families to Casablanca and other new centers. French industrial interests were only very gradually Moroccanized in the second decade following independence, principally to the benefit of the monarchy and its entourage of Fassi business groups. They preserved the "German" model of capitalism that had evolved under the Protectorate. In Israel the victorious Labour Party regime preserved Jewish businesses, including those founded and heavily subsidized during the colonial period by the Histadrut, the Zionist labor federation. Israel's original variant of state capitalism is similar to the French model inherited by its neighbors, Syria and Lebanon, from Ottoman times. Independent Lebanon conserved its entrepreneurs, but they converted to an Anglo-Saxon model to satisfy the American multinationals that set up their regional headquarters in Beirut in the 1950s and 1960s.

The capital-rich, whether in Lebanon or the Gulf, tended to adopt the Anglo-Saxon model, whereas the capital-poor entrepreneurs of Morocco and Turkey gravitated toward the German model, and the Israelis toward the more administrative French model. But predatory states deprived many countries in the region of their respective capitalist traditions. By default, new entrepreneurs were locked into a "French" tradition of administrative favors, although the capital-rich Gulf states are also promoting a third, Islamic way, which is quite compatible with Anglo-American capitalism. Launched in the mid-1970s, Islamic banking and finance offers possibilities for synthesizing moral demands with those of globalization that will be discussed later in this book. The so-called Islamic banks operate in accordance with Islamic law, as interpreted by Muslim legal scholars, and do not accept interest, although they recognize the time value of money in other ways (Vogel and Hayes 1998). They have captured substantial shares of commercial banking markets in a number of Arab and Muslim countries.

To summarize, the structural power of capital was more visible in the democracies and monarchies than in the MENA's military regimes. Lebanon's business elite stayed more or less intact, even through a civil war in the 1970s and 1980s, though Lebanon switched after independence from the French to a less regulated Anglo-American model more in keeping with the country's role as a trading and financial center for the Middle East. Led by third-moment elites, Israel and Turkey were well positioned to maintain their respective capitalist legacies. In Iran a second-moment elite also keeps its indigenous capitalist bazaar, albeit in tension with a strong statist tradition inherited from the shah and expanded after the revolution. The monarchies have also preserved their nascent capitalist legacies. The German model serves the poorer, capital-scarce ones. It facilitates palace control of heavy economic concentrations, whereas wealthier monarchies have more rents to pacify their more numerous and competitive local capitalists and tribal elites. The praetorian republics adopted state capitalism and dismissed much of their private-sector legacies from colonial times. Residues of the Anglo-American model survive in Egypt and the Sudan, as do echoes of French capitalism in Syria. But whatever their domestic political constraints and capacities, extraregional factors push all of the regimes to engage with global capital.

Chapter 2 addresses the extent to which global and regional changes may be leveling the differences between the MENA and other parts of the developing world caused by the MENA's special legacies of rents and foreign intervention. These global and regional changes not only constitute a new impetus for economic development, perhaps reversing recent trends, but also shape the context in which state actors make their political and economic calculations and formulate economic policies. The ebb and flow of relationships with the United States, the European

Community, and the Tokyo/Beijing axis may tilt them toward one or another of their respective models of capitalism, but capitalism has also acquired indigenous roots in most MENA countries and is interacting with global capital in ways that are further discussed in ensuing chapters.

Suggestions for further reading

Richards and Waterbury (2008) comprehensively examine the political economy of the region and are usefully supplemented by El-Ghonemy (1998), whereas Bill and Springborg (2000) and Owen (2004) present comparative political analyses. For political and economic history, see Brown (1984) and Owen and Pamuk (1998), respectively, whereas Ehteshami (2009) focuses on the geopolitical dimension of globalization in the region.

2   The challenges of globalization

The MENA, which hesitated more than any other region of the world to adopt the reforms needed to benefit from the new international division of labor, has progressed considerably since the 1990s in adopting the neoliberal principles of the Washington Consensus as its basis for formulating national economic policies. Global changes are breaking the cocoon that had once protected the region from major structural changes. This chapter first views the degrees to which the region has engaged in the globalization dialectic, and then goes on to analyze the continuing international and regional incentives and counter pressures. Although the MENA continues to attract a disproportionate share of attention from external powers and to receive abundant petroleum as well as strategic rents, the financial flows no longer insulate it from the need to reform. Rapid economic growth is needed to meet the region's spectacular gift and challenge: the youth bulge of record numbers reflecting major demographic changes (Fuller 2004). Although many states such as Algeria, Iran, and Turkey dramatically reduced their birth rates in the 1990s, their baby booms of the 1980s keep enlarging labor markets. Local economies, in wealthy countries such as Saudi Arabia as well as poorer ones, need to offer sufficient employment to preserve social stability in the face of regional and international threats and challenges. Out of self-preservation, they are compelled to seek to attract new businesses, technologies, and compensatory capital flows, which in turn require economic structural adjustments. That this process is proceeding unevenly attests to those states' different internal capacities for reform, the topic that is taken up in Chapter 3.

Global engagement

By economic globalization is meant the removal of barriers to exchanges of goods, people, capital, and ideas. Technology drives the process. Just as steamships and wire transfers made possible the pre-1914 era of globalization, so the information revolution has accelerated the present era

20

of globalization that began in the 1950s with telexes and container ships. In contrast to Western theories of progress and modernization, however, there is nothing inevitable about globalization. It is the product of deliberate government choices to remove barriers to trade and to the movement of people and capital and not to engage in new forms of censorship. Were the Great Recession of 2008–10 to deepen into another Great Depression, the process might yet be reversed. More likely, however, it may be a more universal application of the Washington Consensus that will require the United States to structurally adjust and manage its twin fiscal and trade deficits.

Meanwhile, after some hesitation, much of the MENA engaged in various structural adjustment reforms proposed by the IMF and the World Bank. Policies of import substitution industrialization, often supported in the 1960s by Western development assistance, led to major debt crises by the 1980s. Turkey, without oil revenues, was first to undergo a major crisis, in 1979, followed by Morocco, and then Tunisia, Egypt, and eventually Algeria. All were obliged to undergo stabilization programs with the IMF to curb their fiscal and trade deficits and then to do further structural adjustment over the years. Figure 2.1 illustrates the timing and levels of IMF intervention in the economies of various MENA countries. The biggest borrowers were, in descending order, Turkey, Algeria, Morocco, Sudan, and Egypt. Syria never borrowed from the IMF after 1974, whereas Egypt borrowed continuously from 1970 to 1997, when it finally cleared its accounts. Egypt managed, however, to stall significant structural reforms until the 1990s. Of the MENA's top debtors, only Jordan, Sudan, Turkey, and Yemen remained beholden to the IMF by 2006. They had meanwhile made considerable progress in adapting to the Washington Consensus.

One way of measuring the progress is the KOF Index of Globalization, which offers composite measures of actual financial and trade flows and of restrictions to the movements of goods and capital from 1970 to 2006 (Dreher et al. 2008: 43–4). The actual flows were derived from trade as a percentage of gross domestic product (GDP), stocks and flows of foreign direct investment, portfolio investment, and income payments to foreign nationals. On average, the MENA countries gained 20 percent over the 36-year time period, with Egypt, Israel, Morocco and Turkey gaining respectively 26, 29, 27 and 42 percent. The oil-exporting countries scored below average gains because they were already embedded in the global economy; in fact, the United Arab Emirates declined a little from scores of above 95 percent in the early 1970s. With the exception of Iran, however, all of the major oil exporters joined the others in relaxing restrictions on trade and investment. One of them, Algeria, had also

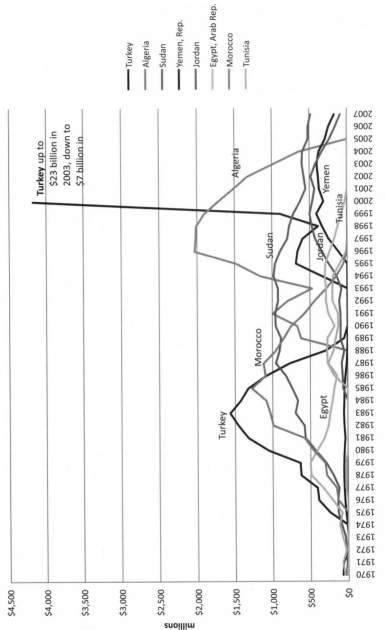

Figure 2.1 Use of IMF Credit, 1970–2007

22

been a major client of the IMF and showed the same dramatic elim-ination of restrictions to trade and capital movements as the other big MENA countries such as Egypt, Morocco, and Turkey. Figure 2.2 shows how these large, heavily populated countries were eliminating restrictions and thereby engaging as much as smaller ones like Jordan and Israel in the processes of economic globalization. Tariffs still remained relatively high, however, in much of North Africa and the Levant. And progress was modest at best with respect to underlying structural reforms that might propel these economies into more self-sustained growth indepen-dent of petroleum revenues and remittances from the "labor importing resource abundant" countries of the Gulf Cooperation Council (GCC) and Libya.

One sign of their limitations was the business climate. Since 2003, the World Bank has annually assessed the "business friendliness" of the developing countries "as a kind of cholesterol test for the regulatory environment for domestic businesses" (World Bank 2008c, vi). Private businesses – small and medium-sized enterprises as well as large corpo-rations – must be able to proliferate and prosper if these economies are expected to sustain the high growth rates necessary for employing a bal-looning workforce. The Bank's Middle East and North Africa Division publishes annual progress reports and remarked in 2008,

Despite notable improvements in some countries (e.g., the Arab Republic of Egypt and Saudi Arabia), as a whole the region has failed to keep pace with business climate reforms elsewhere. In terms of reform effort, it ranks in the bottom third worldwide (29th percentile). (World Bank 2008b: 77)

Even after being celebrated as a top reformer in 2007 and again in 2008 and 2009 Egypt was still, as of 2009, ranked only 106th of 183 countries for the ease of doing business, and Saudi Arabia, rising to 13th place and at the head of the MENA pack, still ranked only 140th in enforcing contracts (World Bank 2009a). The World Economic Forum's *Arab Competitiveness Report 2007* tried to be a bit more upbeat by compar-ing MENA countries to others within their general level of development as well as giving overall rankings, so that Tunisia, for instance, was in third place among its comparators, and Egypt made fourth place within a less developed set (World Economic Forum 2007: vii–ix). But the divi-sion of economies into factor-driven, efficiency-driven, and innovation-driven already told the story: Egypt was still at the primitive stage of factor-driven economies, and Tunisia, the most competitive of the Arab "resource poor" economies, was still stuck in a transitional category between factor-driven and efficiency-driven economies. Its relatively effi-cient administration could not propel the country up the value chain

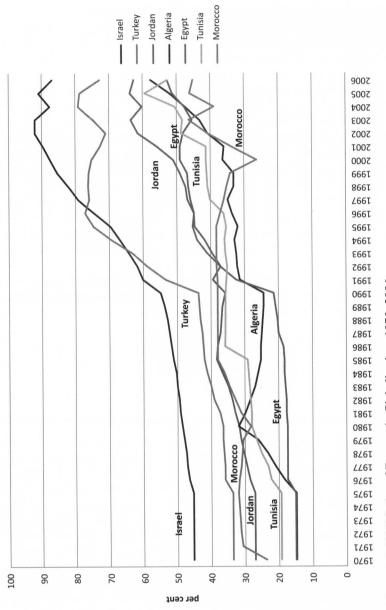

Figure 2.2 KOF Index of Economic Globalization, 1970–2006
Sources: Dreher 2006; Dreher et al., 2008; http://globalization.kof.ethz.ch/

of manufactured goods, much less engage in innovation, and so Tunisia remained vulnerable to fragile export markets.

The region was ever more fully engaged with the global economy, but more structural reforms were clearly needed across the MENA if its economies were to keep up with European and Asian competitors. In terms of human development, too, most of the region still had a long way to go to meet the United Nations' Millennium Development Goals, much less catch up with Greece, Cyprus, Portugal, South Korea, Malaysia, or even Thailand, where gross national per capita income had been less than half Egypt's in 1951. Table 2.1 presents the MENA rankings on the 2007 Human Development Index (HDI), along with those of the other countries. Because HDI indices are composed of life expectancy and educational as well as per capita wealth indices, it is also possible to compare their composite HDI rankings with those of rankings by wealth alone (in purchasing power parity dollars). Many of them do better on wealth than on the composite ranking, as the column subtracting the HDI ranking from the per capita income one reveals. Table 2.1 also compares their rankings on education with those on wealth and reveals that, with the exception of the Jordanians and Palestinians, the MENA populations tended to be ranked as much less educated than wealthy. Adult literacy remained low, especially in Northern Africa and Yemen. Despite some progress since 1997, only bare majorities of Moroccans, for instance were literate or being schooled. Consequently, the region does not yet seem well positioned to build the knowledge-based economies required to take advantage of the demographic "gift" of youth surging into the labor market.

The region, too, has pockets of poverty even in its oil-rich states. Table 2.2 presents the Human Poverty Index assembled by the United Nations Human Development Programme.

Of greater political concern, however, are indications of growing inequality triggered in part by neoliberal reforms to date, because they may intensify the dialectic pitting moralizers against globalizers. Figures 2.3 and 2.4 examine the growing dispersion of salary scales since the 1960s in the industrial sectors of the principal MENA countries (except Saudi Arabia, for which only one data point was available). Although industry is a relatively small part of these countries' respective overall economies, inequality here may reflect parallel inequalities in their much larger services sectors. Inequalities in salaries do not convey a full picture of economic inequalities, but they do seem to reflect the histories of the respective political economies. Figure 2.3, for instance, traces Egypt's evolution from the Nasser era of Arab socialism to President Sadat's *infitah* (opening up) of the economy and Mubarak's consolidation of the

Table 2.1 *Human development index, 2007*

HDI rank	Life expectancy (years) 2007	Adult literacy rate (% aged 15 and above) 1999–2007a	GDP per capita (PPP US$) 2007	Combined gross enrolment in education (%) 2007	Education Index (EI) rank 2007	GDP per capita rank minus HDI rank 2007	GDP per capita rank minus EI rank 2007
25 Greece	79.1	97.1	28517	101.6	11	6	20
26 Korea (Republic of)	79.2	–	24801	98.5	8	9	27
27 Israel	80.7	97.1	26315	89.9	36	7	–2
31 Kuwait	77.5	94.5	47812	72.6	92	–23	–84
32 Cyprus	79.6	97.7	24789	77.6	56	4	–20
33 Qatar	75.5	93.1	74882	80.4	72	–30	–69
34 Portugal	78.6	94.9	22765	88.8	45	8	–3
35 United Arab Emirates	77.3	90	54626	71.4	108	–31	–104
39 Bahrain	75.6	88.8	29723	90.4	64	–9	–34
55 Libyan Arab Jamahiriya	73.8	86.8	14364	95.8	61	2	–4
56 Oman	75.5	84.4	22816	68.2	120	–15	–79
59 Saudi Arabia	72.7	85	22935	78.5	111	–19	–71
66 Malaysia	74.1	91.9	13518	71.5	99	–5	–38
79 Turkey	71.7	88.7	12955	71.1	112	–16	–49
83 Lebanon	71.9	89.6	10109	78.0	98	–7	–22
87 Thailand	68.7	94.1	8135	78.0	74	–5	8
88 Iran (Islamic Republic of)	71.2	82.3	10955	73.2	119	–17	–48
92 China	72.9	93.3	5383	68.7	100	10	2
96 Jordan	72.4	91.1	4901	78.7	94	11	13
98 Tunisia	73.8	77.7	7520	76.2	127	–8	–37
104 Algeria	72.2	75.4	7740	73.6	131	–16	–43
107 Syrian Arab Republic	74.1	83.1	4511	65.7	126	5	–14

110 Occupied Palestinian Territories	73.3	93.8	—	78.3	81	27	56
123 Egypt	69.9	66.4	5349	76.4	138	−20	−35
130 Morocco	71	55.6	4108	61.0	157	−12	−39
140 Yemen	62.5	58.9	2335	54.4	158	−6	−24
150 Sudan	57.9	60.9	2086	39.9	165	−13	−28
154 Mauritania	56.6	55.8	1927	50.6	164	−12	−22
n.r. Iraq	67.8	74.1	—	60.5	139	—	—
Arab States	68.5	71.2	8202	66.2		—	
GCC	74	86.8	30415	77.0		—	
Central and Eastern Europe and the CIS	69.7	97.6	12185	79.5		—	
CIS	67	99.4	10487	81.1		—	
East Asia and the Pacific	72.2	92.7	5733	69.3		—	
Latin America and the Caribbean (UNDP RB)	73.4	91.2	10077	83.4		—	
South Asia	64.1	64.2	2905	58.0		—	
Sub-Saharan Africa	51.5	62.9	2031	53.5		—	

Source: United Nations Development Programme 2009a: 171–175. Education rankings were calculated by the authors from the UNDP's Education Index. Positive numbers in the final columns indicate that HDI or Educational ranking was higher than that of per capita GDP. The Palestinian per capita GDP rank is that of 2006

Table 2.2 *Human and income poverty, c. 2007*

HDI rank	Human poverty index (PHI-1) Rank	Human poverty index (PHI-1) Value (%)	Probability of not surviving to age 40 (% of cohort) 2005–2010	Adult illiteracy rate (% aged 15 and above) 1999–2007	Population not using an improved water source (%) 2006	Children under weight for age (% aged under 5) 2000–2006[c]	$1.25 a day 2000–2007[c]	$2 a day 2000–2007[c]	National poverty line 2000–2006[c]
27 Israel	—	—	1.9	2.9	0	—	—	—	—
31 Kuwait	—	—	2.5	5.5	—	10	—	—	—
32 Cyprus	—	—	2.1	2.3	0	—	—	—	—
33 Qatar	19	5.0	3.0	6.9	0	6	—	—	—
35 United Arab Emirates	35	7.7	2.3	10.0	0	14	—	—	—
39 Bahrain	39	8.0	2.9	11.2	0	9	—	—	—
55 Libyan Arab Jamahiriya	60	13.4	4.0	13.2	29	5	—	—	—
56 Oman	64	14.7	3.0	15.6	18	18	—	—	—
59 Saudi Arabia	53	12.1	4.7	15.0	10	14	—	—	—
66 Malaysia	25	6.1	3.7	8.1	1	8	<2	7.8	—
79 Turkey	40	8.3	5.7	11.3	3	4	2.7	9.0	27.0
83 Lebanon	33	7.6	5.5	10.4	0	4	—	—	—
88 Iran (Islamic Republic of)	59	12.8	6.1	17.7	6	11	<2	8.0	—
92 China	36	7.7	6.2	6.7	12	7	15.9	36.3	2.8
96 Jordan	29	6.6	5.3	8.9	2	4	<2	3.5	14.2
98 Tunisia	65	15.6	4.1	22.3	6	4	2.6	12.8	7.6
104 Algeria	71	17.5	6.4	24.6	15	4	6.8	23.6	22.6
107 Syrian Arab Republic	56	12.6	3.9	16.9	11	10	—	—	—
110 Occupied Palestinian Territories	24	6.0	4.3	6.2	11	3	—	—	—
123 Egypt	82	23.4	7.2	33.6	2	6	<2	18.4	16.7
130 Morocco	96	31.1	6.6	44.4	17	10	2.5	14.0	—
140 Yemen	111	35.7	15.6	41.1	34	46	17.5	46.6	41.8
150 Sudan	104	34.0	23.9	39.1	30	41	—	—	—
154 Mauritania	115	36.2	21.6	44.2	40	32	21.2	44.1	46.3
n.r. Iraq	75	19.4	10.0	25.9	23	8	—	—	—

Source: United Nations Development Programme, 2009a: 176–179

28

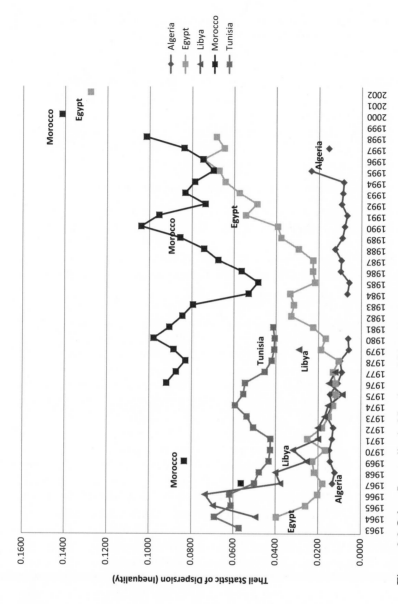

Figure 2.3 Salary Inequality in Northern Africa, 1963–2002
Source: James Galbraith, Inequality Project, University of Texas at Austin: http://utip.gov.utexas.edu/

29

regime of crony capitalists. Even democratic and socialist Algeria began to witness greater wage dispersion in the mid-1990s, suggesting growing inequality.

Figure 2.4 shows how Israel and Turkey, two of the region's more successful reformers, also acquired increasingly dispersed wage structures. Iraq, too, was reforming in a neoliberal direction after the 1980–8 war with Iran (as observed by Chaudhry 1992: 152–4), and Iran was apparently moving toward prerevolutionary levels of inequality, a trend confirmed by extensive household surveys (Salehi-Isfahani 2009).

Strategic rents: foreign aid and arms transfers

Strategic rents, like oil rents, in theory alleviate the pressures for reform. Foreign aid can postpone any structural reform by propping up a regime that is viewed as a vital ally, and arms transfers can pacify its military underpinnings. In our earlier edition we argued that the region's strategic importance had diminished, thereby putting more pressure on governments to reform so as to attract compensatory capital flows from foreign direct investment. The American monopoly on intervention was the principal difference between the new world order and the region's previous more lucrative rent-seeking experiences with foreign powers. The end of the Cold War has, however, reconfirmed the MENA's special vulnerability to external interventions, rather than putting a halt to them. The United States–led military intervention against Iraq in 1991 would not have materialized without a weakened and complaisant Soviet Union and China's abstention in the Security Council. Nor could the United States have so easily attacked and occupied Iraq subsequently, striking without fear of political or military retaliation by any rival power.

Yet historians of the Middle East's exceptionalism have observed that no great outside power long exercises hegemony in this part of the world (Monroe 1981; Brown 1984). In fact, America's "moment" has already passed. The Bush administration transformed America's "moment in the Middle East" into a prolonged death rattle. The Bush administration's first mistake was to have declared a "Global War on Terror," thereby promoting a Saudi playboy into an Islamic Robin Hood. The occupation of Iraq in turn fermented the militant brand of Islamism associated with Osama Bin Laden, leading to ever increasing military involvement in the broader Middle East. Rocketing oil prices, caused in part by American military interventions and threats against Iran, further reinforced the strategic importance of the region that naval geopolitics had singled out as globally pivotal a century earlier. France, Russia, China, and possibly Germany and Japan are awaiting their opportunities to develop

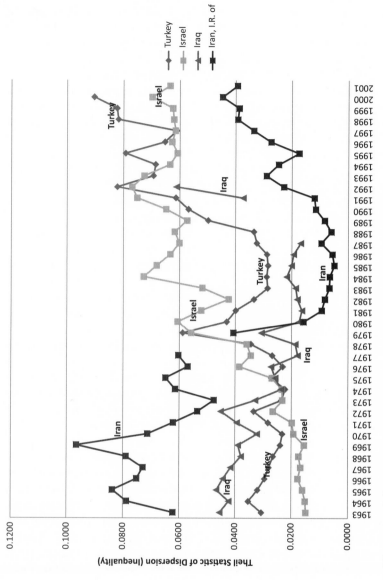

Figure 2.4 Salary Inequality in Iran, Iraq, Israel, and Turkey, 1963–2001
Source: James Galbraith, Inequality Project, University of Texas at Austin: http://utip.gov.utexas.edu/

31

Iraq's bountiful oil fields, once an Iraqi government can agree on the appropriate legislation. If the Obama administration fails to marshal a Palestinian-Israeli two-state peace agreement, U.S. involvement in the region in coming years may focus less on encouraging an Arab-Israeli peace process than on balancing off other contending mediators. A multipolar world is already taking shape in its Middle Eastern energy cockpit.

Why, then, can the region not continue to rest on its geopolitical laurels, suitably irrigated by renewed surges of oil rents? One quick answer is that the Great Recession has rendered all forms of rent uncertain. But even if the Organization of Petroleum Exporting Countries (OPEC) were to stabilize oil prices and profligate outside powers to compete vigorously for political influence (as in the June 7, 2009, elections in Lebanon), the region has paradoxically become too strategically central to escape reform, catching its leaders between the hammer of international pressures and the anvil of political Islam. Polities are penetrated by regional and international influences, and antiseptic technical reforms no longer satisfy impatient donors or restive local populations. The Washington Consensus is as much about good governance as about macroeconomic stability and market incentives for investment. International and regional pressures continue to fuel the competition between globalizers and moralizers within each MENA regime, just as the region seethes with conflicts not only between and among Israelis and the Palestinians but also between Shi'i and Sunni Crescents and, among Sunnis, between global jihadists and their "near" and "far" enemies (Gerges 2005, Burgat 2008).

The ebb and flow of Great Power military and overall geostrategic competition is reflected in the changing pattern of rents that the competitors had previously paid to states of the region, of which foreign aid is a fair measure. Military and economic development assistance of foreign powers had been one of the mainstays sustaining the region's governments' heavy expenditures in the past, supplementing their other traditional means of subsistence to be discussed later – oil revenues earned directly, or indirectly through remittances of guest workers from the petrostates. The international community diminished official development finance to the third world just as the prices of internationally traded oil plummeted from their high points in 1981 to new lows in 1986 and 1998. Not only did development assistance decline in the 1990s, but the MENA region's share of it fell + from 17 percent in 1990 (after an all-time high of 30 percent in 1977) to 9 percent in 1997, reflecting its diminished importance in the world. But then, associated with the Bush administration's military adventures, development assistance swelled after 2003 to new highs of $10.5, $27.6, and $16.8 billion in 2004, 2005, and 2006, most of which went to Iraq. In 2006 the North African countries of Algeria,

Morocco, and Tunisia were all receiving as much or more funding, in current dollars, than in 1990, reflecting America's Trans-Sahara Counterterrorism Initiative, opening a new front in the Global War on Terror. Under the Bush administration, MENA was back in the saddle, receiving more than 16 percent of all official development assistance (ODA). But Figure 2.5 also shows that traditional recipients such as Egypt and Israel had been weaned from the trough, whereas the political flashpoints of Sudan, Yemen, and Lebanon increased their take. International and regional conflicts have given rise to new "gray areas" reminiscent of the nonaligned countries in the Cold War, but they lie for the most part on the region's peripheries.

Other indicators of the strategic importance of the region are military aid and weapons transfers. During the Cold War, the Middle East was the major recipient of arms from the United States and the Soviet Union, but in the 1990s the picture changed. In nominal dollar amounts, inflated by high prices charged to the Gulf states, the region still absorbed 40 percent of the arms in world trade in 1996 (IISS, 1998), conforming to its stereotype as the world's most tension-ridden region. When such trade was measured more accurately, however, it became apparent that Asia had displaced the Middle East as the primary purchaser of arms. According to the Stockholm International Peace Research Institute (SIPRI), which calculates dollar prices for various major weapons systems, the Middle East and North Africa had only one-quarter of the world's conventional arms imports in 1998, whereas East Asia's share was over one-third, and each region's share declined to about 20 percent in 2008. The principal MENA importer during 2004–8 was not Saudi Arabia but rather its tiny neighbor, the United Arab Emirates, whose indigenous population did not exceed 1 million. Its arms imports, lubricated by oceans of oil revenues in need of recycling, were exceeded only by those of China and India. Figure 2.6 shows the principal suppliers to the seven MENA countries who were among the top twenty arms importers over the past decade – Algeria, Egypt, Iran, Israel, Saudi Arabia, Turkey, and the UAE.

The patterns of supply reflect a growing geopolitical competition in the region. France opened a base in the Emirates in 2009, ending, at least symbolically, the American monopoly on Gulf security that arms procurement policies were also reflecting. Although the United States still had almost one-third of the world arms market, some 30 percent of which went to its MENA allies, friendly rivals were already entering the fray, and Russia, too, was regaining the markets of the old Soviet Union while China was acquiring new ones in Algeria, Egypt, and especially Iran. From 2000 to 2008, Russia consistently held over one-quarter of

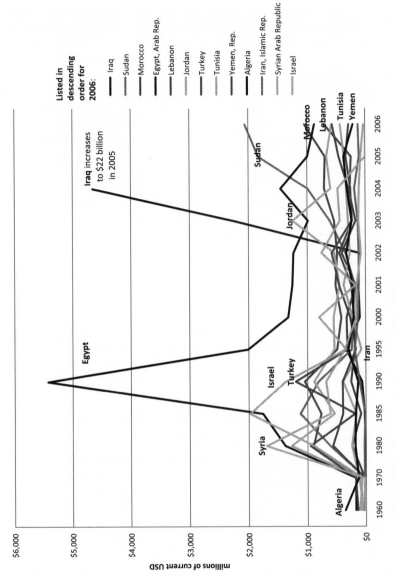

Figure 2.5 Official Development Assistance, 1960–2006

34

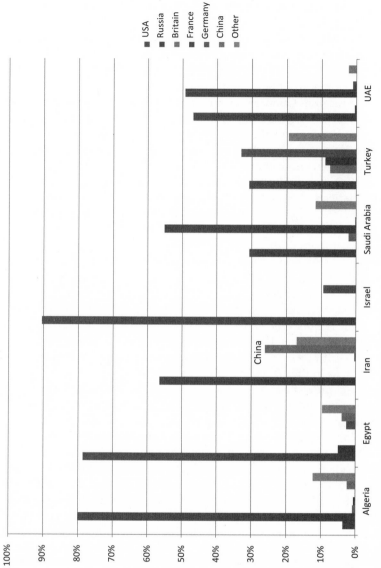

Figure 2.6 Top MENA Arms Importers and Suppliers, 2000–8
Source: SIPRI Arms Transfer Database

35

the world market, competing with the United States as in Cold War times. Although almost half of the arms went to China, some 16 percent went to the MENA, for a cumulative total, as measured by SIPRI, that was almost half that of the United States, and that was channeled mainly to Algeria, Iran, Syria, and Yemen. France, with only 7 to 8 percent of the global market, made more strategic incursions into the lucrative markets of the Gulf Cooperation Council. From 2000 to 2008 it not only rivaled the United States in the United Arab Emirates, where France had already been replacing British suppliers as early as 1973, but temporarily displaced it in America's historic Saudi market. From 2000 to 2008 France provided more than half of Saudi Arabia's arms imports. The events of September 11, 2001, and the 2003 invasion of Iraq had strained Saudi-American relations, and the year following each of these events, 2002 and 2004, also happened to be a year of big Saudi arms purchases. Was it accidental that the United States was asked to supply only 10 to 15 percent of them in those years?

The region still receives an abnormal degree of attention from the outside world because of its alleged involvement with international terrorism and unconventional weapons of destruction. These concerns do not, however, translate into significant strategic rents for allies of the United States in the region. Gone are the Cold War days when the United States bid against the Soviet Union for the favors of their clients. The local allies who still receive American funding, even Egypt and Israel, may once again, as in the 1990s, be subject to cutbacks.

A reinvigorated peace process between Israel and the Palestinians and agreements between Israel and Syria and Lebanon might, however, strengthen Arab support of U.S. goals in the region, notably the non-proliferation of unconventional weapons. Conceivably, were the peace process to be restored, President Obama could dust off a regional initiative originally proposed under the Clinton administration and persuade Congress to finance the United States' proposed share of $750 million in a Middle East Development Bank. Such a sum is small, however, compared with the expected inflow of private-sector funds that depend on a timely implementation of trade aggrements and structural reforms. And if the peace process were to collapse, any public U.S. commitment to financing regional development would be unlikely.

The European Union has maintained an interest in the region because its southern and eastern Mediterranean countries remain Europe's "soft underbelly" in a social if no longer in a strategic sense. North Africa and Turkey are contiguous with Europe, and the potential waves of "boat people" and other illegal immigrants from the countries of the southern Mediterranean basin constitute a threat to Europe's social and political stability. North African guest workers in France and Turks in Germany have already ignited racist backlashes that could one day, if allowed to grow, threaten their respective democratic orders. Turkey, a founding member of the Council of Europe as well as of NATO and the OECD, is almost part of Europe, although the European Union only agreed in 1999 to place Turkey on its waiting list and had originally rejected its application for full membership in 1989. The compromise of a Customs Union, launched on January 1, 1996, "gives the Turks closer economic relations with the EU than any other nonmember countries except Iceland and Norway" (Yeşilada 1998: 182–3). In exchange for opening up its markets to Europe, Turkey receives substantial economic assistance as well as full access to European markets including "reciprocal concessions" on agricultural products. The complex process for accession to the EU began in 2005 with the adoption of a Negotiating Framework.

As for the other southern Mediterranean states, the fifteen foreign ministers of the European Union met with their counterparts in Barcelona in November 1995 to launch a Partnership Initiative calling for a free trade zone (for nonagricultural products) by 2010. In addition to Turkey, the prospective partners were Algeria, Cyprus, Egypt, Israel, Jordan, Lebanon, Malta, Morocco, Syria, Tunisia, and the West Bank and Gaza. Libya, until 1999 shackled by UN sanctions, continues to enjoy observer status. The EU supported its Barcelona Declaration with a budgetary commitment over four years (1996–9) of ECU 4.7 billion (about $5 billion, subsequently cut to €2.8 billion) in grants to finance projects preparing for free trade as well as for other developmental and social objectives. The European Investment Bank, though primarily conceived to finance Eastern European development, committed almost ECU 4 billion in loans.

Europe's new concern with its "Mexico" thus promised additional public funds to the region. Participation agreements signed with Tunisia (July 17, 1995), Morocco (February 26, 1996), and Israel were fully ratified in 1999–2000, followed by agreements with Jordan and the Palestinian Authority. Egypt, Algeria, and Lebanon followed suit, whereas the EU delayed ratification of an agreement with Syria, initialed in 2004, because of political differences that were being resolved in 2009. Some of the programmed bilateral funds also reached Algeria, Lebanon, and Syria, even before formal agreements took effect. In theory, however, EU support does not offer resources for delaying reform, as traditional strategic rents once did. The rapid reformers are supposed to receive greater shares of the allocated funds than the more recalcitrant countries, though size of population (Egypt) and need (West Bank/Gaza) are also taken into account. The funds, however, are limited, and meanwhile the MENA countries are surrendering their preferential access to the EU's agricultural markets, while progressively allowing the EU free access to their markets for industrial products. The countries receiving bilateral assistance are also expected to carry out structural reforms to become more competitive and better able to face the new international competition from Asian textile exports unleashed by the termination in 2005 of the Multi-Fiber Agreement.

The funding was not particularly generous because MENA is less of a European priority than Eastern Europe and Russia and because the EU is not in a financial position to replace declining American aid commitments to the region. Of the total of €8.2 billion allocated between 1995 and 2006, less than two-thirds was actually disbursed by 2007, with up to five-year lags between authorization and disbursement. Figure 2.7 presents only the authorizations by country under MEDA I (Middle East Development Assistance, 1995–9) and MEDA II (2000–6). There were some differences between the proportions committed under MEDA I and MEDA II, but they seemed to reflect the growing needs of the Palestinians after 2000 rather than any rewards for progress in reforms or respect for human rights. The police states of Egypt and Tunisia received lesser shares of commitments under MEDA II, but then so did Morocco, Jordan, and Lebanon. Algeria and Syria were the perennial underdogs, averaging respectively only €1.37 and €1.45 of annual aid per capita and holding small but steady shares of an expanding pie of EU commitments. The total actually disbursed during the twelve years of MEDA was probably less than the foreign exchange that Algerians, Moroccans, and Tunisians working in Europe send back home to their families each year. The EU attempted to inject new life into its partnerships with the Near Neighbor policies of 2003 followed by further attention given to the Southern Mediterranean region in 2008. President Sarkozy's initiative of a Mediterranean Union was diluted, however, by German opposition, and aid levels to the region remained relatively modest.

Remittances from the region's guest workers in Europe and in the GCC countries are indeed a more reliable source of external income for most other MENA countries than any foreign aid. The biggest recipients are Egypt and probably Algeria (where much of the money bypasses official channels). Figure 2.8 shows that Egypt's intake, measured in constant 2000 dollars, increased dramatically after the country's participation in the coalition against Iraq in 1990.

The Egyptians were awarded more jobs in Saudi Arabia. But the remittances then tapered off, probably as a result of their Gulf hosts' and Libya's diminishing oil revenues, before again taking off with the third oil boom. Turkish remittances, by contrast, after weathering recessions in

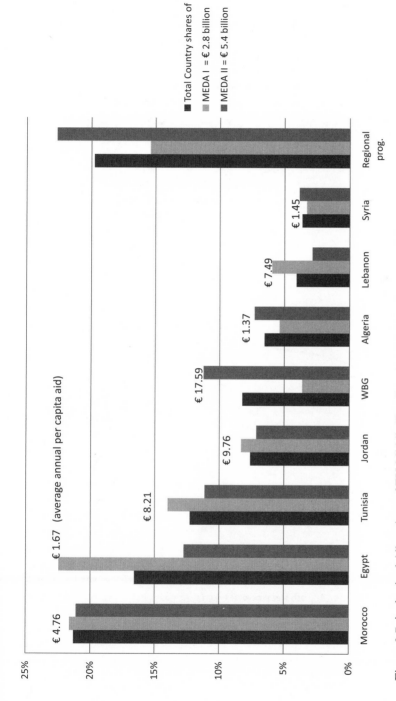

Figure 2.7 Authorized Allocations of EU Middle East Development Assistance, 1995–2006
Source: EU, MEDA I and II Commitments and Payment, Jan. 15, 2007: http://ec.europa.eu/
external_relations/euromed/docs/meda_figures_en.pdf

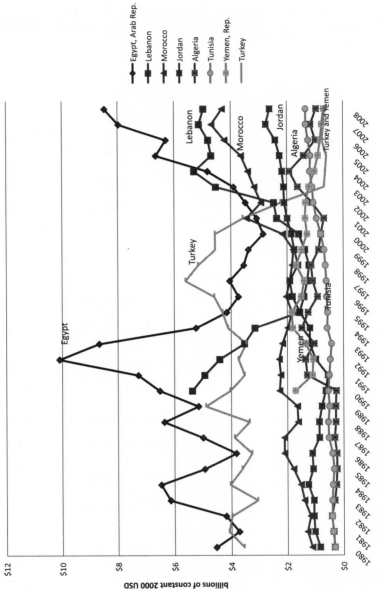

Figure 2.8 Remittances to MENA Countries, 1980–2008
Source: World Bank, *World Development Indicators*

40

Europe and reaching a high of over $4 billion in 2000, shrank drastically to join those of Yemen at the bottom of the pack. North Africa's kept up with inflation. Algeria has twice as many guest workers as Morocco. They are located mainly in France, but their remittances are largely unrecorded, moving through informal channels. Some of the other Arab states were more vulnerable than Egypt to declines in oil revenues, war, and local politics. The Palestinians were especially hard hit after their Kuwaiti hosts claimed that their "guests," many of them installed in Kuwait since 1948, had betrayed them during Iraq's occupation. But Jordan, most affected by the influx of the Palestinian refugees from Kuwait in 1991, was receiving more remittances in 1992 than in 1989, the year before the Iraqi invasion, and remittances regularly constituted 20 percent of the little country's GDP. Yemen was another loser in the war. The Saudis expelled at least 750,000 Yemenites in 1990 because their home government had tried to be neutral. Yet the remittances declined only by one-third and subsequently held steady until recently. The most resilient and dependent of the MENA countries was Lebanon, receiving up to 25 percent of its GDP in the form of remittances – albeit netting much less after withdrawals of foreign businesspeople, workers, and house-hold help – and surpassing Morocco's volume of receipts.

The Great Recession may have an appreciable impact on these receipts as projects in the labor-importing states of the Gulf are delayed or canceled. The jobs of Jordanian engineers, however, are at greater risk than those of Egyptian schoolteachers. The little Levant countries may be hit hard, but Lebanon, at least, was partly shielded by the vast inflows of funds associated with the elections of June 7, 2009, as well as with bank deposits being transferred from GCC banks contaminated by global markets to safe Lebanese havens.

Remittances used to act like strategic rents by cushioning the region from the full effects of globalization. Exposed to European labor conditions or to generous pay scales in the Gulf oil states, guest workers acquired expectations that their home economies could not match. One consequence is that in much of the MENA, labor is priced out of competitive international markets. Its skills, motivation, and productivity do not keep up with nominal wages, making the MENA's real costs of labor comparatively high by the standards of the developing world. Confined to unskilled tasks in industrial economies, or to protected labor markets at home, workers have little incentive to improve their skills. As noted earlier, the MENA countries generally score much lower on the United Nations' Education Index than their wealth would predict – the only exceptions being Jordan and Occupied Palestine. The safety valve of labor migration may be sapping efforts to improve labor competitiveness – in a region otherwise characterized by an abundance of cheap labor that should normally benefit from expansions of world trade (Rogowski 1989). The region confronts the challenge of reducing dependence on foreign labor markets before recessions, wars, social unrest, or substitution of local labor closes them down. For better or worse, remittance "rents" seem bound, like military and economic aid, to diminish in real terms in coming decades, and labor will be obliged to become more competitive.

Oil revenues

The region's other special resource is oil, the value of which is seriously eroded after periodic booms, the latest of which ended in 2008. If El-Gamal and Jaffe (2009) are correct, the world may be headed toward ever more radical volatility in oil prices, as international financial crises amplify the disequilibria between supply and demand that are inherent in an unregulated oil industry. When oil prices are high, too much investment, after long lead times, results in eventual oversupply accompanied by lower prices that in turn discourage sufficient investment, leading to scarcities and price increases, and so on, in twenty-year cycles. In boom times, the petrodollars are recycled in ways that lead to overextensions of bank credit and international crisis, the current Great Recession being the latest in a series of financial shocks that began in 1971 with the floating of the dollar. Further compounding the inherent volatility of the price of oil with a "political risk" as well as a "dollar risk" premium are the competing strategies of the United States and other major oil consumers vying for secure sources of supply. America's invasion of Iraq apparently increased both premiums as well as reducing supply.

More central than ever to the drama are the Middle East and North African oil producers, who hold 65 percent of the world's proven reserves. They are the world's lowest-cost producers, yet produce only 38 percent of total annual global output (BP 2009). At current rates of production the Middle East could keep producing for another 78 years without new discoveries, but the big multinationals prefer to exploit other regions where they enjoy more profitable relations with less well endowed host countries. During the 2003–8 boom, the MENA oil producers, principally the GCC, accumulated an astronomical $1.2 trillion (IMF 2009a: 6) in addition to their normal expenditures and internal investment programs. The United Arab Emirates led the way with the world's largest sovereign wealth fund, but its principal states, Abu Dhabi and Dubai, were also determined to diversify their economies away from dependence on the oil rents. Saudi Arabia, which had seen its oil export revenues plummet from $119 billion in 1981 to $21 billion in 1988 (World Bank, WDI 2008), was more determined to diversify to build an economy that could absorb its burgeoning population. With accumulated reserves of $400 billion it could afford to sustain its industrialization program (SAMBA 2009: 1–2). Despite their vast accumulation of capital, the GCC states were not forgetting lessons from harder times. From a current account surplus of $400 billion in 2008, the IMF projected a net loss for Middle East oil producers of $10 billion in 2009 if oil prices were to average $52 per barrel (IMF 2009a: vi, 5), which they in fact exceeded.

After the dramatic price rises of 1973–4, these economies, as well as some of the others depending on remittances from GCC countries, had been reoriented to the assumption of high petroleum rents. The shift in international bargaining power from Western multinational oil companies to OPEC lasted barely a decade, however. By 1983 OPEC was no longer able to set the price for internationally traded crude petroleum because once supply overtook demand, OPEC could not control the output of its member states. Meanwhile, the industrial consumer states not only had implemented successful conservation policies, but also had gained access to new supplies developed by the multinationals outside OPEC territories. OPEC lost market share in the 1980s without being able to reduce its production sufficiently to keep prices up, and the more market share it lost, the less able it became to protect prices by reducing production. In 1985 the Middle East producers were responsible for only 18.5 percent of the world's crude oil production, and total revenues accruing to these states diminished from $250 billion in 1981 to about $110 billion in 1998, when better Saudi-Iranian relations enabled OPEC to cut production and drive prices and revenues upward into the new millennium and a boom already anticipated by price increases in late 1999.

These countries have learned that oil windfalls are transient and that it is price volatility, rather than any inevitable upward trajectory, that characterizes their underground treasure. They all recognize the need to diversify their economies in efforts to offset the volatility. Sovereign wealth funds (SWFs), anticipated by Kuwait's Fund for Future Generations, which was founded in 1953, are one means of diversification that may be losing its attractiveness as oil prices and investment portfolios become more closely correlated, so that even well-diversified portfolios and oil prices jump more or less in unison to the same tune of global market expectations. A more direct way of offsetting the price volatility of crude petroleum is to integrate upstream production with downstream consumption, the classic formula of the integrated petroleum company pioneered by John D. Rockefeller in the nineteenth century. To some extent, each of the GCC countries is following this path, building refiner- ies and even investing in gas stations overseas, such as Kuwait's Q8 oper- ations in Europe. But not even Saudi Aramco, the wealthiest and best managed of the Arab national oil companies, has the capital or experi- ence – at least not yet – to be another Exxon. As is further discussed in Chapter 6, Saudi Arabia has embarked primarily on petroleum-related capital intensive industries that may to some extent offset diminished petroleum revenues with increased profits in petrochemicals, for instance. Marketing these products has obliged Saudi Arabia to engage in major reforms to become part of the World Trade Organization. Gone are the days, then, when the Gulf petrostate simply collected rents or SWF divi- dends. Operating in the real economy has stimulated the GCC countries to continue their reform efforts despite the favorable oil windfall.

The same cannot be said for some of the other rent collectors. After ambitious efforts in the 1970s to industrialize, Algeria became a cari- cature of the oil rentier state. It deregulated international trade in the 1990s, thereby enabling an import lobby connected with the top lead- ership to block most productive investment outside the hydrocarbon sector, whether for import substitution or a diversification of exports (see Chapter 4). Whatever the industrial policy of the major MENA oil exporters, however, the oil windfall has rendered them ever more dependent on this volatile source of revenue to finance their growing government bureaucracies and services. Table 2.3 shows oil revenues to be covering ever-growing percentages of government revenues for most of them.

Saudi planners cannot forget that in 1998 the government's share of oil revenues plunged to half that of the previous year as total revenues decreased from $45.5 to $29.4 billion, which was even less in constant dollars than the $26.5 billion received in 1985. The budget deficit rose to 10 percent of GDP (SAMA 1999: 95, 101, 276). Every dollar decrease in the price of a barrel of oil increased the deficit by close to 1 percent of GDP in 1998. Oil exporters realize that a prolonged world recession could result in similar fiscal crises in coming years. Table 2.3 also indicates that oil and gas constitute vital elements in the baskets of exports of most of the smaller MENA producers as well. During the decade of the 1990s, such exports accounted annually for almost two-thirds and close to half of Syria's and Egypt's merchandise exports, respectively. Despite declining production, Syria in 2007 still depended on its petroleum exports for 22 percent of the government's revenues.

Table 2.3 Oil and gas revenues, 1972–2007, and as percentages of export earnings and government revenues, 1997 and 2007

| | Oil and gas exports revenues (current billion $) | | | | | | | | As percentages of revenues | | | |
| | | | | | | | | | Export (%) | | Government (%) | |
	1972	1975	1981	1986	1997	1998	2003	2007	1997	2007	1997	2007
Algeria	0.6^f	4.3	14.1	7.6	7.5	4.8	22.7	59.2	96	98.4	62	75.8^v
Bahrain	0.3	1	0	0	0^a	4.5^h	4.8	11	52	80.8	59	80.1^v
Egypt	0.1	0.1	2.1	1.5	1.7	0.8	2.7	8.5	43	52.2	–	23.2^t
Iran	1.6	7.7	–	–	15.7	10.2	26.8	64.1^c	79	83.3^c	55	68.3^w
Iraq	0.1	2.8	13.4	0	4.2	6.1	–	41.4	–	99.6	–	88.5
Kuwait	2.4	8.4	13.4	0	11.8	7.9	15^i	14.9^i	85	–	81	94^s
Libya	2.9	6.8	15.5	8.1	9	5.5	–	43.6^c	95	–	–	93^c
Oman	–	1	4.4	0	5.8	5.2	9	22	29	89.1	74	78.6^u
Qatar	0.8	1.8	3.5^m	2.2^n	4	2.9	12.4	38.2^c	60	90.9^c	57	64.4^d
Saudi Arabia	2^g	29.5	119	26.5^k	45.5	29.4	82.3	210.2	90^a	90.1	75	87.5^r
Syria	–	0.7	1.7	0.6	2.5^b	1.5	4.1	4.4	63^b	40.3^c	38	22^e
Tunisia	0.1	0.4	1.4	0.4	0.5	0.34	0.8	2.4	9	16.2	8	–
UAE	–	–	12.6^m	3.6^j	13.7	9.3	33.3	90.6^c	38	62.3^c	70	70.2
Yemen	–	–	–	0.1^b	1.4^b	–	3.9	6.8	95^b	93.3	68	68

Notes: ^{a} 1996 ^{b} 1995 ^{c} 2006 ^{d} 2006/2007 ^{e} 2007 preliminary data ^{f} 1971
^{g} 1969 ^{h} 2000 ^{i} 2001 ^{j} 1983 ^{k} 1985 ^{m} 1979 ^{n} 1989 ^{p} 1991 ^{q} 1974
^{r} http://www.sama.gov.sa/sites/SAMAEN/ReportsStatistics/ReportsStatisticsLib/5600_R_Annual_En_44_2008_09_23.pdf
^{s} http://in.reuters.com/article/marketsNewsUS/idINLA412340200090510
^{t} Estimated 2007/2008, http://www.imf.org/external/pubs/ft/scr/2009/cr0925.pdf
^{u} http://www.moneoman.gov.om/PublicationAttachment/FACTS_FIGURES.pdf
^{v} http://www.cbb.gov.bh/cmsrule/media/2009/EI%20Jun2009.pdf
^{w} http://www.imf.org/external/pubs/ft/scr/2008/cr08284.pdf
Source: International Monetary Fund Article IV Publications and World Development Indicators, World Bank (online August 2009)

Trade

The impact of volatile oil rents is already reverberating throughout the region, affecting not only the budgets of the oil producers, but also the job security of many other Arab nationals employed in the Gulf. Apart from the petroleum sector and its petrochemical derivatives, the MENA still has little to offer the world economy. Mineral fuels constituted more than three-quarters of the region's exports in 2006, and export diversification, controlling for their respective population sizes, was lower for virtually all of the MENA countries than for most other developing countries (World Bank 2009b: 61–3). The region's ratio of trade to GDP, a conventional measure of the degree of integration of a country or region into the world economy, is relatively high, but much of it is in exchanges of a single raw material for food and manufactured products. Better measures of integration into the world economy are the respective economies' openness to trade and the degree to which the trade is tied to international production processes. As already noted, in the 1960s and 1970s the region was saddled with import substitution industrialization that did not keep up with the explosion of world trade driven by globalized production.

Despite the spectacular rise in oil revenues accompanying the new millennium, however, the leading oil producer, Saudi Arabia, persisted in reforms rather than coasting on its wealth. The Kingdom successfully negotiated its entry into the World Trade Organization in 2005, joining the other GCC states that had acceded earlier, together with Egypt, Israel, Morocco, Tunisia, and Turkey in 1995 and Jordan in 2000. The applications of Algeria, Iraq, Iran, Lebanon, Syria, Sudan, and Yemen were still pending in 2009. With the exceptions of Israel, Turkey, and the GCC countries, even early entrants into the World Trade Organization (WTO) retained high tariff barriers. Despite being the first Arab state to sign an agreement with the EU and among the first to join the WTO, Tunisia keeps its tariffs higher than those of the other MENA members and even nonmembers such as Iran, as Table 2.4 reveals. Cutting tariffs posed special problems for Lebanon, which had relied on customs revenues for up to one-third of its tax revenues in 2000: in 2008, coupled with domestic excise taxes collected at customs, they still constituted 22 percent of the tax revenues (IMF 2009b: 27), but Lebanon had meanwhile reduced its weighted (effective) average tariff duties from 16.5 to 6.1 percent. Table 2.4 also examines the extent to which each country has increased its export of manufactured goods (as measured in constant millions of 2000 U.S. dollars) and the increases of these exports (except for Sudan) as a percentage of GDP and as a percentage of their respective manufacturing outputs.

Table 2.4 *Evolution of manufacture exports, 1985–2006, and weighted tariff rates*

	Manufacture exports in constant 2000 $ millions				As % GDP		As % Mfg value added		Weighted tariff rates	
	1985	1995	2005	2006	1985	2005	1985	2005	Mid-1990s	2006
Algeria	$149.5	$425.9	$416.9	$410.7	0.3%	0.6%	2.4%	10.6%	18.7%	12.5%
Egypt, Arab Republic of	$575.7	$1,795.7	$3,362.1	$3,460.1	1.1%	2.8%	8.0%	16.2%	21.9%	11.8%
Iran, Islamic Republic of			$3,422.6	$4,732.3		2.6%		21.9%	28.1% (2000)	14.4%
Israel	$12,215.5	$17,270.1	$36,422.9	$38,201.8	21.6%	27.3%			5.4%	2.7%
Jordan	$362.3	$925.3	$2,708.5	$3,144.3	6.7%	23.8%	57.9%	130.5%	19.8% (2000)	8.3%
Lebanon (1997, 2004)		$471.2	$1,455.1			7.2%		50.4%	16.5% (2000)	6.1%
Morocco	$1,605.8	$3,287.7	$5,879.5	$6,699.2	6.8%	12.5%	37.0%	72.6%	53.6%	18.8%
Saudi Arabia	$1,032.3	$5,933.4	$10,637.6	$11,182.1	0.8%	4.7%	10.6%	49.8%	11.5%	4.7%
Sudan	$2.9	$43.6	$1.7	—	0.1%	0.0%	18.5%	0.1%	4.0%	15.0%
Syrian Arab Republic	$132.7	$939.7	$1,008.9	$2,092.7	1.2%	4.2%		50.2%	16.6% (2002)	
Tunisia	$973.7	$3,566.1	$6,628.0	$7,089.1	9.2%	27.4%	60.9%	156.2%	30.2%	20.0%
Turkey	$7,714.4	$15,606.1	$40,711.7	$44,912.1	7.2%	16.5%	38.3%	75.8%	7.4%	3.7%

Sources: World Bank, WDI 2008; UNCTAD, *Handbook of Statistics 2008*

The biggest exporters, Israel and Turkey, also demonstrated impressive increases in manufactured exports, with Israel's surpassing 27 percent of GDP by 2005. They each also had the lowest weighted tariff rates in 2006. Turkey reinforced its shift begun in 1980 from a strategy of import substitution industrialization (ISI) to export-led growth, as reflected in the doubling of manufactured exports as a percentage of total manufacture value added. Under much higher tariff walls Morocco and Tunisia also demonstrated the shift in strategy, as did the smaller Jordanian economy, where Qualified Industrial Zones (QIZs) offered preferential access to U.S. markets. Saudi Arabia also cut its tariffs and built up a manufacturing industrial base, half of which was earmarked for export, primarily in petrochemicals. But these exports made up only 4.7 percent of Saudi Arabia's GDP. Manufactured exports constituted even less than those of the other large economies in the region, Egypt and Iran. Indeed, despite widespread tariff reductions, only Israel, Jordan, Morocco, Tunisia, and Turkey appear to be developing diversified export-oriented economies. And it is far from clear to most of the Arab countries whether the benefits of free trade really do outweigh the costs, as the IMF and the World Bank claim.

Many of the MENA countries have few obvious competitive advantages outside the petroleum sector. More free trade will endanger their exports in the short run, regardless of their policy responses. Free trade is also a threat to indigenous manufacturers servicing presently protected local markets. In Egypt, for example, the once export-oriented textile industry is now not only unable to compete on international markets, but needs protection to serve local markets. Significant reduction of tariffs in the absence of major currency devaluation would result in a flood of Asian textiles swamping local markets, a fear shared by many southern Mediterranean countries. Cheap imports have driven many private producers out of business in Tunisia and elsewhere, obliging governments either to increase their burdensome support for public-sector textile manufacturers, or to let them go bankrupt, thereby adding to the already large pool of the unemployed.

Any prospective benefits to MENA countries from free trade depend in part on the degree to which they are already engaged in intra-industry trade (IIT), which is the percentage of their total industrial imports and exports that are concentrated within given industrial sectors. This IIT index tends to be much lower for the Arab countries than for the members of the European Union. With the exceptions of Tunisia and Oman (whose score was inflated by the re-export of tobacco and other products), Arab countries scored lower than their per capita income predicts, either because their trade regimes were more restrictive than the

Table 2.5 *Intra-industry trade index, 1984–2006*

IIT indices	1984–6	1992–4	2006
Algeria	0.051	0.052	0.026
Bahrain	0.107		0.084
Egypt	0.102	0.172	0.107
Iraq			0.008
Jordan	0.207	0.248	0.063
Kuwait	0.192	0.131	0.028
Lebanon			0.063
Libya			0.015
Morocco	0.158	0.204	0.150
Oman	0.164	0.414	0.032
Qatar		0.076	0.030
Saudi Arabia	0.047	0.096	0.070
Sudan			0.009
Syria	0.143	0.125	0.048
Tunisia	0.238	0.301	0.072
United Arab Emirates	0.074	0.081	0.060
Yemen			0.011
Arab countries (weighted averages)	0.159	0.25	
Israel	0.469	0.584	0.430
Turkey	0.159	0.284	0.217
Iran			0.106
Industrial countries	0.876	0.878	
EU	0.86	0.886	
Andean Pact	0.237	0.29	
APEC	0.874	0.903	
Mercosur	0.428	0.519	
NAFTA	0.687	0.773	

Sources: Trade Analysis and Reporting System (TARS), reported by Havrylyshyn and Kunzel 1997; Brülhart 2009: 410–13

global norm or because their industrial structures (in the oil states) were relatively underdeveloped for their income. Controlling for per capita income, their respective IIT indices were substantially lower than those of a sample of Asian countries, but not of Latin American countries. Table 2.5 indicates, however, that Egypt, Jordan, and Morocco, as well as Tunisia, had substantially increased their IIT since the mid-1980s and were catching up with Turkey, even as Turkey and Israel forged ahead. In 2006, when the IIT values were also scored for 3-digit products, defining the same 177 industrial sectors but using a slightly different methodology (Brülhart 2008: 9), the Arab countries were still trailing Turkey and Israel. Morocco had surpassed Tunisia as well as other Arab countries and Iran.

A disaggregated view of the Arab countries' IIT indices also shows substantial increases since the mid-1980s in certain manufacturing categories. In particular, chemical products, soaps, plastics, electrical equipment, ships and boats, aluminum, lead, leather, clothing, and footwear are all sectors with average Arab country IIT indices of 50 percent or more. In theory these and a number of other sectors could benefit from greater trade liberalization. Economic analysts conclude that "the high levels of IIT in so many 3-digit SITC products suggest that the degree of specialization attained enables Arab countries to be competitive in a world market setting" (Havrylyshyn and Kunzel 1997: 21). The Arab countries' IIT indices tend also to be greater for the 10 percent of goods traded among themselves than for their trade with the rest of the world. A further liberalization of intra-Arab trade could therefore enhance the international competitiveness of their respective industrial bases. Israeli economists, too, view intraregional trade, currently a very small proportion of the total even for the Arab world, as having tremendous potential in the event of a full Arab-Israeli peace (Rivlin 2000).

The Great Arab Free Trading Area (GAFTA) formally came into existence on January 1, 2005. Its seventeen founding members, joined later in the year by Algeria, include all the principal Arab countries, but it is too early to tell whether the new agreement, sponsored by the Arab League and superseding other partial arrangements between various groups of Arab countries, will really promote greater interchanges among them. In 1998 intra-Arab trade constituted 8.2 percent of their exports and 7 percent of their imports, much less than regional trade within the EU or even the Andean Pact (Al-Atrash and Yousef, 2000: 4). In 2006 the Arab countries were still only exporting about 8.5 percent of their merchandise to one another, and intra-Arab imports rose to 14 percent mainly because of the high cost of fuel imports from Arab producers (Arab Trade Financing Program 2009).

The liberalization of trade in services was also included in the Uruguay Round, but the MENA countries that have already joined the WTO took advantage of the protective clauses of the General Agreement on Trade in Services (GATS) to maintain some controls over foreign services in their countries, such as international banks or engineering consultant firms. Saudi Arabia, for instance, limited the foreign personnel of most transnational enterprises to 25 percent, including up to 15 percent senior staff (WTO 2005: 4). Only Lebanon, traditionally a freewheeling trading entrepôt before 1975, is negotiating its entry into the WTO, expected in 2010, without referring to the special Article II list GATS exemptions concerning the employment of foreign nationals (WTO 2008: 106).

Further liberalization might enhance the region's services and be of special benefit to the countries that encourage tourism, such as Morocco.

Even wealthy GCC oil exporters, with relatively liberal trade regimes, need to develop more competitive export capacity outside the petroleum sector, where revenues are so unpredictable. The new GAFTA may encourage more intra-Arab trade and help its members to become more competitive and raise their IIT indices. A major challenge is still to attract foreign contributions to the necessary investments in industrial development and renovation and related infrastructure. The specter of volatile oil earnings inclined Saudi Arabia, traditionally a reclusive society, to encourage more private foreign direct investment – except upstream in oil exploration and production – and even to promote tourism.

Capital flows

Most MENA banks were spared the direct impact suffered by the EU and other financial systems that were more closely integrated into global financial markets and exposed to the subprime mortgage securities and packages of derivatives financially engineered in the United States. To become more competitive, however, the MENA still needs to become more closely integrated once the Great Recession subsides.

Major changes in financial flows to developing countries became apparent in the 1990s, and the broad pattern is likely to continue. Official public-sector assistance to developing countries, fueled by the Cold War, was not keeping up with inflation, whereas the private flows of capital became almost indiscriminate torrents in search of emerging markets until the Asian crises erupted in 1997. Figure 2.9 summarizes the major sources of capital flowing into the developing world from 1990 to 2007. More important than the flows, at least for the MENA, could be the technical and managerial expertise accompanying them and better access to international markets and global supply chains.

Official development assistance to developing countries did not keep up with inflation in the 1990s. Despite greater Western largesse since 9/11, it continues to be replaced by the private sector in an expanding pie that increased from less than $50 billion in 1991 to almost $600 billion in 2007. The biggest source was foreign direct investment, but portfolio investments in bonds and equities soared from $14 billion to more than $138 billion in 2007, exceeding all forms of public assistance. Commercial bank lending and trade financing diminished with the turn of the century as earlier debts were being paid off, only to rebound to new heights as petrodollars again became available to recycle. The banks'

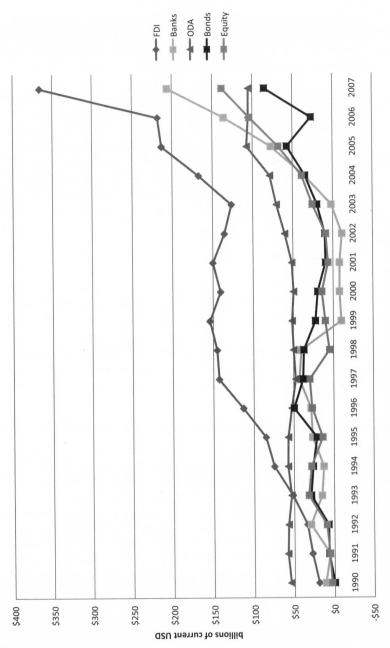

Figure 2.9 Capital Flows to Low- and Middle-Income Countries, 1990–2007
Source: WDI online

share of private capital flows declined from 36 percent to 15.5 percent from 1990 to 1998, but then by 2007 the banks' share constituted more than one-third of these flows of capital, with growing shares reminiscent of the previous oil boom followed by an international debt crisis in 1982.

The MENA region was in large part denied access to the new flows of private capital. As the deputy director of the IMF's Middle Eastern Department observed in the 1990s, "the region has attracted a disproportionately small share of recent international equity flows to developing countries . . . and the total flow of private capital (i.e. equity, bond, and foreign direct investment) to the region has only been about 2 percent of that going to developing countries" (El-Erian 1996: 141). Figure 2.10 shows that the MENA region (excluding Turkey) was faring a little better in the new millennium: although portfolio investment seemed diminished, by 2006 the region attracted slightly more than 10 percent of the foreign direct investment going to middle- and lower-income countries.

Its share of the developing world's population would entitle the region to about 5 percent of the cash flows, but it had on average received less than 2 percent of foreign direct investment (FDI) except in those bumper years of 1992 and 1993, following the first Gulf War, and in 2002–6 as petrodollars poured into poorer parts of the region. The upsurge of capital derived from the international bond market in 2001 and 2002 affected only three countries, Egypt, Lebanon, and Tunisia. In the final analysis ODA was the only source of capital that consistently provided this strategic region with a share of funds greater than its share of population.

Trade barriers and other obstacles discouraged multinationals from investing. Judging from the low IIT indices, there is comparatively little intra-multinational trading in MENA countries, despite the fact that in the world as a whole a full third of all merchandise trade is conducted between affiliates of multinational firms (Sachs 1998). Such trade forms a vital part of global production chains, in which multinational corporations (MNCs) assign specialized tasks in the production of individual commodities to different countries in order to minimize costs. The low IIT indices for the MENA indicate that for the most part MNCs have yet to locate even single links of their production chains there. Investment outside the petroleum and related sectors remains very limited, in part because before the mid-1980s most countries in the region did not need to attract foreign capital. Until the Gulf states' finances were squeezed by declining oil revenues, most of them could count on generous public or private investment flows from these Arab sources. Including workers' remittances, the Gulf states provided $140 billion to other Arab countries between 1973 and 1989, of which over $50 billion constituted official assistance (Boogaerde 1991: 72, 76). Extra rents enabled many of them

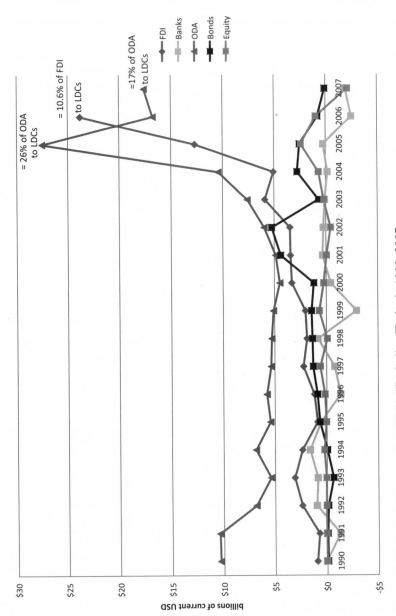

Figure 2.10 Capital Flows to the MENA (Excluding Turkey), 1990–2007
Source: WDI online

to postpone internal reforms toward more market-oriented economies open to foreign investors. Even legislation designed, as in Tunisia, to attract foreign investment is often cumbersome. Investment may exclude certain "strategic" sectors, require too many official permits and favors, and still leave investors unsure of being able to repatriate their profits.

Additional political factors also discourage foreign investors. These factors are examined more fully in Chapter 3, but one deserves special mention: the illiberal, "information-shy" character of most of the incumbent regimes. Investors have information needs that information-shy regimes restrict in a number of ways. In efforts to control all politically related information, they often make it difficult for economic news to be properly disseminated. Of course, information needs for attracting private capital vary, depending on the type of financial flow: international bank lending, bond issues, foreign direct investment, or portfolio investment in local stock markets. International bankers have the least need of publicly available information. They have their own confidential sources, such as their clients, other banks, local government officials, in-house country risk analysts, teams of external consultants, and expensive country risk publications. Commercial banks used to be the principal source of private capital flows to developing countries, and they carry the fewest potential ripple effects on the political structures of borrowing countries. Although they supported IMF and World Bank policies of economic adjustment crafted in the interests of the creditors in the 1980s, their direct impact on host political structures is minimal, and the net effect of their loans may have been to delay needed reforms. International bankers prudently avoid any appearance of involvement in host country politics, and governments can rely on their discretion. But unfortunately for information-shy regimes, traditional commercial bank lending has given way to more open capital markets that require greater transparency if they are to function properly.

All three of the expanding streams of private capital noted in Figure 2.9 – foreign direct investment, bonds, and portfolio investment in local stock markets – require more publicly available information for the private investors than do commercial banks or foreign aid donors. Portfolio investors and managers are particularly demanding, all the more so in the Great Recession. Demands for public information and signals are potentially more troubling and politically destabilizing for information-shy regimes than are the discreet private queries of international bankers or public donors.

Although local stock markets made spectacular progress in the wealthy GCC countries, as discussed in Chapter 3, other stock markets stagnated, especially in countries allergic to the free flow of information.

If Tunisia and Syria suffer the most information constipation, even the wealthy ones enjoying the contemporary "information revolution" with relatively high Internet connectivity, such as the United Arab Emirates, also suffer. Blackberry users were incensed when they discovered that their government-owned service provider, Etasalet, had duped them into "upgrading" their software by downloading a device that censored their email (Wigglesworth et al. 2009). In the wealthy GCC states there are also limits on foreign and even fellow Arab investment, and portfolio investment in the MENA has generally been below the averages in emerging markets. Such investment has the most demanding disclosure requirements of all foreign private investment flows, and it requires reliable regulatory capacities that are not yet proven in these young emerging markets and perhaps are already compromised in some of them. The region was making some progress by 1999, when it attracted 6.8 percent of the investment in "emerging" stock markets, albeit after the Asian collapse had reduced the total equity investment in emerging markets by almost half. Including volatile portfolio investment in Turkey, the region's share approached 10 percent in 1999, only to plummet after the Turkish financial collapse and 9/11. With Turkey, the MENA's share of portfolio equity reached 12 percent in 2005, but the MENA excluding Turkey only managed to attract 3.5 percent that year before again plummeting, as Figure 2.10 indicates.

Figure 2.10 shows that the MENA region was occasionally more successful in financing development through international bond issues, a cheaper form of financing than syndicated loans from international banks. Prices depend on the judgments of the rating agencies, the "new superpowers," as a Lebanese economist once complained (Warde 1997), that survive despite their failures to warn against excessive Wall Street risks in 2007. In the mid-1990s Lebanon, Tunisia, and Turkey scrambled with the other MENA countries to get ratings from Moody's, Standard & Poor's (S&P), and other recognized business authorities. Tunisia, first to make "investment grade," issued sovereign bonds at favorable prices, whereas Lebanon and Turkey had to pay higher risk premiums for their bond issues. In 2009 Israel and all six GCC countries had Moody's ratings in the A's, although Moody's downgraded Dubai's Jebel Ali port in July, for instance, from A1 to A2 because of its parent Dubai World's association with a real estate firm facing hard times (http://www.menareport. com/en/business/249797). Moody's B's included Jordan, Tunisia, Egypt and Morocco, Turkey, and Lebanon, graded in that order. Moody's upgraded Lebanon a bit in April, from B3 to B2, but it was still behind Turkey.

Foreign direct investment is the biggest source of capital for developing countries, but, excluding Turkey, the region's share plummeted from 7.1 percent in 1992 to less than 1.3 percent at the end of the decade. Petrodollars then helped to raise the MENA's share to percentages more reflective of its population, but with the exception of the energy sector, multinationals are deterred from investing because of trade and other restrictions, and also for lack of transparent economic information. Some of the most visible foreign presence, moreover, is not FDI in manufacturing industries, which would increase the IIT indices of MENA countries so that they might better compete in world markets, but rather fast-food chains aimed at local consumers. The MENA seems to be hosting its fair share of McDonald's and Kentucky Fried Chicken, but these franchises do not amount to much, if any, foreign direct investment. Rather, they represent a reverse flow of capital to corporate headquarters from the local investors who buy the franchises.

Figure 2.11 looks at the cumulative net flows of capital into the region (including Turkey but excluding the capital-abundant GCC countries) from 1998 to 2007, by type of resource and by country. The biggest single flow was a cumulative total, in constant 2000 USD, of $67.5 billion in commercial bank loans and trade financing for Turkey, whose outstanding bank debt at the end of the period was $25 billion, or 39 percent of gross national income. Over the decade, however, the international commercial banks extracted, notably from Algeria, more than they disbursed to the rest of the region. Egypt headed the list of ODA beneficiaries, followed by the Palestinian Authority for a much smaller but needier population. In fact Israel, Jordan, and the PA together received more than $18 billion in foreign aid. The region as a whole collected more than $60 billion in foreign aid and – again excluding the GCC countries – also managed to attract $154 billion in foreign direct investment. Much of the latter went to Turkey and Egypt, but a second tier included Morocco, Algeria, and Sudan as well as Israel and Lebanon. Turkey and Lebanon virtually monopolized bond issues during the period, although Egypt and Tunisia garnered small amounts. Over the decade, Israel and Turkey netted a total of almost $35 billion from foreign investors in their respective stock markets, whereas those of Egypt, Jordan, and Morocco incurred small net losses.

The debt problem

The region no longer faces a debt crisis as in the 1980s and 1990s when the IMF imposed harsh conditions of structural adjustment that

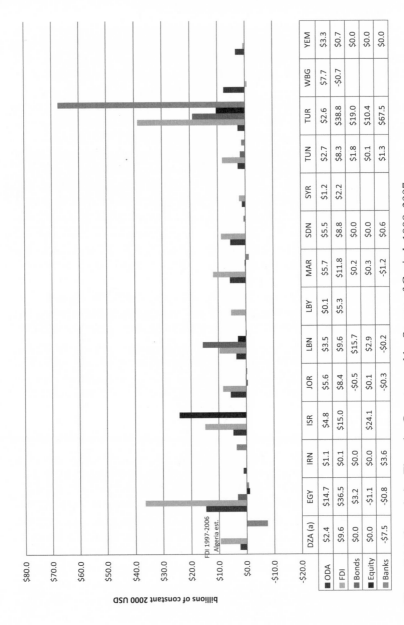

	DZA (a)	EGY	IRN	ISR	JOR	LBN	LBY	MAR	SDN	SYR	TUN	TUR	WBG	YEM
ODA	$2.4	$14.7	$1.1	$4.8	$5.6	$3.5	$0.1	$5.7	$5.5	$1.2	$2.7	$2.6	$7.7	$3.3
FDI	$9.6	$36.5	$0.1	$15.0	$8.4	$9.6	$5.3	$11.8	$8.8	$2.2	$8.3	$38.8	-$0.7	$0.7
Bonds	$0.0	$3.2	$0.0		-$0.5	$15.7		$0.2	$0.0		$1.8	$19.0		$0.0
Equity	$0.0	-$1.1	$0.0	$24.1	$0.1	$2.9		$0.3	$0.0		$0.1	$10.4		$0.0
Banks	-$7.5	-$0.8	$3.6		-$0.3	-$0.2		-$1.2	$0.6		$1.3	$67.5		$0.0

billions of constant 2000 USD

FDI 1997-2006
Algeria est.

Figure 2.11 Cumulative Flows by Country and by Source of Capital, 1998–2007
Source: WDI online; Henry and Saint-Laurent 2007: 9, estimated FDI for Algeria 1996–2006

reminded at least one Egyptian of Superman (Chapter 1) and others of nineteenth-century gunships bombarding Alexandria and besieging Istanbul in the interests of European bondholders. Gone, aside from the bond rating agencies, are most manifestations of the structural power of international capital, although the IMF continues to impose conditions on its remaining borrowers. Up to 2000, however, even the oil states had required external financing to compensate for adverse trade balances, deteriorating oil revenues, and limited prospects for official development assistance. Table 2.6 shows that Saudi Arabia, having preferred to finance its debt from local banks, still averaged a total government debt of 85 percent of GDP over 2000–4. Beginning in 2005, however, escalating oil prices combined with prudent financial management quickly eroded that debt, which fell steadily in absolute terms from 610 billion Saudi riyals to 235 billion riyals in 2008, during which time the debt as a percentage of GDP fell from 65 percent to 16 percent. Despite the dramatic fall of energy prices thereafter, Saudi domestic debt was forecast not to rise above 17 percent of GDP in 2009 and then fall again in 2010 to less than 14 percent (Sfakianakis et al. 2009).

The Great Recession, however, was raising the specter yet again, as in the 1980s, of those terrible twin fiscal and current account deficits. Although it was alleviating commodity import expenses, it was resulting in losses in export earnings and tax revenues as well as collapses in Dubai and elsewhere of real estate markets. This time, if international credit remains tight, much of the debt might have to be financed by the MENA's respective banking systems rather than external sources of capital.

Lebanon is the region's poster child of a debt-ridden economy, in worse shape than Iraq or Mauritania. Table 2.6 shows its total government debt hovering between 160 percent and 180 percent of GDP. In the mid-1990s, then–Prime Minister Hariri, a very wealthy Saudi-Lebanese contractor, fixed the exchange rate of the Lebanese pound to the dollar to enable Lebanese financiers to enjoy fat profits financing the government at high interest rates in Lebanese pounds. Subsequently, the government borrowed more cheaply abroad, floating Eurobonds in dollars bought principally by the Lebanese banks. This diminished the cost of sustaining the high debt, but Lebanon thereby incurred an external debt that amounted in 2007 to 102 percent of GDP, a slight decrease from the 107 percent registered in 2004. Figure 2.12 indicates, however, that debt service charges had diminished from highs of 26 percent to 19 percent in 2007. Hariri's excellent connections with former French president Jacques Chirac as well as with the Saudi royal family resulted in three

Table 2.6 *Total government debt as a percentage of GDP*

Years	2000–4 average	2004	2005	2006	2007	2008	2009 est.
Algeria	53.4%	36.6%	16.0%	23.8%	12.5%	7.2%	8.7%
Bahrain	32.5%	34.4%	28.7%	23.6%	19.3%	15.2%	25.9%
Egypt	97.4%	112.9%	112.8%	98.8%	87.1%	76.5%	73.8%
Iran	23.4%	26.3%	33.7%	19.7%	17.4%	15.1%	14.6%
Iraq		487.3%	361.3%	205.8%	169.8%	108.9%	136.7%
Jordan	97.6%	91.8%	84.0%	77.4%	76.3%	66.1%	65.9%
Kuwait	27.5%	17.3%	11.8%	8.3%	6.9%	5.3%	7.5%
Lebanon	162.8%	167.1%	175.7%	179.9%	167.8%	162.5%	161.9%
Libya	27.8%	1.4%	1.0%	0.9%	0.0%	0.0%	0.0%
Mauritania	227.7%	232.7%	208.6%	110.5%	112.6%	93.7%	95.7%
Morocco	65.9%	59.3%	63.1%	58.1%	53.6%	48.5%	47.5%
Oman	19.7%	15.4%	9.6%	9.1%	6.3%	4.5%	4.9%
Qatar	46.1%	27.8%	19.3%	13.2%	9.4%	7.0%	6.0%
Saudi Arabia	85.0%	65.0%	38.9%	27.3%	18.7%	15.8%	15.6%
Sudan	153.6%	123.0%	106.7%	89.3%	82.3%	70.0%	84.9%
Syria	121.4%	109.8%	56.9%	52.1%	41.1%	30.8%	32.6%
Tunisia	61.0%	59.4%	58.3%	53.7%	50.7%	48.2%	48.4%
Turkey*	75.8%	64.0%	55.3%	51.5%	43.8%		
United Arab Emirates	5.7%	8.2%	9.2%	10.0%	11.2%	9.0%	10.8%
Yemen	57.7%	52.1%	43.8%	40.8%	40.4%	36.1%	39.9%

* 2001–4 average public-sector debt. Sources: IMF 2007, World Development Indicators
Source: IMF 2009a: 46

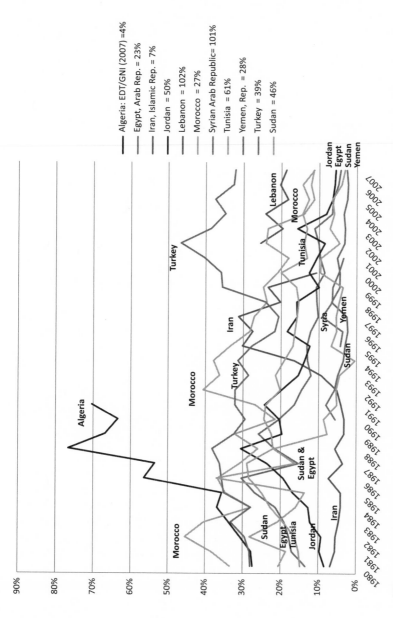

Figure 2.12 Debt Service as a Percentage of Exports, 1980–2008, and Total External Debt as a Percentage of GDP, 2008

Source: World Development Indicators 2009

Paris summits of international donors in 2001, 2003, and 2007 that gave Lebanon some debt relief.

Despite the government's successful efforts to borrow abroad, financing its deficit still crowded out other borrowers at home. Lending in local currency almost exclusively took the form of treasury bills. Lebanon was caught in a debt trap. Interest expenditure on the national debt was costing the government more than 60 percent of its revenues in 1999 (Banque du Liban 1999: 19), and the picture was little changed in 2008. Interest payments on the debt amounted to almost LL 5 trillion ($3.3 billion), or roughly half the revenues and one third of total government expenditures. The huge overall budget deficit, expected to be about 50 percent of revenues and more than 12 percent of GDP in 2009, closely reflected the servicing of the national debt but shows some signs of diminishing (IMF 2010). The commercial banking system and the Lebanese pound survive largely as a result of remittances and relief from the GCC countries. In the late 1990s, Kuwait, Saudi Arabia, and the United Arab Emirates had temporarily rescued Lebanon by depositing hundreds of millions of dollars at the Banque du Liban, Lebanon's central bank. Rescue operations became routine, reinforced by remittances and capital flight from the GCC countries in 2008. Burned by markets in the Gulf, investors were also bidding up Lebanese real estate.

Table 2.6 shows that Iraq and Mauritania are the only countries approaching the Lebanese government's debt levels. Servicing external debt, as indicated in Figure 2.12, also shows how easy the task has become for most of the other countries in the region. Only Turkey, which recently completed a three-year IMF Standby program, must still, as in the late 1980s, set aside one third of its export revenues to repay debt. A number of governments in the region risk being caught in similar debt traps, however, if the Great Recession is prolonged. Egypt's habitual 8 percent fiscal deficit was not, as of May 2009, projected to rise in 2009, but its government debt remains high, and its banks, wobbling under heavy nonperforming loan portfolios (see Figure 3.8), might also need more capital. Tunisia's public finances could also be strained, although its projected deficit for 2009 was only 3.1 percent. Its public debt was less than Egypt's, but its external debt and debt service obligations were higher, relative to exports, and the latter were at the mercy of its European trading partners, whose economies were shrinking.

Part of the attractiveness to Egypt and other countries of substituting domestic for foreign debt is the lack of transparency surrounding internal transactions. Another possible attraction is that the comparatively high interest rates paid for treasury bills and bonds denominated in local currencies guarantee the nominal profitability of public-sector banks that in Egypt, for example, purchase virtually the entirety of such offerings. In Lebanon such loans account for well over half the portfolios of the private-sector banks owned in substantial part by the late Prime Minister Hariri's family, so that in this case, and possibly in others, domestic borrowings guarantee risk-free profits for those in the government responsible for managing the state's finances.

More debt, however, may jeopardize a country's attractiveness to global capital. As a result, MENA governments seek to conceal the real magnitude of domestic borrowings. When external and domestic debt reach substantial proportions, even when much of the domestic debt is to the private sector rather than to government-owned banks, it further increases risk either being inflationary, putting pressure on foreign exchange rates, or crowding out private enterprises to the detriment of economic growth. Despite their diminishing debt service ratios, for example, in 2007 Egypt and Tunisia still had "official" external debts of 23.2 percent and 60 percent of gross national income (GNI), respectively, and outstanding domestic credit, extended in part to the government and public-sector enterprises, amounting to an additional 30.6 percent and 7.3 percent of GDP. Tunisia's total government debt was probably higher than that reported in Table 2.6, because the accounts of the banking system conflate public-sector enterprise with the private sector and hence exclude it from total public borrowing. In 2007, Tunisia was more externally indebted than any country other than Lebanon, although Turkey, with slightly less debt as a percentage of GNI, carried heavier debt servicing obligations. Most governments in the region are likely to discover increasing fiscal deficits and borrowing needs and will be unable to avoid crowding out their respective private sectors.

Pressures for reform

The major MENA countries all have stock markets and new laws to attract foreign investment. They hesitate, however, to implement the reforms that might allow them, as the "serious economists" of the Washington Consensus intimate, to take full advantage of the emerging global economy. Globalization, which offers these countries numerous advantages, also poses very substantial threats. It means opening most domestic markets to foreign competition that is usually better equipped in skills, capital, and marketing power than the local producers. Just as European imports in the nineteenth and early twentieth centuries destroyed much of the MENA's handicraft industries, so a new wave of competition could annihilate years of independent state-led capitalist development in much of the region, including Israel. The economists advise these governments to privatize their state-owned enterprises (SOEs) in order to stop the hemorrhaging of public funds subsidizing their losses and, more generally, to make their economies more competitive in tradable goods.

Even the GCC states feel the pinch of the global economy, not so much because of their gyrating oil revenues as because their small populations are growing and seek employment. Government, the traditional fountainhead of employment in the Gulf as elsewhere in the Arab world, already suffers overstaffing, and private enterprises tend to limit local hires, viewed generally as less efficient and more expensive than expatriates from Asia or from other Arab countries. The wealthy Gulf states, so heavily dependent on foreign management and labor, suffer internal forms of colonialism that more indigenous employment may alleviate in the long run. In the short run, their private sectors face reduced efficiency and possible declines in their modest manufacturing capabilities if they hire nationals. So, for example, textile plants that have been established in the lower Gulf, and which employ Asian labor almost exclusively, would be forced to close their doors if they had to hire local Arab labor.

The employment situations of the GCC countries amplify the general problem, alluded to earlier, that faces the region: underqualified and undermotivated labor forces protected by government regulations. Unemployment is higher in the MENA than in other regions of the world, averaging about 15 percent, but reaching almost half of the labor force in some of the worst performers, such as Algeria. Better-paid and protected workers tend to be clustered in the state-owned enterprises. It is as difficult for governments to privatize them as for the Gulf states to convince their private sectors to hire nationals. Whether in the Gulf or elsewhere, private sectors are reluctant to hire nationals without appropriate qualifications, lest they lose whatever competitive edge they might enjoy. The way out of the employment dilemma involves a combination of short-term policy changes, such as reversing progressive labor legislation that benefits relatively small proportions of workers, and long-term development strategies, such as reform of the educational systems that fail adequately to educate or even train their graduates. But the short-term policy changes are politically problematic, and the long-term developments will not affect the present generation and depend on policy changes that most governments find it difficult to make.

Globalization, in sum, is becoming associated with new forms of cultural confrontation reminiscent of the colonial dialectic. From Casablanca to Tehran, from Istanbul to Riyadh, the MENA states have already moved into the global economy at least at an abstract level. They all have their stock markets, imported (or locally assembled) cars, cosmetics, and other Western consumer items, and they are developing manufacturing capabilities that may in time withstand global competition. Even in Iraq today, they also have their Internet service providers. Indeed, throughout the MENA the use of the Internet is becoming widespread and eliciting new channels of information, including thousands of blog sites, notably in Iran but also across the Arab world. Cybernauts used to be upper middle class, often with university degrees in science or technology and associated at least indirectly with local capitalists and high government officials who were the potential beneficiaries of globalization. These pioneers of cyberspace were sufficiently nimble and polyglot to find niches of comparative advantage in the information age. As the Internet became more available, however, Islamist opponents of incumbent regimes acquired stronger Internet presences. In Iran, where thousands of reformists had taken the lead, the regime was striking back, with "the Islamic Revolutionary Guards Corps' plan to recruit 10,000 Basij bloggers" (Hamid Tehani, cited by Kelly and Etling 2009). In Egypt, blogs linked with sympathizers of the Muslim Brotherhood constituted the largest cluster, surpassing liberal reformists, among some 2,000 Egyptian blog sites surveyed in 2008 (Etling et al. 2009). Certain of the local capitalists and high government officials may, like Iran's Revolutionary Guards, organize their counterattack, but the Anglo-American form of capitalism connoted by the stock markets is more congruent with some forms of Islamism, and notably with Islamic finance, than Egypt's established state capitalist traditions. Egypt is one of the many governments in the region that hesitate to unlock their economic secrets, much less open their protected industries and labor markets to international or internal competition and thereby provoke more opposition.

The incumbent regimes in the region vary considerably in their will and capacity to engage in the reform process. As discussed in the next chapter, political considerations take precedence over economic priorities. The early adjusters, despite their cultivated images of openness to the world economy, cannot engage as radically in the reform process as the World Bank recommends without risking major domestic backlashes and/or the prospects of the steady decline of state-controlled resources that underpin the rule of incumbent elites. Even the ostensible advocates of reform in local business communities tend to advocate liberalization only for others while trying to protect their own market niches and special privileges. Yet international markets supported and oriented by the industrial powers continue to reshape trade and financial markets in ways that oblige even the most recalcitrant regimes in the region to respond positively, or to face ever-bleaker economic prospects.

Suggestions for further reading

Globalization is critically discussed by Gray (1998) and Stiglitz (2006), among many others. Concerning the MENA, Guazzone and Pioppi (2009) offer a rich collection of essays supplementing Noland and Pack (2007) and World Bank (2008b). Concerning oil rentiers, see Tsalik and Schiffrin (2005) and Humphreys et al. (2007).

3   Political capacities and local capital

A state is supposed to be strong and nimble to take full advantage of the accelerated flows of capital, goods, and information associated with the post–Cold War surge of globalization, but few states in the MENA seem to be in the running. Perceived or imagined threats to their survival hobble and tangle a number of them in mushrooming security bureaucracies. Structural adjustment and the rise of political Islam and various ethnic identities have taken their toll, rendering many incumbent regimes ever clumsier, more repressive, and burdened with ever higher costs of police and military establishments. So much so that a representative group of Arab intellectuals issued the *Arab Human Development Report 2002* sparking widespread debate about an alleged "freedom deficit" that was preventing any sustained development in the region. And in Iran, record urban crowds – reminiscent of the massive serial demonstrations leading to the 1979 revolution – protested the irregularities of the June 12, 2009, presidential elections. Indeed, if the World Bank's Voice and Accountability indicator, as reported in Figure 3.1, is a fair measure of the freedom deficit, the region's regimes on average scored lower in 1998 and worse in 2008 than those of any other region except the former Soviet Union, which had helped to shape a number of them to its obsolete security specifications.

This chapter tries independently to compare the capacities of the MENA regimes to mobilize resources efficiently and effectively for sustainable development in response to the challenges of globalization. To recall from Chapter 1, MENA polities consist of three major types – praetorian republics, monarchies, and, last, democracies of varying degrees of institutionalized competitiveness. Each category is in turn composed of subtypes. Praetorian republics are either "bunker" or "bully" states. Praetorian republics ruled by "bullies" have some elements of both civil society and rational-legal legitimacy, which in turn reduce, but do not altogether eliminate, the importance of violence and coercion in political life. The structural power of local capital, although negligible in praetorian republics governed by bullies, is noticeably greater than in bunker states,

67

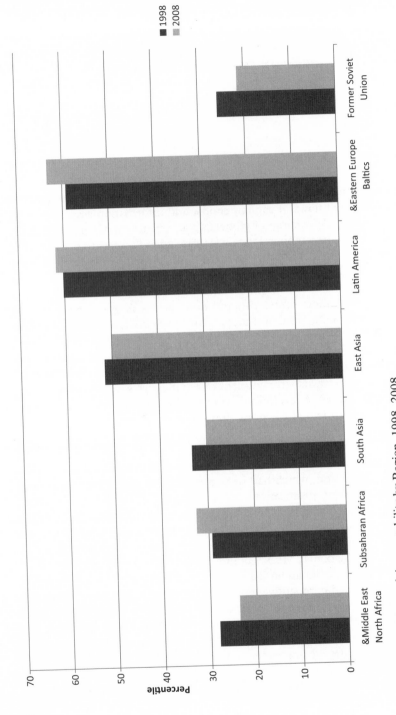

Figure 3.1 Voice and Accountability by Region, 1998, 2008
Source: World Bank, *World Development Indicators* (online 2009)

where security of property is insufficient to permit capital accumulation in the home country. Consequently the "bully" responses to economic globalization are less brutal than those of the bunkers. The limited capacities of the "bully" states, however, and the structural weakness of capital within them, to say nothing of their own political power requirements, have severely constrained their efforts to globalize. Egypt, Tunisia, and post-2005 Iran – after hardliners engineered the election of President Mahmoud Ahmedinejad – comprise the "bully" states of the MENA, whereas Algeria, Iraq, Libya, Sudan, Syria, and Yemen are the bunker states.

MENA monarchies are such largely because the societies in which they persist were not subjected to colonial influence as intense and protracted as those that became republics, where lower strata were mobilized and ultimately removed monarchs or rendered their establishment impossible. Just as traditional political orders in the monarchies were less disrupted by colonial encounters, so, too, their commercial elites typically survived rather than being swept aside by either colonial settlers or radical nationalists. Thus, both state and market in monarchies have had greater continuity than their equivalents among the praetorian republics, and the influence of the market over the state is usually greater in the monarchies than in these republics. It is not surprising, therefore, that monarchical polities and economies tend on the whole to be more open and competitive and hence display greater capacities to respond effectively to the challenges and opportunities of globalization. These capacities, however, are in all cases limited by the prerogatives of royal power, intent as it is on retaining its ruling status. The manner in which that power is exercised varies considerably. Among one group of monarchies, including Morocco, Jordan, and Kuwait, power tends to be relatively dispersed and political competition comparatively institutionalized. Among the other group, the remaining members of the Gulf Cooperation Council (i.e., Bahrain, Oman, Qatar, Saudi Arabia, and the United Arab Emirates), power is more concentrated in ruling families, and political competition is less open, structured, or legitimate.

Finally, the MENA also includes polities that, with qualifying adjectives of various sorts, can reasonably be described as democratic. Turkey and Israel are "ethno-religious" democracies, in which secular Turks and Jewish (especially Ashkenazi) Israelis are privileged participants in their respective political systems, which deny equal rights to Kurds and, until recently, Islamists (in Turkey) and to Arabs and, in much lesser measure, Sephardim (in Israel). Lebanon is a "consociational" democracy, in which elaborate institutional mechanisms based on elite consensus derived from Ottoman historical models and preserved by the French provide political modus operandi to enable competitive religious minorities to cohabit one polity. Conflict arises intermittently as a result of the need to renegotiate those institutional mechanisms, and because of external factors. Last, Iran used to be by name and in fact an Islamic Republic and one in which citizens could change at least part of their government through free and fair elections, hence qualifying it as an Islamic democracy. Befitting democracies, the polities of Israel, Turkey, and Lebanon are more open, competitive, and institutionalized than those of either the praetorian republics or monarchies, and their civil societies are comparatively well developed. Prior to its slide into bully status that commenced in earnest after the reelection of President Khatami in 2001, Iran too had relatively competitive politics buttressed by an active civil society. Political openness and pluralism in the democracies account in considerable measure for their greater capacity to adjust to globalization, but that capacity is also constrained by the intensity of the political identity questions that continue to bedevil these polities and that frequently take precedence over issues of economic management.

That the tripartite categorization of MENA states reflects real political differences is suggested by the relatively close fit between them and "the extent to which country's citizens are able to participate in selecting their government, as well as freedom of expression, freedom of association, and a free media," as measured by the World Bank's Voice and Accountability governance variable. This variable is necessarily a conjunction of subjective perceptions by business and political "experts" that may reflect cultural biases. But if this distillation of attitudes may be perceived by some as "garbage in, garbage out," it also contains a certain reality of international public opinion and is articulated on the World Bank's website even though the Bank issues a disclaimer to the effect that its World Governance Indicators do not reflect its official views.

Figure 3.2, adding Turkey to the MENA region that was depicted in Figure 3.1, shows our democracies, Israel, Turkey, and Lebanon, ranked as the region's leaders in Voice and Accountability. Even our most democratic Israel, however, weighed down by a brutal occupation of Palestinian territories as well as threatened in the eyes of many rightwing Israelis by a Palestinian enemy within, scores well below the 75th percentile of the 208 countries ranked on this governance indicator. Our bullies and bunkers, as expected, are all at the bottom of the scale, along with Saudi Arabia. The monarchies are also in the order our typology suggested, with the relatively liberal ones of Kuwait, Morocco, and Jordan outperforming the five remaining GCC countries. The only very slight discrepancies in our ordering of the regimes concern Algeria, Yemen, and Iraq, three bunker regimes that may not enjoy the very limited "voice and accountability" of the bullies Egypt, Tunisia, and Iran. "Expert" opinion, too, has perhaps

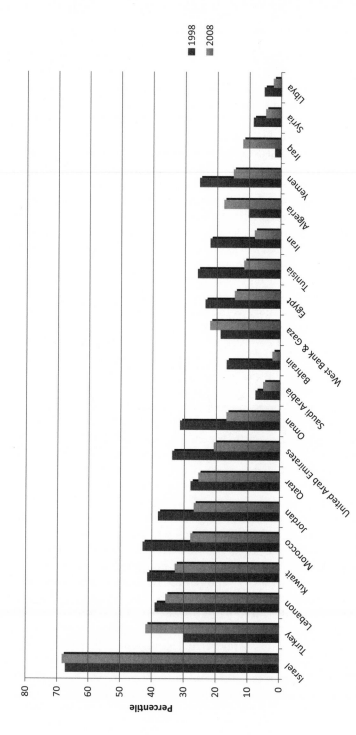

Figure 3.2 Voice and Accountability by Country, 1998, 2008
Source: World Bank, *World Development Indicators* (online 2009)

downgraded Saudi Arabia more than it deserves, a point to be discussed further in Chapter 6.

What is most striking about Figure 3.2 is the decline of "voice and accountability" between 1998 and 2008 throughout much of the MENA compared to the rest of the world,. Only Turkey and Israel among the democracies, the West Bank and Gaza, and Algeria and Iraq among the bunker states received slightly better report cards in 2008 than in 1998. Turkey indeed consolidated democracy with elections in 2002 and 2007 resulting in the victory of a moderate Islamist party, although the country continues to experience tension between the Islamist political leadership and the secular fundamentalist military. The various panels of experts inexplicably also gave Israel slightly, albeit not statistically significantly, better marks in 2008 than in 1998, despite the breakdown in 2000 of the peace process with its Palestinian neighbors and consequent tightening by Israel of its colonial occupation of the West Bank and East Jerusalem and eventual blockade of Gaza. The major trend in the region was toward less voice and accountability as the bullies, Egypt, Iran, and Tunisia, but also more liberal monarchies such as Morocco and Jordan, suppressed the media and political oppositions. The downturn in Iran from the era of President Khatami to that of President Ahmedinejad was statistically significant within the 90 percent probability boundaries of the World Bank's opinion surveys.

All MENA states, however, regardless of how authoritarian or democratic their politics may be, confront major political obstacles that constrain the rate and extent of their economic growth. Polities ruled from bunkers have insufficient state capacities, inadequate civil societies, and business communities that are too dependent to formulate and manage effective strategies of economic development. Praetorian states ruled by "bullies" do have rudimentary civil societies and residual or recently developed capitalists, and hence some resources with which to globalize. But the anxious rulers of these states keep the lid on their rudimentary civil societies and hinder their business communities from interfacing productively with international capital. Although the monarchies grant a little more space to civil society and tend to have more robust capitalists, they also seek to preserve their personal power by imposing oligopolistic control over the market, frequently through family connections. Such control on private business may be less onerous in monarchies than in the praetorian republics, but it nevertheless impedes the development of free, outward-oriented markets. Finally, although the primary business of the MENA democracies is the containment or resolution of disputes that flow from their contested identities, the relatively free flow of information in these democracies, their more robust civil societies, and the greater autonomy of their capitalism from the state provide them significant advantages when confronting the opportunities and challenges of globalization.

Political capacities

"There is by now [in 2009] a strong consensus among both academics and policymakers that good governance provides the fundamental basis for economic development" (FAQs on WGI World Bank website), an argument developed in our book as well (cf. Carothers 2009: 56n10). The World Bank had already broached the importance of political capacity in its 1997 *World Development Report* after discovering the limitations of market forces. In 2003 the Bank zeroed in on the MENA and projected that improvements in various governance indicators would increase the region's rate of growth (World Bank 2003). In friendly rivalry the United Nations Development Programme continued to sponsor a series of Arab Human Development Reports following up on the pioneer 2002 edition that had announced an Arab freedom deficit. The third volume in the series, focusing on governance, depicted the typical Arab state as a black hole "which converts its surrounding social environment into a setting in which nothing moves and from which nothing escapes" (UNDP 2005: 15). The second volume in the series had also plausibly argued that the region's "knowledge deficit" was largely a product of the freedom deficit, preventing the free scholarly inquiry needed to build knowledge-based economies.

MENA states vary considerably in their political capacities. By "capacity" is meant a broad range of dimensions associated with the ability of a regime to mobilize public resources and to use them efficiently and effectively (World Bank 1997: 25). It is not just voice and accountability, code words for liberal democracy, but rather a set of institutions that can promote positive economic outcomes.

The principal component of capacity is the ability to extract taxes. As Ibn Khaldun explained in the fourteenth century, MENA dynasties collapsed periodically because tax bases in this arid region of seasonal migration could not easily support a standing army and self-sustaining infrastructure. His schema applied well to the transhumant societies of his native Maghrib, but less so to riverine civilizations and their sedentary peasant tax bases elaborated as "Oriental despotism" by Karl Wittfogel. Obtaining steady sources of revenue, by hook or by crook, is central to any process of state-building. In the MENA there were some lucrative tax bases associated with Egypt, Mesopotamia, Ottoman Turkey, and, on a smaller scale, the Tunisian Sahel (shoreline facing the East

Mediterranean), but it was primarily foreign powers – Britain, France, and Germany prior to World War I – that completed these processes of extracting taxes for standing administrations: within the past century Europeans controlled the entire region's public finances, except those of Saudi Arabia and Yemen.

If the colonial powers utilized revenues relatively efficiently for their own purposes, they hardly cared to promote accountability and transparency, the mainstays of efficiency and effectiveness in the conduct of public affairs. Accountability, including a relatively independent judiciary, is needed to protect property rights and to restrain the arbitrary behavior of public officials. Transparency, which reinforces accountability, also enhances the efficient allocation of resources by enabling markets to function. As the World Bank observes, "A remote and imperious state, whose deliberations are not transparent, is much more likely to fall into the downward spiral of arbitrary rule and decreasing effectiveness" (World Bank 1997: 28). We have already noted some indications of a downward spiral in Figure 3.2. Without information, neither markets nor institutions nor public opinion can check the descent.

As presently constituted, few political regimes in the region display the combination of transparency and political accountability needed to attract private capital. Most foreign investment that the region does attract goes into sanitized international enclaves such as the hydrocarbon and related sectors, or into tourism and real estate. Rarely outside the energy sector do investors bring new techniques or technologies that would help host countries to climb the value chain of global manufacturing, much less adapt technologies to the needs of expanding labor forces and the knowledge economies needed to absorb them. The biggest challenges to the regimes are internal: to become more accountable and to lift their constraints on the free flow of information. Credible institutions and media are needed. Only then will the necessary external resources become available for economic development.

Israel and Turkey have progressed furthest in these respects, but their political economies, characterized by strong oligopolies and substantial public sectors, limit full disclosure and constrict domestic markets. Both countries are relatively liberal and democratic – although not to their ethnic minorities – and, like other MENA countries, they harbor strong "fundamentalist" social forces among their ethnic majorities that may paralyze economic policy and even challenge the legitimacy of their respective regimes. As with the other MENA countries, their capacity for further reform and integration into the world economy may be constrained by these moralizing challenges to globalization. The influence that globalizers may bring to bear within a given regime depends only in part on their political resources and strategies of coalition building. More crucial to any economic reform program is the available political and administrative infrastructure and its reflective extensions in civil society. Any reform is conditioned by the state's ability to mobilize resources, by the accountability of its agents to abstract rules and procedures, and by the transparency of the markets that they regulate. *Extractive capability* (with its associated instruments of coercion), *credible institutions*, and *reliable information channels* comprise the three distinct vectors of political capacity.

The extractive capability

It is sometimes argued that the oil-rich states have not developed representative institutions and traditions of accountability because they did not need to extract taxes from their populations. If there is "No taxation without representation," then why bother with representation in tax-free societies? Better still, the oil rentiers could distribute some of the oil revenues to their people as social services and benefices in exchange for acquiescence to patrimonial rule. Oil revenues thus completed the work of colonialism in discouraging the transparency and accountability of government institutions. Usually these vectors of capacity are by-products, at least in noncolonial settings, of the administrative penetration of a society to extract taxes. For instance, prior to the oil boom in Saudi Arabia, the monarchy was accountable to the merchants. Kiren Chaudhry (1997) argues, perhaps with some exaggeration (Vitalis 1999: 659–61), that the young Saudi state raised revenues by cutting deals with Hijazi merchants to build national markets; a common currency also facilitated the collection of direct taxes such as zakat, a Muslim tax on property. It was only with the oil boom that the "central extractive and regulatory bureaucracies" atrophied, as distributive ministries acquired priority over the core Ministry of Finance. A major consequence was a loss of economic information and the transparency needed to make national markets work efficiently. Ideological reliance on "free markets" for distributing oil rents resulted instead in a new class of Najdi capitalists linked by family to the midlevel Najdi bureaucrats who allocated oil revenues to them through state banks.

Most of the other MENA states also indirectly benefit from oil and other rents and are commonly viewed as distributive rather than productive states. They, too, preempt any claims for representation or accountability with "social contracts" promising a variety of social services in exchange for loyalty. According to this view, these states face a major crisis whenever they can no longer deliver the goods. As the rents evaporate, they must tax more and therefore presumably be subjected to greater accountability.

Such at least is the theory of the rentier state. And the huge revenues accumulated by the big petroleum exporters until 2009 suggest no current need to increase taxes or even to cut back significantly on investment programs. As for the states depending on remittances and investment from the wealthier petrostates, however, Table 3.1 indicates that most of them, along with the other non-oil states of the region, already tax their citizens "adequately," given their levels of per capita income.

Virtually all of them, except Egypt, Lebanon, and possibly Syria, capture more than 19 percent of GDP, far more than the averages for other regions reported in the table. Algeria and Qatar, big oil and gas exporters, also show high extractive capability, but that is only because they record as tax revenue some of their hydrocarbon rents. Qatar's direct taxes, for example, include levies on foreign companies, taxes that Algeria also used to extract directly from the companies but that now appear as indirect sales taxes on equipment and the like. The other oil rentiers tax much less. The biggest of them, Saudi Arabia, has one of the highest rates of general government consumption in the region, but relies on oil for more than 85 percent of its revenues (SAMA 2009: 132). Its taxation rate is unavailable but might be more meaningfully measured by cuts in subsidized services, such as electricity, rather than by actual taxes. Taxation in Kuwait and the UAE is also negligible. The more diversified and poorer economies of Bahrain, Iran, and Oman tax in the range of 4 to 8 percent of GDP but obviously have other sources of revenue, bringing the government totals of 30 percent or more of GDP. In Iran's relatively diversified economy "more than 50 percent of the economy is legally tax-exempt, and the rest engaging in tax evasion. Subsidies to both consumers and producers amount to nearly 25 percent of the national product" (Amuzegar 2010b).

When compared by type of taxes imposed, some of the MENA states appear to be in the big leagues with high-income member countries of the Organisation for Economic Co-operation and Development (OECD) and East Asian "tigers." Egypt, Israel, Morocco, Tunisia, Turkey, and even Yemen raise over 5 percent of GDP from direct taxes, up to half their total taxes. But a finer-grained analysis of "direct taxes" suggests a different picture. Whereas direct taxes on individual incomes are typically some 10 percent of GDP in Europe, in the MENA, except for Israel, they tend to be much less. In Egypt, for example, taxes on individual income and profits were estimated by the Ministry of Finance in 2009, the fifth year of its campaign to enhance revenues from such taxes, to reach $2.64 billion, which is just over 2 percent of the 2009 estimated GDP of $127 billion. Table 3.1 shows significant progress, however, in

Table 3.1 *Structure of government revenues, c. 2007*

Year	Tax revenue (as % of GDP)	Direct tax (as % of GDP)	Direct tax	(Revenues as percentage of total government revenues)				
				Sales tax	Social security	Customs	Other taxes	Other revenues
2007 Algeria[1]	29.6	2.8	6.9	9.4	–	3.6	0.8	79.6
2006 Bahrain (2006)	3.8	1.2	4	3.2	–	3.7	1.3	87.3
2007 Egypt, Arab Republic of	15.4	7.7	28.5	19.2	–	5	2.9	43.2
2007 Iran, Islamic Republic of	7.3	4.5	12	1.8	11.7	4.9	0.8	80.4
2007 Israel	28.4	13	32.4	28.5	15.7	0.8	5.2	29.4
2007 Jordan	26.7	4	12.5	39.5	0.5	9.3	14.2	17.3
2007 Kuwait	0.9	0.2	0.5	–	–	1.2	0.1	98.1
2007 Lebanon[2]	14.8	3.5	15	25.6	–	14.3	9.2	35.8
2007 Morocco	25.2	9.4	27.1	31	13.2	6.9	6.5	27.6
2001 Oman (2001)	7.4	5.7	21.1	1.25	–	2.8	2.2	73.0
2007 Qatar	23.2	21.2[4]	47.5	–	–	3.3	–	48.1
1999 Syrian Arab Republic (1999)	17.4	9	37.5	19.1	0.3	9.9	6.3	27.2
2007 Tunisia	21.2	8.3	27.5	32.4	18.1	6.1	4.5	29.3
2007 Turkey[3]	18.5	5.6	21.9	38.2	–	1.1	10.3	30.2
1999 United Arab Emirates (1999)	1.7	–	–	17.2	–	–	–	83.0

(*continued*)

Table 3.1 (continued)

| Year | Tax revenue (as % of GDP) | Direct tax (as % of GDP) | (Revenues as percentage of total government revenues) | | | | | |
			Direct tax	Sales tax	Social security	Customs	Other taxes	Other revenues
1999 Yemen, Republic of (1999)	9.4	4.3	17.8	9.1	–	10.2	1.7	60.7
2007 Middle East and North Africa	16.4	4.3	13	32.7	–	6.1	4.5	50.3
2004 East Asia and Pacific (2004)	10.1	3	25.9	34.9	–	6	–	15.5
2007 Europe and Central Asia	17.3	4	13.4	40.3	30.3	1.4	0.3	42.5
2007 Latin America and Caribbean	–	–	16.7	38.3	–	5.1	2.5	
2007 South Asia	11.3	2.4	17.6	29.4	0.3	14.8	2.5	16.3
2007 Lower Middle Income	11.6	2.8[5]	17.3	38.9	–	5.2	0.9	28.4
2007 Upper Middle Income	–	–	15.5	36.8	22.1	4.5	1.2	–

[1] http://www.imf.org/external/pubs/ft/scr/2009/cr09111.pdf
[2] http://www.imf.org/external/pubs/ft/scr/2009/cr09131.pdf
[3] http://www.imf.org/external/pubs/ft/scr/2008/cr08272.pdf
[4] Data from 2006
[5] Data from 2006
Source: World Bank, *World Development Indicators* (online July 2009)

the collection of direct taxes when corporations as well as individuals are included. Each of the major non-oil countries increased their take by 2 percent to 3 percent of GDP over the past decade. Israel still led the pack with direct taxes constituting 13 percent of GDP, but Morocco, Egypt, and Tunisia were already in the range of 8 percent.

Much of the progress in tax collection reported in Table 3.1, however, was due instead to increased sales taxes. Advised by the IMF, a number of countries, beginning with Tunisia in 1997, rationalized a value-added tax to increase their overall tax harvest even while reducing tariff rates on imported goods. Tariffs had constituted 23, 44, 15, and 26 percent of the revenues, respectively, of Jordan, Lebanon, Morocco, and Tunisia in the mid-1990s, but within a decade these countries were able, thanks to sales tax increases, to engage in substantial tariff reductions. By 2007, their taxes on international revenues had steadily declined, with the exception of Lebanon, to under 10 percent of total state revenues, although it was still only Israel and Turkey, among the non-oil exporters, that had virtually dispensed with duties as a source of revenue. In Egypt, taxes on international trade contributed 9 percent of total revenue for the period 2005–9, compared to the 36 percent provided by goods and services taxes and 50 percent by income taxes, of which more than three quarters resulted from corporate taxes (Egypt, Ministry of Finance 2010).

Imposing higher income taxes, however, evidently had not obliged states to become more accountable. Any changes seemed instead to work in the opposite direction: voice and accountability had diminished as tax rates increased, as can be seen by comparing Table 3.1 with Figure 3.2 that registered the diminished voices, replicating an earlier finding from a cross-national sample that gross taxation rates are not related to accountability as rentier theory would have it (Waterbury 1997: 153). Taxes probably do result in greater resistance by taxpayers and stimulate demands for accountability and even participation in decision making about utilization of tax revenues, but authoritarian states can respond by beefing up their security establishments, as was so blatantly the practice of the bully republics.

Institutional credibility and property rights

The transparency and accountability required for economic development in the global economy cannot be directly measured like a regime's extractive capability. But extraction and bureaucratic penetration leave other monetary indicators for measuring accountability. One obvious concomitant of efficient extraction is a common national currency, because it is easier to collect money than bundles of dates or fractions of a goat. Paper or electronic transfers are yet another improvement over hauling sacks of coins or stacks of bills. In the twentieth century the construction of a state's extractive capability is invariably accompanied by progress in commercial banking, and banks are predicated on social trust – which may even survive the collapse of the state, as in Lebanon in the mid-1970s. The scope and reach of commercial banking systems are easily measured by statistics routinely collected by the IMF since 1948. A recent cross-national study of the political capacity to adjust has used these data as a proxy for institutional credibility and accountability. It roughly reflects our theoretical concern and usefully serves as a starting point for comparing the capacities of MENA countries. The "adequacy of institutions" to protect property rights and to guarantee contracts and the rule of law "can be approximated by the relative use of currency in comparison to 'contract-intensive money'" (Snider 1996: 8) that lies within a country's banking system. As Lewis Snider explains,

Where institutions are highly informal, i.e. where contract enforcement and security of property rights are inadequate, and the policy environment is uncertain, transactions will generally be self-enforcing and currency will be the only money that is widely used. Where there is a high degree of public confidence in the security of property rights and in contract enforcement, other types of money that are held or invested in banks and other financial institutions and instruments assume much more importance. (Snider 1996: 9)

Anyone who has lived in Algeria or Syria may intuitively agree. In each of these countries in the late 1980s the cash circulating outside the banking systems exceeded one-third of GDP. People kept their cash under their mattresses and operated in flourishing informal economies of contraband ("trabendo" in Algeria) goods and undercover services. Over the years the bundles have grown bigger as the governments avoid printing denominations of currency large enough to keep up with inflation for fear of counterfeiters. It may be a conceptual stretch to argue that the ratio of "contractive-intensive money" (CIM) in banks to the total money supply (M2) also measures the more general credibility of institutions and property rights, but the results for the MENA seem plausible at the high and low ends of the spectrum.

Table 3.2 shows that all of our democracies, and even the lapsed democracy of Iran, harbor banking systems that attract the highest proportions of the total money supply. Their CIM ratios all exceed 90 percent, although Lebanon's numbers may be more exaggerated than others because of the vast amounts of U.S. greenbacks not counted in its currency supply (Corm 1998: 123). Lebanon is the one country in the region where cash dollars readily substitute for Lebanese pounds wherever one

Table 3.2 *Contract-Intensive Money and World Governance Indicators of MENA countries, 2007–8*

Contract-Intensive Money (CIM)		CIM ranking		World Governance Indicators of the World Bank			
2008	2007			Government effectiveness	Rule of law	Regulatory quality	Control of corruption
97.9%	97.9%	Lebanon	democracy	Israel	Israel	Israel	Qatar
96.8%	96.6%	Kuwait	GCC	UAE	Qatar	Bahrain	UAE
	96.4%	Israel	GCC	Qatar	Oman	Qatar	Israel
	96.2%	Qatar	GCC	Bahrain	UAE	Oman	Oman
95.5%	95.4%	Bahrain, Kingdom of	GCC	Oman	Kuwait	UAE	Kuwait
94.5%	95.4%	United Arab Emirates	GCC	*Tunisia*	Bahrain	*Jordan*	Bahrain
	94.3%	Iran, I. R. of	democracy	*Jordan*	*Jordan*	Turkey	*Jordan*
93.8%	93.4%	Turkey	democracy	Turkey	Saudi Arabia	Saudi Arabia	Saudi Arabia
	90.9%	Saudi Arabia	GCC	Kuwait	Saudi Arabia		Turkey
91.7%	90.8%	Oman	GCC	Saudi Arabia	*Tunisia*	Tunisia	Tunisia
85.6%	86.5%	Egypt	bully	Morocco	Turkey	*Kuwait*	Morocco
86.0%	86.2%	Jordan	monarchy	Egypt	Egypt	Morocco	*Algeria*
86.4%	85.4%	Tunisia	bully	*Algeria*	Morocco	Egypt	Egypt
85.5%	82.3%	Libya	bunker	*Lebanon*		*Lebanon*	Iran
82.1%	81.4%	Morocco	monarchy	*Syria*	Syria	Yemen	Yemen
76.3%	77.1%	Algeria	bunker	Iran	Libya	Algeria	Libya
72.5%	71.9%	Yemen, Republic of	bunker	Libya	Algeria	Libya	*Lebanon*
70.5%	71.4%	Sudan	bunker	Yemen	*Lebanon*	Iraq	Syria
	68.1%	Syrian Arab Republic	bunker	Iraq	*Iran*	Syria	Iraq
49.9%	47.9%	Iraq	bunker	Sudan	Yemen	Sudan	Sudan
					Sudan	*Iran*	
					Iraq		

Sources: IMF, International Financial Statistics; World Bank, World Development Indicators

goes, with an exchange rate fixed since the mid-1990s. The only other countries exceeding CIM ratios of 90 percent are the wealthy GCC states. Their citizens apparently also trust their respective banking systems. Much of the money supply may derive from their hydrocarbon deposits, but oil alone cannot explain high CIM ratios. Other major hydrocarbon exporters, Algeria and Iraq, have much lower CIM ratios. In other words, if CIM really is a proxy for respect for property rights, then property – the lifeblood of civil society – is considerably more secure in MENA's democracies and in wealthy petrostates than in the bunker states. The other monarchies do not appear on the whole to respect property rights more than do the praetorian bullies, but both of these nondemocratic forms of government appear to be significantly more accountable than those led by bunkered elites. If what is really being measured is the informality of the economy, then informal markets seem strongly associated with unaccountable government. A large informal sector may also blunt a state's macroeconomic tools and dull its extractive capability.

Indeed, it is the bunker states such as Iraq, confined in its Green Zone, that cluster at the low end of our CIM scale. Algeria, Sudan, Syria, and Yemen, too, display the weak states, poorly articulated civil societies, and hobbled bourgeoisies that are characteristic of the bunker state. Fierce and authoritarian as they may be, they lack institutional roots in their respective societies, and the people shy away from banks, associated as they are with distant and feared public authorities. There is only one slightly "deviant" bunker, Libya, which displays a slightly higher CIM, having crossed the 80 percent mark in 2007. In fact, all of the bunkers, with the possible exception of Saddam Hussein's Iraq, showed significant progress over the years in increasing their CIM ratios. As government expanded, more employees received official paychecks. Differences still remain, however, between the fierce weak states and the somewhat stronger bullies and non-oil monarchies.

Egypt, Jordan, Tunisia, and Morocco all occupy middle positions on the CIM scale, joined recently by Libya. And indeed their financial systems reflect some of the correlates of CIM, such as more expansive credit to the private sector, a point to which we return later when we discuss the structural power of local capital.

Evidently, then, CIM seems to be a useful indicator of the credibility of public institutions, a major vector of political capacity. The virtue of this indicator is that it is objective, measured by teams of IMF officials ever since World War II. Its weakness lies in its ambiguity. Can we really be sure that it is measuring the credibility of public institutions in general as well as that of commercial banks, their strategies, and consumer preferences (Clague et al. 1997)?

Another way to assess institutional capacity and property rights is to consult the various spectra of opinions of the "experts" tabulated in World Bank's World Governance Indicators. Their most useful measure of capacity may be Government Effectiveness (Kurtz and Schrank 2007: 543), but Table 3.2 examines the rankings of the Rule of Law, Control of Corruption, and Regulatory Quality as well, as they also apparently relate to institutional capacity. Government Effectiveness pretty well mirrors our CIM rankings. It rates the democracies – except Lebanon – and the high-CIM GCC states ahead of the others and puts most of the bunkers, except Algeria and Syria, at the bottom of the pack. Tunisia and Jordan get higher rankings than their CIM scores: some bullies and monarchies can indeed have more efficient administrations than their peer regimes, but along the dimension of effectiveness, democracies and oil rich municipalities seem generally to have the most efficient administrations, at least in the eyes of our experts, and the bunkers tend to be least able to cope with issues not directly related to security.

As for the Rule of Law, it is not clear that the subjective judgments of the "experts" are any closer to political reality than the CIM ratios, which can be interpreted, at least in the MENA, as a useful surrogate for property rights. Of the "misfits" (marked on Table 3.2 in bold italics) ranked higher than their CIM scores on this indicator, Jordan may indeed be as protective of private property as some of the wealthier monarchies, but Tunisia seems out of place. CIM more reliably ranks Tunisia well behind Turkey, whereas putting President Ben Ali's predatory family rule ahead of Turkey's constitutional traditions seems wrongheaded. The other blatant misfits are Lebanon and Iran, victims, perhaps, of political bias on the part of critical majorities of experts. Property rights in Lebanon are perhaps only for the wealthy tens of thousands who can pay to defend them, but few democracies offer better services. As for Iran, CIM seems to be a better indicator of property rights than expert opinion, which evidently overlooked its relatively strong and creditworthy private sector in placing Iran below Syria, Libya, and Algeria as well as Lebanon.

Regulatory quality is another subjective WGI: it "measures the ability of the government to formulate and implement sound policies and regulations that permit and promote private sector development." Again, as on the other WGI indicators, our democracies and GCC countries, with the exceptions of Lebanon and Kuwait, score highest, whereas the bunkers without exception are at the bottom of the heap, along with Iran. Finally, "Control of Corruption measures the extent to which public power is exercised for private gain, including petty and grand forms of corruption, as well as 'capture' of the state by elites and private interests." The story is very similar: the only countries slightly ahead of our ranking order are Jordan, viewed by expert opinion as being closer to the GCC monarchies than to the other monarchies and bullies in the region, and Algeria, viewed as a bully not a bunker. Lebanon, however, is rated among the most corrupt, and private interests indeed captured this problematic democracy, albeit probably no more so than those that captured Algeria and other bunker republics.

To conclude, CIM seems largely to capture the property rights and institutional credibility associated with political capacity, and the rank orders pretty well coincide not only with our typology of democracies, monarchies, bullies, and bunkers, but also with most of the collective subjective judgments tabulated by the World Bank's World Governance Indicators.

Transparency and reliable information

As already observed from Figure 3.2, Voice and Accountability does register our democracies, Israel, Turkey, and Lebanon, as the top three MENA states, followed by the relatively liberal monarchies of Kuwait, Morocco, and Jordan and the wealthy, relatively permissive family regimes of the other set of little GCC oil municipalities. And most of our bunkers, as might be expected, indeed place at the bottom of the expert rankings on Voice and Accountability, but some of these fierce weak states can also permit a greater appearance of Voice and Account-ability than monarchies or bullies. Algeria and Yemen deviate from the other bunkers, suggesting that when the bunker is literally at war with dissidents and civil society is weak and disorganized, displays of dissent do not seriously threaten a bunker.

Voice and Accountability, like the Freedom House or polity scores that it incorporates in its overall rankings, may be a fair measure of liberal democracy and of the "freedom deficit" critically noted in Arab Human Development reports, but it deserves to be supplemented by other indica-tors of information flows. The ability to access reliable information is key to attracting the local and foreign investment needed for economic devel-opment. It may not be possible to censor sensitive political information out of economic information in societies where political and economic elites considerably overlap, so that traditional political freedom remains a major dimension of transparency and reliable information flows. But it is also useful to separate information from the other rights included in the broad Voice variable. The Press Freedom Index annually assembled by Reporters without Borders focuses more specifically on press freedom violations. Figure 3.3 reports the rankings for 2004 and 2009 and com-pares them with the Voice and Accountability rankings for 2008.

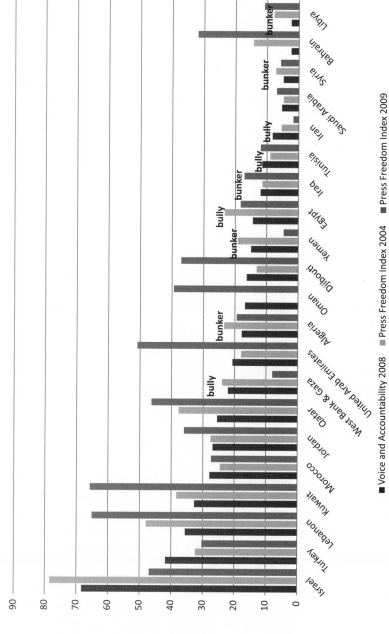

Figure 3.3 Press Freedom Index by Country, 2004 and 2009
Source: Reporters Without Borders

The first thing to note about these percentile rankings is that the dismal showings of Voice and Accountability in the MENA, the "freedom deficit," are largely amplified in the treatments of the press. Even Israel, approaching the 70th percentile on the Voice and Accountability index, scores lower than the 50th percentile on Press Freedom in 2009. Largely the result of the treatment of journalists during the Israeli repression of Gaza in December-January of 2008–9, Reporters Without Borders explains the slide of 47 places in Israel's ranking, from the 73rd percentile in 2008 (as in 2004), to 47th in 2009: "Arrests of journalists (and not only foreign ones), their conviction and in some cases their deportation are the reasons for Israel's nose-dive. Israel's media are outspoken and investigate sensitive subjects thoroughly, but military censorship is still in force" (RSF 2009). The only countries that rise above the median are Lebanon and Kuwait, whereas our other putative democracy, Turkey, sinks to the 30th percentile in 2009, because of "a surge in cases of censorship, especially censorship of media that represent minorities (above all the Kurds), and efforts by members of government bodies, the armed forces and judicial system to maintain their control over coverage of matters of general interest" (RSF 2009). In early 2008, most of the Arab countries agreed to a Charter of Principles for Regulating Radio and Television Satellite Broadcasting and Reception that "in reality aims to muzzle voices and diminish the margin of freedom available" (UNDP 2009b: 57).

As on the Voice and Accountability Index, our democracies and some of the smaller GCC states cluster at the top, whereas most of the bunkers, marked on the graph, largely come in last. Bullies rival the bunkers in their treatments of journalists, as can also be seen in Figure 3.3; in this light Algeria is a liberal paradise compared to its eastern neighbors. Ben Ali's Tunisia, along with Qaddafi's Libya and Bashar al-Asad's Syria, is described as "living hell" for journalists. The bullies discourage newspaper readership almost as much as the bunkers. The Committee to Protect Journalists (CPJ) has consistently rated Tunisia's President Ben Ali among the ten worst enemies of journalism, and in 1997 President Mubarak was also admitted to the select circle of dictators. Tunisia was expelled that year from the World Press Association for failing to defend the freedom of its journalists. The authorities in 1990 had banned what little of an independent press existed and delayed permitting its citizens access to the Internet until late 1997. In 2009 the CPJ reported about the MENA's rising tide of bloggers (see Chapter 2): "Relying on a mix of detentions, regulations, and intimidation, authorities in Iran, Syria, Saudi Arabia, Tunisia, and Egypt have emerged as the leading online oppressors in the Middle East and North Africa" (CPJ 2009). This list of oppressors may help readers to interpret the rankings of the Press Freedom Index.

The region has progressed considerably, however, in expanding lateral means of communication such as telephones and the Internet, which are less easily manipulated by governments than the "heavy" broadcast media. Figure 3.4 examines Internet usage and mobile telephone subscriptions, comparing the country data for 2007 with MENA regional averages and those of East Asia, Latin America, and high-income countries. By that year the MENA had already surpassed East Asian averages. Mobile subscriptions on average exceeded one per person in the wealthier little GCC states and Israel, as in other high-income countries. Mobiles are clearly a reflection of per capita income, but they also offer tools for voicing popular discontent, as evidenced by the massive urban protests in Iran against the apparent manipulation of the June 2009 presidential election returns. Less well known were the massive demonstrations in Algiers in protest both against the Israeli crackdown on Gaza in January 2009 and against the refusal of the Algerian authorities to permit demonstrations. Mobile telephones may have once been the toys of the wealthy, but they are now widespread and enable rapid, low-cost messaging services. The other major communications infrastructure for uncontrolled information flow is the Internet. Here even the wealthier parts of the region lagged well behind Latin America as well as high-income countries. Of course, access alone does not enable free communication. Most of the regimes in the region engage in extensive filtering, and the cyberpolice, already prominent in Tunisia, may be a growth industry throughout much of the region, except in the democracies and some of the smaller GCC states.

A closer look at Figure 3.4 shows that Iran, although it may have become a bully state, was keeping up with the other democracies in Internet usage. In content as well as penetration, the Persian-language blogs seemed to be compensating for Iran's limits to press liberties. A Harvard (Berkman Institute) study of its "blogosphere" identified some 60,000 continuously updated sites in 2007, compared to a total of about 35,000 such sites identified by the same authors in a similar study of the Arab Middle East and North Africa in 2008 (Kelly and Etling 2008, Etling et al. 2009). Figure 3.4 also shows that the other bullies, Egypt and Tunisia, enjoy less Internet access than the monarchies but more than the bunkers – with the surprising exception of Syria, whose president had chaired the Syrian Computer Society before becoming president.

To conclude this discussion of political capacities, our democracies consistently rank high on most indicators, whereas the bunkers get the lowest scores. Oil wealth is associated with a diminished extractive capability, but also with high CIM ratios, more effective administration, and

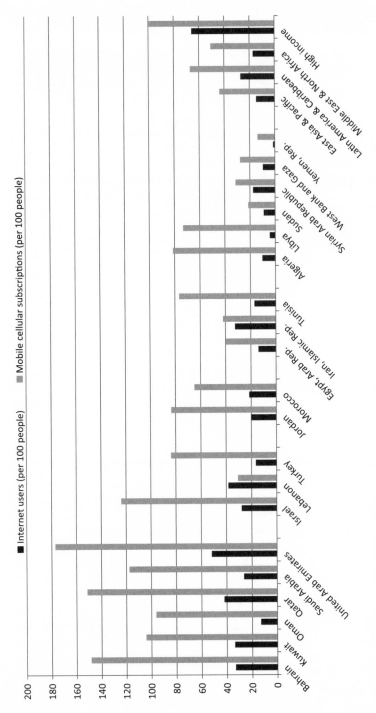

Figure 3.4 Internet and Mobiles by Country and Region, 2007
Source: World Bank, *World Development Indicators* (online 2009)

stronger if not necessarily more liberal information structures. The other monarchies and bullies lie somewhere in the middle on most indicators: generally the monarchies tend to be more transparent than the bullies, although the non-oil monarchies of Jordan and Morocco appear to have less credible institutions, as measured by contract-intensive money, than the small monarchies of the GCC. Egypt and Tunisia score higher than the bunker states, but lower than the monarchies, on most indicators of capacity. At the low end of the spectrum, the bunkers – Algeria, Iraq, Libya, Sudan, Syria, and Yemen – have the largest informal economies escaping administrative control. Algeria and Yemen still enjoy more voice and freedom of the press than the others, but this bottom tier of states also appears, except for Syria, to be least receptive to the Internet. In sum, the data on political capacities suggest that the democracies are best endowed, that monarchies by and large do better than praetorian republics, and that the bunker states within this latter category have the least developed capacities.

These capacities may ultimately depend on the capitalist legacies that the independent states inherited, transformed, or tried to destroy. The states with the lowest political and administrative capacities also turn out to have the most diminished capitalist classes.

The structural power of local capital

Political capacities are conditioned by the structural power of local capital that the respective states try to control. Independent states transformed and sometimes destroyed their capitalist colonial legacies, expropriating dependent local capitalists as well as the foreigners. Whatever the outcome, the structural power of local capital remains a major factor that lengthens the reach yet constrains the power of the respective regimes. Structural power strengthens civil society, which is a capitalist construct shaped by domestic and international capital flows as well as by state regulations. Although nongovernmental organizations (NGOs), political parties, and trade unions are important symptoms of socioeconomic preferences and capacities, the driving force of civil society is finance capital. Any winning coalitions of globalizers or moralizers will depend on the domestic and international capital they can mobilize. Put differently, the politics of economic development does not occur in a vacuum of insulated policy makers, but instead is driven by expectations of financial flows and investments of local and foreign businesses. Such is the structural power of finance capital, which varies considerably, depending on how the economy was colonized and decolonized. How local capitalists and labor interpret and articulate their interests will in turn condition the processes of structural adjustment and economic reform.

The structural power of local capital can be inferred in part from an analysis of the countries' respective commercial banking systems. Commercial banks offer an approximate picture of a country's economy because they finance much of its real assets. Another possible indicator is the stock market, because it, too, is a source of finance capital, albeit a less substantial source than domestic banking systems in this part of the world. These capital markets so central to Anglo-American capitalism have developed rapidly in recent years, as Table 3.3 indicates. Their market capitalization and trading activity appear to be catching up with emerging markets in other regions, even East Asia and Latin America. In 2007, the turnover ratios of the Saudi and Turkish stock markets were in the major leagues with Japan. Saudi market capitalization, too, reached the scale of a number of older emerging and established stock markets. Despite a major correction in 2006, the value of outstanding shares on the Saudi market was 135 percent of GDP in 2007, exceeding the values relative to their respective economies of France, Germany, and Japan, and within striking distance of the United States.

Even so, the numbers of companies listed on the MENA exchanges was limited, with little Israel leading the way with 630 companies in 2008, followed by Egypt's 373, Iran's 329, and Turkey's 284. Despite its higher market capitalization, Saudi Arabia listed only 127 companies in 2008. Relatively democratic and commerce-minded Lebanon listed only 11. Listings seemed to be diminishing because Egypt weeded out companies that had listed for tax breaks but not provided the necessary information about their financial condition. The more active MENA stock markets indeed signify local capital on the move, but they capture the movements of only a relatively small proportion of the region's private enterprises. Firms generally prefer to raise capital through commercial bank loans rather than open themselves up to stock markets where outside investors would require more information. Stock markets require greater transparency than private owners, ever wary of the tax collector, are ready to provide. Unable to finance their own growth through retained earnings, the enterprises become heavily indebted to commercial banks. These in theory have the power to make or break most businesses.

Credits extended to the private sector, which includes most if not all of the companies listed on the stock exchanges, may therefore be a better indication than stock market capitalization of the potential density and power of private-sector enterprise in a broad collective sense. Individual enterprises saddled with huge debts may be sickly dependents, but the collective debt outstanding to the private sector is a measure of its size and

Table 3.3 Stock markets, 1998 and 2008

	Market capitalization (as % GDP)		Stocks traded, turnover ratio (%)		Listed domestic companies, total		Market capital (current billions $)	
	1998	2007	1998	2008	1998	2008	1998	2008
Algeria	–	–	–	–	–	–	–	–
Bahrain	109.5	–	–	12	38	45	$6.8	$21.2
Egypt	28.7	106.8	22.3	58.6	861	373	$24.4	$85.9
Iran	14.5	15.9	9.3	19.7[1]	275	329[1]	$14.9	$49.0
Iraq	–	–	–	–	–	–	–	–
Israel	36.2	144.2	26.4	60.2	650	630	$39.6	$134.5
Jordan	73.8	260.3	11.6	72.7	150	262	$5.8	$35.8
Kuwait	69.9	167.7	144.9[2]	83.2	69	202	$18.1	$107.2
Lebanon	14.1	44.6	12.4	6.9	12	11	$2.4	$9.6
Libya	–	–	–	–	–	–	–	–
Morocco	39.2	100.5	10.1	31.4	53	77	$15.7	$65.7
Oman	31.2	–	33.8	44.2	131	127	$4.4	$14.9
Qatar	37.4	–	–	56.1	19	42	$3.8	$76.3
Saudi Arabia	29.2	135	26.9	137.8	74	127	$42.6	$246.3
Syria	0	0	0	0	0	0		
Tunisia	11.4	15.3	0.9	25.5	38	49	$2.3	$6.4
Turkey	12.9	43.7	154.9	118.5	277	284	$33.6	$117.9
United Arab Emirates	18.7	–	–	89.8	44	96	$9.1	$97.9
West Bank and Gaza	15.1	–	11	31.3[1]	20	35[1]	$0.6	$2.1
Yemen	–	–	–	–	–	–		

(continued)

Table 3.3 (continued)

	Market capitalization (as % GDP)		Stocks traded, turnover ratio (%)		Listed domestic companies, total		Market capital (current billions $)	
	1998	2007	1998	2008	1998	2008	1998	2008
Middle East and North Africa	23.9	55.9[1]	13.1	28.7[1]	1409	1179[1]	66.0	1070.8[1]
Korea	35.1	115.9	184.7	181.2	1079	1798	$121.2	$494.6
Malaysia	136.6	174.4	30.9	31.4	736	977	$98.6	$187.1
Singapore	114.6	219.1	50.5	122[1]	321	472[1]	$94.5	$180.0
Thailand	31.2	79.9	71.2	78.2	418	476	$34.9	$102.6
Latin America and Caribbean	19.5	71.4	42.7	47	2087	1302	$394.4	$1,178.1
Argentina	15.2	33	30.2	19.3	130	107	$45.3	$52.3
Brazil	19.1	104.3	70.9	74.3	527	432	$160.9	$589.4
Chile	65.3	129.9	7.3	21.2	287	235	$51.9	$132.4
Mexico	21.8	38.9	28.5	34.3	194	125	$91.7	$232.6
Venezuela	8.3	—	14.2	1.34[1]	94	60[1]	$7.6	$8.3[3]
Sub-Saharan Africa	78.7	—	20.2	—	1120	912	$183.3	$573.1
Cote d'Ivoire	14.2	42.2	4.5	4.1	35	38	$1.8	$7.1
Nigeria	9	52.2	5.2	29.3	186	213	$2.9	$49.8
South Africa	126.8	294.5	30.4	60.6	668	425	$170.3	$491.3
High Income: OECD	106.9	120.2	91.1	182.7[1]	22165	25334[1]	$24,823.5	$25,581.7
France	67.4	107	68.7	131.5[1]	711	707[1]	$991.5	$1,492.3
Germany	50.1	63.5	144.9	179.7[1]	741	658[1]	$1,094.0	$1,108.0
Japan	64.7	101.6	40.3	141.6[1]	2416	3844[1]	$2,495.8	$3,220.5
United Kingdom	165.6	139.2	53.4	270.1[1]	2087	2588[1]	$2,374.3	$1,852.0
United States	154.7	145.1	106.2	216.5[1]	8450	5130[1]	$13,451.4	$11,737.6

[1] Data from 2007
[2] Data from 1997
[3] Data from 2006

Sources: World Development Indicators, World Bank (online August 2009)

strength. Commercial banks bear the brunt of business financing for the MENA and indeed for most of the developing world, much as five or six Berlin banks did for the German economy a century ago, when capital was scarce and the banks controlled much of German heavy industry. The banking structures are the critical channel through which finance capital exercises structural power. Analysis of the commercial banking structures therefore offers a way of mapping the structural power of local capital in a political economy.

Types of commercial banking structures

The critical dimensions of a banking system are its autonomy and the degree of concentration of its member banks. Autonomous and less concentrated (hence presumably more competitive) systems exemplify an Anglo-American form of credit allocation, in contrast to the German pattern of autonomous oligopoly or to the varieties of "French" state-managed systems that we discussed in Chapter 1. It will be recalled that different models were imposed on the region in the nineteenth century, depending on the timing as well as the nationality of the financial imperialists. Latecomers such as French business groups in Morocco, for example, acquired the oligopolistic characteristics of German rather than French capitalism, so that Morocco's structures resembled those of Turkey more than, say, those of French Algeria.

The structural power of capital will be greater in autonomous than in state-managed systems, and in the less competitive, oligopolistic system "concentration... clearly increases the power of the concentrated segment of the private sector vis-à-vis the government" (Haggard and Lee 1993: 16). These two dimensions, autonomy and the degree of concentration or competitiveness, are ultimately matters of judgment rather than of any single, simple measure, but ownership turns out to be a pretty fair indicator of autonomy. State-owned banks tend to follow political orders and reflect the clientelistic practices of their real bosses, whereas privately owned banks tend to distribute their loans and services by more rational business criteria. Commercial banking systems consisting exclusively or in large part of state-owned banks can therefore be considered less autonomous than those that are predominantly privately owned. Adding up the share of assets controlled by the government-owned banks thus offers a rough and ready indicator of autonomy. The indicator of our other dimension, competitiveness, is the banking industry's structure: the greater the number of middling-sized banks, usually, the more they will be competing with one another. The degree of concentration is readily measured and offers a rough mapping of this second dimension. The

World Bank has recorded the percentage of deposits held by the top five banks in their sample of 143 countries. In the previous edition of this book, we used another indicator of concentration, the sum of the squares of the shares of deposits held by each bank in the system (Herfindahl-Hirschman Index), but the more recent World Bank data pretty much reflect the pattern we discovered from data taken in the mid-1990s.

Figure 3.5 captures the commercial banking structures of the MENA countries for which data were available. To the left are the countries whose banking systems are largely controlled by the government, defined as it owning more than 50 percent of the capital of banks that control over 40 percent of the total assets of the banking system. Government control may be underestimated because in many situations in the MENA, a 20 percent share of the capital – or even less – can give a government the power to dictate, whereas in others, as in the United States during the present financial crisis, larger government ownership does not necessarily translate into allocating the bank's credit to favored government clients.

To the right in Figure 3.5, the banks with less government ownership (along with tiny Qatar, where the government is the ruling family) are ranged in order of their concentration of deposits. Those with relatively high concentrations, such as Kuwait, Israel, Oman, and Morocco, may replicate the "German" sort of system of oligopolistic allocations of credit. Although no contemporary MENA system fully replicates that of imperial Germany a century ago, concentrated systems with strong private-sector financial performance qualify for structural power. In more étatiste systems, the structural power of local capital is more problematic. It must be inferred from the individual financial performances of the banks as well as from the market shares. To the extent that they are really permitted to compete for loans and deposits, the public-sector banks will usually be at a disadvantage, weighed down by nonperforming loans from public-sector enterprises. If they were finally actually to lose their state support, the étatiste system could change into a more autonomous and competitive Anglo-American type, as is the intention, if not necessarily the outcome, of the structural adjustment of the financial sector promoted by World Bank programs. Figure 3.5 shows how Turkey, once an étatist system like Egypt's currently, has evolved along these lines into a system that begins to resemble Lebanon's relatively more competitive freewheeling one.

Exclusively public-sector banking systems

Because state bureaucracies are usually ignorant of commercial banking practices, they find it difficult to establish publicly owned banks but easy

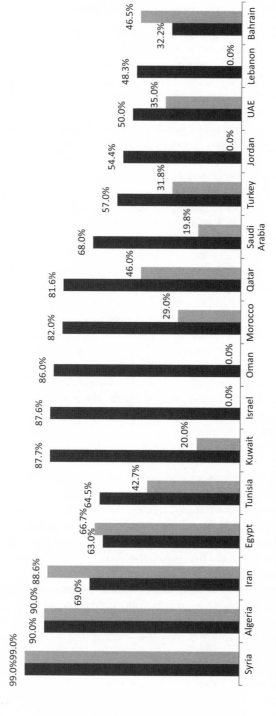

■ Deposits of Top 5 banks   ■ Govt-owned Assets

Figure 3.5 Commercial Banking Structures, c. 2007
Source: Caprio et al. 2008 (World Bank)

to nationalize existing private ones. Exclusively public-sector systems tend by default to be concentrated in a small number of state banks that have absorbed a more complex private sector. In their zeal for bureaucratic rationality, the Algerians and the Egyptians in Nasser's "socialist" years specialized their respective banks by sector, thereby breaking with professional banking practices of portfolio diversification. The Iraqi regime went a step further, controlling all transactions through one big state bank until the late 1980s, when a competitor was invented as part of Saddam Hussein's economic liberalization program. Syria, too, hosted just one big state bank and four small specialized ones, until opening in 2001 to privately owned banks.

In such systems the banks are simply the relays of a central treasury to which the central bank is also subservient. There is no real banking, much less any structural power of private capital. Planners rather than bankers allocate the finance capital, and corrupt officials may siphon off some of it to their brothers or cousins in private enterprises. Any loose investment capital avoids the banking system altogether and simply contributes to a huge informal economy, as indicated by the low CIM ratios discussed earlier. Recent data were unavailable, but Libya's structure mirrored Algeria's in the mid-1990s, just as Iraq mirrored Syria's, and there is no reason to believe that any substantive structural changes have occurred, whether in bunkered down Iraq or in Libya after international sanctions were lifted. It is hardly coincidental that the low-CIM countries, Algeria, Iraq, Syria, and Libya, are also those that have almost exclusively concentrated, public-sector banking systems.

Mixed ownership, but still heavily concentrated in public-sector banks

In this transitional system, the public-sector banks still dominate credit allocation and usually hold more than 50 percent of the market. Whether fragmented or concentrated, private-sector banks remain locked into the public oligopoly. Efforts to break away from it are likely to be suppressed by a regime intent on preserving its patronage networks, even though they are under international pressure in the MENA, as they were in Indonesia, to privatize their banks and clean up their portfolios of nonperforming loans.

Countries in this category include contemporary Egypt, Iran, and Tunisia. Tunisia is included here at the margins, but a finer grained analysis indicated in 1995 that the government could control a bank if it held a 20 percent interest, and that banks in this category controlled more than 80 percent of the country's banking assets. Although two small banks were privatized in the past decade, two large ones still dominate the system in Tunisia, much as in Egypt. The banks finance substantial private as well as public sectors, yet the structural power of local private capital remains minimal, reflecting its fragmentation and subordination to the public sector in the banking system. To the extent that there is any recognizable capitalist system, it is of the "French" étatiste variety.

Significantly, Egypt and Tunisia are the only two countries in the region whose banking systems were viewed by international business analysts as less "open" in 2000 than in 1996 (O'Driscoll et al. 2000), as their political regimes struggled over reforms. In 2007 the analysts gave each country only 30 out of 100 for its banking system, despite better scores on most of their other indices of "economic freedom" – and these bullies fared only slightly better than the 20s awarded our bunker states.

Business lobbies in Egypt and Tunisia do not have independent financial resources. They rely on crony capitalist networks close to their respective political leaders and, to some extent, on aid from external parties. The United States government, for example, fostered the creation and/or sustained the operations of several economic policy think tanks and business associations in Egypt, including the American–Egyptian Chamber of Commerce and the Egyptian Center for Economic Studies. Egypt and Tunisia wish to project themselves as liberalizing in order to attract foreign capital. Business lobbies in these settings lack autonomy because they have few independent resources and depend largely on their connections with influential cronies, political leaders, and foreign governments for credit and other favors.

Predominantly private sector and concentrated

This category approximates the classic German syndrome if the banks are privately owned and universal, operate like an oligopoly, and provide most of the finance capital to the real economy. However, a high degree of formal concentration is also compatible with the Anglo-American variant of capitalism if it is supported by an active stock market. Britain has a highly concentrated retail banking system, consisting of four big national banks, but the City also features one of the world's leading stock exchanges and many merchant or investment banks. Formal levels of concentration do not indicate how competitive a banking system really is without taking other variables into account. Some of the less concentrated systems may behave as oligopolies, and some of the more concentrated ones may behave competitively.

The MENA's relatively concentrated, predominantly privately owned banking systems include some but not all of the Arab monarchies as well as Israel. The rich Arab oil states do not need the capital rationing associated with Germany's industrialization a century ago. Their ruling families, however, seek to retain control over budding capitalists by keeping the banks in reliable hands and allocating capital through them. Others, notably Kuwait as well as Israel, may be in a process of transition toward the British model of highly capitalized stock markets. In East Asia a more developed "British" illustration would be Singapore, which is also included in the emerging capital markets documented in Table 3.3.

The most striking illustration of the German model in the Arab world is the Moroccan system, consisting of one relatively large state bank, the privatization of which has been delayed for a decade for the sake of politically critical constituencies, and six others that collectively dominate the market. The Casablanca Stock Exchange is almost as much under · the sway of the commercial banks as is its sister in Tunis. The German model of universal banking had been assimilated by earlier generations of French capitalists who colonized Morocco, and decolonization left the system relatively intact when the monarchy acquired control in 1980 of the Omnium Nord-Africain (ONA), the colonialists' principal industrial conglomerate. The ONA subsequently bought controlling shares of Morocco's best-performing bank and minority holdings in some of the others before Morocco embarked in 1991 on financial liberalization and the easing of various credit constraints. In Morocco, the commercial banking oligopoly articulates the structural power of private capital, but the king reserves enough of it to keep discipline from within.

The Moroccan variation lends itself to family domination with collusive bankers expected to keep the family business secrets. Without much analysis of the oligopoly, a World Bank study, *From Privilege to Competition*, reports far greater business dissatisfaction in Morocco than the other countries surveyed – even Algeria – with access to credit (2009b: 113, 185–6). Paradoxically, in the rich Gulf petrostates, where oil rents have been partially distributed among merchant families, control of a banking system may have less strategic significance than in poorer countries, such as Morocco and Jordan. Kuwait is an obvious example of competitive markets and competitive politics as families compete for influence in commercial banking, on the Kuwait Stock Exchange, and in parliament. Although Kuwaiti commercial banking appears more concentrated than Morocco's, its real behavior may be more competitive (see Figure 3.6).

In Israel as well, concentrated banking is attenuated by a vibrant stock market and further alleviated by venture capital raised by NASDAQ. These forces might, however, work together to expand capitalism in Israel. The banks had fallen under state receivership in 1983 after they had bid up their shares to unsustainable levels on the Tel Aviv Stock

Exchange. Earlier, the public/private distinction was never clear in Israel, where Ha'Poalim Bank, Israel's largest bank, had been controlled by the Histadrut, the trade union federation, and Bank Leumi appeared to be a parastatal emanation of the Jewish National Fund. A prominent Israeli political sociologist once argued that Israeli statism dwarfed any real private-sector capitalism and stunted the development of civil society until the late 1970s (Doron 1996: 210–12). However, Ha'Poalim was fully privatized in June 2000 and is controlled by a conglomerate, the Arison-Dankner Group. Israel's banking authorities rightly restrict the Group's use of the bank to finance its big construction company (Gerstenfeld 2000: 12) and thereby pressure the bank to cooperate with its competitors. Plans to sell off the government's 43 percent of Bank Leumi and 53 percent of Israel Discount Bank still depended on negotiations with suitable core investors in 2000 (Berger 2000: 11), but finally in 2005 the government divested itself of the controlling shares in both banks. A consortium headed by former U.S. vice president Dan Quayle gained control of Israel's second largest bank, and earlier in the year Matthew Bronfman, the Canadian Seagram heir, acquired a controlling interest in Israel Discount Bank. Might these outsiders forge alliances with influential business groups within Israel? Israel's system seems to have shifted from a French to German model; certainly it was pumping substantial credit into Israel's growing private sector. It was too soon to tell whether the structural power of private capital might ultimately support a peace process, just as South Africa's powerful private sector broke apartheid in 1986.

Predominantly private and relatively competitive

The World Bank and other mainstream economists view this "American" structure of commercial banking as optimal for credit allocation because it connotes competitive financial markets. Saudi Arabia, rich in capital like America, appears to be the best exemplar of this structure in the region. Its commercial banking system looks similar to Kuwait's, but it is less concentrated, suggesting a greater potential for competition. It also commands the resources of much of a quasi continent, not just an extended city-state. The Saudi financial system finances the greatest potential capitalist power among Arab states of MENA, as shown in Table 3.4 by the credit it extends to the private sector.

Much of the Saudi system has integrated Islamic finance into its conventional banks. For instance, the National Commerce Bank, traditionally the leader with a 25 percent market share, was reorganized to make much of its activity conform to the norms of Islamic banking. Other banks, such as Saudi American Bank (SAMBA), originally founded by Citibank, opened Islamic windows in response to the growing demand in the Kingdom for Islamic products. For at least a decade, two major conglomerates of Islamic banks had attempted without success to establish commercial banks in Saudi Arabia. Each was Saudi-owned, one by a son of the late King Faisal and the other by a self-made businessman, but permission was stalled on the grounds that their recognition would have discredited other banks that Saudi Arabia, defender of Islam, had permitted. Eventually Islamic financial products were licensed through the conventional banking system in a compromise that strengthened the system, close to 40 percent of which was "sharia-compliant" by 2009. However, the Saudi system is also hybrid in another sense: the privately owned commercial banking system coexists with specialized state lending agencies. The five state agencies offer concessionary lending for most kinds of private-sector business activity. Although their relative importance has diminished since 1998, when they were lending almost as much as commercial banks to the private sector (SAMA 35th Annual Report, 1999: 46, 83), their outstanding loans were still close to one-quarter those of the commercial banking system's credit to the private sector in 2007 (SAMA 44th Annual Report, 2008: 54, 100, 341). The étatist regime funneling subsidized credit to its protégés still coexisted with the more competitive commercial banking system, but the state subsidies did not keep pace with explosive private-sector growth associated with the oil windfalls.

The structural power of capital is evident in the Saudi commercial banking system, but the country's politics are much less open than Kuwait's or Morocco's. One reason why civil society in Saudi Arabia has yet to emerge strongly from this material base is that much of that base remains under the direct or indirect influence of the Saudi ruling family and its Najdi allies. The Saudi family, moreover, is far larger than its royal counterparts elsewhere in the GCC and exerts more direct control over ministries than the ruling families of Morocco or Jordan. Nevertheless, the existence of a substantial material base on which civil society ultimately could draw suggests some potential for political as well as economic liberalization in the future.

Until the 1980s, Turkish capitalism seemed largely inspired by the German model, yet its commercial banking system also retained a significant public sector. Turkey's structural adjustment loan for the financial sector was not fully disbursed in 1988 because the government could not carry out certain commitments concerning the reform of Ziraat Bankası, the public-sector agricultural bank that held a quarter of Turkey's commercial bank deposits and still, as of December 2008, held 18.5 percent. Ziraat remains the government's principal patronage vehicle for rallying votes from the countryside, whereas Halk Bank, with another 8.9 percent of the nation's deposits, is the state's vehicle for funding small businesses. Some shares of Halk were sold on the Turkish Stock Exchange and, encouraged by the IMF, the government was planning eventually to privatize Ziraat. After completing a three-year $10 billion Stand-by Arrangement with the IMF in May 2008, the global financial crisis could result in yet another loan accompanied by further pressure to privatize these banks. Apparently, too, their "loss-making duties" – that is, subsidized lending – are no longer required (Standard and Poor's 2006: 12/15).

Turkey's commercial banking system also features a core of dynamic private-sector banks linked to major industrial conglomerates, but it has become considerably less concentrated than Morocco's. Despite its historic ties to the German model (Henry 1996: 100–6), Turkey has moved toward the diversified Anglo-American model, as the high turnover rate as well as the capitalization of its stock market shown in Table 3.3 suggest. It is by far the most active market in the MENA and offers an alternative to finance capital dominated by a small number of holding companies and commercial banks. Whether through its business conglomerates represented in the Turkish Industrialists' and Businessmen's Association (TÜSIAD) or through impersonal market forces, private capital seems to have acquired some structural power. TÜSIAD has a much greater voice in economic policies than the Egyptian Businessmen's Association, for instance.

Finally, the least concentrated and apparently most freewheeling banking system in the region is Lebanon's. Despite increases in its concentration ratio since the mid-1980s, the top five banks held only 48.3 percent of the deposits in 2005. Originally converted during the postwar boom from French- to American-style capitalism, the banking system became more concentrated under the impact of Lebanon's billionaire prime minister, the late Rafiq Hariri. Coupled with lucrative government borrowing, Hariri's private conglomerate acquired control over much of the banking system and the real economy. After Hariri was assassinated in 2005, allegedly by agents of Syria, Banque Audi's acquisition of Bank Saradar propelled it ahead of the other top banks identified with Hariri and with Syria, resulting in a greater concentration of the system. Figure 3.5 also shows the newer banking systems of Jordan, the UAE, and Bahrain to be less concentrated, but they were not necessarily more competitive. A better indication of competition were the net interest margins, or profits earned from bank loans after paying off depositors. A World Bank study offers such information since 1991, and the results are reported in Figure 3.6, comparing these systems to Morocco's banking oligopoly. Lebanon and Bahrain appear to have the lowest spreads, whereas

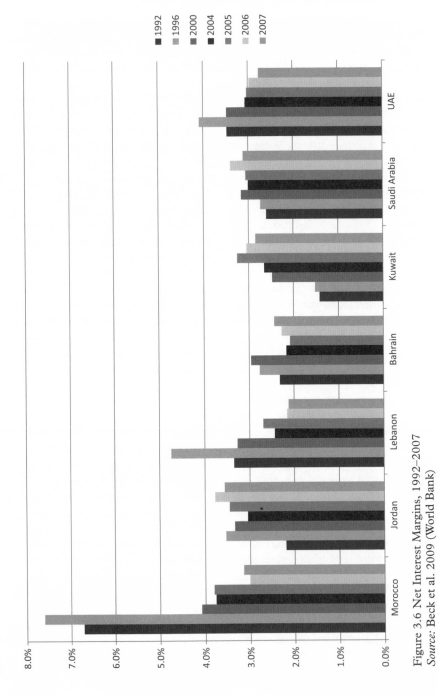

Figure 3.6 Net Interest Margins, 1992–2007
Source: Beck et al. 2009 (World Bank)

Jordan's were slightly exceeding Morocco's after 2005. But spreads had also substantially diminished in Morocco since the 1990s, suggesting increasing competition among the banks for credit-worthy clients in each of the region's major kingdoms.

Structural power of capital – summary

From this brief inspection of the MENA's stock markets and commercial banking systems, it is possible to come to some preliminary conclusions about the potential of business interests to influence government policies and encourage greater accountability. The greater the structural power of capital, the greater the possibility that the business community can engage in effective collective action, articulating the interests of various economic sectors – and the greater, too, the resulting developmental capacities of the state. Local capital both reinforces and constrains these capacities. It strengthens them by offering a tax base, information, and economic opportunities, but constrains state choices by presenting a variety of interests to be satisfied.

Structural power may be envisioned as the collective outstanding credit given to the private sector. Credit is a measure of the confidence the banks and public authorities have in their borrowers, just as contract-intensive money is a measure of the people's confidence in their banking and other public institutions. Credit to the private sector is usually a set of voluntary contracts, unlike the state financing of public-sector enterprises. In the MENA, however, the distinction between the public and private sector is only as strong as respect for private property rights, and these distinctions become especially blurred in family regimes such as Qatar's, where government ownership of 46 percent of the banking system, for instance, may be less relevant than a sublineage within the ruling (al-Thani) family, or in corrupt presidential family regimes such as Tunisia's as well. For Morocco, Israel, and Tunisia, the available financial statistics do not distinguish between public and private sectors, whereas Algeria, Egypt, Iran, Jordan, Saudi Arabia, Syria, and Turkey have made the necessary distinctions at least since the early 1990s, when the IMF apparently encouraged better financial disclosure.

Table 3.4 presents the available data both in the total credit to the private sector for the years 1998 and 2007, measured in constant 2000 U.S. dollars, and as a ratio of private-sector credit to GDP for these years. The countries are grouped according to our classification of their respective banking structures, as outlined in Figure 3.5. In absolute amounts of credit allocated to the private sector, Israel, Saudi Arabia, and Turkey tower over the others, although Israel's amount may be overstated.

Table 3.4 *Private-sector credit, 1998, 2007*

	(Constant 2000 millions USD)		(As percent of GDP)		Bank disclosure index (World Bank 2006)
	1998	2007	1998	2007	
Concentrated government-owned					
Algeria	$2,370.8	$9,745.6	4.6%	13.3%	53
Libya	1999 $11,262.0	$3,265.3	29.4%	7.2%	29
Syrian Arab Republic	$1,791.7	$4,315.2	9.2%	16.2%	35
Yemen, Rep.	$471.4	$977.0	5.4%	7.9%	51
Less concentrated government-owned					
Egypt, Arab Rep.	$47,044.4	$68,805.9	52.7%	50.6%	55
Iran, Islamic Rep.	$25,706.4	$74,628.1	27.2%	49.2%	28
Tunisia*	$11,545.3	$17,435.0	65.9%	64.3%	62
Concentrated private ownership					
Israel*	$80,324.3	$137,371.1	73.0%	90.1%	79
Kuwait	$24,059.6	2006 $35,279.1	65.6%	69.6%	62
Morocco*	$15,900.2	2006 $36,521.3	43.9%	69.9%	62
Oman	$8,931.9	2006 $8,562.7	47.3%	2006 32.0%	
Qatar	2000 $4,768.4	2005 $9,222.6	38.8%	2006 41.6%	83
Less concentrated private ownership					
Bahrain	$4,569.7	2005 $6,686.3	63.0%	2006 78.4%	84
Jordan	$5,916.1	$12,731.2	75.3%	99.0%	74
Lebanon	$12,670.6	$15,822.2	75.4%	75.6%	76
Saudi Arabia	$115,538.1	$97,777.2	63.8%	40.4%	69
United Arab Emirates	$37,225.1	2006 $68,851.6	57.5%	2006 64.3%	79
Turkey	$46,624.5	$108,772.8	18.0%	29.1%	80

* Credit to public-sector enterprises is also included
1. Kuwait credit is for 2006
2. Oman, Bahrain and UAE credit and credit as % GDP are for 2006
3. Qatar credit is for years 2000 and 2005, credit as % GDP for 2006

Sources: World Bank, WDI online (July 2009); Rocco Huang, "Bank Disclosure Index: Global Assessment of Bank Disclosure Practices," World Bank, Sept. 2006

Generally, the privately owned banking systems offer more credit to the private sector than state-owned systems, and the concentrated government-owned systems characteristic of bunker states offer the least amount of credit. An additional column in Table 3.4 presents their respective scores on the World Bank's Bank Disclosure Index, which is developed from an elaborate set of criteria. It shows that the privately owned systems are generally more transparent than their predominantly government-owned counterparts. As usual, our bunkers fare worst, along with Iran. A more recent World Bank study (not including Iraq) scores Syria, Yemen, and Algeria lowest with respect to various criteria of credit "efficiency" (2009b: 110).

Part of the reason for bunkers' inability to finance the private sector may be that their banking systems are saddled with obligations to their respective public sectors. Figure 3.7 examines the recent evolution of credit to the public sector as a percentage of credit allocated to the economy. Syria and Algeria indeed seemed trapped, like Egypt many years earlier, into providing the working capital needed to keep their public enterprises running, whereas Iran and Egypt, less concentrated and government-owned than the banking systems of the bunker regimes, have steadily reduced their obligations to points approaching the less indebted public sectors of Saudi Arabia and Turkey. These "French" étatist banking systems still suffer, however, from their clients, be they public or private enterprises, who do not repay their loans.

Figure 3.8 examines the evolution of nonperforming loans as a percentage of total loans from the year 2000, when the World Bank first began systematically to publish these indications of financial heath. It is readily seen that Tunisia as well as Egypt, like the bunker states of Algeria, Libya, Syria, and Yemen, had acquired considerable portfolios of nonperforming loans, despite efforts under World Bank structural adjustment programs since the mid-1990s to clean them up. Iran, too, under Ahmadinejad presidency, was becoming more burdened with nonperforming loans, as if anticipating its transition into a bully praetorian state. But although the Bank correctly points to striking correlations between the state ownership of banks and nonperforming loans in the MENA (World Bank 2009b: 118–19), differences between public-sector and private-sector management may also get blurred in systems of crony capitalists. In Tunisia, for instance, the IMF Article IV report shows a certain convergence in the mismanagement of public-sector and private-sector banks, because the latter are also obliged to lend to regime favorites. Although the proportions of nonperforming loans were gradually diminishing (but still remaining high, between 15 percent and 20 percent of total risk assets), in the last two years for which data were available,

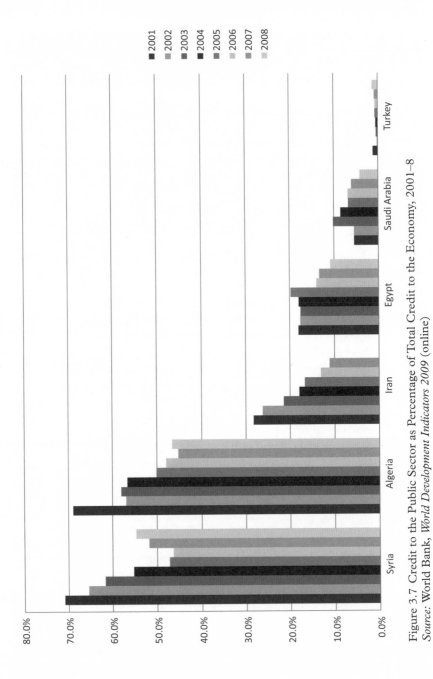

Figure 3.7 Credit to the Public Sector as Percentage of Total Credit to the Economy, 2001–8
Source: World Bank, *World Development Indicators 2009* (online)

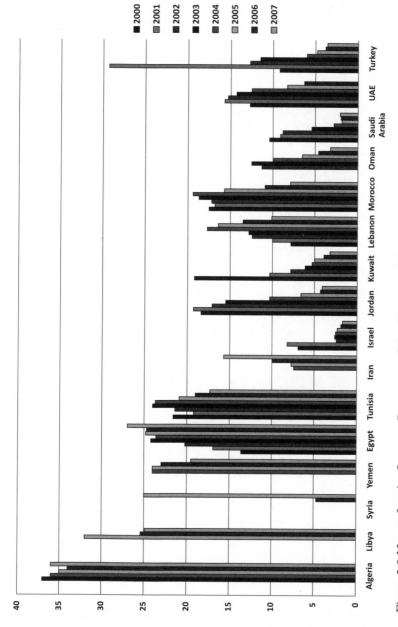

Figure 3.8 Nonperforming Loans as Percentage of Total Loans, 2000–7
Source: World Bank, *World Development Indicators 2009* (online)

107

the private-sector banks had precisely the same percentages of bad loans, and they were less well provisioned than their public-sector counterparts (IMF 2008: 12).

The "French" étatist model, despite some reform in Egypt and Tunisia, still operates under a set of constraints stemming from the region's legacy of state capitalism, which curtailed commercial banking and drastically limited private capital or eliminated it altogether. Regimes with big public-sector banks, including all of the praetorian republics, go through the motions of structural adjustment, but they prevent the rise of autonomous private sectors in order to keep control of civil society so as to preserve their own patronage networks. The policy outcomes safeguard these regimes at the expense of long-term development.

The structural power of capital is still limited in the region. The "German" model is confined outside of Israel to monarchies that control nascent financial and industrial cartels. The banking system is a major asset for these regimes as long as insiders hold the levers of financial power, for they then extend the regime's reach and patronage networks into the private sector. Because the system rests on oligopoly, however, it is inherently unstable. If the system were opened to international capital, the newcomers could undermine it, or insiders could become more independent and use their financial power to make the regime more accountable, as may be the case in Israel.

Only Israel, Turkey, and the GCC countries stand out as financial environments in which private capital enjoys relative autonomy and can support various articulations of business demands. Figure 3.8 also shows how quickly Turkey was able to recover from the financial crisis of 2001. Unlike the bunkers and bully republics, it reduced its portfolio of nonperforming loans within four years from a peak of 29 percent down to levels below 5 percent. And as for Israel, despite having consolidated a "German" orientation by privatizing its four major banks, its system may be moving, like that of Turkey, toward the Anglo-American model. Saudi Arabia's healthy and apparently competitive commercial banking system suggests that it, too, might support a limited articulation of business interests, albeit within a less liberal political framework.

Facing the challenges ahead

The countries that face the greatest problems of adapting to globalization are those with minimal capacity, small private sectors, and big state banking systems – the bunker states – to be further discussed in Chapter 4. Civil society is weakest in these countries, further limiting the potential for effective responses to globalization. Algeria, Iraq, Libya, Sudan, Syria, and Yemen, all praetorian republics ruled from bunkers by political military elites, display the lowest levels of capitalist development. They are also the countries with the largest informal economies. Many of the most dynamic elements of their civil societies have emigrated. Although capital flight and labor migration are not confined to these countries, they may be its most prominent exemplars. Algerian workers, for example, have a longer history and a more substantial presence in France than do their Moroccan or Tunisian counterparts. Private Algerian capital stays in France, not Algeria, and the real development of the private sector in Algeria, if it is to occur, may depend on its return. Algeria does have capitalist traditions, but they are French, and its painful adjustments to the new world order will be along "French" lines like Egypt's and Tunisia's. Syria, too, enjoys close historic ties with France, whereas Lebanon, though no longer quite French, serves as a proxy for the old metropole, a haven for private Syrian capital and outlet, despite the departure of the Syrian army, for up to a million Syrian guest workers. But whether these special ties to the former colonial power pave the way to broader globalization, or lock these countries into relations of bilateral dependency, remains to be seen.

On the domestic front, most of the regimes seem to have effectively contained their nascent capitalist classes. Either they tie them into public-sector or political networks, as in Egypt or Tunisia, where the state still dominates credit allocation, or they give them a semblance of autonomy in conglomerates directly or indirectly under patrimonial control, as in Morocco. Chapter 5 focuses on the dilemmas of the bully regimes in keeping control over, yet encouraging, the development of their respective private sectors. Each variety of capitalism threatens the incumbent regimes, but the Anglo-American variety of capitalism being promoted by international financial institutions appears to be the most threatening to them. It offers more ready access to foreign capital than do the French or German models, but at the cost of giving up decisive control over the private sector.

Chapter 6 then examines the monarchies, beginning with Morocco, the one that best exemplified the oligopolistic German model. There may, however, be some slippage in Saudi Arabia away from royally favored merchants toward new combinations of capitalists financed by a relatively competitive banking system. Ironically, the most effective guarantor of the Anglo-American model in the region may be Islamic banks and businesses, whose capacity to mediate with global capital and markets may empower some countries successfully to engage in globalization, a subject also to be developed in Chapter 6 with regard to Saudi Arabia and the other Gulf monarchies.

For most of the MENA, the major structural challenges to incumbent regimes lie both outside and inside the respective countries. The globalization of capital has major implications for every political economy in the region, including those traditionally financed by oil rents. Oil revenues are not expected to return soon to their peak in 2008, and the Gulf states with their burgeoning populations might again be strapped for funds for current expenditures and long-term investment if the Great Recession is prolonged into a double dip. Every country needs to attract substantial local and foreign private capital if it is not to risk potentially destabilizing increases of either domestic debt or unemployment. Globalization also works the other way; a major stimulus to reform may be the fear of capital flight. Despite controls, it is increasingly difficult to trap capital in any of the MENA states. One rigorous study of capital flight based on open public sources estimated capital flight from the oil exporting states of the MENA between 1972 and 2002 to have totaled almost $1 trillion with accrued interest (Almounsor 2008: 44), and McKinsey consultants reckoned that total holdings of Arab investors, including $1 to $1.3 trillion of sovereign wealth funds, had reached $3.4 to $3.8 trillion by 2008 (Farrell and Lund 2008:1).

To attract more of this capital, governments in the region have spruced up their stock exchanges. Syria, the last holdout, opened its stock exchange in 2009. Yet the banks, which tend to dominate local stock markets, may resist greater transparency; so also may their political authorities, whose patronage networks would be exposed. Economic and political information do not lend themselves to easy segmentation in MENA political economies. In the smaller states, especially, political and economic elites may be too intermixed for them to accept the transparency of open markets. Yet the regimes face pressures to open up more in order to attract more investment – from their own citizens as well as from foreign enterprises.

If the MENA were to gain a fair share of the expanding pie of global capital, the new investments would probably reinforce local capitalists and other elements of civil society more than they would help to sustain their incumbent, information-shy regimes. It is true that the "German" model has been employed in defense of patrimonial rule in Morocco, and even cruder state oligopolies service political networks supporting other MENA regimes. Accelerated global flows of capital, however, would tend to undermine any oligopoly's control of capital markets. If activated sufficiently to attract significant foreign portfolio investment, stock markets would become alternative sources of financing for local capitalists, whom local oligopolists would no longer be able to exclude. As the capital pie expanded, governments would become less able to control its allocation either directly through public-sector banks or indirectly through crony capitalist conglomerates.

Turkey, the region's bellwether, best illustrates this transition toward more competitive capital markets. Turkey has come closest to taking these risks just as it has benefited the most from influxes of foreign port-folio capital as well as other forms of private investment. Lebanon, by contrast, is a parody of the Anglo-American model; until recently, at least, its capital structures were becoming concentrated into those of a banana republic. Chapter 7 will examine each of the region's precarious democracies in turn, including the one that already got away, after expe-riencing real revolution and a partial democratic transition, from being a monarchy to joining the region's other bullies.

Transitions to democracy, alas, are not inevitable, nor are transitions to more competitive capital markets. The challenge of attracting more foreign capital will lead regimes to devise new strategies and frameworks for balancing or playing off local and international capital. The pre-dominantly public-sector commercial banking structures of the region's statist and post-statist economies are under siege, as credit rating agen-cies and international financial institutions call on their governments to clean up their public-sector bank portfolios and then to privatize them. But besieged regimes will delay, privatize in ways that keep state man-agements intact, and try through the banks and parastatal investment funds to retain control of stock markets. Rather than develop more trans-parency, they are likely to engage in a rhetoric of economic and political liberalization while trying to coopt foreign as well as local capitalists into their patronage networks. If international portfolio managers could be bought into Thailand's corrupt and opaque financial markets in the 1990s, then why not promote more MENA countries by corrupting more of Wall Street?

In sum, global capital markets have structural power to which regimes are presently fine-tuning their responses, because even the wealthier need better access to these markets and to the technological and world mar-keting capabilities with which they are associated. Most of the regimes hesitate, however, to open themselves to the indiscriminate workings of Anglo-American capitalism and its requirements, in theory at least, for timely information and accountability. Yet the hesitations may have severe opportunity costs, by delaying the capital investments and asso-ciated economic growth needed to attack the region's unemployment problems and to contain its rising social movements. First we turn, then, to the bunker regimes most in need of reform and change.

Suggestions for further reading

Ayubi (1995) and Snider (1996), supplemented by Clague et al. (1998), present interesting insights into the political capacities of countries that remain a concern of the UNDP (2005, 2009b) as well the World Bank (1997, 2003, 2009b). Zysman (1983) still deserves to be read for his insights into political and economic development in a variety of capitalist contexts, as of course do Bagehot (1904) and Hilferding (1910). The World Bank (2009c, 2008b and preceding three years) have useful summaries of the MENA's economic reforms and prospects.

4   Bunker states

The critical political weakness of the praetorian republics ruled physically or metaphorically from bunkers is that their states have little if any autonomy from traditional social forces that managed, typically during the turbulent nationalist phase that followed the end of colonial rule, to seize control of those states. Algeria's "deciders," for example, represent political clans anchored in both society and state institutions. Muammar Qaddafi of Libya and Ali Abdullah Saleh of Yemen rule their countries through military/security/party structures that are in turn controlled by alliances of these leaders' families and tribes. Although Saddam Hussein had relied heavily on tribes and tribal alliances to rule Iraq prior to 1991, after that time the weakening of the state apparatus resulted in a dramatic increase in tribal power and Saddam's reliance on it (Glain 2000; Jabar 2000). Confined to the Green Zone in Baghdad, the bunker liberated by the Americans for returning political exiles still relies on tribal alliances and sectarian militias to manage the fractured society. The same is true in Syria, where the Alawi sect, of which Syrian President Hafez al-Asad was a member, has come to control virtually all important state structures, although other Alawis have opposed the regime now led by Hafez's son Bashar (Perthes 1997: 181–4). In the Sudan, tribal alliances lurk behind General Omar Bashir's military organization and Hassan Turabi's National Islamic Front, reorganized in 2000 as an opposition party, the Popular National Congress.

In each of these cases except Algeria, the social forces that have penetrated and come to control the state are tribal or religious minorities, typically ones distrusted if not despised by much of the remainder of the population. Their rule is, therefore, seen by much, if not most of the population as being fundamentally illegitimate and intended to serve the interests of that social force, rather than the country as a whole. In these circumstances, coercion is necessarily the primary and, in some cases such as that of Iraq or in much of Sudan, virtually the only means by which government can ensure the public's compliance. In Algeria, 132 years of colonialism pulverized the social forces, but the national liberation struggle fostered new clans based on friends and cousins. The society is "'folded' into its State and *vice-versa*" without those blankets connoted by civil society (Jean Leca, foreword to Liverani 2008: xii).

Bunker praetorian states are in a potential state of war with the societies they rule. These states dare not permit the freedom of information or autonomy of economic action necessary for globally competitive economic growth. Outside the bunkers, their civil societies and business entrepreneurs, to the extent they ever existed, have been deactivated, silenced, forced into exile, or eradicated. Just as these states cannot adopt and then implement consistent and effective policies for economic growth, so are their societies too weak to respond quickly and dramatically to opportunities that policy changes, were they to occur, might offer. It is conceivable, however, that bunker states could evolve into a less virulent form of praetorian republic, were the political elite through accommodation or some other means to come to represent a broader coalition of social forces. In this event, they would begin to take on the characteristics of the praetorian republics to be discussed in Chapter 5.

The six bunker states – Algeria, Iraq, Libya, Sudan, Syria, and Yemen – display the least institutional capacity of any of the MENA states to manage their economies. These countries have the largest informal economies, reflected in the relatively high proportion of their money supply that escapes their respective banking systems. Tax revenues outside the petroleum sector are low, and some of those revenues are being siphoned off to ruling factions. Import monopolies, whether official or "private" sector, largely escape the official controls of economic decision makers or planners. The technocrats of these regimes have little opportunity to make or even influence policy, because the ruling clans typically filter and distort economic information. No significant economic establishment, public or private, eludes the predatory rulers, although some firms, notably in the petroleum and military industrial sectors, may enjoy special protection. Private entrepreneurs may accumulate capital, but only so long as they enjoy the special favor of those who control the military or security services. Indeed, a major difference between bunker state capitalism and its more sophisticated "French" variant is that the latter's favored entrepreneurs may buy protection that is more durable.

Although indices of domestic violence and disorder distinguish these MENA countries from the others, so also do their underlying financial structures. These are less contingent than episodes of civil violence, because they reflect underlying political economies that are difficult to change. Financial data provide a clue to distinguish these bunker states from the rest of the MENA. Specifically, they fall to the bottom left in Figure 4.1, low with respect to "contract-intensive money" (CIM) that

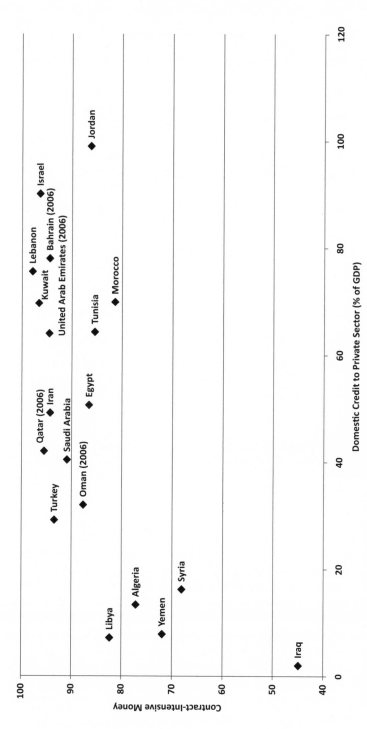

Figure 4.1 Credit to the Private Sector by Contract-Intensive Money (2007)

115

obviously limits their commercial bank credit allocated to the private sector (as a proportion of GDP).

This contract-intensive money, discussed in Chapter 3 as a proxy for property rights and institutional credibility, is the proportion of money held inside the banking system, rather than outside it, in the form of currency. As seen in Figure 4.1, the low-CIM countries also (with the marginal exception of Morocco, which is not a bunker state) have the least viable private sectors underpinning their respective civil societies. Without the shock absorbers, or even blankets, of effective political or civic associations, much less the support of private capital, domestic or foreign, adjustment is bound to be rough and the dialectics of globalization less amenable to resolution.

The bunker regimes, however, are under pressure because their dependence, direct or indirect, on volatile oil revenues has rendered them vulnerable: when, as in 2005–8, the revenues are high, they raise their populations' expectations for better services; when they collapse, as in 1986, or wave volatile blinking red flags as in 2008–9, they may nudge the decision makers in the bunkers into thinking about diversifying their source of income. Yet economic reform is bound to be more painful in the bunker states than in countries already enjoying more integration with the global economy and its financial markets. The bunker states still monopolize oil rents, but any tacit "contract" offering welfare and security in exchange for allegiance has been revised. Their menu of state services has necessarily diminished with the decline in oil revenues, at least on a per capita basis. Their way of keeping up any tacit contract in most of the bunkers, beginning with Algeria, was to increase the value of security – "empowering" themselves by tolerating a small amount of insecurity. Recent spikes of high revenues have not diminished their dependence on insecurity.

Algeria is the most vivid and bloody illustration of how bunkered elites manipulate economic policy for political ends. Algeria in some respects adjusted far more quickly in the late 1990s than did Egypt or other star pupils of the IMF. The mindless massacres of tens of thousands of civilians enabled the regime to carry out draconian economic policies. The economy has undergone structural change while a hard core of illegitimate military rulers has retained power on the pretext of widespread insecurity. Raw power struggles between the ruling factions as well as between them and Islamist guerrilla forces diverted attention from the economic policies being implemented, sometimes in the 1990s with advice from the IMF. Economic policy makers have enjoyed a relative autonomy of sorts, but virtually no resources in civil society with which to implement economic reforms, other than the emergence, ultimately costing billions of dollars as we shall see, of an imaginary, invented private sector headed by crooked cronies of the regime.

Algeria's bunker

Algeria is, to be sure, an exceptional case, but its very exaggeration sheds greater light on many of the problems faced by other MENA states. It endured the region's most protracted and destructive colonialism. Not only were its indigenous elites suppressed or hopelessly compromised by the French authorities of colonial Algeria; its culture was virtually destroyed. Its own "French" politicians could not negotiate their country's emancipation as did Lebanon's and Syria's urban families and Tunisia's more broadly based national movement; instead, guerrilla forces overran Algerian civil society. Far from refashioning associational life as in neighboring Tunisia, Algeria's protracted struggle for independence marginalized its small educated elite and destroyed most fledgling organizations, even the Front of National Liberation (whose principal political founder inside Algeria was strangled to death). Deprived not only of its intellectuals but of its high culture as well, Algeria's civil society was among the weakest and most fragmented in the Arab world. Much of it is still located in France and Switzerland, rather than Algeria.

Independent Algeria was militarized from the start, unlike other MENA countries that underwent military coups. The general staff of the external Army of National Liberation seized power in 1962 and placed a prestigious figurehead, Ahmed Ben Bella, in the presidency. When he in turn tried to encourage independent power centers to bring the army under control, Colonel Houari Boumédienne removed him from power. Boumédienne tried to develop political institutions, but he died suddenly in 1978 before his revised blueprint for the Front of National Liberation and various ancillary bodies could be acted on. The army command, not the civilian leadership, selected his successor, Chadli Benjedid, more or less on the basis of seniority. Chadli's peers then prevented him from consolidating power as his predecessor had done. As long as the Algerian economy appeared to prosper, the colonels – French-trained professionals as well as former guerrilla commanders – promoted themselves to general and extracted enough legitimacy from the revolution to stay comfortably in power. Indeed, Algeria was not perceived from the outside as having a particularly militaristic regime. It did not ever appear to be in the same league as Nasser's Egypt and Ba'athist Syria and Iraq. The most visible Algerian military leaders were homegrown guerrilla politicians, and their governments were largely composed of civilians. Colonel Boumédienne appeared to be managing a mildly authoritarian administrative state. Military expenditures amounted on average to barely 3 percent of GDP, quite low compared with other bunker regimes or Egypt, Jordan, or Israel. "Algeria today is governed by a complex network of interactive structures that provide institutional stability, direction, and predictability to the political system," a well-informed American academic wrote in the mid-1980s (Entelis 1986: 168). Government budgets continue to convey this impression: in 1993 the military's share was lower in Algeria than anywhere else except Sudan, Tunisia, and postwar Iran. Despite civil war, Algeria's military expenditure as a percentage of GDP barely exceeded Morocco's in 1997 and subsequently declined below Moroccan levels, albeit not in actual expenditures. Figure 4.2 also shows that the other bunker states were steadily reducing the military drag on their respective economies and that their expenditures as a share of GDP were no higher than those of the much wealthier GCC states. Even Syria, despite continued confrontation with Israel, reduced its ratio of military expenditure to GDP in the face of a much richer and bigger spending adversary supported by the United States.

From the inside, however, narratives of economic decision makers record a very different perception of Algeria's system. Two such accounts present the same picture from opposing viewpoints and different positions in the hierarchy. Belaid Abdesselam was Boumédienne's chief architect and manager of the Algerian economy from 1970 to 1977. Ghazi Hidouci was a professional economic planner until 1984, when he was called to head the Department of Financial and Economic Affairs in the presidency. He then served as minister of the economy in Mouloud Hamrouche's government from 1989 to 1991. A third narrative, that of Abdelhamid Brahimi, is politically less informative but offers evidence of the massive corruption implied by the first two accounts. Brahimi was appointed planning minister in 1979, after Chadli Benjedid became president, and he served as prime minister from 1984 to 1988. He publicly declared in March 1990 that corrupt officials and intermediaries had pocketed some $26 billion, the equivalent of Algeria's external debt at the time, in commissions and inflated invoices during the Boumédienne years (Brahimi 1991: 152–5). The timing of his revelation diverted attention to corruption and helped to undermine Ghazi Hidouci's efforts to attack its roots with market reforms.

Belaid Abdesselam views Algeria's industrial technocracy from the summit during the golden Boumédienne years. Like his counterpart planners in Tunisia, Libya, and Senegal (Belkhodja 1998: 78), he was inspired by the French economist Gérard Destanne de Bernis's vision of "industrializing industry" and gained Boumédienne's enthusiastic approval. One of a small number of Algerian university students who joined the maquis

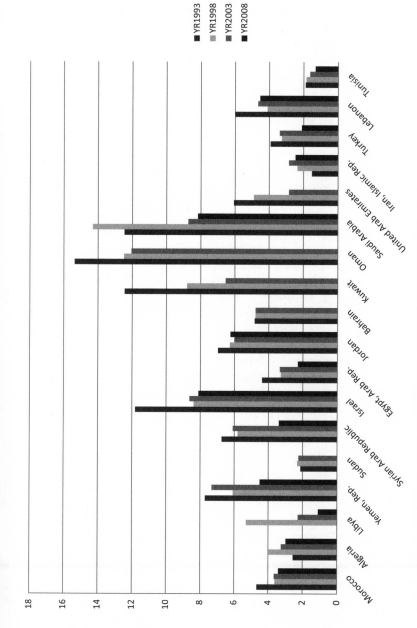

Figure 4.2 Military Expenditure in MENA States as Percent of GDP, 1993–2008
Source: World Bank, World Development Indicators 2009 (online November)

Legend: YR1993, YR1998, YR2003, YR2008

119

in 1956, Abdesselam had political as well as scholastic credentials but had studied medicine, not economics. He oversaw the accumulation of Algeria's oil revenues and their reinvestment in natural gas liquefaction plants, a step intended to accumulate more export revenues, and in a heavy industrial base, including iron and steel. The vision of an industrialized Algeria was Boumédienne's legitimating myth, much like the Aswan High Dam for Gamal Abdel Nasser. Consequently, Abdesselam enjoyed the president's protection.

From his political memoirs (Bennoune and El-Kenz 1990), however, it is clear that Abdesselam's authority was seriously constricted by contending military clans and their business extensions – a set of veritable "mafiosi" in his words. He could sometimes cross one of them, with support from the president, but he dared not provoke them collectively. Abdesselam's own following consisted of industrial technocrats, not the regime's core military players. The "turf battles" had a peculiarly Algerian flavor, but they may ring a familiar bell with Syrian or Iraqi insiders. Abdesselam recalls the day, for instance, when the Gendarmerie, backed up by special military units, surrounded the oil fields of Hassi Messaoud. All those working in the fields – most of them just wearing shorts in the hot desert sun – were asked for identity papers. Many, including oil executives from Europe inspecting their field operations, were carted off to a police station and held for 24 hours or more because they had left their passports back at camp. When Abdesselam protested against this arbitrary and economically destructive police roundup, Bencherif, the minister of the interior and head of the Gendarmerie, primly responded that nobody, not even in the industrial sector, is above the law. Then Abdesselam understood. A few days earlier some crony of an important political personality had asked a European enterprise working with Algeria's national oil company, Sonatrach, whether he could become the firm's representative in Algeria. The Europeans responded that they were agreeable, as long as Sonatrach also agreed. When Sonatrach did not agree, however, the company did not feel obligated to hire him. Abdesselam suddenly understood that Bencherif was teaching the European companies a lesson on that hot day in the oil fields. Sonatrach could not protect them. They had to cut other power centers in on any deals (Bennoune and El-Kenz 1990: II, 43–4). Writing of his experiences as minister of industry and energy, Abdesselam concludes:

One is almost up against a system penetrated by a Mafia type of incrustation! When one is responsible for a sector like industry, which engages enormous interests, evidently it arouses much envy and many people want to profit. I have told you how one can get the profits... First you have the intermediaries, the compradores who want mandates from large foreign companies to get their percentage on every contract. Then there also has to be complicity within the system. These individuals have to show that they have enough influence within the power structure to influence a deal. All of which necessitates support within the system. If you are opposed to such things and wish business to work normally, you become an adversary. Either you go along with them and get some needed peace or you work according to certain rules and counter certain people's appetites. Then you become an enemy to be shot down (II, 200–1).

Ghazi Hidouci presents a complementary snapshot of economic decision making from below during the halcyon years of great industrial projects. Entering the planning ministry as a junior economist at about the time Boumédienne seized power in 1965, Hidouci had a backstage view of economic policy making in Algeria. In theory his ministry was the brain behind Boumédienne's centralized economy. In practice it sat on the margins. It was consulted about the budgets of the economic ministries but never empowered to engage in real central planning, much less to make other ministries implement a national plan. Inside the planning ministry, the macroeconomic planners usually generated three data sets: a relatively prudent one for the president, an "approximately sincere" one for internal use, and a "highly manipulated" set for dealing with the other ministries (Hidouci 1995: 36). During the 1970s the planning minister, Abdallah Khodja, contested the economic viability of many of Abdesselam's projects. Once the oil revenues surged in 1974, Abdesselam usually had his way, but he symptomatically regarded criticism as a sign that Khodja had the support of powerful cliques of officers and their compradores, or finally of Boumédienne himself (Bennoune and El-Kenz 1990: II, 258). Hidouci, loyal to his minister, describes the clandestine operations of the planners to obtain information about the industrial enterprises and other matters.

In the often empty corridors of the Treasury and Tax [departments of the Ministry of Finance] we developed the habit during these dark years of digging up missing pieces of information on the spot, where the poorly paid, often demoralized bureau chiefs, indifferent to the incongruity of displaying the secrets of prebendal administration, opened up everything to us. It was nevertheless more difficult to penetrate the ministerial cabinets . . . (Hidouci 1995: 39).

Subsequently, Hidouci gained access to the inner workings of economic policy making at the highest levels. He presents a remarkable picture of the climate of mutual suspicion pervading the corridors of power in the mid-1980s. Much of the relevant information was filtered and manipulated; for instance, the personnel files of public-sector managers were secrets in the hands of competing security agencies. Part of Hidouci's job was to gather information that could be used against public-sector officials, and he had latitude to build his own channels through the banks and enterprises acquired through his years in the planning ministry. Because he did not have access to the security files, he learned "less about interest networks and people than about the administration of things" (Hidouci 1995: 118). Through his own network of former planners and other reform-minded individuals in strategic places, however, he acquired more reliable economic data than were provided in official reports, which he quickly learned to file without reading (Hidouci 1995: 117).

Algeria's centralized planning was a myth. The reality, once Boumédienne consolidated power, was a centralized system for distributing the rents and prebends, controlled by the presidency and managed by close collaborators in the Ministry of Finance, not Planning. The Ministry of Finance was originally headed by military commanders close to the president. They directly controlled the credit and allocated the grants and subsidies, with little need for administration, much less a banking system. The minister and his personal cabinet made the decisions and left the rest of the ministry in a "shocking state of disrepair" (Hidouci 1995: 39). The French settler assets, virtually the entire modern economy, were up for grabs when almost a million settlers departed "on vacation" before July 5, 1962 – Algerian Independence Day – never to return. Boumédienne brought political order to the anarchic appropriations of the Ben Bella years. After his 1965 coup, he distributed the loot to pacify the numerous guerrilla commanders and their followers, while he concentrated political power in the hands of his victorious "Oujda clan" (named after the Moroccan city near the Algerian border where Boumédienne had assembled the beginnings of an external army of national liberation before moving to Tunisia in 1958). Once the resources of the European economy were depleted, oil revenues took up the slack. Driven by political considerations, allocations of property, rents, markets, and import licenses had little or no economic rationale. By 1972, Boumédienne had consolidated control over the allocations and redistributed some of the patronage to the provinces where the prefects enjoyed similar powers independent of the Ministry of Planning and other central ministries.

Abdallah Khodja, denounced as a rightist by Abdesselam (Bennoune and El-Kenz 1990: II, 221), waged a rear-guard action until 1974 in favor of a more critical evaluation of industrial projects and greater investment in agriculture. Projects were occasionally stopped or at least delayed, despite pressures from the foreign beneficiaries of the turnkey projects as well as the Ministry of Industry and Energy. Hidouci reports a series of meetings in early 1974 chaired by Boumédienne himself to air the differences between the planners and the industrial technocrats (Hidouci 1995: 65–6). But after a few months oil prices again doubled, terminating any critical economic discourse. "The planners picked up their tools, for nobody was disposed any longer to talk about necessity and economic constraints, and everyone was now supporting adventurism and indebtedness. Expenditure is immediate; management deferred" (Hidouci 1995: 67). Hidouci is "convinced that Boumédienne long believed that progress and modernity could simply be bought from those who had it and that he had no need for entrepreneurs in local markets nor of economic regulation" (Hidouci 1995: 55).

Oil revenues conveniently supplemented the proceeds of the modern economy abandoned by the settlers, rendering economics, in the sense of allocating scarce resources, superfluous for Algeria's political leaders. Algeria, nevertheless, was not a classic rentier state like those of the Gulf Cooperation Council. Until 1972, substantial private sectors of "traditional" Algerian agriculture, wholesale commerce, transport, and small-scale industry survived on the peripheries of the centrally allocated modern sector. "In contrast to the deserts of the Persian Gulf before petroleum, the least developed, where everything was a new creation, in Algeria one destroyed an economy and a preexisting equilibrium to promote a new myth" (Hidouci 1995: 43). The Algerians could then exaggerate their vision of "industrializing industries" well beyond those of other Promethean modernizers such as Bourguiba or Nasser because their oil revenues exceeded the capital available for investment in all but the wealthiest Gulf oil states.

A related impact of Boumédienne's industrial, agrarian, and cultural revolutions launched in 1972 was to drive much of the private sector underground or across the Mediterranean (Hidouci 1995: 73). Figure 4.3 shows Algeria's contract-intensive money ratio increasing in the early Boumédienne years, when he stabilized the political economy, but then contracting in the early 1970s with his triple agrarian, cultural, and industrial revolution, and again in 1979–80, after Boumédienne's death. The money supply can be understood as government policy, whereas CIM may be interpreted as a response of merchants and others who decide whether to keep their money in the banks.

Chadli Benjadid, Boumédienne's successor, encouraged economic discourse and criticism of Algeria's industrial experience by appointing Abdelhamid Brahimi to be his planning minister. Boumédienne had himself experienced some doubts about industrializing industry and divided up Abdesselam's ministry, demoting him in 1977 to take charge of the light industries that were supposed to have arisen in the wake of Algeria's heavy industry. Brahimi subsequently carved up Abdesselam's old empire, including Sonatrach, into smaller enterprises. Extracting evidence from the planning ministry, he attacked and discredited the

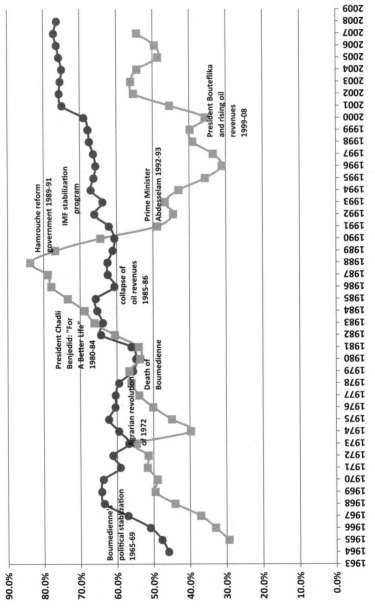

Figure 4.3 Algeria's Money Supply and Contract-Intensive Money, 1964–2008
Source: IMF *International Financial Statistics;* World Development Indicators, World Bank (online August 2009)

entire experience of industrializing industries. But after Abdesselam and his technocrats were purged, economic analysis had no further place in Algerian policy making. Hidouci, who remained in the planning ministry until 1984, claims that by this time it did little more than issue national accounts statistics – "to illustrate official speeches about growth in this unconstrained period" – and compile routine public investment programs (Hidouci 1995: 85). Chadli's slogan, "For a Better Life," generated ever more rents from import monopolies tied to military clans – until the oil revenues sharply plunged in the mid-1980s.

Chadli's early reform efforts to cut up the state enterprises and give them greater autonomy amounted to little more than softening them up for the rent seekers – "assassinating industry," as one purged technocrat exclaimed at an international conference in 1990. The high military command dramatically expanded in numbers and in rank – by 1998 Algeria counted 140 generals – and Chadli could never be more than their front man. Consequently, Abdelhamid Brahimi, whom he appointed prime minister in 1983, could not become Algeria's Gorbachev despite his impressive academic and military credentials (a doctorate from Ohio State University as well as previous service as a guerrilla with Chadli inside Algeria). Even when they agreed, neither the president nor the prime minister took decisive action in the face of collapsing oil revenues. Instead of rescheduling the debt, they resorted to more expensive short-term loans in the hope that oil prices would increase. The scarcity of foreign exchange led to widespread shortages of basic consumer items. It also had the interesting effect of extending the state's patronage networks, as a growing group of black marketeers thrived under the protection of the military mafiosi. Algerian dinars circulating outside the banking system jumped in 1986 from 34 percent to almost 40 percent of the money supply, and foreign exchange cost about four times more on the black market than at the official rate. "Trabendo" (contraband) commerce, already part of Chadli's "Good Life" in the early 1980s, boomed in the late 1980s, further widening the gap between the official and unofficial foreign exchange rates. It would double again – to a factor of 8 and even 9 – after the October 1988 riots finally shook the regime's bunkers. Figure 4.3 shows further withdrawals from the banking system in 1986, when the government was printing money to compensate for the decline in oil revenues, and also in 1999 and 2000, after the riots.

By sending in the tanks to quell demonstrations in 1988, killing more than 600 people in several cities (Hidouci 1995: 162), the army lost any remaining shreds of revolutionary legitimacy and discredited the single-party regime. The civilian edifice, so carefully codified in the 1976 National Charter and "enriched" in the 1986 Charter, was now beyond repair. Until 1988 the real leaders – les décideurs, or "deciders," as Algerians call them – remained faceless, extorting favors from officials much as they had constrained Abdesselam in happier years. Military rule in Algeria, however, was still relatively benign. The very fact that a few urban riots shocked the generals into major constitutional and economic reform distinguishes them from the military rulers of Syria (who destroyed a major city in 1982) or Iraq. Indeed, after Chadli introduced a new multiparty constitution, Mouloud Hamrouche led a government from 1989 to 1991 committed to democratic political reforms and economic liberalization.

The story of this first serious reform effort, although known to Algerian specialists (Entelis and Arone 1992; Corm 1993; Ghilès 1998; Dillman 2000), has not received adequate attention in the political economy literature. Algeria almost succeeded in simultaneously moving to constitutional democracy and a market economy. Although its failure illustrated the tenacity of a bunker regime, it still serves as the rough draft of a dialectics of globalization that may be rewritten elsewhere.

Algerian springtime: reform and democracy (1989–91)

The reform efforts began by stealth, "putting sand" (Hidouci 1995: 108) into Algeria's dysfunctional administrative engines by offering new sources of information. Better informed and weakened by Algeria's deteriorating economic conditions, the president lent the reform team official support in late 1987, less than a year before the October 1988 riots. The reformers had a "global institutional and juridical vision" of the necessary changes: to move to "contractual relationships between the administration and the producers of goods and services, including social services, and also to a transparent 'commercializing' of economic transactions" within the public sector (Corm 1993: 13). The virtue of this solution in the late 1980s was its perfect fit with the political liberalization to which the deciders, huddled in the presidential crisis center, had apparently agreed in October 1988 when they called in the reform team (Hidouci 1995: 161). After drafting legislation and disseminating the *Cahiers* (Hadj-Nacer 1989), five pamphlets giving guidelines for reform, Hamrouche's reform team became the official government in 1989; meanwhile a transitional government supervised a constitutional referendum and legalized the components of Algeria's new multiparty system, including the Islamic Front of Salvation (FIS).

The economic reforms were a bold attempt to change the rules governing economic decision making. Previous efforts under Brahimi to "decentralize" the public sector had not worked because a small number of deciders, including the dreaded Sécurité Militaire (renamed the Département du Renseignement et Sécurité – DRS), kept the real levers of command. Their powerful clans dominated the state monopolies over foreign commerce, domestic credit, and many lucrative domestic markets, as well as the public-sector personnel files. Hidouci's solution was to abolish the monopolies, deregulate prices, and establish a framework for each public enterprise, including the banks, to operate as an independent self-supporting firm responsive to market forces. A flexible system of state holding companies was set up in 1988 to replace the supervision of public-sector enterprise by parent ministries. Transparency and open markets were intended to curtail the pervasive rent-seeking by eliminating much of the spoils. A gradual devaluation of the dinar was planned to eliminate the gap between official and parallel rates and with it much of the trabendo commerce. Foreign direct investment, or Algerians repatriating their capital, was to be encouraged. Algeria, in sum, was to become more openly integrated into the global economy.

The reforms predictably enjoyed little support among public-sector officials or labor. Liberal commentators dismissed them as yet another legalistic exercise (Addi 1991), and the reformers actually attacked Algeria's small private sector for being protected, rather than cultivating it (Dillman 1997: 171 n20). Despite support from the IMF and the World Bank, the reforms did not receive adequate funding from the conservative French banks because Algeria rejected rescheduling, with the external constraints that it would impose, in favor of an informal "reprofiling" to lighten the servicing of its heavy international debt. In their twenty months in office, however, the reformers did succeed in abolishing the foreign commerce monopolies and establishing a strong central bank to replace the Ministry of Finance's opaque methods of controlling the money supply and credit allocation. Developing a true market economy would inevitably be a slow and painful process. The banks, for instance, could hardly become autonomous agencies overnight when 65 percent of their loans, almost exclusively to public-sector companies, were nonperforming (Nashashibi 1998: 36); nor could the latter suddenly become operational economic entities in Algeria's tangled, partially deregulated markets. Devaluing the dinar also posed problems. The reformers wished to move decisively to reduce the gap between the official and parallel market rates and shared the IMF's antipathy to inflated official rates. Yet devaluation had to be gradual in order to limit its inflationary impact.

Each public enterprise was to be released from its parent ministry and given its autonomy to operate in partially deregulated markets. But the new "participation funds" established as holding companies to supervise the public enterprises had few staff and little expertise. The annual report of one of them reflected a widespread misunderstanding that they were simply "implementing a new system of economic planning." Obviously it would take many years for new institutions and market-driven behavior to take root in Algeria's vast bureaucracy. Obstacles to change were and remain far greater than in other bunker capitalist regimes, such as Nasser's Egypt. Regimented only for a decade or so (1961–74), the Egyptians had active memories of a market economy that helped to facilitate some reform in the 1970s, whereas the Algerians have none.

Yet the Algerian reformers had one tremendous potential source of support in 1989–90. They enjoyed the tacit blessings of the FIS. The Islamic Front of Salvation has been accused of not having an economic program (Roberts 1994), and indeed its priorities were cultural purification and political power. Their program of March 7, 1989, however, offers an "economic doctrine" calling for a market economy in almost perfect accord with Hidouci's reform program (Al-Ahnaf et al. 1991: 179–87). Originally published abroad after the FIS was officially recognized, the FIS program may have been fabricated after the fact to gain some credit with the reformers. Yet the "economic doctrine" seems consistent with other fragmentary FIS commentaries and with the actions of the party during the reform period. Any formal alliance would have embarrassed both the reformers and the FIS, yet they served each other's political objectives. By defeating the FLN in the municipal elections of June 1990, the FIS strengthened the reformers' hold over the FLN parliament and other ruling circles; by pursuing political liberalization, the reformers opened up political opportunities for the FIS.

The latter's ill-considered call for a general strike in May 1991 unfortunately gave military leaders, threatened by the economic reforms, a pretext for obliging Chadli to proclaim a military emergency, even though the strike was fizzling out. The reform government resigned in the face of a virtual coup (Entelis and Arone 1992). It still should be noted that that FIS's economic prescriptions were almost identical with those of the reformers. Like Hidouci, the FIS's economic program attacked Algeria's centralized state economy as "discouraging the spirit of initiative... in favor of mediocrity and incompetence... penalizing small enterprises... In our country industry is actually making the economy more dependent." Although in favor of "industrializing industries," as long as they were internationally competitive, "the Islamic Front of Salvation insists that industry, crucial as it is, should never be at the expense of agriculture, as it has been in the past." Khodja and Hidouci had made similar arguments in Boumédienne's time. The FIS, too, opposed industrial and commercial monopolies. FIS favored not only limiting state intervention in the industrial sector and protecting private property but also "watching that the latter not be transformed into monopoly infringing on the public interest, for this would be an open door for economic, political and social parasitism." In addition to specifically Islamic economic reforms such as legalizing zakat (Muslim taxes on property for charities) and opening Islamic banks, the FIS joined the reformers in advocating the dismantling of state import monopolies and price controls. "Commercial monopoly should be prohibited except when the State needs to intervene to safeguard major political or economic interests." The FIS advocated export-oriented growth because many of its supporters were in small industry or commerce. Like Hidouci and the International Monetary Fund, the party also specifically favored eliminating the gap between the official and parallel market exchange rates. Evidently the moralizers and globalizers were working together in Algeria at this critical juncture. In a sense, the reformers had anticipated the FIS's principal specific demand, the opening of Islamic banks, by encouraging the establishment of Algeria's first Islamic bank, Banque Al Baraka Algérie, a joint venture, legally incorporated in May 1991, of the international Al Baraka group with one of Algeria's big public-sector banks.

Reforms from the bunker (1991–)

A variety of governments with various economic policies succeeded the reformers. First, Sid Ahmed Ghozali maintained the IMF program of his predecessors while freezing many of the domestic market reforms and replacing some of the public officials identified with the reform team. He also offered prospects of joint upstream oil ventures to attract international, especially American, capital. Even while he stayed as prime minister, however, the specter of a decisive victory by FIS in the 1991–2 parliamentary elections gave the military the excuse to terminate President Chadli Bendjedid as well as the elections. Some political formations in Algeria's burgeoning civil society were determined to prevent a FIS victory, and the most outspoken of these parties also enjoyed close ties with military "deciders." Seeking civilian cover, the latter brought Mohammed Boudiaf back from exile in Morocco. Boudiaf had quit Algerian politics in 1963 but, as one of the "historic" founders of the National Liberation Front (FLN), was perceived as a useful figurehead. Prime Minister Ghozali preserved some continuity as presidents changed, but he was succeeded by his original patron from the Boumédienne years, Belaid Abdesselam, after President Boudiaf, enormously popular after only six months and no mere figurehead, was assassinated. The new prime minister stubbornly resisted calls by the IMF for a depreciation of the Algerian currency in return for debt relief. While fully servicing its external debt – 80 percent of its export earnings – without rescheduling, Abdesselam's government abandoned any semblance of fiscal or monetary discipline, printed money to cover widening deficits (Figure 4.3), and tightened price controls while keeping subsidies on basic consumption items amounting to 5 percent of GDP (Nashashibi et al. 1998: 6). His policy efforts to salvage his industrializing industries might have worked, had oil revenues begun their surge in 1993 rather than 1999. He still defends his resistance to the IMF and to the Algerian military "brain" that supported his removal from office so that a more pliant civilian prime minister could negotiate a Standby arrangement with the IMF (www.belaidabdesselam.com). His industries continued to be sabotaged: for instance, cement plants were operating well below capacity despite his allocation in 1993 of sufficient funds to import the equipment and services needed to increase production. Because demand outran supply, imports provided a free market price floor that could be bid up, generating rents for regime cronies. In this vein, a need to import cement was created yet again in 2009 after increases in local industrial capacity could have easily met local demand.

All efforts ceased between 1991 and 1993 to realign Algeria's foreign exchange rate. Despite expansionary fiscal and monetary policies, unemployment increased and there were growing shortages of consumer items. Finally in May 1994, following a drop in oil prices, a balance-of-payments crisis seemed imminent. By this time the guerrilla warfare and counterinsurgency, unleashed by the canceling of the 1991-92 parliamentary elections and intensified with the assassination of Boudiaf, facilitated a radical reorientation of the Algerian economy. Under a new president and new prime minister Algeria embarked on another IMF structural adjustment program and formal debt rescheduling, engendering a slight rise in public confidence in Algeria's financial institutions as reflected in the CIM ratio (Figure 4.3). After some quick relief under a one-year standby arrangement with the IMF, followed by public debt rescheduling with the Paris Club, it successfully negotiated a three-year Extended Fund Facility in May 1995 and further rescheduled the public debt in July. It concluded a rescheduling of private commercial banking debts with the London Club in September.

Once the military lost its constitutional cover, the opposition's resort to guerrilla warfare played into its hands. When in January 1995 the major Algerian political parties, including the FLN as well as the FIS, agreed to the Sant'Egidio (Rome) Platform, which would have restored constitutional order, the junta rejected the deal. Even more macabre, however, is the way the guerrilla warfare and counterinsurgency then facilitated Algeria's necessary policies of economic adjustment, deprived of the buffer of any internal vision of economic reform, and justified a state of emergency that still, in 2010, serves to reinforce the bunker state.

President Zeroual fielded a succession of governments of varying political complexions, all of which faithfully implemented the IMF program out of necessity, but none of which could project any vision of comprehensive economic reform, much less political institutions to sustain it. For instance, Minister Ahmed Ouyahia, whom Zeroual assigned in 1995 to accelerate the IMF program by imposing greater fiscal austerity, stated in 1998: "We cannot introduce a market economy which is not in working order. If we need it, we will have it but if we do not need it we will abandon it" (Dillman 2000: 142 n22).

The IMF proudly reported, however, that Algeria "has adjusted faster" than MENA's earlier starters (Egypt, Jordan, Morocco, and Tunisia) and that its macroeconomic performance had "equaled or even surpassed" them by the end of 1996. "Real growth was 4 percent; inflation was declining to single digits, both the budget and the current account posted surpluses; foreign reserves were at five months of imports; and external debt indicators had improved markedly" (Nashashibi et al. 1998: 64). But unemployment was increasing, not decreasing, although government officials, including the security forces, increased between 1985 and 1995 from 4.1 to 4.4 per hundred inhabitants. Government employment was still higher on a per capita basis in Algeria than in Jordan, Morocco, Syria, and Tunisia, not to mention various East Asian states (Nashashibi et al. 1998: 25). The middle classes, however, were being "laminated" by the rising cost of living without commensurate salary increases (*El Watan*, May 9, 1999). Between 1990 and 1995, more than 400,000 Algerians emigrated, including tens of thousands of professionals and managers (Dillman 2000: 143 n25). Small private businesses fled to Tunisia to escape extortion by military clans (Dillman 2000: 58), whereas others went out of business for lack of credit, being crowded out by the public sector.

The restructuring of Algeria's public enterprises ultimately eliminated many of them. State enterprises were subjected after 1994 to tighter budgetary constraints, and the construction sector was especially hard hit, shedding 93,000 workers between 1995 and 1997 (Nashashibi et al. 1998: 50). At least 76 large public companies out of more than 400 were dissolved, with estimates as of April 1998 running as high as 400,000 people thrown out of work (Dillman 2000: 83). In December 1997, 250 of the companies were placed on a list to be privatized. Prime Minister Ouyahia, while squeezing Algeria's budget deficit into a small surplus, also cracked down on the public-sector managers. Two thousand of them were jailed after 1995, as much for being on the wrong side of power struggles among military factions as for any alleged wrongdoing. One notorious case involved the top management of SIDER, the iron and steel company. Its crime was to have inexpensively imported large quantities of iron bars for reinforced concrete, upsetting monopolies run by people close to President Zeroual (El Kadi 1998: 66). The brother of the manager, however, was an army general who interpreted the attack on his brother as really aimed at himself for having crossed Zeroual on other matters (*Algérie confidentielle* no. 76, June 1996). So many injustices were committed that some of those finally released from prison constituted an "association of incarcerated cadres" in May 1999 (*El Watan*, May 23, 1999). Such a "civil society" initiative in a bunker state was only possible because other generals supported a political offensive against General Mohammed Betchine, whom Zeroual had promoted as his possible successor. Betchine, who had favored negotiations with the FIS, was anathema to hardliners within the military. In 1998, after barely three years, they obliged their president to resign. In his place they resuscitated Abdelaziz Bouteflika, who had been Boumédienne's secretary before becoming foreign minister.

New presidential elections in 1999, had they been free, might have preserved at least a fig leaf of legitimacy, but six of the seven contenders withdrew at the last moment in a remarkable display of consensus that the elections were being rigged (*Jeune Afrique* no. 1997, April 20–6, 1999). The winner, Abdelaziz Bouteflika, had served as Algeria's foreign minister from 1963 to 1979 after being a charter member of the Oujda clan. He recovered no more legitimacy than the officers who had brought him out of retirement, and the vote rigging reinforced doubts about the earlier elections of the incumbent parliament and regional assemblies (*El Watan*, May 24, 1999). Although reelected president in 2004 and again, after passage of a constitutional amendment permitting him a third term, in 2009, Bouteflika was still dependent on a shadowy and changing cabal of military officers. Yet without a cover of legitimate government, the décideurs were vulnerable to their own internal divisions as their clans openly competed for economic spoils.

Indeed, since the previous edition of this book, little changed on the ground in Algeria. The shadowy terrorist groups morphed into Al Qaeda of the Islamic Maghrib (AQIM) and committed sporadic atrocities, including the simultaneous bombings of the United Nations Development Program's Algiers office building and the Constitutional Court in December 2007, following an earlier explosion close to the prime minister's office overlooking downtown Algiers. AQIM no longer poses a serious threat but rather gives credence to "managing instability," the subtitle of an excellent study of Algeria's political elite (Werenfels 2007). Signs of popular frustration were mounting. Only 35 percent of the electorate – by generous official count – bothered to vote in the 2007 legislative elections. In January 2009 unprecedented and illegal public demonstrations against Israel's war on Gaza overtook Algerian security services in Algiers and other cities. Yet the well-funded local authorities engineered a respectable turnout for Bouteflika's reelection in May 2009, supported behind the scenes, as in the presidential elections of 2004, by Algeria's dominant military faction.

The deindustrialization of Algeria was well underway. Algerian sources cited by the IMF indicate that public-sector industry, excluding hydrocarbons, produced only 69.3 percent as much in 1997 as in 1987, when they were already operating well below capacity. The biggest declines came after 1993 (IMF 1998: 44, Table 10). Textile production was down by more than half, and even food processing diminished by 17 percent from 1993 to 1997 despite effective rates of protection in 1996 of respectively 60 and 110 percent in these two sectors (Sorsa 1999: 10). Private industry did not appear to be taking up the slack. As Bradford Dillman explains, "a liberalized economy [is] operating through a circulation of rent between the military, a deficient public sector and a largely commercial private sector" (2000: 3). In Algeria liberalization and the breaking up of state import monopolies was accompanied by new private oligopolies of importers. Although in theory anyone was free to import goods, in practice certain lucrative sectors were reserved for the regime's favored clients. The general climate of violence ensured a relative stability of market shares.

The pharmaceutical sector, cornered by six large importers, is of special interest. Not only did the importers manage to limit local production of generic drugs – Algerian local production was far less than that of its Maghrib neighbors – but they also offered a marvelous learning experience and window of opportunity for Abdelmounem Rafik Khalifa, Algeria's "golden boy" for the first two years of the twenty-first century. This young pharmacist (born in 1966) inherited not only his late father's pharmacy but also some of the latter's political connections. Laroussi Khalifa had managed the offices of the Abdelhafid Boussouf, the founder in 1958 of Algeria's military intelligence service and patron of Boumédienne. Boussouf left politics for business at the end of the war, but his office manager became Algeria's first minister of commerce and industry. Boussouf's "*Malgaches*" (named after his wartime Ministère des Armaments et Liaisons Générales) constituted powerful political clans after independence and still wielded residual influence after three decades, enabling young Moumen, as friends called him, to make useful connections when he started to import generic drugs in 1991 with small amounts of family savings.

After learning the import business, Algeria's "golden boy" took advantage of new laws encouraging private-sector banking. His Khalifa Bank, legally recognized in 1998, grew rapidly to acquire 7 percent of Algeria's commercial banking deposits by 2003. Offering higher interest rates than his public-sector competitors, he persuaded various public entities as well as a broad Algerian public to park their funds with his bank. He then used the funds to establish Khalifa Airlines by leasing airliners and luring some of Air Algérie's most experienced, competent, and frustrated staff of pilots, attendants, and administrators with higher salaries. The writer of these lines was astonished, on returning to Algiers in 2002 after more than a decade, to see more planes bearing the insignia of El Khalifa Airways than of Air Algérie parked on the tarmac of the Houari Boumédienne Algiers Airport. High Algerian officials pointed proudly to its superior service as a sign of a brilliant future for Algeria's burgeoning private sector. Many Algerian youth also identified with Moumen as indicating "finally, we can have the good life, too," as an Algerian advertising consultant put it (Crumley 2003). No expenses were spared, and both Khalifa Bank and Khalifa Airways employed many children of the Algerian elite; meanwhile, in France, Moumen hobnobbed with Catherine Deneuve and Gerard Depardieu among other French stars and staged media circuses supposedly to celebrate Algeria's entrance into global fantasy land. Indeed, the consultant, whom Moumen had tried to recruit, saw it clearly: "This company was a fantasy creation by and for an Algerian élite – an artifice certain to collapse." But most Algerians, their economic senses atrophied by so many years of French colonialism and Algerian socialism followed by the dark decade of the 1990s, expected miracles. Hundreds of thousands of them, lured by high interest rates, invested their savings in Khalifa Bank.

The crash finally came in 2003, but Khalifa Bank should have been stopped two years earlier for not submitting proper reports to the Central Bank and ignoring earlier warnings. At the show trial of the Khalifa Group in 2007, an array of high officials made the former governor of the Central Bank a scapegoat for their own mismanagement, and the full story has yet to be told. Moumen had fled to London and so was condemned in absentia to life imprisonment, but the Algerian authorities were not in a hurry to get him extradited. He could insist on a new trial and then implicate too many high officials in his pyramid schemes. After the Central Bank, in November 2002, finally did freeze Khalifa exports of currency to finance Moumen's failing enterprises in France – which included a lavish cable TV station, a soccer team, a luxury car leasing agency, and several villas, not to mention an apartment in Paris reserved for President Bouteflika's brother Said – top bank officials were then caught at the Algiers airport in February 2003 carrying out suitcases of hard currency.

Local press sympathetic to the tycoon even then argued that the attacks against his enterprises were politically motivated because the cable TV station might have upset the president's plans for reelection in 2004. Top décideurs, including General Larbi Belkheir, were trying as late as May 2003 to rescue the bank (Hachemaoui 2009b: 231). Perhaps indeed Moumen had a strategy that might have worked. He had used his bank's funds to purchase a German construction company that could be positioned to take advantage of Algeria's heavy investments in infrastructure, funded by surging hydrocarbon revenues, and thereby regain liquidity and eventual solvency for his business empire. In 2003 two other private banks failed, their fraudulent schemes also exposed. The failure of the Khalifa Bank was the most spectacular, with losses estimated at $3 to $5 billion, but the other banks lost at least an additional $1 billion – not that the costs mattered much to a regime that was raking in the hydrocarbon revenues and had accumulated reserves estimated at over $140 billion by 2008.

These private-sector adventures had come when, as Algerian political scientist Laouari Addi (1999) observes, competing clans were losing some of their mutual solidarity as well as their pecuniary resources. The clans were becoming too brittle and exposed in the late 1990s to survive increased competition over diminishing spoils. An imaginary private-sector booty served for a time to hold them together, but once the vast investment projects in infrastructure afforded by surging revenues opened new opportunities for plunder, the enterprise became expendable. As Mohammed Hachemaoui, another rising Algerian political scientist (also based in France not Algeria), observes, the regime is built on ill-gotten gains to finance critical patron-client networks in support of the bunker (Hachemaoui 2009a).

Increasing spoils in the 2000s seem only to have further whetted elite appetites. In January 2010, a major corruption scandal decimated the leadership of Sonatrach, Algeria's principal patronage resource, and Algeria's police chief was murdered in late February, ostensibly by an associate he had suspended for alleged bribery concerning the import of spare parts for police helicopters. Some local journalists interpreted the crime as a response to the Sonatrach scandal, which had targeted a nephew of one of Bouteflika's inner circle. One commentator speculated, amid rumors that Bouteflika was planning for his brother's succession, whether the ruling clans were self-destructing

For several years it's been a real tempest blowing in on the pyramid of power and striking down its most visible godfathers. Some are taken by old age and illness, others coldly liquidated or victims of plots. And the most recent financial scandals are not about to settle matters. The decapitation of Sonatrach's top personnel has in turn provoked a "management crisis" for the top circles (Benfodil 2010).

Lessons for other bunker regimes

Reform is highly problematic in any bunker regime because economic liberalization requires a major political change. Reformers within such a regime need outside support. In the MENA, as in Eastern Europe and other transitional settings, the softline reformers need alliances with "moderate" opposition forces that can isolate the hardliners within, while also containing the more radical opposition factions opposed to a political reform process. Under more effective leadership, Algeria's FIS could have played such a role in 1991. Algeria's situation is extreme, but not atypical of other bunker regimes in the region. With the exception of Sudan, the principal opposition forces to bunker regimes since the 1970s have been Islamist. The Algerian case suggests that they can be allies of political and economic liberalization. The economic policy of the FIS concorded with the Ten Commandments preached by the Washington Consensus, and contemporary Islamic economics remains broadly congruent with more flexible reinterpretations of the Consensus. *Ijtihad* or reinterpretation has happened on both sides of the aisle, and "Islamism" obviously has no single blueprint, most Islamist movements having little to say about the economy. But bunker regimes unfortunately do not promote political moderation among Islamist oppositions. In the other, gentler forms of political economy to be discussed in subsequent chapters, alliances with Islamic business sectors have greater chances of success than in bunker states. In Syria, by contrast, the residual private sector's sympathies for the Muslim Brotherhood seem to have caused both Hafez al-Asad and his son-successor Bashar to proceed extremely cautiously with economic reforms, finally legalizing Islamic finance in 2005 as had Algeria by 1991, and to avoid political ones altogether (Lawson 1992: 130–2; Ayubi 1995: 262–3; Lawson 2009).

The danger to a bunker regime is that adjustment to the global economy, however economically necessary, will undermine it. These regimes lack strategic depth. There is little civil society with which officers might ally to leverage a reform program. Chadli, Hamouche, and Hidouci tried to pull off an almost impossible stunt. Their implicit ally, the FIS, had little economic base beyond small shopkeepers and trabendo commerce. As for Zeroual's reform efforts, maybe "his remarkable political stabilization programme in 1995 was in part a result of his shrewd policy of assuming the same political ground as the FIS. Politically he repositioned himself outside the state while at the same time standing at its centre" (Stone 1998: 252). But there was simply no ground on which to stand. Abdelmounem Khalifa and others tried to build new ground that turned into quicksand.

Civil society, to be sure, is not only a capitalist construct but a public sphere in which political regimes try to project their image of legitimacy. Even the military dictators reach out of their bunkers and, whether or not they have read Jean-Jacques Rousseau, try to "transform might into right." Algeria saw a series of attempts under Boumédienne and his successors to erect a façade of constitutional order so as to camouflage their guns. In Syria, Adib Shishakli (1949–54) ruled securely behind the scenes, only to fall after his rule became more exposed. His many military successors stumbled until Hafez al-Asad (1970–2000) institutionalized the Ba'ath regime, with its complex of allied parties and associations that enabled his son Bashar to succeed him. In Iraq Saddam Hussein (1968–2003) also commanded a complex of civil institutions designed to legitimate his leadership and an eventual succession of one of his sons. Saddam Hussein, in fact, had risen to power through the Ba'ath Party, not the military. The successor regime has yet to replace these structures destroyed by fiat from Rumsfeld's Pentagon.

In the Sudan the military has alternated with civilian rule since 1958. After Numeiri's fall and a brief interval of civilian rule (1986–8), Sudan's military strongman, Omar Bashir, could not rule with military force alone. To legitimate his regime and keep his fellow officers in line, he coopted Hassan Turabi to provide an Islamist cover, but then dismissed him in 1999. Ali Abdullah Saleh has veiled his tribal-military rule of Yemen with the General People's Congress, which has been reinforced, at least in opposition to various rough Yemeni political forces, by tactical alliances with the Islamist Islah Party. In Libya, too, Muammar Qaddafi (1969–) created a facade of legitimacy. First he created a Libyan Arab Socialist Union modeled after the schema of his late mentor, Gamal Abdel Nasser. When the LASU failed, Qaddafi became more creative: the *jamahuriya* of popular assemblies enabled him as revolutionary leader to retire from all official positions. But Rousseau's lessons about participatory democracy evidently did not inspire him to assume the position of Legislator, described in the conclusion of *The Social Contract*, and retire from politics altogether. He might indeed be unable to resist a popular upsurge reflecting a regional trend begun in Syria to appoint one of his sons, presumably either Saif al Islam or Mutasim, head of state.

The visible manifestations of civil society are the media, civic, cultural, and human rights associations, political parties, trade and professional unions, even tribal associations and football clubs. They exist in most bunker states and have positively flourished in Algeria since 1988, when "literally thousands of associations were created" (Zoubir 1999: 36). Yahia Zoubir observes that "civil society has resisted either being reabsorbed by an ascending powerful, authoritarian state or being swept away by yet another populist, totalitarian movement," as he views the FIS (Zoubir 1999: 39). Being the most open and "vibrant" of the civil societies tolerated by a bunker state, in fact, Algeria perhaps also best reveals their limitations (Liverani 2008). Sandwiched between guerrilla bands and a rapacious counterinsurgency, civil society has no institutional guarantees. Although many free-spirited, mostly middle-class Algerians learn the arts of association, their aspirations are constrained by economic as well as political realities. The media and the various associations rest on a very narrow economic base. A private sector of shopkeepers and small enterprises funds some associations, including the FIS, but most politically significant groups, including the press, are funded almost exclusively by the government. In addition to the usual censorship, there are more subtle controls. What is published or not published reflects the balance of power between the clans. Stories of Mohammed Bechtine's abuses of power surfaced in late 1998, for instance, because Lamari clan leaders gave the press the green light to embarrass their rival. This is not to deny the personal bravery of the Algerian press corps: at least fifty-eight journalists were killed in the line of duty by either security forces or oppositions in the 1990s. But civil society lacks a private-sector base. Thus, newspapers connected with leading clans get the subsidies and state advertising accounts, while those of their opponents go bankrupt.

The only capital enjoying structural power in a bunker state consists of the rents accumulated by its janissaries and their networks of friends and cousins. The bunkers cannot mobilize their business communities or develop durable arrangements with elements of civil society. Without an independent private sector to support it, civil society is largely fictitious or subject to a high degree of manipulation from the bunkers in countries such as Algeria. Libya used to be the reductio ad absurdum of a civil society. In 1976 Qaddafi tried to abolish money altogether and destroy the institution of private property on which civil society rests. "Libyans call the years from 1978 to 1988 the 'dark decade' because of the political repression and the extreme economic hardship" (Al-Kikhia 1997: 94). In 1978 Libya's CIM ratio plummeted to 63 percent but subsequently recovered as the Revolutionary Leader's revolutionary appetites waned. Like Algeria under the French, the Libyans had suffered a devastating colonial experience at the hands of Mussolini. Although the oil boom of the late 1950s resulted in some capital accumulation by rent seekers around King Idris, Qaddafi easily leveled the private sector in the early 1970s. At this time, Boumédienne was cutting down the remnants of a native Algerian capitalist class left over from the colonial period. In both countries the colonial situation eased the way for bunker capitalism by destroying the elites that might otherwise have articulated a stronger civil society.

In the other bunker states, too, the private sector seems too feeble to support much civil society. Yemen has not one but three scattered bourgeoisies (Chaudhry 1997). Much of the original merchant class escaped the exactions of the monarchy in the 1930s for British protection in Aden. Many of the old landed classes and merchants of Aden and the Hadramout in turn emigrated to Saudi Arabia in 1967, when a radical nationalist faction gained control of the People's Democratic Republic of Yemen. A further wave escaped the state monopolies organized by the Yemen Arab Republic in the 1970s. Many returned with unification in 1990, but the triumph dissipated amid increasing taxation and declining remittances from Saudi Arabia, followed by a wave of regime-instigated Islamist violence directed against them. Yemen's workers also displayed remarkable mobility, departing for Saudi Arabia in the 1970s only to be expelled back home en masse in 1991 – some 750,000 to a million economic casualties of the Second Gulf War. In the Sudan a small, wealthy bourgeoisie is more firmly implanted, but it is overshadowed by a public sector that consumes much of the available credit. Returning to power in 1989, the military cracked down on civil society (Lesch 1996). Rents from cotton exports and arms imports from the Taliban accrued instead to Al-Mahfazah ("The Portfolio"), a business group associated with Hassan Turabi (Hirst 1997). Poor societies with relatively small middle classes, such as Sudan or Yemen, are perhaps more easily plundered than wealthier ones, but Syria and Iraq also lost most of their respective bourgeoisies. In the 1960s successive Ba'athist revolutions scared away much of Syria's vaunted manufacturing as well commercial entrepreneurship. President Asad's controlled infitah (opening of the economy) of the early 1970s, to be sure, did result in an expanded private sector, but it was heavily dependent, like its weaker Algerian counterpart, on military patrons. In the 1970s and 1980s, Saddam leveled Iraq's class structure and created new entrepreneurs primarily from his family and village.

Algeria and Iraq were the bunker states of renown in the 1990s, as their embattled rulers conducted wars from their literal bunkers against their own people, practices that continued under changed leaderships in the twenty-first century. But in the late 1970s and early 1980s, Syria held the dubious distinction of being the Arab state whose leadership was most hunkered down in bunkers out of fear of attack by its citizens. That Syria ultimately emerged from its civil war with its political elite still intact, but subsequently made little progress in liberalizing its economy or stimulating economic growth, underscores the tenacity of political obstacles that impede effective responses to globalization in the bunker states. The Syrian case suggests that Algeria could win the battle against internal violence, but still lose the war against economic stagnation. In both cases, as in the other bunker praetorian republics, the lack of state autonomy from social forces results in the state becoming an instrument of one or more of those social forces in their domination of others. This in turn prevents those bunker states from developing or implementing economically rational policies. They lack broad, institutionalized support in society, so they must subdue it, which entails extracting resources from civil society both to prevent it from supporting autonomous action and to pay for the coercive capacities of the state. The primary concern of these states, in short, is political control, not economic growth.

Syria: succession in the bunker

From the first postindependence coup d'état in 1949, until 1970, various political movements and cabals of officers, with greater or lesser independence from the religious and ethnic groups of which Syria is constituted, struggled to control the state. Finally, in the late 1960s, army officers drawn from the most "compact" of the religious minorities, the Alawis, who had provided the backbone of locally recruited military forces under the French, gained control of the state. Hafez al-Asad, who ruled Syria for thirty years, quietly overthrew another, more radical Alawi in 1970, after refusing to support his military adventures. Before the end of the decade, the Muslim Brotherhood, which represented the majoritarian Sunni Muslim community, began to violently challenge what they saw as Alawi usurpation of "their" state. The denouement came in 1982, when the Brotherhood instigated a mass revolt in the northern city of Hama, hoping thereby to spark unrest in Damascus and throughout the country. In the event, their effort failed, in large measure because the regime, deploying troops under the command of kinsmen of the president and including large numbers of other minorities, especially Kurds, pulverized the center of Hama, killing some 20,000 of its inhabitants. For the next several years Sunni Muslim activists were hunted down by the regime, imprisoned, or liquidated. For more than thirty years the Syrian state has been controlled at its apex, in descending order of importance, by the family, clan, tribe, and minority religious sect of the president. Commands of the vital military and security organs are virtually exclusively Alawi preserves, while another religious minority that tends to be favored by the regime, the Christians, provides a disproportionate number of domestic intelligence officers.

In the wake of the 1982 bloodbath, the government embarked on a hesitant economic reform, necessitated by declining oil prices and made possible politically by the intimidation of the Muslim Brotherhood. The destruction of Hama was fresh in the minds of any Sunni Muslims who might have been tempted to use their economic skills and resources to take advantage of the limited economic opening for political purposes. In need of economic assets that the Sunnis possessed in greatest measure, the regime essentially struck the same bargain with them as the "deciders" in Algeria did with Algerian capitalists. That bargain consisted of deals between individual Alawi patrons and Sunni capitalist clients, whereby the former provided protection, contacts, and permissions while the latter did the business, paying their patrons appropriate rents for services rendered. That bargain underpinned the political economy of Syria through the remainder of the Hafez al-Asad era, but weakened with the succession of his son Bashar in 2000. Thirty-four years of age when he became president, Bashar had replaced most of his father's aging compatriots with his contemporaries well before he was reelected president in 2007 with more than 97 percent of the vote. Many of his recruits into the elite, such as his brother Mahir, placed in charge of the Republican Guards, or his brother-in-law Assef Shawkat, appointed as deputy director of military intelligence in 2001 and promoted to director four years later, were drawn from his immediate or extended family, the latter especially on his mother's (Makhluf) side, and still more from his generation of the predominantly Alawi elite who had been exercising political and economic power for thirty years. These *awlad al sultah*, or "children of power," typically well educated and self-confident, rapidly extended their influence into the economy, thereby marginalizing some of the second-tier Sunni businessmen who no longer could claim a monopoly on relevant skills. The ring of crony capitalists around the presidency has thus tightened yet further into the Alawi regime core under Bashar, while the scope of its activities has expanded (Ismail 2009: 20).

Although Syria benefitted like all other MENA countries from the third oil boom, GDP growth peaked at 6.7 percent in 2004 and fell back to below 5 percent even before the boom ended. For much of the period of the Asads' forty-year regime, GDP per capita has stagnated. The endemic problem of capital flight, which the Minister of Finance estimated in 2007 to total some \$60 to \$70 billion and which was further aggravated by Bashar's displacement of Sunni by Alawi cronies, has contributed to Syria's persisting failure to achieve even average MENA growth rates (Raphaeli 2007: 42). In the early 1950s Syria's was one of the most rapidly growing economies in the third world, and most observers judged its prospects to be extremely bright, in part because of the country's favorable factor endowments. Its continued failure to realize that promise attests to the shackles that Syrian governments have placed on autonomous business activity generally and on the allocation of capital specifically.

Capital has no structural power in Syria because its accumulation is not protected by law or institutions, as reflected in the low ratio of contract-intensive money to the total money supply that was shown in Table 3.2 and is traced out over time in Figure 4.4, reflecting Syria's bumpy political road. Only broken Iraq was a worse performer than Syria on this measure, which is a surrogate indicator for the degree of rule of law and security of property. Moreover, although the Syrian ratio, like Algeria's, improved somewhat over the years, as is shown in Figure 4.4, it slumped between 2002 and 2005 before recovering slightly, suggesting that any nominal liberalization signified by the opening of foreign bank branches has not succeeded in inducing those with money to entrust it to official financial institutions. Indeed, under Bashar Syria's CIM ratio, after an initial spurt, flattened out, reflecting the continuing lack of trust in the state and the institutions directly or indirectly controlled by it. An assessment of the banking system as "an appendage of the state budget" (Waldner 1999: 122), prior to the legalization of private banks by Law 8 of 2001, remains essentially true. State banks in 2009 continued to hold more than four-fifths of total bank assets (IMF Staff Report 2009, 8) and to account for more than 90 percent of private-sector lending (Syrian information on economic freedom 2009). Figure 3.5 reveals that it is the most concentrated and government owned of the MENA's banking systems, a result in part of the requirement that 51 percent of a private bank's shares be owned by Syrians. According to one analyst, "every Syrian knows that the majority of these (banks) are controlled either by Gulf investors or wealthy members of the president's inner circle" (Marshall 2009: 112). The central bank is not independent, and the eight private-sector banks by 2009 held only some 15 percent of total assets and liabilities in the banking system. On the Heritage Foundation's index of economic freedom, Syria in 2009 ranked 16th out of the 18 MENA countries it assessed (Table 7.1). Of the ten measures that constitute the overall index, the lowest score was on financial freedom

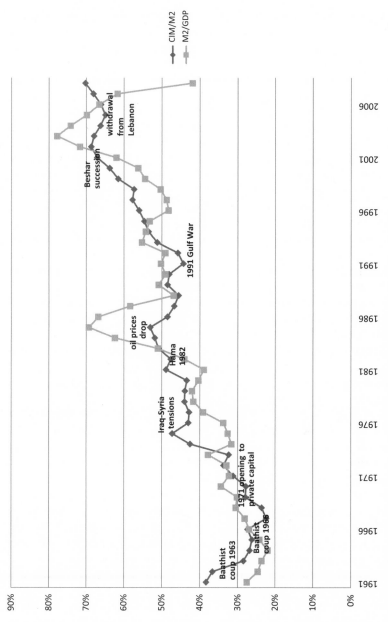

Figure 4.4 Syria's Money Supply and Contract-Intensive Money, 1961–2008
Source: IMF *International Financial Statistics*; World Development Indicators, World Bank (online August 2009)

and was also the lowest among the Arab countries (Heritage Foundation 2009b).

Not surprisingly, the emergence of private banks after the first was established in 2004 – it taking three years for Law 8 to be implemented – has failed to fundamentally alter the allocation of credit. Credit to the private sector as a percentage of GDP stagnated at 15 percent between 2005 and 2009 (IMF Staff Report 2009: 5). Conversely, credit to public-sector firms as a percentage of credit to the entire economy, as shown in Figure 3.7, is, along with Algeria, the highest in the region. The public sector's share actually increased between 2006 and 2008 while Algeria's declined, thus making Syria's share in 2008 equal to Algeria's four years earlier. The World Bank's *Doing Business* report in 2009 ranked Syria 181st out of 183 countries on ease of getting credit. Syria's Central Bank reported in 2008 that domestic private businesses received a scant 7 percent of all bank lending (Marshall, 2009: 108). Given the government's tight embrace of the banking system and Syria's rank in 2009 of 147th out of 184 countries on Transparency International's Corruption Perception Index – with only Sudan and Iraq in the MENA being less transparent – it was surprising that nonperforming loans were only 5 percent of total bank loans when first reported in late 2007, when the IMF also claimed that the system is "hampered by serious data deficiencies in public banks" (IMF Staff Report, 2009: 8). The problem was possibly corrected the following year (World Bank 2009b: 118) when nonperforming laws reached a staggering 25 percent, almost attaining Algerian and Egyptian heights (Figure 3.8).

The Syrian government sought in 2009 to augment the trappings of its nascent private financial system by adding a stock exchange and by bolstering its small but growing Islamic banking sector. Launched in March, the Damascus Stock Exchange is the smallest in the MENA, having six listed companies, of which four are banks. It is overshadowed by the Islamic banking sector, the growth of which is accelerating after a slow start. Legalized in 2005, the first Islamic institution, Cham Bank, was not founded until 2007. Within a year it had attracted $100 million in deposits and planned to open an additional eight branches. The following year the $100 million Syrian-Qatari joint venture Syrian International Islamic Bank opened for business, and in October 2009 Bahrain's Baraka Islamic Bank launched a $35 million initial public offering for a new branch in Damascus. The Central Bank has approved five more licenses for Islamic banks, all of which are joint ventures, primarily with Gulf investors. By November 2009 Islamic banks had attracted 12 percent of personal deposits in private-sector banks and almost 4 percent of total assets of the entire commercial banking system (Dagge 2008; *Syria*

Banker '09 2009). One tiny straw in the wind was that contract-intensive money exceeded 70 percent of the money supply for the first time ever, suggesting that Islamic finance was tapping new markets of pious depositors who distrusted conventional banks, whatever their ownership.

In Syria the security of property, hardly guaranteed by the legal/judicial system, is sought through personal connections. Thus the power and influence of key members of the core of the elite ultimately determine the outcome of even relatively minor disputes, as claims are pushed up competitive personal networks by the disputants, until one ultimately prevails by virtue of having reached a more powerful patron. Business transaction costs in Syria, like those in Algeria, are extremely high, impressionistic evidence suggesting a qualitative difference between such costs in those two and other bunker states, on the one hand, and those in the bully praetorian republics on the other. Relevant surveys confirm these impressions. *Doing Business* reported in 2009 that it was more difficult to enforce a contract in Syria than any other MENA country, it ranking 176th out of 183 countries on this measure. On the overall *Doing Business* ranking, Syria dropped from 130th to 144th out of 184 countries between 2007 and 2009. The World Economic Forum reported a similar decline in the country's business environment on its Global Competitiveness Index, which showed Syria slipping from 78th out of 134 countries in 2007 to 94th two years later, the lowest in the MENA. In 2008 Syria had lower scores on five of the six World Bank's governance indicators than it had had when the Bank first issued its governance scores in 1996, with the biggest falls occurring in government effectiveness and corruption. More than 95 percent of countries ranked by the Bank in 2008 on voice and accountability scored higher than Syria.

Syria's capacity to compete regionally and internationally is further undermined by pervasive restrictions on information flow. All typewriters had to be registered with the government and a sample of their typeface provided until the early 1990s. Fax machines were prohibited until the latter part of that decade, and the Internet only became available in the country just prior to Hafez al-Asad's death. The combination of censorship and a dull, state-controlled press reduces newspaper circulation to the second lowest on a per capita basis in the Arab world – only largely illiterate Yemen has proportionately fewer newspaper readers. Permission for the publication of private newspapers and magazines was accompanied in 2001 by the passage of legislation that required them to adhere to various principles, including respect for the Syrian people, the Ba'ath Party, national unity, the armed forces, and the president's policies. Although Syria in 2009 as indicated in Figure 3.4 had about the same number of Internet users per 100 people as bully states Egypt and Tunisia and rather more than the bunker states of Yemen, Sudan, Libya, and Algeria, Reporters without Borders notes that "Syria is one of the world's most repressive countries toward Internet users." It filters all Internet communications, blocks many websites, and requires all website owners to maintain personal details of those who post articles and comments and to make public the names of contributors. In 2007 YouTube was blocked, apparently either because it showed the dress of the President's wife flapping in the breeze at an official function, or because it posted clips of mistreatment of the country's Kurds. In May 2008, access to Wikipedia's Arabic language site was blocked. Since 2007, the government has arrested bloggers on such charges as "damaging national prestige," "publishing false news," and "weakening national sentiment" (Syria 2009). In 2009 the Committee to Protect Journalists ranked Syria among the ten worst countries in the world in which to be a blogger (Committee to Protect Journalists 2009). On the World Press Freedom Index, Syria ranked 159th out of 173 countries in 2009, with the only lower performers in the MENA being Libya, Saudi Arabia, and the Palestinian Territories.

Restrictions placed by the narrowly based ruling elite on private capital accumulation, business activity, and information flow have undermined what may have been in any case only half-hearted efforts to globalize the Syrian economy. Unwilling to implement various provisions of the draft association agreement with the EU that was initialed in 2004, Syria has been forced to forgo improved access to and various other benefits from its largest trading partner, which until October 2009 refused to sign the agreement. When the EU then declared its readiness to sign, Syria delayed its response, apparently because the document contains provisions regarding human rights that no other Arab country has been asked to sign. Syria thus remains the only signatory of the Barcelona Declaration that has failed to sign a partnership agreement with the EU. Syria has also been unwilling to meet terms for membership in the WTO, with which it began negotiations in 2005. Syria had previously withdrawn from GATT a year after it had become a founding member. One of the sticking points in its negotiations with these bodies is persisting high tariffs and nontariff barriers to trade. Effective duty rates in 1997 were 29.7 percent, the highest in the MENA region. In 2006 the weighted mean tariff on all goods was 15.5 percent, exceeded in the MENA only by Tunisia. Syria's tariffs, some three times the average for all lower-middle-income countries, were almost twice that of the MENA ones, but Syria's participation in GAFTA has boosted trade since 2004.

Coupled with Syria's failure to take full advantage of other trading opportunities globalization might provide has been stagnation of its industrial sector. Manufactured goods as a percentage of GDP actually declined from 15 percent in 1995 to a meager 7 percent in 2006, the latter figure only 1 percent above MENA-trailing Sudan and about one quarter of the average for lower-middle-income countries and just over one-half of the MENA lower-middle-income country average. As shown in Table 2.2, it is the only MENA country, other than Kuwait, in which the intra-industry index dropped between the mid-1980s and the mid-1990s. By 2006 Syria's intra-industry trade outperformed only the oil exporters Algeria, Iraq, Libya, Oman, Qatar, and Kuwait, in all of which oil dependency militates against intra-industry trade, as well as impoverished Yemen. The relatively low output of manufactured goods results not from a lack of investment in industry, which has been comparatively substantial, but from an almost complete absence of productivity increases (Waldner 1999: 188). In a report commissioned by the German government development assistance agency, GTZ, Syria's total factor productivity (TFP) across all industrial sectors was calculated in comparison to nine other emerging country comparators, ranging from India to Brazil and including one MENA country, Egypt. Syria's TFP was 70 percent less than Egypt's, which in turn was about 25 percent below China's and almost 40 percent below Brazil's. Syria's TFP was much the lowest of the ten countries, which is hardly surprising given the fact that overall unit labor productivity has long had a negative annual growth rate of around one percent (Bruck et al. 2007: 6). Possibly further contributing to low productivity in industry is Syria's poor performance in developing its human resources. In 2009 in the MENA only Egypt, Morocco, Sudan, and Yemen were ranked lower than Syria's 107th place on the UNDP's Human Development Index. But since 1980 all of those countries have improved their HDI scores more rapidly than has Syria. In any case there are few employment opportunities for educated Syrians outside the lumbering public sector, which employs 81 percent of men and 78 percent of women with university degrees, and to which more than 80 percent of unemployed youths aged 15–29 look for jobs (Kabbani and Kamel 2009: 200–1).

In the 1950s the region's second largest agricultural exporter with the most rapidly expanding industrial base in the Arab world, Syria's decline is also due in some measure to a minor case of the Dutch disease. Oil production increased from 250,000 barrels per day (bpd) in the mid 1980s to a peak of almost 650,000 bpd in the mid-1990s, at which time oil exports accounted for some two-thirds of exports. But by 2007 Syria had become a net oil importer because of stagnating production and rising domestic consumption, with its 2.5 billion barrels of proven reserves the lowest of any oil-producing MENA country, suggesting that the prospects for increasing production were very limited. The oil windfall was thus more of a curse, in that it contributed to the delay of economic reforms while sustaining an overvalued currency. Other rents, derived from Syria's geostrategic position, whether from the Soviets during the Cold War, the United States as reward for the country's participation in the first Gulf War, Saudi Arabia and other Arab Gulf states as a result of its "front line" status vis-à-vis Israel, or subsequently from Iran for maintaining the alliance first forged in 1980 between Hafez al-Asad and Ayatollah Khomeini, have also provided the regime with resources, and hence with disincentives to reform the domestic economy and to engage with the international one. Ranked 107th out of 156 countries on the KOF Economic Globalization Index in 2009, Syria was less globalized than all other MENA countries except Algeria and Yemen.

Paradoxically, if Syria had fewer natural endowments and less ability to generate rents, its economy might have developed more rapidly. But the regime has managed to sustain its almost autarchic economic policy for some four decades precisely because it has been the beneficiary of strategic and petroleum rents and an agriculture that is reasonably productive. Syria is almost able to feed its own population, no small achievement in this region of food dependency, although a persistent drought was putting pressure on the entire agricultural sector by 2009. Unwilling for political reasons to unleash capitalists, the regime has tethered them to the military/security state, using them as cronies in rent-generating activities, primarily through telecommunications and import licenses and exports of raw materials, including agricultural products, not the least of which have been illegal drugs. The options for Syrian businesspersons are thus to cultivate relations with the Alawi elite and share rents with them, or to conduct as much business as possible beyond that elite's reach, which means outside Syria. Thus Syrian capitalists, who are reputed to be among the most astute in the MENA, have spread their family business conglomerates into the Gulf and Europe, especially the old eastern bloc countries, but their primary base is usually in Beirut, not Damascus or Aleppo. And these family businesses tend to be in trading rather than industry. Fixed capital is not safe in Syria, nor is it easy for foreign Arab nationals to establish industrial firms in other Arab states, as they tend to be more at the mercy of those states than are foreign multinational corporations.

The Syrian political economy today, replete with a ruling single party, almost 30 percent of the labor force employed by the state, and its own cold war with Israel, more closely resembles a classic eastern-bloc, communist one than any other remaining in the MENA. This raises the question of its future, especially because sustaining adequate rents is proving increasingly difficult as economic challenges mount. Each year, 300,000 new entrants to the labor force need jobs, while the existing unemployment rate is about 20 percent by independent estimates, more than twice official figures. About half the population depends on wages or pensions from the state (Raphaeli 2007: 46). One in three Syrians lives in poverty as defined by the $2 per day income threshold (Bruck et al. 2007: 1) Whereas most other MENA states were able to reduce their debt burdens during the third oil boom, Syrian governmental debt doubled to some 40 percent of GDP between 2001 and 2007 (Raphaeli 2007: 44).

Rents in the meantime have not been keeping pace with ever-mounting economic needs. Absent unlikely new discoveries, oil revenues will not be significant in the future. They are already on a precipitous downward slide, dropping from 38 percent of government revenue in 1997 to 22 percent in 2007, despite the fivefold increase in prices over that period (World Development Indicators 2008). Public foreign assistance as recorded by the World Bank fell from $683 million in 1990 to $27 million in 2006 (World Development Indicators 2008). Although remittances doubled between 1990 and 2006, their total of some $800 million in that latter year is less than one-fifth the amount currently received by Egypt, where remittances are not the vital source of national income they were some twenty years ago. Although the Iranian relationship generates some revenue, it does not appear to be substantial. Its investment in Syria over the past several years is estimated at a rather unimpressive $1 billion, whereas trade between the two countries totaled only $200 million in 2007, with a scant 10 percent of that trade being Syrian exports to Iran (Raphaeli and Gersten 2008: 2). The economic loss to Syria of its ejection from Lebanon is unknown, but must be sizeable and probably exceeds benefits provided by Iran. Syria did enjoy a boomlet of FDI, principally from GCC states, between 2003 and 2007, with Kuwaitis and Qataris in particular investing in the tourism and real estate sectors. But the Great Recession brought that boomlet to a close, with FDI dropping in 2009 to some $700 million (Marshall 2009: 110).

So like Algeria, only more so, the Syrian regime is desperately in need of resources to sustain the state and economy as currently constituted. Traditional sources of rents seem unlikely to suffice in the face of increasing demands. One way out of the squeeze would be a dramatic volte-face in Syria's regional posture, which would be based on a peace treaty with Israel and a severing of the Iranian tie, which might in turn serve as the catalyst for dramatic economic reforms supported by foreign assistance. Such a scenario does not strain credulity to the breaking point. A peace deal with Israel with substantial direct and indirect "peace dividends" might both enhance regime popularity and underpin economic reform that would receive further support from the more benign regional environment, which, among other things, would reduce the need for military expenditures. This optimistic scenario begs the question of whether a rejuvenated Syrian economy would pave the way for political reform, or for consolidation of regime power currently threatened by inadequate resources.

If comparative regional history is any guide, the chances are high that the Asad regime could benefit from rather than be displaced by a dramatic foreign policy opening to the West, and that an infusion of additional resources would be unlikely to propel fundamental reforms, especially of the polity. Libya's Qaddafi is riding high after he engineered an accommodation with the West. The promise of more rapid economic growth resulting from renewed western involvement in the oil industry has presumably been well received by Libyans, but the Libyan economy remains as chaotic as ever. Similarly, Sadat's peace with Israel was lubricated with generous U.S. foreign assistance, which relieved mounting pressure on his regime, but did nothing to accelerate the pace of his economic *infitah*. In neither case was a reorientation in foreign policy accompanied by a political liberalization.

If indeed Bashar al-Asad were to seek a way out of his current economic difficulties through a peace with Israel and reorientation of Syria toward the West, he would presumably do so with the intent of preserving his regime's incumbency and the system it directs. An increase in the pace of economic liberalization would be consistent with that objective. Assurances to Syrian capital backed up by new external relations could invigorate the private sector and stimulate capital repatriation and domestic investment. Sunni capitalists might well benefit disproportionately from such an opening, thereby relieving some of the pressure on the regime from this quarter while providing it with greater capacities to benefit from regional and global trade and financial links. But economic success is unlikely to be matched with dramatic political innovation. In Syria, as in the other bunker states, antagonisms between social forces are deep and structures of sociopolitical control are so firmly in place that engineering a gradual, peaceful transition to more inclusive government would be a risky undertaking. Fear on the part of the elite that a gradual, top-down engineered decompression could gain momentum and become uncontrollable would presumably constrain experimentation. So political transformations in bunker states, including Syria, remain unlikely regardless of economic windfalls and new foreign alliances. In fact, the pressure to liberalize the political economy resulting from deteriorating economic circumstances might have more profound effects than a liberalization propelled by a new infusion of resources. But in the event that the Asad regime chooses to tough it out rather than cut a deal with the West, it could also be the case that with its back to the wall it becomes yet more vicious, rather than seeking to relieve economic and political pressure through appropriate relaxations. The choices before Syria, as with the other bunker states, are clearly difficult, reflecting as they do the relative fragility of these regimes and the weakness of their civil societies in the face of global competition.

Iraq: back to the bunker

A declared purpose of the U.S.-led invasion of Iraq in March 2003 was to destroy Saddam's metaphorical bunker and erect a democracy in its stead. Paradoxically, Baghdad's fortified Green Zone encompasses one of his former palaces and serves as the new bunker from which the Iraqi government, constituted under U.S. guns, seeks to impose itself on the country. This paradox attests to the contradiction of an external actor seeking to use military means to impose democracy, to the cavalier, ill-informed approach in Iraq of Bush, Rumsfeld, et al., and to the durability of social formations. The ethno-religious triangle of Iraq, with the minority Sunnis dominating Shi'a and Kurds from independence, with increasing ferocity from the onset of Saddam's consolidation of power in 1979, was simply rotated by the U.S. invasion onto the longer Shi'a, majority base. But the Shi'a empowered by the U.S. proconsul Paul Bremer, head of the Coalition Provisional Authority from May 2003 to June 2004, virtually all of whom were returned exiles and who had legitimate grievances against Saddam's Ba'athists, but who seem to have generalized it to the Sunnis as a whole, are even less inclined to politically include their perceived religious antagonists than were their Sunni predecessors. So the Green Zone bunker, in which various Shi'a factions struggle against one another, is naturally besieged by Sunnis, who may or may not ultimately be subordinated or included. In the meantime the Kurds have built their own bunkers in the north, with the Barzanis' KDP based in Arbil and Talabani's PUK in Sulamaniya. Thus Iraq has gone from a country ruled from a single, overpowering bunker into one with multiple bunkers, each plagued with internal divisions. The key question is how those hunkered down in their bunkers seek to impose their will, over the whole country in the case of the Shi'a in the Green Zone, or over northern Iraq in the case of the Kurds.

The strategy pursued by Nuri Kamal al Maliki, a former exiled Da'wa Party activist elected Prime Minister in May 2006, is instructive. Carefully balancing the need for continuing U.S. support with concessions to nationalist sentiments, al Maliki's primary objective has been to gain control of the levers of state power, implanting Da'wa Party activists and fellow travelers into key ministries and agencies, especially those with coercive capacities, including the reconstituted army, or direct control over financial resources, such as the Ministry of Oil. The purpose of this strategy is not only to gain control over material resources of the state, but to utilize state power to capture a greater share of total societal resources, much as Saddam had done after 1991.

More astute than his two principal Shi'a competitors – the Supreme Council for the Islamic Revolution in Iraq (renamed the Islamic Supreme Council of Iraq, or ISCI) led by the erstwhile al Hakim family and backed by Iran, and the Sadrists, the eponymous followers of Muqtada al Sadr – al Maliki has utilized carrot and stick while seeking to subordinate them. ISCI has been allowed to control much of the lucrative trade with Iran, and its Badr Brigade has entrenched itself in the Ministry of Interior. For their part the Sadrists, along with an offshoot, Fadilha, a Basra-based party, were for several years permitted to virtually monopolize the smuggling of oil from the south. In 2005-07, when they were part of the governing coalition, they were awarded the ministry of health from which they engaged in "corrupt and criminal activities as well as to promote sectarian policies, such as allowing sectarian forces to murder Sunni patients in hospitals. . . ." (Davis 2010: 350). When al Maliki perceived that he finally had the muscle to subdue the Sadrists and Fadilha, he launched in March 2008 the "Charge of the Knights," which succeeded in overwhelming his foes, driving Muqtada al Sadr into exile in Iran and bringing much of the export of southern oil under al Maliki's control. The investment of 74 percent of the central government's $58 billion budget in 2008 in the salaries and operations of the more than 640,000 security personnel clearly had paid dividends for al Maliki, if not for Iraq, as it helped enable him and his associates to capture a greater share of societal resources. Of the 200,000 to 500,000 barrels of oil a day estimated to be smuggled out of the south, the lion's share until the "Charge of the Knights" had gone to Fadilha, the Sadrists, various small tribal groupings, straight-out gangsters, and Basra's governor and his brother, the latter of whom fled to Kuwait although the former, apparently reconciling with al Maliki, was allowed to retain his position (Williams 2009a: 82). By early 2009 it was reported that "figures in al Da'wa" had brought that smuggling under a single shipping authority the party controlled (Moore 2009: 11). Some two years previously al Maliki's government had "severely inhibited" the Commission on Public Integrity by demanding that it obtain the permission of his office before investigating ministers and other government officials and preventing it from sending cases to courts until they had permission from the minister under whom the alleged offender worked. In dramatic testimony to the U.S. Congress in October 2007, the head of the commission, Judge Radhi Hamza al Radhi, stated that thirty-one of his commission members had been assassinated, that only 241 cases out of more than 3,000 they recommended had gone to trial, and that under his watch some $18 billion had been stolen from the government. He ended his testimony with the announcement that he was seeking political asylum in the United States (Williams 2009a: 206–7). Not surprisingly, Transparency International in 2009 ranked Iraq fourth from the bottom of its 180 country index of corruption, while on the World Bank's ease of doing business index Iraq was worsted in the MENA only by Sudan.

Just as in the final decade of Saddam's rule, the contemporary Iraqi state is too weak to extract resources directly, and so it relies on various intermediaries with which it shares the spoils. Some of these are in fact legacies of the Ba'athist era. The Shahid al Mihrab Corporation, for example, was created by the intelligence services to manage the flow of pilgrims from Iran and what little trade there was between the two countries. Ammar al Hakim, the head of ISCI, gained control of that corporation in 2005 and has, like his Ba'athist predecessors, used it to manage the flow of Iranian goods and people into the South (Moore 2009: 5–6). Even U.S. occupation forces, unable directly to control Iraq's political economy, have resorted to intermediaries. As part of its strategy to counter the Sunni insurrection and reinforce the Iraqi state, the U.S. military, like the Iraqi government, farmed out patronage to various tribes, including one of Saddam's favorites, the Dulaimi. One of its subtribal shaikhs, Abdul Sattar Abu Risha, who had contested with al Qaida for control of roads around Ramadi in order to rob travelers and had then moved into the oil smuggling business, was appointed "counter insurgency coordinator" by the U.S. military and head of the Anbar Salvation Council. His status was further elevated by a much-photographed meeting with President Bush, shortly after which he was assassinated by al Qaida (Williams 2009a: 244–6). By comparison to Saddam, the U.S.-al Maliki alliance has produced results that seem to attest to yet greater depredation by those in government. The informal economy, which accounted for about 35 percent of GNP in the final years of his regime, has grown to an estimated 65 percent (Looney 2007a). Those among the Shi'a parties and militias who have become millionaires as a result of this expansion of illicit activities are, according to one Iraqi trader, yet more ruthless than their Ba'athist predecessors, for "under Saddam you could be robbed by the public sector or forced to pay bribes. Now you can lose your money and your life or your brother's." One of his compatriots observed that the Iraqi business environment "is about getting your money as fast as you can and getting out." To the extent that fewer bullets are flying, it attests to the consolidation of patronage networks directly under al Maliki's control or at least affiliated with a faction entrenched in the Green Zone (Moore 2009: 7).

Capital is clearly not secure in Iraq, as reflected by the fact that the formal financial sector, which was opened to private banks in 1992 but remained overwhelmingly dominated by the two giant public sector banks through the end of the Saddam era, has developed little. The small private banks and minuscule bond market account for a contract-intensive money ratio that is the lowest in the MENA. Rafidain and Rasheed, the two public sector banks that outlived Saddam, in 2009 still accounted for 86 percent of all banking sector assets (SIGIR 2009). Iraq's is a cash economy, in which the shrink-wrapped packages of $100 bills flown in by the U.S. military in the wake of the invasion are still utilized for large transactions (Moore 2009: 8). The biggest private financial organization in Iraq is Nipal, which is a money transfer service. The 22 private-sector banks operating in 2010 are owned by individuals who live outside the country, typically "lack credit departments," charge a 2 percent fee on deposits, and make virtually all of their profits not from loans but from fund transfers and processing transactions for public sector companies (Cordesman 2010: 53). The treasury bill market is restricted by the fact that no purchasers can be found for local currency bonds with maturities in excess of six months. Credit allocation is thus virtually exclusively the preserve of government, for which economic development is a lower priority than paying soldiers and police, as reflected by the operating budgets of the ministries of defense and interior, which at some $10 billion in 2009 consumed almost a quarter of all governmental expenditures (Cordesman 2010: 39).

Private business is thus figuratively and even literally dying on the vine, as the collapse of the overwhelmingly private agricultural sector attests. Date production has fallen by half, in part because the government, the primary purchaser of the crop, claims to have insufficient resources to pay even the costs of production or to maintain the irrigation and drainage systems. Iraq in 2008 became a net food importer for the first time in modern history (Williams 2009d). Private-sector employment is negligible, while the government employs an estimated 2.5 million people out of a total potential labor force of some 7.7 million, suggesting that of those Iraqis working, about one-half are working for the government (Kukis 2009).

But lack of security and credit are only part of the economic problem. A misguided and inadequate policy framework, the product of both U.S.

and Iraqi efforts, is also to blame. The flood of imports that have drowned local producers results in part from Paul Bremer's abrupt cancellation of most tariffs. Attempts by the Ministry of Finance to draft a new tariff law that meets WTO requirements have thus far been insufficiently detailed to meet that organization's requirements (Chon 2009). Possibly the failure to provide even minimal tariff protection for Iraq's struggling producers of goods is due to the fact that "ministry officials have little interest in doing this . . . (they) would rather dole out millions each month in import contracts. The contracts deliver cash in hand" (Moore 2009: 6). The Dutch disease, due primarily to oil but further exacerbated by the infusion of $38.5 billion of U.S. foreign assistance between 2003 and 2010, is another culprit, driving inflation and currency appreciation as it has (Cordesman 2010: 30). Other than oil, Iraq exported in 2007 less than $200 million in goods, while it imported some $4 billion.

And the oil industry itself, exports of which in 2008 were equivalent to three quarters of GDP and provided some 90 percent of government revenues, has yet to regain production levels of the Saddam years. These peaked at 3.7 million barrels a day (mbd) in 1979 and are now less than 2.5 mbd, having declined slightly since 2008. The failure to expand production between 2003 and 2006 was due primarily to security problems. Since then the absence of a clear legal framework to structure contractual relationships with foreign oil companies has become the more important obstacle. The draft oil law presented by the cabinet to parliament in February 2007 has yet to be passed. The first round of bidding for oil service contracts in June 2009 resulted in only two bids being offered by international oil companies – one by BP and another by the Chinese National Petroleum Company (CNPC) for regenerating the giant Rumaila field. Others, such as Exxon-Mobil, Shell, and Total, hung back because of perceived unfavorable terms, lingering worries about the absence of an applicable legal framework, "and the lack of infrastructure and graft" (Williams 2009c). But, fearful of ultimately being excluded from subsequent exploitation of the lucrative Iraqi fields, they subsequently came forward in a second bidding round in the fall. In the meantime, the 100,000 barrels per day produced in the Kurdish-controlled north were prevented from being exported as a result of a disagreement between the central and regional governments, the former refusing to pay the producing companies. International oil companies continue to be leery of the challenges posed by uncertain political and legal contexts: "There are always fears that the parliament will nullify a contract and exert state control over the oil industry or that the central government will stop issuing payments if it deems an agreement illegal" (Cordesman 2010: 19). The precipitate drop in oil prices from 2008, combined with a decline in exports, left the government in 2009 with a $20 billion budget deficit just as U.S.-supplied reconstruction funds were dwindling. Iraq has the third largest proven oil reserves in the world, but is only the thirteenth largest producer, suggesting that there is huge potential but that its realization is far from adequate.

The state of the Iraqi economy, in sum, is parlous. About one quarter of the labor force is unemployed. Of those with jobs, as many as two-thirds work for the government (Cordesman 2010: 31), which, with a budget deficit in 2009 of some 20 percent of GDP and virtually wholly dependent on stagnating oil revenues and rapidly falling U.S. financial support, began cutting back on employment. The productive sectors of the non-oil economy are largely idle as imports have undermined them. Forced to turn to the IMF, in March 2009 the government concluded a Standby Arrangement that provided for a substantial reduction of debt owed to the Paris Club of creditor nations, coupled with required economic reforms inspired by the Washington Consensus. In October the government announced it would need further assistance from both the World Bank and the IMF.

The country's economy is thus stagnating as the intensity of violent conflict subsides but that of political contestation within the bunkers increases. As a result the population has become disaffected from the principal political factions that have exercised power under the American occupation. The elections in the Kurdish north in July 2009, in which the Goran (Movement for Change) that had split off from the PUK, won a surprising 41 seats in the 111-member Kurdish regional parliament, indicated that even in this comparatively tranquil part of the country the population, when given a chance, would manifest their displeasure with those ruling them. In the county's principal bunker in Baghdad's Green Zone, jockeying in late 2009 turned on the law to govern the March 2010 elections. Grand Ayatollah Ali al Sistani, reflecting the popular will and the fact that the Shi'a community is divided, called for voters to be able to choose their own candidates through a first-past-the-post, district-based electoral system. Party leaders, led by Prime Minister al Maliki, on the other hand, preferred a list system that would enable them to select winning members on their slates. Accompanying that attempt to ensure that independent voices not be heard in the election, the government commenced a crackdown to stifle voices in the media as well. It moved to ban Internet sites "deemed harmful to the public," to require Internet providers to register users with the government, and to censor books and other publications. Ahmad Mohammed Raouf, formerly chief censor of electronic communications under Saddam, was placed in charge of implementing the new decrees (Williams 2009b).

Not surprisingly, the insurrection seemed once again to be intensifying, as the al Maliki government steadfastly refused to include members of the Sunni Awakening in military, police, and security forces, although he did forge an electoral alliance with some minor Sunni political figures prior to the March 2010 parliamentary elections in order to strengthen his hand against his Shi'a compatriots in ISCI, the Sadr movement, and Iraqiya, the Iraqi nationalist grouping headed by the Shi'a secularist and former prime minister, Iyad Allawi. Al Maliki responded to massive suicide bombs that destroyed the ministry of justice and Baghdad city council buildings within the Green Zone in October 2009 by undermining the minister of interior, one of his rivals, and by replacing General Muhammad Shahwani, head of the National Intelligence Service, which is a competitor to the Ministry of National Security, which al Maliki controled through his client, Shirwan al Waili.

But al Maliki's tightening grip on power may have been counterproductive electorally, for in the March elections Iyad Allawi, whose Iraqiya reached out to Sunni voters, won two more seats than al Maliki's paradoxically named "State of Law Coalition." Thus in spring 2010 as jockeying over the formation of a new government commenced in earnest, Iraq appeared to confront two starkly different political choices. A benign scenario whereby secular Shi'a, Sunnis, and even reform-minded Kurds might form an inclusive coalition seemed possible. But so, too, did a malignant one, in which Shi'a hardliners allied in greater or lesser measure with Iran, entrenched in the Baghdad bunker and in coalition with the PUK and KDP, would continue to seek to exclude all but the most quiescence Sunnis. Whichever the outcome, any government constituted on the basis of the existing institutions of coercion and implicated in the pervasive system of corruption that permeates the economy would be unable to safely emerge from its bunker. Nor would it probably feel sufficiently confident to grant the space in which a private sector could begin to flourish, for that would deprive it of direct control over resources and possibly make them available to political opponents. So Iraq seems destined to continue in a state of conflict and insecurity, with the only immediate hope for the economy being an increase in oil prices and production. It is still the gun, not capital, that has structural power in Iraq, just as it did under Saddam.

Conclusion

Bunker states fragment their upper and middle classes into masses and migrants. Trade unions and business associations exist, but are not permitted to acquire roots in their societies from which to negotiate with governments or render them accountable. Civilian entrepreneurs, whether in business or politics, must remain loyal to their protectors. The one who strikes out on his own for an autonomous power base risks being assassinated, like Algeria's Boudiaf. No viable economic or political pacts are possible in the absence of credible interlocutors, such as the FIS's Abdelkader Hachani, killed at his dentist's office in downtown Algiers in 1999. It is instead up to the ruling clans to cut their own deals and divide up rents and other economic spoils of domestic and international commerce. When official state monopolies are dismantled, the clans reappropriate the ostensibly privatized and deregulated ones (Dillman 2000: 94–6). In Libya and Syria, as earlier in Saddam's Iraq, the clans have imploded into extended families and related tribes of the ruler.

The ultimate test of the new asabiya, or clan solidarity (Salamé 1990: 61) is a succession crisis. Some of the bunker states, whatever their political rhetoric, resemble hereditary monarchies without a private sector. Hafez al-Asad's ultimate triumph was posthumous, passing political power to his son Bashar in June 2000 in a succession that had been deemed "highly unlikely" by one of Syria's best-qualified observers, as well as most people inside and outside the country, only five years earlier (Perthes 1997: 269). One godfather has finally passed the keys to his son, and similar preparations may be underway in Tripoli and Sanaa. The keys of bunker states no longer open many doors, however, because the private sector's treasuries have fled elsewhere along with much of their respective civil societies.

It is not so much the volatile oil rents as the disconnection between bunkers and their private sectors that explains these regimes' difficulties with globalization. Their officials and entrepreneurs smuggle much of their private capital abroad. Bunker states are not the only ones in the region to be affected by capital flight, but they seem to experience greater difficulty than the others do because their domestic money markets are also less inviting. As their low CIM ratios indicate, they do not have much control over their currency flows. As political economists from Montesquieu to Kiren Chaudhry observe, mobile assets are harder to police than fixed, tangible ones that can be fenced off or occupied. Yemen during the boom years was a more extreme case than Algeria; remittances in the form of various currencies circulated by the money-changers may have exceeded North Yemen's GDP (Chaudhry 1997: 244). With or without booming remittances, however, Yemen's CIM was always low. It reached a new low in 1994, in fact, as Yemen suffered civil war. More ominously, "before, during, and after the war Ali Abdallah Saleh and his faction were purging the key organizations of all opposition groups, arranging for mass and individual assassinations of dissidents . . . and setting up a brutal security state constructed on the model, and, by many informal counts, with the advice of the Iraqi Ba'ath" (Chaudhry 1997: 304). Crackdowns merely decentralized the money-changers' informal system, further rupturing any business-state relations and limiting the bunker's economic capacities. Fierce military and security forces can terrorize merchants or money-changers, whether in Yemen or Baghdad, but the large informal economies defy any sustained economic controls.

The bunker states still have to adjust, as Algeria illustrates, once they become heavily indebted and dependent on imports for their necessities. Lacking in strategic depth, however, the best they can do is to serve as gunships for the IMF. Their nineteenth-century predecessors were the British and French fleets that patrolled the southern Mediterranean, collecting Ottoman debts and establishing colonies or protectorates. In 1995 Algeria adjusted more quickly than its neighbors because it rode roughshod over its budget deficits under cover of an insurrection. Iraq between the Gulf wars also rammed through many reforms of economic liberalization (Chaudhry 1992: 152–8). The chronic civil war and starvation in the southern Sudan allowed General Bashir the chance to adjust his deficits, according to a program worked out in 1997 with the IMF. In the Yemen, too, civil war enabled Colonel Saleh not only to crush his oppositions, but also to engage in a major IMF structural adjustment program. Indeed, the only laggards were Libya and Syria, and each had an excuse. Until 1999 Libya was subject to international sanctions, and Syria remained technically in a state of war with Israel. Most economic reforms of bunker regimes appear to be hollow exercises. The missing piece is the export-oriented private sector that is supposed to benefit from trade liberalization and be the internal dynamo attracting investment and generating employment. In a bunker state, however, any dynamic sector outside the official rent producers must stay underground. Not only in oil rentier states is the petroleum sector an enclave disconnected from the rest of the economy (Mahdavy 1970); the bunker state, whether or not it also has mineral wealth, is also disconnected, so that abstract legal initiatives of economic liberalization cannot promote greater productivity outside its enclaves. In Algeria, manufacturing value added, measured in constant dollars, declined by more than one-third from 1985 to 2005 (calculated from Table 2.4) – a striking illustration of the negative impact of economic liberalization on economic growth. Neither Sudan, striving despite civil war to exploit its oil resources, nor Yemen, unified largely for the sake of oil, can expect better results. Neither oil nor its related "Dutch disease" but rather politics determines these outcomes, although oil may reinforce the bunkers (Karl 1997; Ross 1999; Ross 2008; Lowi 2009).

A final point about bunker regimes is that they sharply limit the possibilities of fruitful economic integration with their neighbors. Algeria shattered efforts in the late 1960s to build a united Maghreb; the final blow was Qaddafi's coup in Libya. The Union du Maghreb Arabe (UMA), proclaimed in 1988 when Algeria and Morocco had repaired their relations, was stillborn. Since Chadli's removal from power in 1992 by his fellow officers, Algerian-Moroccan disputes over the ex-Spanish Sahara have festered. Syria and Iraq, despite a common Ba'athist legacy, have waged their internal wars since each bunker was consolidated. And the removal of Baghdad's Ba'athists did not repair the relationship. Syria apparently permitted large numbers of insurgents to pass back and forth into Iraq after 2003, before then tightening controls under U.S. pressure in 2006 (Williams 2009a: 165). But by 2009 the government of Nuri al Maliki was accusing Syria of once again "supporting terrorism," a claim on which the U.S. government remained conspicuously silent, suggesting it viewed the charge more a result of feuding between the two countries than as a reflection of reality. Libya has been at odds with all of its neighbors, and Sudan intermittently has been at loggerheads with Egypt. The political economy of bunker states explains a significant part of the problem. Having castrated their private sectors and civil societies, the bunkers lack the cover of nongovernmental intermediaries serving to cushion processes of economic integration and developing mutual interests.

Globalization may strengthen civil society and its underlying financial flows, but these new forces escape the bunkers' reach. These states seem destined to decay amid their internal wars unless they cultivate their private sectors. The longer they stagnate, the greater the social fragmentation and proliferation of social movements in defiance of the economy, and the greater the violence as the movements in turn are suppressed. Algeria may be exceptional only in that it is so close to Europe and has such a vibrant "European" civil society inside and outside the country that the external pressures to change may prove irresistible. Syria and Libya, also facing the Mediterranean, may face greater pressures if their excuses for the bunkers – war with Israel and various economic sanctions, including unilateral American ones – are removed. Syria, like Algeria, has substantial human and capital resources outside the bunkers that might facilitate reform. So, for that matter, does Iraq. But the mobilization of those resources within these countries is unlikely without credible guarantees of security and prospects for profitable undertakings. Given the profound distrust between these states and their at least partially exiled civil societies, it is doubtful that these gaps can be bridged.

Suggestions for further reading

The sociological reflections of Ali El-Kenz (1991) deserve all the more attention in light of Algeria's subsequent tragedies. Dillman (2000), Quandt (1998), Ruedy (2005), Werenfels (2007), Liverani (2008), and Lowi (2009) offer further insights into Algeria. Batatu (1999), Perthes (1997), Waldner (1999), Zisser (2006), Hinnebusch and Schmidt (2008), and Lawson (2009) analyze Syria from a variety of perspectives. Al-Kikhia (1997) and Vandewalle (2008) focus on another bunker state, Libya. Carapico (1998), Chaudhry (1997), Phillips (2007), and Mahdi, Wurth, and Lackner (2007) present contrasting views of Yemen. Chandrasekaran (2006) describes life in the Iraqi Green Zone "bunker"; Tripp (2007) provides an authoritative history; and Herring and Rangwala (2006), Springborg (2007), and Mahdi (2009) address the contemporary Iraqi polity and economy.

5   Bully praetorian states

Egypt, Tunisia, and the area controlled by the Palestinian Authority are not ruled from bunkers by elites beholden to clans, tribes, or other traditional social formations. In the case of Egypt and Tunisia, and the prospective Palestinian state, the ruling elites are at once both more narrowly and broadly based. Their rule rests almost exclusively on the institutional power of the military/security/party apparatus, but because these elites are not drawn from a clearly identified social formation, they are at least not unrepresentative of their relatively homogeneous political communities. Because the state provides the primary underpinning for these regimes, they have relatively little incentive to build and maintain ruling coalitions based in their respective political societies. The rulers of each of them seem content to restrict their extrastate coalition building to the placation of rural and traditional elites. Rent-seeking arrangements with crony capitalists are more for the purposes of serving state-based patronage networks than for broadening ruling coalitions.

The differences between bunker and bully praetorian republics, other than the key issue of the lack of autonomy of the bunker states from social formations, are not great. The leaders of Egypt and Tunisia, not having been forced to forge societal as opposed to state-based coalitions to come to or maintain their power, lack the political legitimacy that flows, as Max Weber described, from tradition, charisma, or rational-legal procedures. Yasser Arafat used a combination of his coercive capacity based in the Palestine Liberation Organization (PLO) and support from Israel and the United States, as well as political alliances on the ground in the West Bank and Gaza, to assert control over Palestine. By virtue of having built those alliances and because of his historical role as state builder, Arafat personally enjoyed considerable legitimacy, but after his death in 2005, the Palestinian "state" lost much of its legitimacy. Fatah, the party he had founded, was attempting in 2010 to restore that legitimacy, but it also required credible progress toward a two-state solution. Meanwhile Iran, discussed in Chapter 7, was apparently losing any semblance of democratic legitimacy and relying ever more on police and paramilitary power like the other bully praetorians.

This chapter focuses primarily on Egypt and Tunisia, given the destructive occupation of the Palestinian political economy and the novelty of the Iranian presence, yet to be fully consolidated as a bully praetorian republic. Dependent primarily on state-based patronage networks, the Egyptian and Tunisian rulers seem politically unable to radically downsize their states or dramatically privatize their economies. Parenthetically, the Palestinian Authority (PA) also rapidly expanded public employment while subordinating what little private economic activity there was to rent-seeking relationships to key members of Arafat's entourage. In the first four years of its existence, the PA created more than 65,000 government jobs, such that by 1997 the percentage of the labor force it employed (18.7 percent) was virtually level with that of construction (19 percent), making these two sectors the largest employers. In 1998 almost half of all new jobs were in the PA, taking central government employment to more than one-fifth of total employment and accounting for some 60 percent of the PA's budget (Roy 1999: 64–82). With the breakdown of the economy as well as the peace process after 2000, it no doubt surpassed Egyptian levels, where total government employment accounts for about one-third of the nonagricultural labor force. Tunisia, although heralded as a model for the region by the World Bank, also retains a public sector that is among the most costly to the public purse in the MENA.

With insecure political footings in the societies they rule, the elites of the bully states are compelled to rely on economically irrational, overgrown governmental and public sectors. They cast about for ways to generate patronage from private economic activities, rather than engage in the political coalition building that would obviate the need for their leviathans in the first place. But the drain on aggregate economic performance resulting from the gargantuan appetites of these leviathans, combined with the need to garner rents from private economic activity and reluctance to grant any economic or political space to independent actors, inhibit economic growth. These factors also deter political elites from devising creative strategies that would help perpetuate their rule while encouraging economically beneficial responses to globalization, as happened, for example, in Morocco, a case which is discussed in the following chapter.

Rent-seeking arrangements that have been struck between the political elite and capitalists in Egypt discourage broad export-led growth, for the elite can rig local but not international markets. Crony capitalists are provided either local oligopolies and monopolies that they exploit, sometimes providing them a base from which to expand outside of Egypt, or access to highly subsidized hydrocarbon resources or energy, which virtually guarantee international competitiveness and profitability, but at the expense of the economy as a whole and the vast majority of those who comprise it. Unlike the developmental states of Asia, which foster the growth of labor intensive manufaturing industry, Egyptian policy directs the most capitalized private enterprises into hydrocarbon rather than human resource dependent sectors. The vast bulk of the private economy consists of microenterprises, large proportions of which are in the informal sector. They lack the capital, technology, productive capacity, and, in the case of informal operations, the legal status even to consider exporting.

Tunisia has enjoyed proportionately greater export success than Egypt; closer to European markets, it pioneered offshore sweatshops in the 1970s and has developed an impressive manufacturing base over the years. But the Ben Ali regime that succeeded Bourguiba's party-state building has retained its overgrown state and strategic public-sector enterprises, notably banking, for patronage and control purposes. The domestic market is too small to support much import-substituting manufacturing, so the scope for it to generate substantial patronage through rent seeking is limited, although continuing high tariffs suggest that selective permissions for importation may still offer some patronage resources. The ruling elite has encouraged the development of export manufacturing, but, unlike its counterpart in Morocco, has not succeeded in integrating these activities into a tightly structured oligopoly linked directly to that elite. The Tunisian rulers are thus more wary than the Moroccans of both civil society and capitalist activity, although most enterprises remain small, and the large and visible ones tend to come under the umbrella of the ruling family. Lacking the legitimacy and means to direct and to benefit from civil society and capitalist activism, as enjoyed by its Moroccan neighbor, the Tunisians hesitate to open any wider the doors to either political or economic competition. The regime selectively favors trusted, individual capitalists, rather than capitalism as a concept and practice. Large banks and enterprises have fallen prey to the president's family members (Beau and Graciet 2009).

That the economic performance of these bully republics differs considerably, despite the structural similarities of their political economies, attests also to the importance of regional factors for the MENA's economies. The Palestinian economy is hostage to the peace process, and as that process has broken down, so has it. Checkpoints segmented the occupied territories of the West Bank and Gaza into collections of small enclaves cut off from the outside world – and Gaza was tightly blockaded even after the formal occupation ended in 2005. Regional factors worked favorably for Tunisia, on the other hand. Far removed from the Arab-Israeli conflict and only eighty miles from Europe, it was tagged as a "Mediterranean Tiger" in the late 1980s as the World Bank and others were looking for success stories to parallel those of the East Asian "tigers." Although it has in fact remained an economic pussycat by comparison, it nevertheless substantially outperformed Egypt until recently in globalizing its economy, thanks in large measure to the eager European embrace, propelled as much by fear of potential North African boat people as by any other considerations. Unable to take to boats from their own well guarded Mediterranean shore to reach Europe, and situated much closer to the Middle East's "Arc of Crisis," the Egyptians have been proportionately less favored by Europe than have the Tunisians, and by 2009 nonmilitary foreign assistance from the United States had declined to $200 million, some $2.60 per capita, compared to over $40 per capita to Jordan. Egypt has also felt compelled to devote a substantially greater proportion of its budgets to the military.

The capitalist legacies of Tunisia, Egypt, and Palestine also account for some of the variance in their economic performance. Palestinian capitalism went offshore after the *naqba* (disaster) of 1948 when Israel was founded. Arab Bank, founded in Jerusalem in 1930, set up branches in the West Bank and Gaza but most Palestinian businesses, including large transnational enterprises, stayed away from the PA rent seekers. Egypt's capitalists have not had to deal with occupation and an intifada, but the Egyptianized minorities among them, including Jews, Greeks, Italians, Syro-Lebanese, and others, were essentially forced into exile, while the native capitalists were subject to expropriations and other indignities by Nasser's Arab socialism. Still, Egypt's capitalist legacy is both more substantial and more continuous than Palestine's or Tunisia's. The Tunisian capitalism that existed at the end of French rule, although substantially disaccommodated by Ahmad Ben Salah's planned economy in the mid-1960s, has remained much more closely linked to the former colonial metropole. Indeed, it is those linkages that account in part for the comparatively rapid rise of Tunisia's manufactured exports over the past decade, but which also pose the greatest threat to them. Having agreed to the EU's terms as laid out in Barcelona in 1995, Tunisia is losing preferential access to European markets. It will have to open up its nascent manufacturing sector to European competition by lowering its tariffs, which still averaged 20 percent in 2006, almost double Egypt's and tops in the Arab world (see Table 2.4).

At the core of the explanation of the economic performance of these and other MENA states, however, is the nature of their political regimes.

Egypt and Tunisia have different factor endowments and locations, but they share in common rule by elites whose primary base of support is within state structures, rather than in political organizations anchored in society at large. Compelled to service and maintain these structures, these elites are politically incapable of surviving free and fair elections or permitting truly free economic markets to operate. Egypt, seven times as populous as Tunisia, perhaps best illustrates how economies in praetorian republics ruled by "bullies" are hostage to their power requirements. But the evolving political structure also closely resembles Tunisia's, as we will note in passing while focusing on Egypt.

From Paris to "tiger along the Nile?"

Belle époque Cairo was a "Paris along the Nile," as a 1999 book attests by title and by photographs of the city's European architectural legacy (Myntti 1999). A veritable Mediterranean melting pot as Albanians, French, Greeks, Italians, Syro-Lebanese, and others were attracted by the accumulation of wealth first stimulated by the early nineteenth-century reforms of Mohammed Ali, Egypt at nominal independence in 1923 could boast one of the largest, most successful, and certainly most ethnically and religiously heterogeneous capitalist classes in the Mediterranean world. Unlike the Italian and French *colons* who exploited Tunisia after the establishment of the French Protectorate in 1882, the *mutamassirun*, the Egyptianized foreigners who originally led Egypt's capitalist development under the aegis of British imperial control and French and Belgian investment, were joined as the twentieth century progressed by increasing numbers of native Egyptians, a process that accelerated as the nationalist movement gained strength. With the ultimate triumph of that movement under Nasser, followed by the Suez War of 1956, most of the mutamassirun fled the country, leaving what remained of the capitalist economy in the hands of native Egyptians. But it did not remain in those hands for long, because in the early 1960s the government, devising a homegrown ideology of Arab socialism to justify one-party rule, seized large and even medium-sized holdings of property, stocks and bonds, and other forms of capital that had escaped nationalization until that time. Many Egyptian capitalists joined the mutamassirun in exile, external or internal, while the regime-sanctified "national capitalists," who ultimately formed the core of the crony capitalism that first emerged under Sadat, were awarded niches within the public-sector-dominated economy.

Parallels with Tunisia are striking, including the colonial settler architecture of its capital, however provincial by Cairo standards. Habib Bourguiba, who gained political independence from the French in 1956, accelerated Tunisia's economic decolonization in 1961 as neighboring Algeria appeared to be winning its independence struggle. Bourguiba, like Nasser, launched his takeover of the economy ("Destour Social- ism") in 1961, and in Tunisia, as in Egypt, new private entrepreneurs would emerge from the shadows of planned industrialization. Despite Nasser's efforts as late as 1967, after the pace of industrialization slowed for lack of foreign exchange even before the Six-Day War, to nationalize all contractors, even small ones, the heavy state investments inevitably generated a private sector of rent seekers. So also in Tunisia, private con- tractors would constitute the nucleus of a new private sector that was then officially encouraged after 1969, when angry and politically well- placed rural property owners stopped Tunisia's state socialism. Tunisia's opening to private capital preceded Egypt's by four years.

In Egypt, faced with an economy that was, as he put it, "below zero," and an Israeli occupation of the Sinai that was corroding what precious little political legitimacy he had, President Sadat, who succeeded Nasser in 1970, saw that he had to come to terms with the United States. To do so would require at least some modification at both the rhetorical and operational levels of the Arab socialism then in effect, a price Sadat was willing to pay as he had never been a supporter of that socialism which had, in any case, run its economic course. So in the wake of the semi-successful October 1973 war, Sadat launched his economic infitah, or "opening," which he claimed would wed Arab petrodollars, Western technology, and Egyptian labor and management for the purpose of giv- ing birth to a dynamic, industrialized, mixed public/private economy. Although awash in capital and enjoying fulsome support from the United States and other Western nations, the reconfigured Egyptian economy did not develop at the pace its architect had hoped for and the Egyptian pub- lic had been promised. On the political front, too, Sadat was in increasing need of new sources of patronage to substitute for the partial dismantling of the Marxist-Leninist political structures he had inherited from Nasser and to compensate for the loss of resources from the declining public sector.

Sadat accordingly incubated a system of crony capitalism, key to which was Osman Ahmad Osman, boss of the huge Arab Contractors con- struction company. With help from a fellow engineer who was Nasser's minister of housing and would consequently get much of Osman's busi- ness as his principal design consultant, Osman had obtained a special decree in 1964 defining a uniquely ambiguous public/private status for his company that in turn shared its prosperity with key members of the elite (Moore 1994: 124). Sadat elevated this inherited crony capi- talist to heights unimaginable under Nasser, to which Osman gratefully responded by generating private wealth and political patronage, and the image, if not the reality, of dramatic and rapid economic development including overpasses for Cairo traffic. The image seemed sufficient at a time when oil revenues were flowing in record amounts and per capita income in Egypt and throughout the MENA was increasing at rates envied by the rest of the world.

Mubarak succeeded Sadat in October 1981, after the high point of oil prices had already been reached and within months of their rapid descent. During much of the remainder of the decade of the 1980s he struggled to keep the ailing economy afloat, in danger as it was of capsizing because of its heavy load of external debt. At the end of the decade, when still no major economic reforms had been undertaken, luck of almost the same magnitude as the oil boom rescued the Egyptian economy and maybe Mubarak, whose decision to support the U.S.-led coalition against Iraq netted $25 billion in almost immediate debt relief. This in turn paved the way for an IMF-led stabilization package that both the IMF tutor and its Egyptian student heralded as a textbook case of financial reform. Spokespersons for the latter began referring to the "Tiger along the Nile," a premature characterization at best. Indeed, it was to be more than a decade of lackluster economic performance before the combination of a dramatic increase in world energy prices with more thoroughgoing economic reforms finally resulted in a noticeable acceleration of the per capita growth rate. But even this optimistic interlude was destined to be short-lived. The global financial crisis of 2008 and the following worldwide recession brought it to an end before fundamental transformations were achieved.

Tunisia, more modestly endowed with hydrocarbons than Egypt, had also benefited from surging oil prices in the 1970s and, with their collapse in the 1980s, experienced major fiscal and trade deficits leading in 1986 to a structural adjustment program with the IMF. Mansour Moallah, a leading Tunisian technocrat who served in 1982 as finance minister, had tried to keep the budget under control and resigned when his efforts failed to curtail military and security expenditures. These had escalated in part because of regional threats but also because of a loss of confidence in the ability of the ruling party, notably the Neo-Destour Youth, to serve as a reliable paramilitary force. The financial crisis of 1986 was thus at least in part due to increasing costs of maintaining the bully regime in power as Habib Bourguiba, who had refused to institutionalize internal party democracy in 1971, aged into the caricature of a charismatic leader. His successor Zine al-Abidine Ben Ali, who seized power in a quasiconstitutional coup in 1987, was a military intelligence officer who would develop Tunisia into a fully fledged police state.

Tunisia and Egypt both engaged in structural adjustment programs in 1986 and 1987, but Tunisia far outperformed Egypt over the following two decades. Ben Ali fully supported the structural adjustment, and the Tunisians forged ahead, whereas Egypt did not complete its 1987 Standby with the IMF and continued to procrastinate with reform programs until 2003. Participation in the Allied Coalition to liberate Kuwait in 1991 gave Egypt's staggering economy massive debt relief conditioned on some progress in privatizing its state enterprises. Although the 1991 bailout and accompanying stabilization program significantly improved Egypt's macroeconomic position, its failure to pursue structural adjustment, combined with global economic dislocations and the sharp downturn of energy prices from 1998, ensured that the ten years after 1991 were a lost decade of development. By spring 1999, the prime minister announced that fewer than 10 percent of state-owned enterprises (SOEs) had been privatized, and the privatization program was grinding slowly to a halt as further economic liberalization was being reversed. The Egyptian pound came under attack, government debt ballooned, and as the economy slid downward, the Government of Egypt imposed more controls on it, further dampening private activity and isolating it yet more from global markets. These backward steps were taken just as Egypt faced growing competition in its domestic markets as a result of joining the WTO in 1995 and in 2001 committing to reduce protectionism in agreement with the EU under the terms of the Barcelona Accord of 1995, a promise Tunisia had made six years previously. Foreign assistance, which throughout the 1990s had been providing about one fifth of central government revenue, had already begun a scheduled decline. The Egyptian economy, in sum, was in crisis by 2001. But as in 1991, crisis proved to be the stimulus for reform.

Although the 1991 "Economic Reform and Structural Adjustment Program," as it was officially dubbed, did not actually result in profound structural adjustment, it did further legitimate private economic activity and its champions within the political/economic elite. As the decade wore on, this "lobby" began to assume more coherence and capacity to assess economic ills and provide solutions. Much of that capacity was centered in the Egyptian Center for Economic Studies (ECES), a think tank created as a result of a USAID initiative and involving key figures from the country's business elite. Toward the end of the decade the President's son, Gamal Mubarak, recently returned from his stint in London as an investment banker and searching for platforms on which to build his political career, adopted the ECES as his economic brain trust. ECES leadership, recognizing in Gamal a conduit to the president for their policy prescriptions on economic reform, was glad to oblige.

Paralleling the emergence of this "change team" was the growing salience of business elites within the broader political system, as symbolized by the victory in the 2000 parliamentary election of a still larger contingent of businessmen than had been brought into parliament in 1995. Shortly thereafter, Gamal Mubarak made the strategic decision to utilize the ruling National Democratic Party (NDP) as the vehicle in which to ride to the top. His first foothold was in the Party's Policies Secretariat, into which he recruited a galaxy of business and economic policy stars, with many of whom he had established relationships within the ECES. From this new strategic perch, Gamal and those reformers who had tied their fates to him launched a barrage of policy recommendations, the timing for which was ideal precisely because of the parlous state of the economy. From 2001, these policy prescriptions, which were founded in neoliberal orthodoxy, began to be officially adopted. By July 2004, at which time the formation of a new government brought the change team associated with Gamal into the key economic decision-making portfolios under fellow-traveling Prime Minister Ahmad Nazif, some of the key pillars of a new program of economic liberalization had already been put in place. The currency had been successively depreciated from 2001and then floated in 2003, the Central Bank had been afforded much greater autonomy under Law 88 of 2003, and tariff reductions commenced. In September 2004, the new government further reduced and rationalized tariffs, after which it commenced reform of taxation, subsidies, and business regulation. By 2008 Egypt had gone from being one of the most closed of the MENA economies to becoming one of the more open ones. In the previous year in its annual *Doing Business* survey, the World Bank ranked Egypt as the world's best performer in improving its business climate.

Tunisia had meanwhile engaged in its structural reform earlier and more rapidly than Egypt. The first MENA country to have its partnership agreement with the EU ratified, Tunisia received more aid and credits per capita to upgrade its manufacturing than any other southern Mediterranean country. In fact, between 1995 and 1999 the EU disbursed more funds to Tunisia, despite its relatively small population, than to any other southern Mediterranean "partner" (European Commission 2000: 5). Its responses to globalization were more timely and effective than Egypt's, largely because it has a more efficient administration (see Table 3.2), garners fewer international rents, has a greater need to export, and enjoys a tighter embrace of Europe, both historically and contemporaneously.

Both countries registered relatively impressive economic performances by MENA standards, Tunisia during the entire reform period from 1987, with Egypt almost catching up by 2008. Table 5.1 presents an overview of their respective performances, compared to the MENA average and to that of lower- and middle-income countries more generally.

Egyptian growth rates exceeded Tunisia's after 2004, and the former's average annual growth rate since 1987 almost caught up with Tunisia's cumulative average of 4.68 percent in 2008, although it hardly matched Tunisia's twenty-year average annual per capita growth rate of 3 percent, tops in the MENA, much less the 5 percent of lower-middle-income countries more generally that included real Asian tigers and the like. Still, Egypt and Tunisia were at least preserving their manufacturing bases, which amounted to roughly 17 percent GDP for each. As Table 2.4 indicated, Tunisian manufacturing was considerably more export oriented than Egypt's, its much smaller infrastructure of facilities exporting double the constant dollar value of Egypt's manufactured exports. Until Gamal Mubarak's team pushed through their reforms, Egypt seemed if anything to be deglobalizing. Whereas Tunisia steadily increased its manufacturing exports so that overall trade was finally exceeding GDP by 2006, Egyptian trade as a percentage of GDP sharply diminished in the late 1990s and only picked up after 2003 to earlier levels, surpassing them in 2007 and 2008. And even so, manufacturing value added as a percentage of GDP seems to have peaked in both countries. Gross capital formation and gross fixed investment in plant and equipment seem also, apart from speculations in 2008, to be languishing in both countries, an important point to which we return later, and foreign direct investment inflows, although stronger than for most of the MENA and abundant in 2005–8, seemed unable adequately to supplement flagging domestic investment, as shown in Table 5.1. Whereas the MENA on average and developing countries more generally were surpassing their 20-year averages in 2007 and 2008, Egypt and Tunisia seemed to be moving in the wrong direction. Both countries, moreover, retained selective high tariff barriers to protect their vulnerable textiles and other exports: more vulnerable, Tunisia's barriers were almost twice as high as Egypt's (see Table 2.4).

Tiger sustained

Even as the rising economic tide of the third great oil boom was floating virtually all of the region's economies, the sustainability of Egypt's rapid growth was being questioned. True economic transformation of Egypt would be manifested in a reduced reliance on its traditional "big four" sources of income – energy exports, tourism, remittances, and Suez Canal

Table 5.1 *Indicators of financial performance, Egypt and Tunisia, 1987–2009*

	1987–91	1992–6	1997–2001	2002	2003	2004	2005	2006	20 yr Average 1987–2006	2007	2008	2009
GDP growth (annual %)												
Egypt, Arab Rep.	3.9	4.2	4.9	2.4	3.2	4.1	4.5	6.8	4.3	7.1	7.2	3.6
Tunisia	4.1	4.5	5.2	1.7	5.6	6.0	4.0	5.7	4.6	6.3	5.1	3.3
Middle East & North Africa	3.2	3.4	4.0	3.6	2.4	6.2	4.5	5.4	3.7	6.0	5.8	
Lower middle income	5.1	6.9	5.3	6.3	7.8	8.6	8.5	9.5	6.6	10.3	7.6	
GDP per capita growth (annual %)												
Egypt, Arab Rep.	1.6	2.3	3.0	0.4	1.3	2.1	2.5	4.9	2.2	5.1	5.1	
Tunisia	1.9	2.7	3.9	0.5	4.9	5.1	3.0	4.6	3.0	5.3	4.1	
Middle East & North Africa	0.5	1.2	2.0	1.6	0.5	4.2	2.6	3.4	1.5	4.1	3.8	
Lower middle income	3.3	5.5	4.1	5.0	6.5	7.2	7.2	8.3	5.0	9.0	6.3	
Manufacturing, value added (% of GDP)												
Egypt, Arab Rep.	17.3	17.1	18.8	19.6	18.2	18.0	17.3	16.6	17.8	15.7	16.9	
Tunisia	16.5	17.9	18.4	18.6	17.9	17.7	17.1	17.1	17.6	17.2	16.5	
Middle East & North Africa	13.6	14.3	12.5	12.3	11.9	13.7	13.0	12.6	13.6	12.3	12.5	
Lower middle income	27.2	27.1	25.6	23.9	24.4	24.9	25.0	25.4	25.0	25.8	25.5	
Trade (% of GDP)												
Egypt, Arab Rep.	50.9	52.6	40.6	41.0	46.2	57.8	63.0	61.5	49.5	65.1	81.9	
Tunisia	85.2	89.3	91.9	94.7	91.5	96.8	99.8	103.1	90.9	110.7	133.5	
Middle East & North Africa	50.2	57.1	51.6	58.3	58.1	64.2	68.6	68.1	54.7	69.7	79.4	
Lower middle income	43.0	52.4	54.5	53.8	58.8	65.6	69.8	70.9	49.3	71.4	64.5	

Gross capital formation (% of GDP)

Egypt, Arab Rep.	28.6	19.6	19.7	18.3	16.9	16.9	18.0	18.7	21.4	20.9	23.7
Tunisia	24.2	26.6	27.0	25.7	25.1	24.2	21.8	23.9	25.5	24.8	25.1
Middle East & North Africa	25.9	25.6	24.5	25.5	26.7	27.2	26.0	25.7	25.9	27.7	28.1
Lower middle income	31.9	34.4	29.9	29.9	32.0	33.9	35.1	35.7	31.5	35.7	36.0

Gross fixed capital formation (% of GDP)

Egypt, Arab Rep.	28.3	18.9	19.3	17.8	16.3	16.4	17.9	18.7	21.0	20.9	23.7
Tunisia	22.6	25.9	25.4	25.4	23.4	22.6	22.2	23.5	24.4	23.6	24.1
Middle East & North Africa	24.0	22.7	22.6	22.6	23.1	23.3	23.2	22.9	23.3	24.2	25.3
Lower middle income	26.4	29.9	28.1	28.3	29.9	31.5	32.9	33.5	28.3	33.3	33.4

Foreign direct investment, net inflows (% of GDP)

Egypt, Arab Rep.	2.3	1.3	1.1	0.7	0.3	1.6	6.0	9.3	2.1	8.9	—
Tunisia	0.8	2.5	2.6	3.8	2.2	2.3	2.7	10.7	2.6	4.6	—
Middle East & North Africa	0.5	0.9	1.0	1.2	1.7	1.5	2.6	4.1	1.1	3.7	—
Lower middle income	1.0	2.9	3.0	2.5	2.2	2.2	3.0	2.9	2.1	3.4	—

Sources: World Bank, World Development Indicators 2009; IMF 2009a: 36 (Table 5.1)

earnings. Presumably this would require rapid growth of manufactured exports, underpinned by productivity growth. Sustainability would also require prudent macroeconomic management, combined with a responsive financial sector and improvements in Egypt's notoriously recalcitrant public bureaucracy. Underpinning all of this would need to be an upgrading of the country's human and physical infrastructures so as better to compete internationally. Sustainability, in sum, required structural changes rather than just the adoption of a partial package of neoliberal reforms and the infusion of petrodollars, which fortuitously for the credibility of the reformers, occurred more or less simultaneously.

Key to assessing the degree of structural change in the economy that has occurred is an appreciation of the important direct and indirect roles that hydrocarbons play, hence the degree to which Egypt's is a "monocrop" economy, depending heavily on energy prices for its wellbeing. The evidence suggests that the direct and indirect impacts on the Egyptian economy of hydrocarbon exports have been increasing after dipping as a result of comparatively low energy prices from the mid-1980s through the early 1990s and again in the late 1990s. As for direct impacts, hydrocarbon and hydrocarbon-related products became vital to Egypt's economy and export performance in the 1970s and have remained so despite the near-total collapse of oil exports after 2000. Having reached a maximum capacity of somewhat less than a million barrels of oil per day in 1996, oil production commenced a steady decline then as domestic consumption tripled between 1980 and 2005. But just as Egypt was becoming a net importer of oil in the new millennium, its production and export of natural gas, based on discoveries first made in the early 1990s, began to escalate, increasing a thousandfold between 1980 and 2005 (Selim 2006). By 2008 Egypt had become the world's fourteenth largest producer of natural gas. Hydrocarbon extraction and processing had become the single largest industrial activity, alone accounting for some 8 percent of GDP. As natural gas was replacing oil as Egypt's leading hydrocarbon export, with gas production tripling between 1995 and 2005, the share of fuels in the country's exports rose from an average of 38.4 percent in 1987–91 to 52.2 percent in 2007, as Table 5.2 indicates.

Liquefied natural gas exports went from $17 million in 2003 to almost $3 billion in 2006, a boom virtually equivalent to that enjoyed by Egypt in the heady years following the 1973 war. Although during the first five years of the 1980s oil had made up some 60 percent of total exports, energy and energy-related exports by 2009 actually exceeded that ratio. Oil and gas exports, reported in current dollars in Table 2.3, actually in constant 2000 dollars earned for Egypt $8.8 billion in 2007, compared to $3.6 billion at the height of the oil boom in 1981. Construction of

Table 5.2 *More economic indicators, Egypt and Tunisia, 1987–2007*

	1987–91	1992–6	1997–2001	2002	2003	2004	2005	2006	20 yr Average	2007	2008
Fuel exports (% of merchandise exports)											
Egypt, Arab Rep.	36.5	43.5	38.4	33.5	43.1	43.2	51.3	55.5	41.0	52.2	
Tunisia	18.3	11.0	8.8	9.4	10.0	9.6	12.9	13.0	12.3	16.2	
Middle East & North Africa			71.3	63.8	67.9	67.7	70.6	75.4	69.8	–	
Lower middle income	17.0	12.2	15.5	13.5	14.5	11.8	12.6	18.7	12.3	11.5	
Workers' remittances, receipts (BoP, current billions U.S.$)											
Egypt, Arab Rep.	$3.8	$4.4	$3.2	$2.9	$3.0	$3.3	$5.0	$5.3		$7.7	
Tunisia	$0.5	$0.6	$0.8	$1.0	$1.1	$1.3	$1.2	$1.3		$1.4	
Workers' remittances and compensation of employees, received (% of GDP)											
Egypt, Arab Rep.	9.8	8.8	3.6	3.3	3.6	4.2	5.6	5.0	7.1	5.9	5.8
Tunisia	4.5	3.6	3.9	5.1	5.0	5.1	4.8	4.9	4.1	4.9	4.7
Middle East & North Africa	7.7	6.0	3.6	3.8	4.5	4.4	4.1	3.7	4.9	3.7	3.1
Lower middle income	1.4	1.6	1.9	2.2	2.4	2.2	2.3	2.3	1.7	2.4	2.4
Trade in services (% of GDP)											
Egypt, Arab Rep.	21.2	25.7	17.8	18.2	21.2	28.2	28.0	25.8	22.3	26.3	–
Tunisia	20.9	21.6	20.5	19.6	18.2	20.0	21.4	21.8	20.8	22.0	–
Middle East & North Africa	9.3	14.9	12.1	–				–	12.4	–	–
Lower middle income	7.6	10.5	9.9	9.6	9.5	10.8	11.2	11.4	9.0	10.5	–

(continued)

175

Table 5.2 (continued)

	1987–91	1992–6	1997–2001	2002	2003	2004	2005	2006	20 yr Average	2007	2008
International tourism, receipts (% of service exports)											
Egypt, Arab Rep.	36.5		43.7	44.3	42.5	44.6	49.2	50.4		51.8	
Tunisia		72.6	71.5	68.3	65.9	67.0	69.6	69.8		68.7	
Middle East&North Africa											
Lower middle income	47.6		51.9	53.5	47.4	46.3	42.1	40.8		39.7	
Foreign direct investment, net inflows (BoP, current billions U.S.$)											
Egypt, Arab Rep.	$0.9	$0.7	$1.0	$0.6	$0.2	$1.1	$5.3	$9.9		$10.9	
Tunisia	$0.1	$0.4	$0.5	$0.8	$0.5	$0.6	$0.7	$3.2		$1.5	
Manufactures exports (% of merchandise exports)											
Egypt, Arab Rep.	36.4	35.9	38.5	35.2	30.5	30.5	23.6	20.7	34.6	18.6	
Tunisia	66.4	76.6	79.5	81.3	80.8	77.5	74.9	73.3	75.0	69.8	
Middle East & North Africa			19.1	20.5	20.2	19.8	18.6	16.1	19.4	–	
Lower middle income	52.3	64.9	67.5	70.8	70.9	73.4	73.2	67.6	66.5	71.5	
High-technology exports (% of manufactured exports)											
Egypt, Arab Rep.	0.0	0.3	0.4	0.8	0.5	0.6	0.4	0.5	0.5	0.2	
Tunisia	1.0	1.8	2.6	3.7	3.8	4.9	4.4	6.6	2.9	5.3	
Middle East & North Africa	0.3	0.7	2.5	3.1	3.1	3.1	2.9	4.2	3.0	–	
Lower middle income	2.9	10.9	18.2	19.8	21.2	23.2	23.1	22.8	16.9	23.3	

Source: World Bank, World Development Indicators 2009

energy-intensive production plants, including those for petrochemicals, iron and steel, cement, and fertilizer, has resulted in rapid increases in their share of total exports, with iron and steel exports, for example, quadrupling in the four years after 2003. Already by 2004 chemicals and "other manufactures," the vast majority of which were energy intensive, had grown to some 60 percent of total manufactures, as the share of food and beverages, clothing and textiles, and machinery and transport equipment dropped after 1995 from 45 to 40 percent. Petrochemicals and fertilizer were the two fastest-growing sectors of the Egyptian economy in the twenty-first century. Egypt's direct dependence on exports of hydrocarbons, and goods manufactured there because of access to hydrocarbons at prices far below those obtaining in Europe and the United States, thus became a more central feature of its economy during the boom years from 2003 to 2008.[1] Indeed, the gas bonanza accounted for a dominant share of that boom, at least as far as exports are concerned. Table 5.2 compares the direct contribution of oil and gas exports to Egypt's merchandise exports with Tunisia's, where oil and gas peaked in 2007 at a modest 16.2 percent of Tunisia's thriving exports. The Great Recession intensified the centrality of hydrocarbons to Egypt's economy, as reflected by the fact that FDI in that sector rose from $4.1 billion in 2007–8 to $5.4 billion in 2008–9, whereas total FDI dropped 39 percent in that year, from some $13 billion to $8.1 billion, below the 2007 levels recorded in Table 5.2. Investment in oil and gas thus accounted in 2008–9 for two-thirds of all FDI in Egypt (Wahish 2009).

Hydrocarbons also have significant indirect impacts on the Egyptian economy, such as remittances from Egyptian expatriates working in the GCC countries, and from FDI and tourism from those countries. Remittances rose from $2.9 billion in 2002 to $7.7 billion in 2007, at which point they constituted 5.9 percent of GDP, well above the world leading rate of MENA lower-middle-income countries of 2.4 percent. Although remittances' share of exports of goods and services had fallen from as much as 40 percent in the 1980s to about 15 percent by 2006, growth in tourism from Arab countries has made a steadily increasing contribution to Egypt's service exports, rising overall from 36.5 percent in the mid-1990s to 51.8 percent in 2007. The skyrocketing of FDI from an annual $1 billion or less in the 1990s to $9.9 billion in 2006 and $10.9 billion in 2007, at least half of which is estimated to have originated in the Gulf, is further suggestive of the substantial indirect effects of MENA

---

[1] In 2008, for example, selected industries were being offered gas for $1 per million BTUs, compared to an international price that reached $11 per million BTUs in that year (Elmussa and Sowers 2009: 3).

hydrocarbons on the Egyptian economy. Tunisia also enjoys comparable tourist revenues, as the trade in services reported in Table 5.2 suggests, but they depend more on European than on Gulf Arab markets.

The Egyptian economy thus went from being highly dependent on the production and export of oil from the late 1970s through the mid-1980s, through the fallow years of the 1990s, and then to the gas-fired boom of the early twenty-first century. This sequence suggests that the vagaries of hydrocarbon deposits, combined with prices for them, have been a key determinant of the overall well-being of the Egyptian economy since the Sadat era. This hydrocarbon dependence is a mixed blessing. Although it has underpinned much of the country's economic growth, including the development of its energy-intensive manufacturing in recent years, it has resulted in growth being highly cyclical, responding to ever more volatile and unpredictable energy prices. Despite having sizeable gas production capacity and reserves, Egypt's growing dependence on utilization of gas has already led to policy dilemmas reflecting the value of the resource but also its limits as the principal motor of economic development. As the government's need for revenue intensified in the spring of 2008 to cover increasing expenses for food subsidies and civil servants' salaries, both of which had been increased out of fear of public discontent sparked by inflation, it suddenly announced a significant reduction in energy subsidies, including to industrial consumers. The Cairo stock market immediately plummeted, shares in energy-intensive companies leading the way down amid widespread complaints about the government's arbitrary and precipitous pricing policies. The government apparently was seeking not only to reduce its energy subsidy bill, but also to obtain additional gas supplies for export. Before the year was out, however, it was forced to backtrack and restore subsidies to industrial consumers, probably primarily because the captains of energy-intensive industry were some of the best politically connected crony capitalists in Egypt. The need to regain investor confidence may also have played a role, as might have the desire to maintain employment and domestic growth in the face of the global financial crisis. Competition between the need for governmental revenues through exports of gas and the need to stimulate domestic production by providing it at subsidized prices to industry will be further intensified as demand from household consumption and electricity generation steadily expands. Egypt is thus in a race against time to develop alternative productive capacities before its reserves of hydrocarbons are insufficient to simultaneously sustain governmental revenues, a reasonable balance of trade, domestic industrial growth, and adequate household energy consumption. The dramatic downturn of energy prices in late 2008 further accentuated this need, as did the decoupling of oil and gas prices to the detriment of the latter.

Despite rapid growth from 2003 to 2008, the four pillars of the economy – hydrocarbons, remittances, Suez Canal earnings, and tourism – remain predominant, especially if the definition of hydrocarbons is extended to include the basic energy-dependent processing industries of cement, ceramics, iron and steel, fertilizer, and petrochemicals. Egypt's exports are suggestive. In the four years ending in 2005, propane and natural gas grew by 90 percent, cement by 237 percent, and iron and steel by 44 percent. Clothing and textile exports declined, their total value falling from $741.3 million in 2000 to $523.3 million in 2005 and their share of all manufactures declining from 13 percent to 10 percent between 1995 and 2004. Table 5.2 shows how manufactures have steadily declined over the past decades as a percentage of merchandise exports, whereas relative decline of Tunisia's manufactures – from much higher levels – dates only from 2004. With respect to high-technology exports, defined by the World Bank as "products with high R&D intensity, such as in aerospace, computers, pharmaceuticals, scientific instruments, and electrical machinery" (World Development Indicators 2008), Egypt's showing is minimal and Tunisia's, though strong by MENA standards, reached barely one-quarter of developing country average shares of merchandise exports in 2007. Multinationals clearly avoided assembly lines in this part of the world.

A closer look at two critical sectors – clothing and textiles, and finance – may illustrate the degree of reform achieved in each country. In Egypt the clothing and textile sector continues to be the largest employer in the industrial sector, its 1 million workers accounting for almost a third of total industrial employment (Ghoneim and Pigato 2006: 2). It also contributes almost one third of industrial value added. But the industry as a whole remains inward looking and dominated by the public sector. It had been unable in the 1990s to fill its EU or U.S. quotas under the expiring Multi-Fiber Agreement, suggesting its lack of competitiveness in even these protected markets. The industry is fragmented, with public-sector firms still responsible for most of the weaving and spinning, but with the private sector now producing about 90 percent of ready-made garments (RMGs) (Kheir-El-Din 2008). The RMG subsector has performed reasonably well and has attracted considerable FDI, but problems resulting from backward and forward linkages within the overall sector continue to constrain growth of textiles and clothing as a whole. The industry has failed to make the transition from being an inward-looking industry focused on domestic markets to being a dynamic exporter. Indeed, it continues to enjoy more tariff protection than any other industry in Egypt, which is quite substantial given that in 2006 the weighted mean average tariff for all products was 11.8 percent, compared to the lower-middle-income median of 5.3 percent.

Between 1997 and 2004, as the scramble to supply European markets for clothes and textiles intensified, Egypt's market share remained below 1 percent as its total exports to Europe increased by only about $100 million during that time, compared to increases by Morocco of some $1 billion, Tunisia of $1.1 billion, Turkey of almost $7 billion, and China of some $12 billion (Pigato and Ghoneim 2006: 4). During that same period and despite enjoying preferential access to U.S. markets, Egypt's share of American imports of clothing and textiles dropped from an already paltry 0.72 percent to 0.65 percent (Pigato and Ghoneim 2006: 5). Jordan, which had virtually no such exports to the United States in 1997, by 2004 had some 80 percent more than Egypt. With the oldest textile and clothing industry in the MENA, Egypt has a lower global market share in all the subcategories of textile and clothing exports than its regional competitors Jordan, Turkey, Morocco, and Tunisia.

Unlike Tunisia, which had taken advantage of EU cooperation to bring many of its enterprises up to standard ("mise à niveau"), inefficiencies still abounded, resulting in high costs. The Egyptian industry seemed unable to extricate itself from the conundrum already noted in 1991 by the World Bank: "the private units are too small to benefit from economies of scale, while the public sector mills are too large to be managed efficiently." Inefficiencies resulted in high costs. Lack of modern computer-aided designing in the garment subsector resulted in fabric wastage rates of 17 percent compared with an average rate of 8 percent and time loss 15 to 25 percent higher than the standard for developing countries (World Bank 1991: 77). The average operating efficiency for spinning in Egypt was less than 60 percent, as compared with a global standard of 85 to 90 percent. This inadequate performance was due to both poor management and obsolete equipment, with some 850,000 of the total of 3 million spindles in use being uneconomic (USAID 1993b: II-3). Nominally low wage rates placed Egypt among the lowest labor cost producers, with a revealed comparative advantage in the vital EU market that was higher for textiles and clothing than that of any other country of the world. Yet, wage costs per worker increased faster in the 1990s than either real production or real value added per worker (Kheir-El-Din and El-Sayed 1997: 7). The labor costs in yarn production were 16 percent of total costs, putting them among the highest percentages for competitive producers. The authors of the most thorough review of the textile sector undertaken in the 1990s observe that "this is ominous for a country that has wage rates among the lowest in the world" (USAID 1993a: II-47). It was ominous because it indicated low total factor productivity resulting from out-of-date technology and bad management, both of which were in turn the products of inappropriate public policies.

In sum, although Egypt's RMG industry has been largely privatized and is increasingly focused on exports, its achievements are below those of Tunisia or other countries in the region with similar or less favorable factor endowments. The Egyptian failure, however, is rooted in misguided policies rather than any inherent political needs of the bully regime to sustain strategic patron-client networks. In Tunisia, the industry adapted to the new global competition unleashed by the termination of the Multi-Fiber Agreement in 2005 not only by retaining high protective tariff barriers, as noted previously, but also by developing new strategies taking advantage of its geographical proximity to European markets. Closer to the clients, Tunisia could develop offshore apparel exports: the bully regime liberated them from local textile suppliers, so that European firms could freely import low-cost inputs and stay competitive. The Tunisian government also took the initiative in guiding the upgrading of favored companies and industrial clustering, whereby they might benefit from economies of scale (Cammett 2007: 144–5, 216–17).

Finance, however, was another matter. Neither bully regime seemed capable of undergoing the necessary reforms of their respective banking systems to liberate the allocation of credit from their respective systems of political favors. The Egyptian change team that consolidated power within the cabinet formed in July 2004 viewed the financial sector as key to increasing rates of growth, principally by allocating capital more effectively to the private sector. This in turn required further privatization and upgrading of banks, enhancement of the equity market, and improvements in relevant legal and regulatory structures and processes. Although considerable progress was made in each of these areas, the financial sector continues to exhibit weakness, as manifested by a shrinking share of private-sector domestic credit of GDP, which fell annually by 6.9 percent in the five years up to 2008, taking it to a level of only about 60 percent of the median for lower-middle-income countries (55.3 percent as compared to 81.3 percent), and by increasing spreads in interest rates between deposits and loans, which widened from 4.5 to 6.6 percent in the four years to 2006. Egypt's real interest rate was 4.8 percent in 2006, one full point above the MENA lower-middle-income average. The wide loan/deposit spread coupled with high interest rates points to persisting inefficiencies in the banking sector, despite the fact that by 2008 more than half of it had been privatized.

The declining share in GDP of credit to the private sector documented in Table 5.3 reflects a much-discussed reluctance to grant credit to private-sector clients, a product of macroeconomic policies that make lending to the government a low-risk, profitable undertaking for banks; the continuing inability of banks accurately to assess risk; a legacy of non-performing loans; and possibly a paucity of credit-worthy private-sector clients. It also results from chronic weaknesses in the most credit-relevant aspect of the legal/regulatory system – the protection of legal rights of borrowers and lenders. On the World Bank's index, Egypt continues to score one out of a possible ten points, placing it at the bottom of the already low MENA tables. The combination of impediments to private-sector credit result in it being commonly ranked by businessmen and others as the single greatest obstacle to private-sector expansion (Lopez-Claros, Porter, and Schwab 2005). Small and medium enterprises, or those numbering between ten and fifty employees, rely on self-financing for more than 90 percent of their total capital, with both formal and informal institutions accounting for less than 10 percent, of which the bulk is from suppliers and most of the remainder from informal money lenders (El Mahdi and Rashed, 2009: 103). That Egypt's financial sector has failed to deepen over the past two decades is reflected in the flattening out of the ratio of CIM to money supply, which reached a plateau of 85 percent in 1990 from which it has barely budged.

Tunisia's CIM ratio also stagnated in the 85–86 percent range, and although its banking system was somewhat more accommodating to private-sector clients than Egypt's, it suffered similar problems with non-performing loans, as discussed in Chapter 3 (Figure 3.8). Significantly, too, state banks and private banks were equally affected as they were all subjected to the control of President Ben Ali's family members, making personal wealth a function of one's proximity to power (Beau and Graciet 2009: 136). Tunisia's strongest privately owned bank had been the Banque Internationale Arabe Tunisienne (BIAT), founded by a group of entrepreneurs from Sfax, Tunisia's second largest city and a principal incubator of private agribusiness and other enterprises. Concerned in 1993 that its CEO Mansour Moallah might be a possible presidential rival, Ben Ali ordered Tunisian public enterprises such as Tunis Air to withdraw their deposits from the bank until Moallah stepped down from the bank into forced retirement and virtual house arrest. The bank was then brought under the control of presidential clients, downstream with a financial subsidiary belonging to Belhassan Trabelsi, the president's brother-in-law, and upstream in 2008 with the president's son-in-law's Mabrouk Group acquiring over 30 percent of BIAT's shares. By then most major Tunisian businesses, including Trabelsi's Karthago Airline,

Table 5.3 *Financial indicators, Egypt and Tunisia, 1987–2008*

	1987–91	1992–6	1997–2001	2002	2003	2004	2005	2006	2007	2008
Domestic credit to private sector (% of GDP)										
Egypt, Arab Rep.	31.6	32.9	55.4	61.9	61.1	60.4	57.4	55.3	50.6	42.8
Tunisia	54.3	66.5	66.1	68.5	66.7	65.4	65.6	65.0	64.3	
Middle East & North Africa	39.3	29.9	37.3	40.1	39.5	38.6	38.5	41.3	–	
East Asia & Pacific	69.7	87.5	102.8	105.4	110.5	105.3	100.5	98.7		
Lower middle income	54.6	62.4	77.3	76.1	79.7	77.8	75.9	76.1	77.8	82.3
Contract Intensive Money (in banks) as % of money supply (M2)										
Egypt, Arab Rep.	82.8%	86.4%	85.7%	86.4%	87.0%	87.3%	86.8%	86.2%	86.5%	85.6%
Tunisia	82.0%	82.9%	84.8%	85.2%	85.3%	85.3%	84.5%	84.5%	85.4%	86.4%
External debt, total (% of GNI)										
Egypt, Arab Rep.	105.5	61.4	33.4	32.3	35.5	39.6	33.6	27.4	23.0	20.9
Tunisia	69.6	62.2	61.5	77.0	76.9	74.5	65.0	64.5	57.4	51.1
Middle East & North Africa	62.9	59.9	41.3	37.9	36.7	34.3	26.2	21.9		
Lower middle income	40.6	40.4	35.7	29.5	27.9	25.8	22.3	19.9		
Central government fiscal balance as % GDP										
Egypt, Arab Rep.				–6.0		–8.3	–8.4	–9.2	–7.5	–7.8
Tunisia				–3.2		–2.6	–3	–2.9	–2.9	–0.8
Total government debt as % GDP										
Egypt, Arab Rep.				97.4		112.9	112.8	98.8	87.1	76.5
Tunisia				61.0		59.4	58.3	53.7	50.7	48.2
Internet users (per 100 people)										
Egypt, Arab Rep.			0.4	2.6	4.0	5.2	11.7	12.5	13.2	15.4
Tunisia			1.7	5.2	6.4	8.4	9.5	12.8	16.8	27.1
Middle East & North Africa			0.6	2.8	4.1	7.6	10.5	11.2	13.4	24.2
Lower middle income			1.0	3.0	4.0	5.4	6.6	9.0	11.7	–

Sources: World Bank, World Development Indicators 2009, IMF 2009a, IMF International Financial Statistics online

183

were under the thumb of the president's family, principally that of his wife's Trabelsi clan but also the sons of two of Ben Ali daughters by a previous marriage. Tunisia's small stock exchange languished, its market capitalization as a percentage of GDP remaining in the teens (Table 3.4).

By contrast, Egypt's stock market, revitalized in the 1980s, quickly passed the long established banking sector by standard performance measures. But despite a market capitalization ratio soaring over 100 per cent in 2007, the exuberant stock market continues to be overshadowed by the lumbering banking sector as the provider of credit to businesses. For most businessmen, neither is to be relied on. A recent survey of firms revealed that 70 percent draw on retained earnings as their main source of financing, 24 percent turning to banks, but only 4 percent resorting to the stock market (Abdel-Kader 2006: 14). Not surprisingly, the stock market remains remarkably thin, with a handful of companies' shares accounting for the bulk of capitalization and turnover. The number of listed companies actually fell from 1,076 in 2000 to 373 in 2008 for reasons noted in Chapter 3. Egypt was still well ahead of Tunisia, where the stock market showed little turnover with only forty-nine listed firms worth 15 percent of GDP.

The macroeconomic context within which private business operates in Egypt has improved, but aspects of it remain problematical. Private-sector access to credit, as just discussed, remains a key issue and one that results in some measure from the need for government credit crowding out the private sector. As credit to the private sector peaked in 2003, the government, with fiscal deficits averaging 8.2 percent of GDP for the five years ending in 2008, was coping with awesome amounts of domestic debt, as Table 5.3 also indicates. Underlying these persisting budgetary imbalances have been disproportionate expenditures on government wages, which rose from 26 to 28 percent between 1995 and 2006; subsidies, which rose from 21.7 to 36.8 percent from 2003 to 2007; and interest payments, which were in the 15 to 20 percent range for several years, but which jumped up dramatically in 2009, from LE52.9 to LE71.1 billion, as Egypt's public finances deteriorated sharply (El-Gibali 2009). The balance of funds remaining for capital investment declined at an average rate of almost 13 percent from 2002 to 2007. Demands for domestic credit to cover fiscal imbalances steadily displaced credit to the private sector, which fell from almost 62 percent in 2002 to 50.6 percent in 2007. Coupled with high budget deficits has been a sustained, high growth rate in money supply, which grew on average more than 15 percent annually after 2002, reaching almost 19 percent in 2008. Combined, budget deficits and high monetary growth resulted in a steadily increasing inflation rate, which averaged 7 percent annually from 2002 to 2006, then reached 11 percent in 2007 before virtually doubling in the following year.

These fiscal and monetary policies make the task of improving the business environment yet more difficult, but these policies are deeply rooted in the political economy. Government wages and subsidies are the chief remnants of the frayed social contract. The change team in the cabinet has repeatedly signaled its desire to reduce those budgetary burdens and indeed, took steps to do so regarding energy subsidies in 2008. But fears of negative political reactions, based on the hard evidence of demonstrations, strikes, and other manifestations of public protest, all of which have increased in number and severity as reforms have progressed, combined with reactions by crony capitalists and their state-based patrons, led the change team's political masters to veto further reforms and even to roll back those already implemented. And as with most systems of entitlements, special interests grow up within them that make them yet more difficult to reform. In Egypt's case, those benefiting disproportionately include not only the middle and upper classes generally, whose consumption accounts for a much greater proportion of ill-targeted subsidies than does that of the poor, but crony capitalists who are able to extract rents from those subsidies. From the beginning of the new millennium with the rapid expansion of natural gas production, the most profitable rent has been access to highly subsidized energy to use in downstream production processes. It may not be coincidence that key members of the ostensible "change team," which includes the most important backers of Gamal Mubarak, are also prime beneficiaries of these rents. The most well known case in point is Ahmad 'Izz, an iron and steel magnate whose firms dominate that industry and who serves as Secretary for Organizational Affairs of the NDP and Chairman of the Budget Committee of the *Maglis al Sha'b* and who is widely thought to be the main supplier of funds for the patronage that Gamal needs to dispense to bolster his undeclared presidential candidacy. Reported improvement of the business environment ignores the fact that reforms have been primarily formal and legal in nature, their application impeded by institutional shortcomings, the removal of which would negatively impact entrenched political and economic interests.

Tunisia's macroeconomic environment is healthier than Egypt's, as Table 5.3 suggests. The central government's deficits are kept below 3 percent, and the government does not appear to squeeze credit to the private sector as tightly as in Egypt. As noted in Chapter 3, however, the "private sector" in Tunisian accounting included public-sector enterprises as well as private-sector enterprises and households. Private businesses still suffer from the same predatory rent-seeking environment.

Bank managers must bow to the Trabelsi clan and to other members of Ben Ali's extended family, as the apparently incorrigible bad loan portfolios of private as well as public-sector banks attest. Smaller state-owned banks were at least nominally privatized, although their management still must be vetted by the authorities. BIAT finally in 2009 became Tunisia's largest bank, overtaking two big public-sector banks, but it was no longer under the control of the Sfax entrepreneurs who had founded it. The new principal shareholders, Marouane Mabrouk and his wife Cyrine, Ben Ali's second of three daughters by an earlier marriage, also owned substantial retail outlets and Tunisia's largest private Internet service provider (Beau and Graciet 2009: 43). After hesitating for years over how to use the country's Internet node acquired in 1990, Ben Ali had finally decided in 1997 to give the public access through a company he could trust, owned by his son-in-law.

Tunisia in fact exercises more draconian controls over the Internet and other sources of information, even fax machines, than Egypt. Table 5.3 shows that per capita Internet usage is slightly higher in Tunisia, but Tunisia is smaller and wealthier, albeit not as small and wealthy as Israel and the GCC countries that, with Turkey, have the highest usage (see Figure 3.3). Tunisia's cyberpolice are extraordinarily efficient in filtering out any online information that might be critical of Tunisia. They also track down and filter out "anonymizer" sites that enable one to surf the net without filters or traces. Tunisia's press controls are also among the toughest in the region, as noted in Chapter 3. Newspaper circulation runs neck and neck with Syria for lowest honors. The heavy atmosphere of censorship in turn affects the financial system, as is evidenced by the anemic performance of Tunisia's stock market. Indeed, were it not for its history and surviving shreds of a legitimate state order, Tunisia would qualify as a bunker, its presidential palace in Carthage coming to resemble Baghdad's Green Zone.

The heavy fog also suffocates Tunisian university life and prevents the country from engaging in research and development and climbing the ladder of production chains toward a knowledge-based economy. Without liberty of association, scientists can hardly interact with one another, much less with businesses that might finance applied research and innovation (Siino 2004). Abdeljail Bedoui, a distinguished Tunisian economist, also observes a related phenomenon of a diminishing portfolio of exports, reduced from twelve to seven products between 1987 and 1990, four of which are concentrated in the textile sector (Lamloum 2006: 143). Tunisia is apparently unable to climb the production chain because in his view it has "an institutional environment and a mode of governance that discourages entrepreneurial liberty and supports social inequalities." As in Egypt, partial neoliberal reforms failed to generate structural reform.

The package of such reforms that Egypt finally adopted after 2000 has not substantially accelerated the development of more competitive human and physical infrastructures, on which yet more rapid economic development ultimately would have to depend. The most directly economically relevant aspects of human resource development are education and employment. As for the former, Egypt, like Tunisia, is a comparatively generous spender, with public expenditure on primary education of 4.1 percent of GDP in 2007 being almost twice the lower-middle-income country median. Private spending may be as much s 3.6 percent of GDP (Mattina and Cebotari 2007: 38). Its net enrollment rate of 93.7 percent in 2005 was slightly higher than the rates for MENA and global lower-middle-income countries. Its net secondary enrollment rate of 82.1 percent compared even more favorably, with the rates for MENA and global lower-middle-income countries being 65.2 and 66.8, respectively. And its gross tertiary enrollment rate of one third was about double the lower-middle-income country median.

Despite these comparatively high commitments to education, Egypt's youth literacy rate in 2006 was only 84.9 percent, well below the medians for both MENA and global lower-middle-income countries, which were 92.2 and 97.1 percent, respectively. Other evidence also suggests underperformance of the educational system. A World Bank study in 2005 found that at the primary level, Egypt has one administrator for every teacher and a further nonteaching staff member for each eight teachers (Egypt: Economic Performance and Assessment 2008: 33). In 2009 the World Economic Forum ranked the quality of Egypt's primary education 124th of 133 countries. Egypt's university faculty have relatively few research opportunities, as total spending on research and development has remained at around 0.2 percent of GDP for several years, about one quarter of that of Turkey, which in turn is about one fourth of that of OECD countries. No Egyptian university ranks in the top 500 in the world (Noland and Pack 2008: 64).

The structure of employment both contributes to and results from the broader economic context. Although unemployment gradually declined as the new millennium progressed, officially falling from 11 percent in 2003 to 9 percent in 2007, the nature of jobs being created suggested an economy that was adding more of the same rather than undergoing a transformation. Unemployment continued to be positively correlated with education, with those least likely to be employed being university graduates and those most likely to find jobs having minimal educations. Although this inversion of the relationship that obtains in developed economies reflects the fact that those without means simply must work, it also suggests that the growing economy had comparatively little need of the highly educated, who continued to be employed disproportionately in the public service, whose share of total employment declined only marginally. After more than three decades of ostensible economic reform, one half of wage workers in 2009 were still employed in the government and public sector (*Egypt and the Global Economic Crisis*, 2009: 7). The private sector does not generate adequate demand for the highly trained and educated, nor seem to care too much about developing skills. A global World Bank survey in 2007 found that only 13.4 percent of Egyptian firms offered formal training to their employees, with only firms in Guinea-Bissau, at 12 percent, being less likely to do so (World Development Indicators 2008). Firms in all MENA countries were more likely to offer such training, with the next worst performer, Syria, having 21 percent of its firms providing training.

Jobs being created are primarily in services, both public and private, as the proportion of males working in industry dropped from 25 to 23 percent in the period from 1990 to 2006, and that of women from 10 to 6 percent. Between 1998 and 2006 the manufacturing sector's share of total employment fell from 17 to 15 percent (Assaad, 2009, 36–7). The hydrocarbon sector, which is the motor force of the merchandise economy, employs only some 30,000 each in the oil and gas industries, or about one-quarter of a percent of the labor force in 2007 of some 23,000,000. Not surprisingly, productivity growth "has been lagging," a result according to USAID of "inadequate and inefficient investment in human capital" and "insufficient investment in physical capital in certain sectors" (Economic Performance and Assessment 2008: 6–7). Low productivity rates do not reflect rapid expansion of the labor force, because the overall labor force participation rate of just over half of those in the eligible age group has not appreciably expanded and is far below the lower-middle-income median. Real wages in 2006, after they had been driven up for some three years as a result of the third oil boom, had not quite reached their 1988 level (Said 2009: 54). The rise in any case was due primarily to wage increases in the public, not the private sector, as the former increased by 40 percent from 1998 to 2006, whereas the latter only rose by 17 percent (Said 2009: 76). One third of the country's informal workers earned less than $1 per day in 2006, while another third earned between $1 and $2 daily (El Mahdi and Rashed 2009: 108).

The failure of the economy to move up production chains and create jobs requiring more skills and providing greater material rewards, possibly thereby attracting more Egyptians, and especially females, into the labor force, is also reflected in the structure of employment. Participation in the labor force by educated women declined steadily between 1988 and 2006, a factor which contributed to Egypt's ranking of 120th of 128 countries ranked by the World Economic Forum on the gender gap (Assaad and El Hamidi 2009: 219, 253). According to the World Bank, Egypt has a very high proportion of what it terms "vulnerable employment," which is unpaid family work and own account workers, who constituted 21 percent of all male and 44 percent of all female workers in 2005 (World Development Indicators 2008). In 2006 the self-employed and those working for household enterprises accounted for 36 percent of total employment. The growing share of this sector of the labor market, combined with a decline in real earnings within it, indicates that "household enterprises . . . have served in recent years as a sort of sponge that absorbs excess labor . . . with as much as one-third of new entrants finding work in unpaid family labor" (Handoussa et al. 2008: 32). Three-quarters of new entrants to the labor force in the first five years of the twenty-first century took jobs in the informal sector (Assaad 2009: 2). The proliferation of micro and small enterprises, or those that employ fewer than fifty workers, which now account for more than 98 percent of all private-sector firms and 81 percent of the labor force in the private sector, is suggestive of a widespread need for those facing bleak employment prospects to eke out a marginal living on their own or with a few family members. This interpretation is reinforced by the growing importance of micro firms, which employ fewer than five persons. They accounted for 54 percent of employment in 1988 and just short of two thirds by 2006, by which time they employed 5.2 million workers in 2.4 million microestablishments, for an average of fewer than three workers per firm. These micro firms remained the dominant source of employment creation during the third oil boom (Handoussa et al. 2008: 150; El Mahdi and Rashed 2009: 92). More than 80 percent of employment in these firms is informal (Assaad 2009: 40). A longitudinal study of small-scale enterprises in Cairo revealed that in 1986 the average number of people employed in them was 3.6. Twelve years later this rate had declined to only 2.5 workers per firm. During the same period the share of firm owners and their family members of total employed rose from 45 percent to 63 percent of all those working in these enterprises (Meyer 2001). Just as a very high proportion of workers are informal, so are the vast majority of micro and small firms informal in the sense that they are not officially registered, and hence not entitled to benefit from either public- or private-sector credit and most other forms of support. The third great oil boom thus swept over Egypt from 2003 to 2008 leaving the structure of its labor force largely unchanged, other than the relative growth of employment in tourism and construction.

Invoking the tiger metaphor to suggest that Egypt's development tra-jectory would be similar to those of East Asian countries was, despite the acceleration of growth from 2003 to 2008, misleading. The econ-omy benefited directly and indirectly from the rapid increase in energy prices and from the comparatively tepid neoliberal reforms it imple-mented after 2000. But neither the third oil boom nor the reforms brought about structural changes to an economy that remained heavily dependent on the four principal sources of income on which it has relied since the 1970s. Macroeconomic performance improved but remained shaky, whereas human and physical infrastructure remained below those of comparators. Egypt had failed to take advantage of yet another golden opportunity for development and was now facing the Great Recession, during which its "big four" sources of revenues inevitably would decline substantially. Key to the limit of reform was the political system, which, with some minor fluctuations, remained unchanged despite the partial economic liberalization.

Egypt in the early twenty-first century was thus, like Tunisia, a text-book case of economic liberalization pursued by an authoritarian regime anxious to retain political power in the face of a deteriorating economy. After the brief economic fillip stimulated by the writedown of its foreign debt and the adoption of an economic reform and structural adjust-ment program in 1991, falling energy prices, combined with declining remittances and shrinking foreign aid, were squeezing the economy. The limited reforms did little to relieve that pressure, but they did stimulate the further growth of "globalizers." This steadily expanding group, which first began to emerge as a result of the slight economic opening at the end of the Nasser era, and which grew slowly and erratically over the next thirty years, was constituted of crony capitalists seeking to build more ambitious business empires while retaining at least some of their rents, autonomous businessmen who had been able to prosper as a result of increasing space in which the private sector could operate, and a collec-tion of Westernized academics, journalists, and other intellectuals who were in all cases committed to the fundamentals of the Washington Con-sensus and in some cases to the belief that its adoption would also pave the way for political reform.

Given the concentration of political power at the top, the key to policy change in Egypt is access to the president, and for this group of glob-alizers it was provided fortuitously by the president's son, whose back-ground in banking, along with his personal political ambitions, caused him to become their champion. It is unknown whether he, too, saw eco-nomic reform as a stepping stone to political liberalization, or simply as justification to replace the old guard entrenched in the state and party apparatuses, who were blocking his rise to power, with his more modern, liberal acolytes, who would facilitate his ascension. But having the ear of his father president and against the backdrop of a growing economic crisis, Gamal and his change team began to engineer some tentative reforms in the wake of the 2000 parliamentary elections. Then, as the economy began to pick up with the rise in oil prices in 2003, father essentially handed the cabinet over to son Gamal and his team, thereby opening the door to further economic reforms while ensuring that a close check could be kept on any efforts to liberalize the polity.

In the event, the partial political liberalization that commenced more or less simultaneously with the formation of the new cabinet was stillborn, raising the question of its true purpose. It may have resulted from the naïveté of Gamal and his globalizers, who thought that a growing economy would underpin their appeal to the broader public while disarming their old-guard antagonists. Alternatively, because it occurred at the very height of the democratization campaign by the Bush administration, it may have represented acquiescence to Washington. Yet another explanation is that the president himself, facing reelection in 2005, sought to burnish his image by allowing a competitor to contest that election and by promising a range of reforms, including revisions of the constitution. Cynics offer the explanation that the president permitted reasonably free and fair elections in 2005, at least in the first of their three stages, out of the calculation that by performing well, the Muslim Brothers would frighten Washington and many Egyptians, thus enabling him to use the justification of the threat of Islamism to crack down on one and all.

Whatever the correct explanation, postelection reneging on promised political reforms was accompanied by divisions within Gamal's change team, some of whom were committed if not to thoroughgoing political reforms, at least to embedding improvements of "the quality of administration" in greater "public accountability," which would include reforms of state institutions and reductions in rents for crony capitalists and their allies within the state. A manifestation of the division within the ranks of the globalizers over whether reforms should be limited to procedural ones intended to improve the business environment, narrowly defined, or should be more thoroughgoing and include leveling the playing field between businessmen, surfaced in parliament in 2008. Ahmad 'Izz, the tycoon who enjoys a near monopoly over the iron and steel industry and is the chief financial backer of Gamal, using his position as chairman of the Planning and Budget Committee of the People's Assembly and drawing on his multitudinous connections, defeated an antimonopoly bill that key members of the prime minister's own team of technocrats, led by

Minister of Trade and Industry Rashid Mohammed Rashid, were trying to push through parliament. The law that ultimately was adopted was a watered-down version of the initial bill, in which both penalties against monopolistic practices and the likelihood that such practices would be exposed were significantly reduced.

Thus the ostensible change team could not change the system of rent seeking connecting some of their nominal globalizing allies to state elites, thereby suggesting the narrow limits of the economic reform to which they could aspire. As for political reform, the primary institutional power base of the change team was the cabinet, which is at a level well below where such weighty matters are decided. Unable even to broach matters of "public accountability," the change team could only watch as limits imposed from above on political reform became yet stricter, possibly out of the regime's fear that partial economic reform was stimulating an ever-increasing number of strikes, demonstrations, and other manifestations of discontent by those in specific vocational categories and even by the general public. The pressure for further liberalization of both the economy and the polity had, in other words, run up against the bedrock of "bully praetorianism," which consists at its deepest, most powerful level of the triumvirate of ruler and his entourage, the military, and the security forces, riding on top of which is the executive branch, which along with the ruling party presides over the other branches of government and the polity as a whole.

Evolution of Egypt's bully praetorianism

The broader evolution of roles and relationships between Egypt's military, security intelligence agencies, and its president since the coup d'etat of 1952 disguises fluctuations within each of the three administrations. The broad pattern is one of the military retreating from a direct governance role as "ruler" to being a "guardian" and then "moderator," to use Kirk Beattie's terms, although "all post 1952 regimes have been fundamentally praetorian, i.e., regimes in which military officers are major or predominant actors by virtue of their actual or threatened use of force" (Beattie 1988: 201–30). The percentage of military officers in the cabinet and other key governmental posts traced a more or less steady decline from the Nasser through the Mubarak eras (Dekmejian 1971; Karawan 1996: 107–22; Cooper 1982: 209). Military involvement in the economy has evolved from officers managing civilian state-owned enterprises under Nasser, to the emergence under Sadat of a military economy with a steadily expanding and civilianizing product range, to strategic relationships with the private sector under Mubarak, although elements of these three forms overlap the three regimes (Vayrnen and Ohlson 1986: 105–24; Springborg 1989: 95–134; Cook 2007: 131–52; Dunn 1986: 119–34; Sfakianakis 2004: 77–100). As for the power of the president vis-à-vis the military, it now favors the former more than it had under Mubarak's predecessors, as suggested by the 2007 constitutional amendments that render a constitutional succession by a military officer improbable.[2] Similarly, the role of security intelligence agencies is more expansive under Mubarak than under either of his predecessors. But these differences are largely just nuances. Since 1952, the Egyptian polity has been described in terms that reflect the emphasis of the power of one of these three actors – as being a praetorian state or "military society," a dictatorship or one-man regime, or a police or *mukhabarat* (intelligence) state. The Egyptian government, in other words, has for more than half a century been a triumvirate of these three elements, and the changes that have occurred in the power relationships between them have not fundamentally altered that reality.

But even minor fluctuations may signal sources of future instability. Interestingly, within the broader evolutionary pattern, each of the three regimes followed a similar trajectory. In the early years of their rule Nasser, Sadat, and Mubarak all sought to downplay the roles of the military and security services, while devoting their energies to projecting their own political personalities and forging alliances with civilian political forces. Whether this was only a tactical maneuver intended to cement their personal preeminence, or was based on the belief that politics could substitute for coercion, is unclear. But what followed for each was a similar, seemingly unexpected, profound learning experience. Its first step was a challenge from the military. In the case of Nasser, it was his old comrade in arms Abd al Hakim Amer who managed to win the loyalties of the officer corps and thereby pose a threat. For Sadat, it was a tactical alliance between the Minister of War, Muhammad Fawzy, and leftist acolytes of the Soviets that posed the initial threat at the time of his succession, followed by a lingering suspicion of the president's capacities within the officer corps that caused him to retaliate by cashiering a series of top commanders. For Mubarak, the first eight years of his regime were characterized by a behind-the-scenes struggle between him and his charismatic Minister of Defense, Field Marshall Abd al Halim Abu Ghazala, who ended up under house arrest from 1989 until his death in 2008.

---

[2] Another possible indicator of the balance of power between Mubarak and the military is that the budget of the latter was reduced from almost 7 percent of GDP in the late 1980s to some 3.5 percent by 1996.

As their struggles for power with the military were in progress, these presidents undertook three countermeasures. First, they employed a variety of strategies to bring the military under their direct control, key to which was purging and even liquidating (in the case of Amer, for example) the ringleaders of their opposition within the officer corps. Second, they reached out politically, engaging directly with both supporters and potential opposition forces, while projecting an image of civilian political leadership, although the styles varied substantially reflecting their personalities and their times. They also toyed with political organization. Nasser sought to inspire the nation with anti-imperialist rhetoric, while creating a series of mobilization instruments, including the single party that has lasted, albeit under a different name, until today. Sadat, who portrayed himself as the "believing President," lifted the security shackles from the Muslim Brotherhood and Islamists more generally and facilitated their entry into a wide range of institutions, meanwhile creating a substantial façade of political liberalism.[3] For his part, Mubarak in the 1980s rekindled Sadat's failed reforms, while portraying himself as a man above politics, ready to listen to others' views while granting the opposition access to representative institutions. For the first five years of his rule, his Ministers of Interior, first Hassan Abu Basha and then, from 1984 to 1986, Ahmad Rushdi, had reputations for being liberal and believing in dialogue with rather than repression of the opposition (Basha 1990). Indeed, the latter is reported to have apologized to the then Supreme Guide of the Muslim Brotherhood, Omar Tilmisani, for torture of members of the organization under Nasser (Al-Awadi 2004: 43).

Whether these were political masks hiding cynical maneuvers to elevate presidential power over that of military challengers, or reflected true beliefs that competitive politics was important in its own right, is not clear. But in each case dalliances with civilian politicians did not last. Nasser ultimately gave up on widespread political mobilization. Sadat imprisoned Islamists and others who had responded to his invitation to resume political activism. After less than a decade in power, Mubarak decisively reneged on commitments to free and fair elections and pluralism more generally, substituting an increasingly severe repression, punctuated with brief interludes of relaxation. He had already signaled his shift to the right in 1986, when in the wake of the January Central Security Force insurrection, he replaced the Minister of Interior, soft-liner

---

[3] Sadat in fact took personal control of the Muslim Brotherhood "file," cutting his Minister of Interior out of the relationship (Al-Awadi 2004: 43).

Ahmad Rushdi, with the heavy-handed, tough-talking former governor of rebellious Asyut, Zaki Badr.

Moreover, for Nasser, Sadat, and Mubarak, abandoning a strategy of engaging with political forces was coterminous with increasing dependence on security intelligence services, presumably both to serve as a counterbalance to the military and to contain civilian political forces. Nasser brought in the East Germans to upgrade his intelligence services and then created a barracked security force under the Ministry of Interior both to contain street riots, which broke out in 1968, and to obviate the need for the military's presence in the capital. Sadat upgraded the Central Security Force that Nasser had created and placed increasing weight on the domestic intelligence agency that reports to the Minister of Interior, State Security Investigations, and correspondingly less weight on military intelligence. This trend reached its apotheosis under Mubarak. An indicator of the increasing weight he has placed on security intelligence is indicated by the increase in spending on it, which rose from 3.5 percent of the budget in 1987 to 4.8 percent in 1997; by the expansion of police personnel from 9 to 21 percent of total government employment during that time; and by the ratio of security intelligence personnel, including police, to military manpower (Soliman 2005: 84). The last total in fact declined slightly during the Mubarak years, dropping to less than 450,000 in all branches of the military. The Minister of Interior, by contrast, was reported to command a total of some 1.7 million men in 2009, up from just over 1 million in 2002, including 850,000 police and Ministry of Interior staff, 450,000 Central Security Force troops, and 400,000 secret police (Zuhur 2007: 15–18; Qandil 2008: 19; Faruq 2009).

In 2009 it was estimated that Ministry of Interior employees constituted slightly more than one fifth of all government employees and that the ratio of security forces to population was 1:37, twice what it was at the end of the Shah's reign (Faruq 2009; Qandil 2008:19). Possibly most menacing and symbolic is the creation of an altogether new deterrent to direct political action in the mid-1990s in the form of plainclothes auxiliaries within the Ministry of Interior, similar to if not actually modeled on Haiti's Papa Doc's Tonton Macoutes. These goon squads, directed by officers of State Security Investigations (SSI) and coordinated with Central Security Force troops, carry barely concealed side arms and truncheons and move among demonstrators, beating them, occasionally molesting females, and intimidating all and sundry. Even more sinister and damaging to the rule of law is its internal legal/judicial/incarceration system, which consists of prosecutors and emergency state security courts and their attendant personnel, as well as a network of prisons. This is a Kafkaesque world into which suspects enter and may never return, the "black hole" already noted earlier (page 73).

And as if that were insufficient, SSI also has, in addition to the Central Security Force, a barracked riot-deterrent force of unknown numbers, but probably in excess of 100,000 personnel. Finally, SSI agents are typically seconded to other ministries, governmental agencies, universities, public-sector companies, media outlets, and so on, not only for purposes of monitoring their activities and those of their members, but for determining their policies and operations. The annual internal security budget in 2006 reached $1.5 billion, substantially more than the sum spent on health care (Bradley 2008: 140).

The parallels with Tunisia – informers, goon squads and all – under Ben Ali were remarkable. Early in his rule Ben Ali multiplied the number of police and rural constabulary fourfold and since 2000 has seemed to be competing with Egypt on a per capita basis, probably reaching 1 for every 70 Tunisians (Camau 2003: 203–205), compared to 1 for every 50 in Egypt. By contrast Italy, the most heavily policed of the large European countries, has only 1 for every 175 inhabitants, despite the fact that they must contend with the Mafia, whereas the ruling family is viewed as one in Tunisia. Even talking to foreigners is risky. In May 2010 Tunisia's cabinet discussed a draft amendment to the Penal Code to imprison any Tunisian "who establishes . . . contacts with foreign sides instigating to harm Tunisia's vital interests," defined as "anything that has to do with its economic security" (*Tunis Afrique Presse*, May 19, 2010).

The presidents of both Egypt and Tunisia, then, were political failures in that they apparently tried without success to build bases of power outside the executive branch of government. In addition, each of them ended up bolstering security intelligence forces to fill political vacuums, to counterbalance the military, and to keep the ruling party under surveillance. Over the course of Egypt's three presidencies, the net effect of their similar trajectories has been to enhance the power of security intelligence, while retaining that of the military as a counterbalance to it, and gradually reducing the military's capacity to exert influence over the president. Less is known about the political dynamics within Tunisia's ruling party, which has stronger historical roots than Egypt's National Democratic Party. But in Egypt the presidency has taken the state ever closer to the Eastern European communist model. How close it is to becoming a pure police state, in which the military and president are unable to control the security intelligence services, is a key issue.

Whereas Sadat bolstered the Ministry of Interior's domestic undercover capacities at the expense of the military's, hence police at the expense of military officers, Mubarak, by contrast, has sought to establish a balance between the two, albeit one in which the military is preponderant. To that end over the past several years he has bolstered General Intelligence (*mukhabarat al 'amma*), which is headed by the former chief of Military Intelligence and fellow graduate of Moscow's Frunze Military Academy, General Omar Suleiman, and includes in command positions numerous military officers, so that it has become a counterweight to SSI. It reports directly to the president and now is heavily involved in domestic counterintelligence, primarily of a political nature. However, because of its origins in the military and military domination of key recruitment, General Intelligence is considered to be the military's equivalent to the SSI, albeit one situated in the presidency. Each branch of the military also has its own intelligence department. In addition, whereas Sadat had begun to diversify recruitment into the presidency, Mubarak reverted to Nasser's practice of recruiting exclusively among the military for posts in the presidency, probably both because of his background and contacts there and because this would reassure the military of its priority access to his person. Mubarak's use of the Presidential Guard similarly can be seen as reassuring the military of its preeminence in his regime, while simultaneously bolstering his personal power. Not only has he expanded the size of the Guard, but he appointed its commander as his long-serving Minister of Defense, Field Marshal Muhammad Husayn Tantawi, and also appointed from it the former Chief of Staff, Magdy Hatata.[4] Mubarak placed a military general in charge of counterinsurgency operations in Upper Egypt in the 1990s against the Gama'at al Islamiyya (Islamic Group) and appointed former military officers as governors in those provinces swept by the insurrection.

Mubarak has thus skillfully integrated the military into a behind-the-scenes role in domestic political management, thereby heading off discontent within the military resulting from the expansion of the SSI and growth of power of the Ministry of Interior and the police forces on which it is built. Moreover, he has done so while bolstering the security intelligence capacities of the presidency. Finally, Mubarak has constructed a parallel balancing act between the military and police forces by his appointments of governors. Whereas Nasser appointed a majority of military officers to these key posts and Sadat preferred civilians and police officers, Mubarak has over the past two decades gradually reduced the

---

[4] Hatata's replacement, Lt. General Sami Hafiz Enan, is a former Commander of the Air Defense Forces, which is a separate branch of the Egyptian military. It may be significant that the top positions in the military hierarchy are not occupied by those who formerly occupied command positions within line army units, such as Field Marshal Abd al Halim Abu Ghazaleh, for those positions provide possible bases for broad loyalties within units that could pose political threats.

number of civilians, while increasing in tandem the numbers of governors with military and police backgrounds. He has, in sum, created a carefully balanced security intelligence triumvirate in which the Ministry of Interior, the military, and the president along with his entourage, despite competition and rivalries, are all engaged and from which they must derive some common sense of purpose in defending the nation, to say nothing of themselves, from internal threats.

Undercover economies and crony capitalism

The economic assets and interests of the security intelligence services differ from those of the military. The latter is a direct owner and operator of productive units, whether factories producing armaments, civilian durables and consumer goods; construction companies building civilian and military infrastructure; agribusiness enterprises that grow crops and livestock, bottle artesian water, or bake bread; or networks of tourism and real estate facilities. Economic resources provided to the military and to active-duty and retired officers from these operations are a major source of the institution's power and its members' and former members' incomes. Probably even more profitable at both the institutional and personal levels has been the military's selling, leasing, or directly utilizing for income-generating purposes land under its jurisdiction. Transfer into private hands of prime real estate on the Mediterranean, Red Sea, Suez Canal, and Sinai coasts has netted vast sums for the officer corps and for the developers to whom they have sold or leased it.

As in Pakistan, one can truly speak of "milibus" in Egypt as a self-contained sector of the economy and a major concern of the organization and its members (Siddiqa 2007). From the outset of the privatization program, military enterprises were explicitly excluded, so the military's primary interests remain centered in the public sector. But as privatization has proceeded, a growing number of strategic relationships with crony capitalists, especially in the construction sector, have linked the military, or at least those officers in positions to benefit from such linkages, more closely to the private sector. This transitioning poses a potential threat to the coherence of the military, for whereas the military public sector provides opportunities even for enlisted men as well as virtually the whole of the officer corps, strategic alliances with the private sector are the preserve of a much more limited military constituency. Retention of the stagnating military public sector and especially its non-armaments components therefore probably results primarily from the need to avert intramilitary tensions as a consequence of differential access to material benefits.

The economic resources of security intelligence agencies do not consist of direct ownership of assets, whether land or productive enterprises.[5] Instead those resources are derived from the information and strategic networks of agents as individuals or small groups.[6] The ethos that permeates the undercover community appears very similar to that of "dirty togetherness," described by Andrzej Zybertowicz as the feeling of esprit de corps that being above the law gives to those engaged in intelligence activities (Zybertowicz 2007: 65–82). As in communist Poland, Egyptian intelligence operatives have become more deeply engaged in political activities, so their direct dealings with citizens have steadily increased. Thus academics, reporters, bloggers, students, union members, NGO activists, members of political parties, and many others now commonly report that they have been contacted by an officer from SSI or General Intelligence, who discussed this or that matter with them. Running through these reports is the attitude of these agents, which is reflected in approaches along the lines of "Come, be reasonable, we can do business together. You are a smart person so appreciate that the law is irrelevant."[7] The bargaining approach security intelligence frequently takes in its dealings with activists is reflected in a conversation reported by Issam al Aryan, a former member of Parliament and leading member of the Muslim Brotherhood whom the regime has jailed intermittently for several years. When the Brotherhood was distributing blankets to those who had suffered as the result of the 1992 Cairo earthquake, a security officer informed al Aryan that it was permissible, but that he was "unhappy with our slogans and banners" (Al-Awadi 2004: 150).

The "dirty togetherness" of feeling to be above the law, while defending the nation from its own weaknesses, reflects the role of Egypt's security intelligence forces. They are ubiquitous within government, constituting a shadow state behind the façade of civilian authority reminiscent of Saddam's Iraq (Tripp 2007) and Turkey's "deep" state (*derin devlet*)

---

[5] There are some exceptions to this general rule, of which the Ministry of Interior's ownership of an Arabian horse stud farm is one. Ownership and operation of tourism facilities by that ministry for the benefit of its employees does not distinguish it from, say, the Ministry of Foreign Affairs, so these installations are not properly classified as productive assets.

[6] In a recent case investigated by State Security Prosecutions, for example, it was reported that a bribe was paid to an Administrative Court judge by security officers acting on behalf of a prominent businessman who also serves in the lower house of parliament. (*Al Masri Al Yawm*, 2008).

[7] Such conversations have been reported to one of the authors by numerous individuals. The head of SSI on the University of Cairo campus was reported as telling an organizer of a student protest that he and his colleagues were essentially wasting their time with their strike against the university administration and should deal directly with SSI because their power transcended that of the university president (Students in Action 2007).

perceived by some observers (Skinner 2008: 21–3; Freely 2007) as the bedrock of the real regime that could replace the civilian governmental leadership if it so desired. There is, therefore, no security intelligence economy as a collective undertaking in the same form as the military economy. The economic interests of security intelligence agencies and their members are thus different from those of the military and potentially in conflict. In Poland, for example, these services took advantage of their engagement with various components of the public-sector economy and with foreign involvement to facilitate the emergence of private enterprises from which they could benefit. The Polish military, on the other hand, was not a proponent of the transition to capitalism (Zybertowicz 2007: 71).

A similar phenomenon is occurring in Egypt. An SSI general, for example, recently complained to a Western ambassador about the problem of retaining personnel. He noted that the expansion of SSI's role had increased the workload of his agents and, equally importantly, that they were able to utilize their personal assets, including strategic relationships and knowledge of the inner workings of the bureaucracy, to obtain remunerative employment in the private sector or to establish their own businesses. Former agents, in other words, become "fixers" for others, or operators in their own right. In either case their interests lie in the privatization of state assets and the growth of a private sector, for, unlike the military, they derive comparatively few direct material benefits from the public sector.

Tactical conflicts of economic interest between the military and security services also become more likely as both become more directly engaged in the private sector. A case that came to public attention in 2008 illustrates the nature of competition between the two. Ayman Abd al Monaim, director of the Ministry of Culture's restoration work in Islamic Cairo and a key assistant to its controversial minister, Faruq Husni, was sentenced to ten years in jail and a LE200,000 fine, a sentence upheld by the Court of Cassation in July, 2009, for accepting bribes to award a contract to a construction firm for the preservation of a mamluke-era house in Islamic Cairo. This judgment and the publicity surrounding the case, including details about the North Coast villa, luxury apartment, fleet of trucks, and urban land he was given, struck observers as unusual, for kickbacks to firms involved in such work are known to be commonplace, as is the fact that most of the firms involved are controlled by the military. The mystery was that Abd al Monaim apparently was double dealing, having taken bribes from two companies, one owned by former military officers and another by former security intelligence agents. When he then awarded the contract to the former, presumably in the belief that he would be protected by the military officers, his patron the minister, and his patron's patron, the first lady, he failed to anticipate the response by security intelligence. The aggrieved parties drew on the prosecutorial service of SSI to launch an investigation. Thanks to their connections within the media, it was covered widely in the press, which threw in innuendos about other such kickbacks and, for the careful reader, about sexual relationships between the accused and the minister, who is widely thought to be gay.[8] In sum, security intelligence raised the stakes to Abd al Monaim's protectors to levels they could not afford, so they stood aside as he was sent off to break rocks.

Presumably it is only the high profile that renders this case of economic conflict between military officers and security agents unique. As the private sector's share of GDP steadily grows, the potential for both structural and case-by-case conflicts of interest between them also expands. The situation is rendered yet more complex by the involvement of the third member of the ruling triumvirate, the president and his entourage, the core of which is provided by his wife and sons. All three political actors utilize their base in the state to forge economic relationships, but the military's are most concentrated in the public sector. Thus the fault line of material interest divides it on the one hand from the president and the security intelligence services on the other, a division that could assume importance in the presidential succession.

But the crony capitalist system that Mubarak inherited from Sadat and then expanded also ties together the three pillars of the regime. In order to secure his direct, personal control over the sources of patronage, Mubarak dismantled some of the Osman Ahmad Osman empire that was the key to Sadat's patronage network. He fostered the creation of several additional Osman-like empires, based primarily on construction, an undertaking that provides ample opportunities for generating capital through strategic relationships with state elites, requiring as it does their approval to secure loans, permissions, and contracts. Crony capitalism, which was almost in the singular under Sadat, became "cronies capitalism" under Mubarak, starting first with Osman and his clones, and then spreading out into various other sectors of the economy.

As in Indonesia, Tunisia, or Palestine for that matter, crony capitalists in Egypt are the instruments of powerful political forces lurking in the background. Chief among them are the president and his family, through which President Mubarak has mediated business relations with some two to three dozen leading cronies. The Mubaraks provide the

---

[8] The Abd al Monaim case did not dissuade the First Lady from strongly supporting Faruq Husny's failed candidacy in 2009 to lead UNESCO.

necessary rent-generating facilities, such as access to satellite communications, monopolies over telecommunications markets, or contracts for services to state-owned enterprises, while the cronies do the rest. But the Mubaraks have permitted military and, to a lesser extent, security service officers to replicate their linkages to cronies, albeit on a smaller scale. So the Bahgat Group, for example, is tied not only to President Mubarak himself and his sons, but also to military officers who have provided Ahmad Bahgat both access to military factories to assemble electronic goods and protection from others who might want to assemble competitive appliances, by closing the factory gates to them (Sfakianakis 2004: 93). Dream TV, which is Egypt's most popular private channel and is owned by Ahmad Bahgat, regularly invites security agents to debate with political activists on its most popular program of political commentary (Drummond 2007: 8). Mubarak, in sum, has diversified the crony capitalist system he inherited from Sadat and reaped considerable benefits by so doing. He has gained direct or indirect control over the flow of resources, such that his dominance over the elite is unchallenged. He has been able to present, more or less convincingly, accomplishments of crony capitalism as manifestations of Egypt's economic liberalization, thereby reducing pressure to really liberalize.

The power of capital in bully praetorian republics

If fundamental transformations of the Egyptian and Tunisian political economies appear unlikely in the near term, what are the prospects that private capital accumulation, which has been occurring slowly but steadily since the Nasser era in Egypt and the Bourguiba era in Tunisia, might alter the basic dynamics of these political economies, freeing them from praetorianism?

The historical legacy is not encouraging. Egyptian and Tunisian capitalists were both much weakened at the hands of their radical nationalist states, the decimation of nativized foreigners in Egypt being replicated by the gradual decolonization of businesses in Tunisia, although the nationalizations were not so thoroughgoing. The uneven resuscitation of capitalism in Egypt and Tunisia has been too incomplete and too discontinuous to generate a new class of independent capitalists, although private capital accumulation is accelerating in both, as suggested by the rising share of profits and rents and declining share of wages in both economies. But accumulations of capital do not translate directly into political power. Although regimes in bully states are not as hostile to capitalist accumulation as they are in bunker states, bully regimes jealously guard their monopoly on political power. As Jean-Pierre Cassarino observes with regard to Tunisia, "The 'challenges of globalization'... have encouraged the emergence of a group of highly visible entrepreneurs... but in doing so [have] strengthened their connection with the state, through the distribution of financial resources, 'titles of nobility,' and media visibility." He further notes, "As for the government, there is no question that by mobilizing the 'Captains' of these corporate groups, it enhances its control over economic liberalization" (Cassarino 1999: 69–72). Tunisia's chief captain, textile magnate Hedi Djilani, became part of the Trabelsi clan by marring off his daughter to a brother-in-law of Ben Ali (Cammett 2007: 124–5) and then another daughter to a close relative of the president.

Both impersonal and personal methods are used to restrain the political autonomy of capital, as evidence from both Egypt and Tunisia suggests. The banking sector, about half of which remains in the state's hands, continues to favor well-connected clients tied to the regime. The private component derives steady profits from lending the government money at what are comparatively high interest rates by both regional and global standards. Public finance is extremely concentrated, such that virtually all allocations of public money for civilian purposes, even those by local governments, must be approved at what in practice is the prime ministerial level. In the case of the Islamic financial sector, in which the potential for conversion of capital into autonomous political resources is much greater, the degree of governmental control is qualitatively higher. The "informal" component of that sector consisted of the "Islamic investment companies" that proliferated in the mid-1980s and came to control a substantial share of private savings, largely by serving as channels for remittances from the Gulf. The government, suspecting Ponzi schemes and fearing connections with the Muslim Brotherhood, cracked down on it in 1988, and depositors were still struggling to obtain some portion of their frozen funds years later (Henry 1996: 263–75). The government's renewed attack on the financial assets of the Muslim Brotherhood that intensified from 2008 suggested both its lingering fear of the organization's capacity to convert financial into political resources and its intent to weaken the organization in the lead-up to parliamentary and presidential elections in which the long-awaited presidential succession might occur. In April of that year, successful businessman, financial manager, and First Deputy of the MB Khairat al Shatir and his partner Hassan Malek, along with some forty others to whom they were allegedly linked in various business and financial undertakings, were convicted in military courts and sentenced to five years in jail and the confiscation of their business assets. In July 2009, the government swooped in on another member of the MB's Executive Guidance Bureau, Abd al Monaim Abul Futuh, charging him with receiving money for the MB from Hizbollah. In follow-up dawn raids, it arrested various owners and employees of foreign exchange companies allegedly linked to the MB.

The formal Islamic sector, which consists of Islamic banks, cannot be dealt with as harshly as were Islamic investment companies and enterprises with direct links to the MB, for those banks have international credibility and linkages and, in any case, comply with all central bank regulations. The Faisal Islamic Bank, which commenced operations in 1977, is the oldest and largest of the three Islamic banks. In addition, eleven private commercial banks and one public-sector bank (Bank Misr) have opened Islamic branches over the past fifteen years. Islamic banks' deposits of LE7.4 billion amounted to 5 percent of total deposits by 1997, having achieved slow but steady growth throughout the decade. The rate of growth of deposits and lending would probably have been substantially higher in the absence of governmental efforts to contain such growth. Those efforts have consisted of attempting to tarnish the Islamic legitimacy of the institutions, as well as placing legal obstacles in the path of their operations. The three major Islamic banks, for example, were forbidden to open new branches. The country's official Islamic establishment, which is under direct governmental control, conducted a campaign against the banks. Sheikh al Azhar Muhammad Sayid Tantawi issued a string of fatwas favoring conventional banks. In 1997 he contributed a series of articles to *Akhbar al Yawm* in which he argued against the religious credentials of "so-called Islamic institutions." He referred to those who do not set fixed interest rates as "thieves" and banks that have Islamic branches as "ignorant and hypocritical," causing one of his al Azhar colleagues to observe that his statements may be "politically rather than divinely inspired" (Mostafa 1997: 52–8). Paradoxically, the state itself, as another tactic to contain Islamic banking, opened its own Islamic branches operated by the state-owned Bank Misr; free to organize throughout the country, they succeeded by 1998 in attracting more deposits than any of the fully fledged Islamic banks (Galloux 1999: 494–6).

So also in Tunisia, an Islamic bank jointly owned by the Al-Baraka Group and the Tunisian state gained onshore status in 1988 (Henry 1996: 188–9) but did not receive permission to open branches outside Tunis for fear of possible association with Tunisia's opposition Islamist Nahda Party. Despite market research indicating important potential demand, it remained a marginal actor, virtually contained in offshore activities. In 2009, however, a second Islamic bank was recognized, a sign of the times reflecting the rise of Islamic banking in the GCC countries. This time the Ben Ali regime jumped on the bandwagon, with his son-in-law and potential successor Sakhr Materi founding Banque Az-Zitouna, complementing his Zitouna radio station that was also spreading the call of Islam while putting any Islamic capitalism under strong presidential family control.

Potential or actual manifestations of autonomous political behavior by Egyptian business elites are strongly discouraged. Leadership of the principal business associations, such as the Egyptian Businessmen's Association, the Federation of Industries, or the American-Egyptian Chamber of Commerce, is exercised by businessmen with close ties to the political elite. Informal political "red lines" are made evident to businesspersons lest they cross them and earn the government's ire. One such red line is support for opposition political parties, which is widely known to invite problems with the authorities for those businessmen who do provide it. All but a handful of the scores of businessmen elected to parliament in 1995, 2000, and 2005 were either members of the ruling National Democratic Party or "independents" affiliated with it. The one prominent businessmen who won election in 1995 and again in 2000 for the Wafd Party, Munir Fakhri Abd al Nur, was defeated in 2005 as a result of a concerted NDP campaign against him (Shehata 2006). The Muslim Brotherhood's leading businessman, Khairat al Shatir, was, as described earlier, imprisoned in 2008. Private capital is indeed accumulating as the economy is gradually liberalized, but the power of that capital remains too limited to be exercised independently of the state. A study of the behavior of deputies in the 1995–2000 parliament revealed that those who were businessmen "performed poorly," lagging behind their colleagues in attendance and submission of legislation. Significantly, they did not take unified stands on key economic issues (El-Mikawy and Mohsen 2006).

In Tunisia, liberty of association and parliamentary representation were even more restricted than in Egypt, and there was a disturbing indication of the structural weakness of Tunisian capital. The World Bank observed in its 2007 progress report concerning the Country Assistance Strategy mutually agreed with the Tunisian authorities that rates of private investment were inadequate. "The main concern of the authorities, which is shared by Bank staff, is the poor performance of private investment, particularly domestic private investment, which threatens future income growth and employment creation." The Report continues:

Weaknesses in economic governance, particularly regarding the predictability and transparency of the regulatory framework and limited market contestability constitute an important constraint for private investment. Discretionary intervention by the government, low levels of public accountability, voice and participation contribute to weakening the investment climate and strengthening the hand of "insiders", mostly in the absence of strong competitive forces. This contributes to reducing market contestability and discouraging risk taking by less well connected entrepreneurs.

Although Tunisia ranks well on a number of competitiveness and business climate indicators, special treatment of well-connected individuals is a growing concern of the Tunisian business community and may partially explain the low level of domestic private investment (World Bank 2007a: 3–4).

The Tunisian governance practices observed by the World Bank (but contested by the Tunisian government) largely explain the problem of capital accumulation noted earlier (see Table 5.1) concerning both bully regimes. Private investors simply withhold the investment needed to expand fixed plant and equipment. Consequently, there is an ever-present need for increased borrowing to stimulate higher rates of growth. Burdened with mounting security expenditures and skittish private investment, both Egypt and Tunisia walk a tightrope between inadequate capital accumulation on one side and unsustainable debt levels on the other. When they shrug off local capital's structural power, however feeble it may be, the bullies lose its possible benefits.

Prospects for bully praetorian republics

Because globalization unleashes forces that reduce the control of states over their national economies, it poses a particular threat in the MENA, where virtually all states are, by global standards, overgrown. Paradoxically, bunker praetorian republics appear to have greater latitude than their bully counterparts to formulate policies in response to globalization. This is because those bunker states are less constrained by their civil societies and the power of capital, a freedom that comes at the price of effectiveness of any economic policy these states adopt. The policy choices of regimes in bully praetorian republics are more constrained by civil society and the structural power of capital, but the probable effectiveness of their policies is greater. They at least have the possibility of renegotiating state-society relations to make them more conducive to sustainable, broad-based economic growth. The line between ruler and ruled in the bully praetorian republics is drawn only by their respective relations to the state, not, as is the case in bunker praetorian republics, by their ascribed membership in clans, tribes, or other social formations. Thus redrawing those lines does not necessarily involve a complete reconfiguration of the political community, or possibly a civil war.

A renegotiation of state-society relations will ultimately be required if bully praetorian republics are to respond really effectively to the threats and opportunities of globalization. The analogy of the colonial dialectic suggests, however, that time is required before the balance of power between them becomes more equal, and hence propitious for either negotiations or a breakthrough into power by a new social force. At present the rulers of Egypt seem to be operating on the premise of business as usual. They appear to believe they can reconcile globalization with a political regime based almost exclusively on state institutions, with all the costs such a regime imposes on capitalist development. The one noticeable change is the expansion of the roles of crony and smaller, independent capitalists since the end of the Nasser era and at a steadily accelerating pace, which itself reflects the pressure and opportunities of globalization. Thus far the capitalism that has developed has enabled the regime to have its cake and eat it, too – to retain state control while giving the appearance of adopting the Washington Consensus. But this crony capitalism is too enfeebled and state dependent to drive economic and political transformations. The failure to increase exports of manufactures outside energy-dependent subsectors, the steady deterioration of public finances, the continued reliance on traditional sources of foreign currencies, and the failure to even begin to build a "knowledge economy" that would, along with targeted investments, increase productivity, are all indicators that Egypt did not utilize the third great oil boom to develop a more sustainable, independent capitalism that might in turn foster a political liberalization. Yet the shift of the locus of rents from protected domestic markets for goods and services, to utilization of energy, at least in part for exports, has also induced the cronies with access to that energy to develop strategies that are in some measure globally competitive, much as their counterparts in the Gulf have done.

For Egypt, and Tunisia, too, for that matter, crony capitalism does not have to be the end of the line. It could be a way station on the road to a more genuine, effective capitalism. As economic competition is increasing, such as in the telecommunications industry where new service providers have received operating licenses, it stimulates efforts to enhance returns through both rents and productivity improvements. Egypt's leading telecommunications company, for example, having generated vast profits from its early monopolization of the domestic market, has moved offshore to become a serious contender in telecommunications markets in Algeria, Iraq, Italy, and various Sub-Saharan African countries. Increased competition at home has also caused it to improve service in Egypt. These and some similar examples suggest the possibility that today's crony capitalists may become tomorrow's entrepreneurs, the calculation of their own economic interests causing them to support the creation of "level playing fields" as more profitable alternatives to sharing rents with political elites. And an increasing number of those in the business elite and even on the margins of the political elite, such as some of the members of Gamal's change team, are sincerely committed not only to improving public administration, but to anchoring those improvements in public accountability. This desire might in turn dictate a strategy of support for alternative political actors, including those who speak directly on behalf of this emerging and transforming capitalism.

International pressures of various sorts that impinge on the domestic economy will also enhance domestic competition and provide opportunities for new entrants to the system. Privatization, although still incomplete in Egypt in the crucial financial and textile and clothing sectors in particular, will ultimately erode some of the economic power base of the state. Economic success and political stability could in turn feed the confidence of incumbent political elites, especially those following the Husni Mubarak era, who might then respond by permitting steadily greater latitude for investors. Rent-seeking mentalities would, in this scenario, steadily give way to the understanding that broadly based economic growth will pay the greatest economic and political benefits. In short, crony capitalism could be a developmental phase in the gradual economic reform of a command political economy in which the political elite is insufficiently confident to suddenly throw open the doors to rapid economic and political change. As such, crony capitalism would play a functional, transitional role for the further development of the political economy.

An alternative, less benign scenario is also possible. It is that the present state-dependent crony capitalism is not a way station on the road to a more open, competitive free-market system, but is an alternative and hindrance to other, more productive forms of capitalism. The nexus between the executive – at the heart of which is the ruler and his entourage, the military and security and intelligence services – on the one hand and successful businesspeople on the other is, in this view, too central to the system, too institutionalized, and too remunerative to both sides for it easily to be broken. Neither side would ever have an interest in modifying rent-seeking arrangements, and outsiders, whether Egyptians or foreigners, will have insufficient leverage to do so. Entrenched in power and protected by purposeful lack of transparency, cronies and their guardian "mamlukes" in the state will ensure that competitors do not arise. They will succeed, for example, in perpetuating comparatively high tariffs and nontariff barriers to trade to protect monopolized domestic markets secured through rent-seeking arrangements, and they will successfully lobby to retain energy subsidies to their own enterprises, thus obtaining private profit from the public energy resource. According to this scenario, crony capitalism will continue to shape the market's relation to the world, thereby perpetuating both itself and inadequate rates of development, possibly until the strategy ultimately collapses as a result of economic calamity or political chaos.

Reference to the possibly analogous case of the colonial dialectic might help resolve whether the benign or malignant scenario is the more likely of the two. The globalization dialectic has created a first generation of aspiring capitalist imitators – cronies – equivalent in both substantive and sequential terms to the Westernized "compromisers" of the colonial dialectic. Were the door to power to be opened to them now, presumably they would consolidate an imitative system in the shadow of the Washington Consensus – a successful conversion of crony capitalism into a more dynamic, outward-oriented version, à la the first scenario.

But the globalization dialectic has already thrown up a second generation of moralizers, most of whom are searching for radical, noncompromising, nativist solutions of which Islamist ones are far and away the most prevalent. Because the globalization dialectic is proceeding at a faster pace than its colonial predecessor, this generation of moralizers has been on the scene for about as long as the capitalist accommodators, with whom they are in competition. But their very radicalism, which has alienated large portions of the population, and the relatively greater power of national as opposed to colonial states seem to have undermined their chances of a breakthrough. The way may thus have been paved for a third-generation antithesis to the thesis of globalization – that is, unless an economic or political crisis swamps these systems in the meantime.

This third generation is also that of moralizers, but one that is relatively moderate and seeks a synthesis between nativist Islam, on the one hand, and the globalist Washington Consensus of free markets and (implied) secular polities, on the other. With regard to the economy, mention was made in Chapters 1 and 2 of the role of Islamic financial institutions, which are growing throughout the region. On the political level the most rapidly expanding sector of civil society, including political parties, appears to be moderate Islamism, a movement that eschews the radicalism of underground terrorist groups and seeks political office, where possible, through the ballot box and an Islamicized yet modernized society through voluntaristic activities. But neither the economic, the social, nor the political manifestations of this third generation of synthesizers have yet matured sufficiently to assume major financial or political responsibility. The current contest is defined by incumbent elites, who minimize the importance of those who would synthesize Islam and the pressures of globalization, associate them with more radical Islamist oppositions, and marginalize them in Egypt, for instance, by supporting public-sector and crony competitors. But Islamic finance and the capitalists it may spawn, who might in time bring about a qualitative change in the political economy, are probably the best defense against other, radical or revolutionary Islamists.

For both Egypt and Tunisia, the scenario of a renegotiation of power between state and society, with the nascent, as yet largely crony capitalism steadily assuming more power and gradually being transformed into a more robust, more independent capitalism, seems possible. The constant economic pressure resulting from globalization may push toward a renegotiation. In Egypt and Tunisia, both the state and society have considerable strengths, suggesting that Islamist radicals are unlikely to prevail. The state has its well-articulated structure, its tradition of rule by law if not of law, its sheer size, and its history of centrality to the country. But society can also draw on a long tradition of structured political participation, of some independence of civil society and of capital, and on the resources and impacts of globalization itself. The justification for military or police rule, even indirect, has steadily eroded, and the transition back to civilian government is a central issue in current speculation over the next presidential succession – especially in Egypt, where the corruption that has eaten away at the state has not passed over the military. Divisions between beneficiaries of patronage networks and those outside them undoubtedly exist. The historic military mission, rendered largely irrelevant by the signing of a peace treaty with Israel in 1979, has yet to be redefined. To the extent that Egypt has a national security policy, it is one that subordinates the country to American interests, a matter that must affront the pride and aspirations of many in the officer corps. The continuation of officers well above retirement age in the positions of Minister of Defense and Chief of Staff suggests the president's anxieties about allowing younger, more dynamic military leadership to have public exposure.

The temptation must be increasing for both countries' nascent capitalists to seek to play more independent and important roles in shaping public policy for both the economy and the polity. With the advantages of a broader middle class and some traditions of contestation between a once-powerful trade union and the dominant nationalist party, Tunisia might be better positioned than Egypt to renegotiate state-society relationships and institutionalize some forms of accountability and transparency, including control of the military and security services. Because Tunisia is less geopolitically significant than Egypt, its American and

European protectors might be more willing to countenance political change, even at the expense of cherished security alliances.

Suggestions for further reading

Galal Amin (2004 and 2006) is always stimulating in his observations of Egypt's political economy and critique of neoliberal reform. Relations between the state and the mainly Islamist opposition are analyzed by Al-Awadi (2004), Utvik (2006), Moustafa (2007), Brownlee (2007) and Rutherford (2008). Bowker (2010) addresses issues of economic reform, whereas Handoussa (2008) provides information and analysis on Egypt's civil society. Hamidi (1998) offers the perspective of a disappointed sympathizer on Tunisia's Islamist opposition, and Murphy (1999) and Zartman (1991) present its political economy. Rocard (1999) critically analyzes the Palestine National Authority; Brand (1998) and Brown (1997) offer comparative analyses of political liberalization and the rule of law. Cammett (2007) deals with Tunisia's economic response to global-ization, whereas Henry (2007) describes the country's deepening author-itarianism, and Alexander (2010) offers a general overview.

6   Globalizing monarchies

The monarchies in the region are better positioned than praetorian republics to take advantage of the opportunities of globalization. They have more active private sectors, some of which have joint ventures and other constructive relationships with multinational companies, in petroleum-related industries for the most part. Many of them also have concentrated financial systems, discussed in Chapter 3, that enable them to engage in a controlled liberalization consonant with the Washington Consensus. However, the monarchies are also politically more vulnerable than the praetorians because they did not undergo the full political transformation of a colonial dialectic. And they depend almost as much as the other regimes discussed so far in this book on their military and police forces to stay in power – rather than on any deeply rooted traditional legitimacy to which their official propaganda machines lay claim.

Most of them are relics of British imperialism. Britain generally preferred to intervene as little as possible in the internal affairs of these possessions because their prime importance lay in their geographical positions, astride passages to India, not in any intrinsic worth. It was easier to deal with ruling families by anointing them as monarchs than to reorganize their territories as crown colonies. Borders were matters of chance and political opportunity. As colonial secretary in 1921, for instance, Winston Churchill invented Jordan for the sake of one of the sons of the Sharif Hussein of Mecca. The father was owed favors for sponsoring T. E. Lawrence's Arab Revolt against the Turks in World War I. Abdullah, the son in question, had been promised Iraq, but the British gave this plum instead to his younger and more cosmopolitan brother Faisal, who became "available" after the French expelled him from Syria in 1920. The British protected other ruling families, the Sabahs of Kuwait, the Khalifas of Bahrain, the Thanis of Qatar, and the Qabbous of Oman, as well as other tribal notables along the Arabian coastline of the Persian Gulf, helping them to assume the trappings of monarchy and to limit the field of Saudi expansion. Only Morocco's ruling dynasty has roots in the precolonial past, whereas Saudi Arabia, defined by the conquests of its ruling family, only fully emerged with defined borders in the early 1930s. Despite receiving British subsidies, the Saud family retained its independence first by winning the holy lands of Mecca and Medina in 1926 and then by offering oil concessions to the Americans.

With the exception of Morocco, the monarchies surviving independence enjoyed relatively superficial and positive colonial encounters, barely touched by nationalist movements. They consequently retain close business links with their old colonial mentors and new American advisors, while encouraging local private entrepreneurs to benefit from the overseas connections. Unlike bunker or bully capitalist regimes, they rarely nationalize foreign or indigenous assets. Even the nationalizations of the American, British, and French oil companies came late, gradually, and reluctantly. In Bahrain and the United Arab Emirates, the foreign companies retain minority shareholdings. Aramco, a consortium of American oil companies, managed the Saudi oil business until 1990 (Vitalis 2007), and Americans still provide critical technical assistance.

Private capitalists, perceived as a threat by secretive and unaccountable praetorian regimes, offer the monarchies strategic depth. Active private sectors help them to attract the international and national capital needed to be more competitive in the global economy. Local business elites act as part of a big extended family, for the ruler retains the ability to alter the pecking orders of power, privilege, and wealth. There is no true distinction between public and private property. What a wealthy ruler gives away may be taken back; he can manipulate the private-sector resources of his more or less vibrant civil society and the nongovernmental organizations (NGOs) that formally reflect it. The semblance of civil society buffers political opposition and can facilitate crafty strategies of cooptation for economic development and globalization. It enables the monarchies to project more open business environments than those of the bunker or bully capitalist regimes.

Monarchies, in sum, remain wedded to the international order that founded them and facilitated their development. Unlike the military regimes with their state enterprises, the monarchies and their principal businesses are relatively well integrated into the global economy through joint ventures. They are consequently more exposed to potential populist backlashes against globalization. Because the structural power of local capital is greater, the rulers cannot bully it. They instead negotiate with their business notables so as to discourage them from making alliances with populist Islamists. Their economic strategies are more constrained by the interests of local capital, which may sometimes be expressed in civil society, than are those of the bully or bunker regimes.

Within these parameters, the monarchies display considerable variation. Morocco, with more than 30 million inhabitants, has almost twice the indigenous population of Saudi Arabia, five times Jordan's, thirty times Kuwait's and the UAE's, fifty times Bahrain's, and more than 150 times Qatar's. Morocco's ruling dynasty, the Alawis, achieved power and spiritual hegemony by 1666, centuries before the Saudis, not to mention the Hashemites of Jordan and Iraq. The monarchies vary not only with respect to their legitimacy and longevity but also in the degree of sophistication of their civil societies. Morocco, Kuwait, and Jordan have highly articulated party systems (although informal in Kuwait's case), more or less regular elections, and a relatively free press. Morocco and Jordan do not have the mineral wealth of Saudi Arabia or the other Gulf Cooperation Council (GCC) states of Bahrain, Kuwait, Oman, Qatar, and the UAE and perhaps compensate by according somewhat greater political freedom to their citizens. But Kuwait, with huge oil wealth, did not need to compensate its citizens with political liberties for diminished economic privileges. Its government supports social services, including sinecures in Kuwait's vast bureaucracy and public sector, at least as extensive as those of the other petrostates, but the sophistication of its merchant class and the shadow of Iraq have also influenced its politics since the 1930s, generally toward a semblance of democracy. The Kuwaiti parliament has a unique if discontinuous history. The other rich monarchies of the GCC keep a tighter lid on their respective oppositions, but Bahrain's new emir pardoned hundreds of detainees and exiles, held a referendum in February 2001 for a National Charter, and then promulgated a constitution, albeit less liberal, establishing a more controllable bicameral parliament, than the one abrogated in 1975. Not to be outdone, Qatar's emir followed suit and established his constitutional monarchy but has not yet, as of 2010, convened the parliamentary elections promised for 2007. Saudi King Fahd (1982–2005) finally appointed a consultative council in 1993 – but only after suffering the traumas of Desert Storm and local petitions against arbitrary government (Gause 1994: 94–8). His successor King Abdullah enlarged the consultative council and also established an Allegiance Council in 2006, consisting of the sons of King Abd al-Aziz (1902–53) or their heirs, to pledge allegiance to future kings and to nominate future crown princes by secret ballot. He instituted elections in 2005 for half the seats of the kingdom's seventy-eight municipalities, the first elections held in Saudi Arabia since the early 1960s. More cautious, with much greater stakes than the family-run city-states on its Eastern borders, the Saudis tolerate the political experimentations of their neighbors as a sort of laboratory for sustaining family rule in the era of big oil and massive development plans. The thirty-five-member

Allegiance Council, by including each of King Abd al-Aziz's recognized sons or male heirs, ensures that no one set of full brothers, such as the Sudeiri Seven, has a majority.

Morocco and Saudi Arabia are not only the most populous and influential of the monarchies. They also mark extremes on the continua of longevity, wealth, and civil sophistication. In one respect Morocco is unique among Arab monarchies. It alone weathered a relatively intensive and protracted colonial situation without either, as in Tunisia, being superseded by a mass nationalist movement or, as in Egypt or Iraq, being overthrown by radical military officers. As already mentioned in Chapter 1, the French colonial authorities unintentionally transformed Mohammed V, their reclusive, protected sultan, into a national hero by exiling him and his family to Madagascar in 1953. His son, the late Hassan II (1929–99), then repressed and subdued Morocco's second- and third-moment elites. After physically eliminating his most intransigent opponents in the 1960s, he coopted much of Morocco's political class into a parliamentary system that reserves most significant powers for the monarch. Thus Morocco is not only the oldest but also the most experienced and effective of the Arab monarchies in coping with contemporary nationalist and Islamist oppositions. Jordan, by incorporating the West Bank and receiving hundreds of thousands of Palestinians expelled from Israel in 1948, is the only other surviving Arab monarchy facing comparable internal opposition. The monarchies of the GCC, of interest primarily for their oil, were not colonized extensively, and Western education came much later than to Iran, Iraq, and the Mediterranean states of the region. Consequently "the new middle class" is weaker, so that Saudi Arabia and the other GCC monarchies deal with less articulated civil societies and have less experience coping with organized oppositions than do their northern neighbors. But all of the monarchies are experiencing major social problems that may render them vulnerable to the challenges of traditionalist and radical oppositions.

Morocco

The king's royal household, the *makhzan*, not the official government, dominated economic policy making until recently. In precolonial times this makhzan, or magazine, stored the grain collected as taxes that the sultan then redistributed in hard times to favored tribes. It remains the central source of patronage in Moroccan politics. The French Protectorate preserved the venerable institution but deprived it of its ruling functions. With independence, however, the king acquired new authority and power, and, with the departure of many colonial landholders and businesspeople, substantial properties as well. By the time Hassan II succeeded his father, in 1961, the royal household included some of the most fertile lands and a variety of businesses purchased from departing settlers. The monarchy also effected an alliance with rural notables, many of whom were Berber, with the intention of curbing the political ambitions of urban nationalists. The notables came in large part from the very families that France had mobilized in the final years of the Protectorate against the sultan and his nationalist allies. The monarchy consolidated its power by distributing ex-settler land and other benefits to the client notables and to military officers, many of whom were also of the same Berber families as the notables. Hassan completed his father's work and confounded most political observers by surviving in power for thirty-eight years rather than the six months they had predicted.

Whereas the Algerians had anarchically grabbed the spoils of their departing settlers, most of whom vanished when independence was proclaimed, the Moroccan monarchy very gradually appropriated much smaller spoils without precipitating any rapid departures of the settlers. The colonial properties were carefully allocated to supporters of the monarchy. By 1973, when much of the land had been quietly redistributed, it was time to Moroccanize commerce, especially after two attempted military coups, in 1971 and 1972, had almost eliminated King Hassan. The law promulgated in 1973 encouraged private Moroccans to gain majority shares in French businesses and thereby diversified the makhzan's patronage resources. Senior administrators could be shuffled off to the private sector, opening the way to government promotions for a new generation of king's men (Leveau 1985: 255). In the mid-1970s, positions in ministries and public-sector enterprises were multiplied with the help of record revenues from phosphates, Morocco's principal export. Although Moroccan phosphate rents pale in comparison with Gulf oil, Morocco enjoyed a modest boom until 1976, when phosphate prices collapsed. It then experienced fiscal deficits comparable to those that affected the Gulf states with the collapse of oil prices. Its balance-of-payments deficits were far more serious, however, and Morocco was impelled into a series of agreements with the IMF to reduce government expenditures and curb credit. Royal opportunities to dispense patronage were consequently diminished. After 1983, freezes on government employment, tariff reductions and freer trade, the elimination of most price controls and some state trading monopolies, and various other measures of economic liberalization required by either the IMF or the World Bank tended to erode the makhzan's traditional patronage resources. These were, after all, derived from the allocation of official posts and selective implementation of government regulations. The monarchy gained considerable legitimacy in 1975 by orchestrating the Green March to take over the former Spanish Sahara, but it still needed tangible as well as psychic resources to balance the political parties and elite factions and maintain political control. It gained them in the private sector by buying into a final icon of the French Protectorate.

In 1980 the makhzan acquired a major interest in the Omnium Nord-Africain (ONA). This holding company, founded in 1934, exemplified "German" capitalism under the auspices of the French Protectorate. By gaining control and putting his son-in-law in charge of it, King Hassan, who was already Morocco's leading landowner, gained a dominant position in private-sector industry and finance. The industrial conglomerate's gross revenues account for more than 5 percent of Morocco's GDP. The ONA acquired major stakes in Morocco's leading commercial banks and thereby enabled the makhzan to dominate the economy indirectly behind the scenes. In other words, the king regained in the private sector the influence that policies of economic liberalization were progressively eroding in government and the public sector. He could ardently engage his country in globalization without risking any serious defections in the business community. The Confédération Générale des Entreprises Marocaines (CGEM), official mouthpiece of Morocco's business leaders, is quite naturally "in a symbiotic partnership with the state" (Patton 1999). Clothing exporters, however, acquired some independence in the 1990s from the "big families" that dominated less efficient textile producers for the home market (Cammett 2007: 148–89). Within the CGEM it was possible to articulate sectoral interests when they coincided with economic reforms favored by the government, but the big families retained control of the CGEM until 2009, when a new reform team headed by the CEO of Hightech Payment Systems, a software firm, took charge in uncontested elections, and, representing the modern face of Moroccan management, removed most of the association's previous leadership. Joined by the chairman of the clothing exporters, the new team also enjoyed the discreet backing of the ONA.

The makhzan's principal instrument of control, however, is the commercial banking system. As in the German model, a small number of Moroccan banks operate a tight oligopoly. Reinforced in 1976 by the imposition of credit ceilings, these banks selectively control credit allocation and can make or break most businesses. In 1987 ONA acquired a major stake in the Banque Commerciale Marocaine (BCM), the leading privately owned one, as well as in other banks. Other Moroccan conglomerates close to the palace, the Kittani and Lamrani groups, controlled two of the remaining five privately owned banks until 2004, when the BCM absorbed Kittani's Wafabank into Attijariwafa Bank.

Consequently, the king could promote further economic liberalization, including the lifting in 1991 of credit ceilings and formal controls on interest rates. Unlike the Tunisians or Egyptians, he could also afford to privatize one of Morocco's two public-sector banks, holding half of Morocco's domestic deposits, without losing control over the allocation of credit and patronage. In 1995 Othman Benjelloun acquired a core stake in the Banque Marocaine du Commerce Extérieur (BMCE). Although internal management problems have delayed the privatization of the Banque du Crédit Populaire (BCP), perhaps indefinitely, the Moroccan banks were in better shape with fewer nonperforming loans than their Tunisian or Egyptian counterparts (see Figure 3.7). These loans, primarily legacies of state ownership, almost reached 20 percent of Morocco's total portfolio of outstanding loans in 2004, but were brought into line, below 8 percent by 2007, when the patronage driven portfolios of the bully and bunker states were still at least twice as nonperforming.

Privatization in Morocco poses neither the political nor technical problems experienced by the bully capitalists. The Moroccan owners and principal managers form a tight and exclusive circle, for the most part of Fassi origin like the Benjelloun family. Outsiders such as Miloud Chabbi, who had bid for control of the BMCE and whose Ynna Holding would be deemed "successful" by the World Bank (2009b: 28), were clearly unacceptable. Benjelloun's winning offer for the BMCE was priced so high that he may have received special encouragement to join the select circle and to keep Chabbi out of it. Chabbi was not even allowed to acquire Shell Oil's downstream operations because the Ministry of Privatization disqualified him, though he has extensive investments in Tunisia and Egypt. But the bankers are the major gatekeepers. Coordinated by the Groupement Professionelle des Banques Marocaines (GPRM), the banking system ensures the loyalty of Morocco's capitalist class.

Economic liberalization resulted in ever greater concentrations of market power in the hands of financial conglomerates. In the face of globalization, the leaders reinforced their presence in Europe, attracted more minority participation in their capital from major European and Japanese banking consortia, and took over some of their weaker Moroccan sisters. The conglomerates then reorganized in 2010 in anticipation of further liberalization of international banking services under the General Agreement on Trade and Services (GATS). One "megadeal" infused the BMCE with cash from the government's Caisse de Dépôts et de Gestion (CDG) to fund some of the latter's numerous enterprises ("CDG-BMCE Bank" 2010); the ONA then merged on March 25, 2010, with the Societé Nationale des Investissements (SNI) to constitute "a group of international dimensions" (Lahlou 2010: 3). Evidently the field for royal patronage expanded rather than contracted. Privatization offered it further scope. A politically reliable financial system enabled Morocco to privatize substantially more of its public enterprises in the 1990s than Tunisia, even though its public sector had never been as large. In addition to foreign bank competition, however, Morocco's "German" model faces another challenge at home. The Casablanca stock exchange, reinvigorated to facilitate the privatization efforts, offers an alternative source of financing for enterprises beholden to the banks. It also represents an alien Anglo-American variety of capitalism that insists on the full public disclosure of the sorts of information that commercial banks deem to be confidential. Indeed, the merger of the SNI with ONA was the occasion for these major holdings to cover up by repurchasing their shares and withdrawing from the Casablanca Stock Exchange (SNI-ONA 2010).

During King Hassan's final years, the political system became sufficiently liberal to tolerate some of the required flows of information. The contrast with Tunisia could not be more striking. Four of Morocco's thirteen approved brokerage houses issued periodic bulletins in the late 1990s analyzing not only the traded companies but also their respective industries, market shares, and competitive strategies. Analysts fresh out of business school presented case studies worthy of being taught in the classroom. Behind them, too, are a young generation of journalists specialized in economic affairs. *L'Economiste* was fielding thirty-four investigative reporters and analysts in 2010, and its Arabic daily sister had an additional forty. Founded in 1991 as a weekly to compete with a prestigious journal left over from the time of the Protectorate, this paper owned by a Moroccan political scientist and a prominent economic analyst is a sign of the times. It expanded to become a daily in 1998 and, supported in part by ONA and other prominent groups, generates sufficient revenues from publicity to finance its presence online and to organize its archives, which are also available online. Together with its Arabic daily, the media group has roughly one-third of the market and supports an FM radio station and a monthly magazine as well. In 2008 it opened a private three-year school of journalism that is projected to graduate some 20 journalists annually.

These enterprises could not flourish in an illiberal environment. *L'Economiste* retains its credibility, in fact, by being staunchly independent. In 1996, for instance, it left its editorial page blank (February 8, 1996) rather than toe the official line that all was going well with Interior Minister Basri's crackdown against corruption in the port of Casablanca. The crackdown was actually so clumsy and draconian that businesses stopped importing, but at least *L'Economiste* was not sanctioned for preserving its professional reputation within the business community, while the regime "cleaned up" the private sector to prepare for "*alternance*" (turnover), the inclusion of opposition parties in a new government (Saaf 2010). In July 1998 *l'Economiste* broke a taboo when it reported news taken from a brokerage firm's information sheet that DGAS (Direction Générale des Affaires Sociales of the Royal Armed Forces), which manages officers' pension funds, had taken a major position in a rather poorly performing bank stock. Normally, as in praetorian republics, no civil, political, or economic action of the military is open to independent reporting. On July 20, 2009, *L'Economiste* again joined other Moroccan dailies in a blank editorial page protest against the seizure of 100,000 copies of *TelQuel* and its sister Arabic-language publication *Nichane* ("Straight Talk," written, unlike most of the Arabic language press, in colloquial Arabic understood by most Moroccans) for publishing the results of poll that gave the king favorable ratings from 91 percent of those interviewed. The Ministry of the Interior was insisting that the monarchy "can't be an object of debate"(Lindsey 2009).

King Mohammed VI inherited a monarchy that presented some signs of becoming genuinely constitutional. King Hassan had handed most economic decision making over in 1998 to the new government headed by Abderrahmane Youssoufi, a leader of Morocco's once-radical secular opposition. The makhzan retained control over foreign affairs, defense, internal security, and religious affairs, but an alliance of seven opposition parties held the rest of the ministries. The young king, building on this apparent liberalization, dismissed Driss Basri, his father's long-serving minister of the interior, and promoted human rights. Mohammed VI might have preferred a more constitutional, less politically engaged role than his father, but he soon discovered that Juan Carlos could not be his role model. The king of Spain had defended his country against military coups as he presided over the transition from Franco's authoritarian regime to constitutional democracy, whereas King Mohammed VI listened to his advisors, brought some new blood into an expanding makhzan, and ruled through a variety of royal commissions that tended to undercut elected constitutional bodies. A selective crackdown on the press in April 2000, though modest by regional standards, already reflected the rising influence of his military and security services (*Middle East International*, May 5, 2000: 6–8). By 2003, as terrorist operations in Casablanca announced an El-Qaeda presence in Morocco, the press crackdowns were disappointing liberal observers inside and outside the country who had hoped for greater freedom under the new king than his father. Still, however, it was possible to hold meetings of the Association of Moroccan Journalists and the Legal Defense Committee for Journalists Rights, for instance, to defend frail liberties and protest measures imprisoning or fining journalists or banning them, as in the case of Ali Lmrabet, from practicing journalism in Morocco (he went to Spain instead). Human rights violations, the most egregious of which had been exposed toward the end of Hassan's reign, resumed in the wake of the Casablanca suicide bombings in 2003, compounded by those in Madrid in 2004 and again in Casablanca, with less damage, in 2007.

Morocco's traditional political parties were weakened over the years by cooptation and collusion with the monarchy. King Hassan gave his coalition government of "opposition" parties headed by Prime Minister Abderrahmane Youssoufi of the Union Socialiste des Forces Populaires (USFP) full responsibility for economic policies, but the government was weak and divided, without adequate means to carry out economic reforms and weighed down by military and economic commitments associated with the occupation and colonization of the former Spanish Sahara. The prime minister was eventually replaced by a technocrat and then, in 2007, by an Istiqlal leader, after the USFP performed poorly in the parliamentary elections and then fell victim to internal divisions. Meanwhile a new Islamist party, the Party for Justice and Development (PJD), won ten seats in parliament in 1997 and many more in 2002. It survived the fallout from the Casablanca bombings but did less well than expected, coming in second after the Istiqlal in the 2007 parliamentary elections although winning in the cities. These elections mark a nadir in Moroccan political life that even upset the World Bank economists, who noted the abstention rate to be "an additional risk factor" for Morocco (World Bank 2007b:8). By official count only 37 percent of the registered voters turned out to vote, and turnout was much lower in Rabat and Casablanca. One response of the monarchy was to revert to a political strategy pioneered by King Hassan at the beginning of his reign: the formation of a new party by a close political associate known to have the ear of the king. Fouad Ali El Himma, one of the king's twelve former palace schoolmates, resigned from office as Minister of the Interior to run for parliament in 2007. Then in 2008 he founded a new party in opposition to the Istiqlal government and outran all the other parties in the local elections of June 2009, confirming the traditional makhzan hold over rural Morocco and thereby "enabling the resurrection of the Makhzen version 2.0" (*North African Journal*, July 15, 2009, p. 23). Interestingly, the party chose a tractor as its symbol during these elections to show its rural constituents its desire to modernize the Moroccan countryside.

The economic challenges remain daunting, however, for any prospective prime minister. Although poverty was diminishing, 45 percent of the population aged 15 and above remained illiterate in the early 2000s. Because King Hassan had deliberately neglected schooling in the countryside, famously saying in 1967, "If we all become intellectuals, we'll only have pencils to eat" (Moore 1970: 267–8), illiteracy drove Morocco further down the Poverty Index than income alone would have predicted; but in 2006 17 percent of the population was still deprived of adequate water supplies, and 14 percent lived on less than $2 per day. Morocco still ranked 96th out of 135 countries, below Tunisia (65th), Algeria (71st), and Egypt (82nd) on the Human Poverty Index (Table 2.2), by which the UNDP measures a combination of unhealthy living conditions, illiteracy, and low life expectancies. Unemployment officially averaged under 10 percent in the late 2000s but was over 20 percent among secondary school and university graduates, some of whom habitually manifested their need for work on the main street of the nation's capital.

The World Bank reported in 2007, however, that the reforms undertaken since 2002 "make of Morocco a leading reformist country in the MENA Region and beyond" (World Bank 2007b: 1). Focused on alleviating the country's problems of poverty and "social exclusion" as well as unemployment, the government undertook a series of reforms in education, transportation, low-income housing, the water and energy sectors, trade policy, public finance, and the banking sector. When the Great Recession hit Morocco in 2009, cutting demand for its exports by 34.4 percent during the first half of the year, remittances by 12.5 percent, tourism revenues by 12.5 percent, and FDI by 34.5 percent (Bank Al-Maghrib 2009: 6), Morocco still seemed better placed than its neighbors to survive the crisis. Although central government debt remained relatively high, at 48.5 percent of GDP at the end of 2008, 0.2 percent greater than Tunisia's, its current account and fiscal deficits and inflation rate were less than those of any other oil-importing country in the MENA, and external debt was only 21.3 percent of GDP, whereas Tunisia's was 51.1 percent (IMF 2009a: 52).

Morocco's Royal Institute of Strategic Studies released a report in July 2009 that spelled out the short-term measures taken to alleviate the impact of the crisis, including subsidies to business enterprises to keep their workers. Although the report had an upbeat tone, stressing how the nonagricultural sectors of the economy had developed momentum, averaging 5 percent growth until 2009 under the impetus of dynamic private-sector investment levels attaining 30 percent of GDP, the report also recognized downside risks including social unrest and diminishing foreign exchange reserves. Continuing massive investments in infrastructure expenses and expensive social safety nets could still lead to dangerous foreign exchange shortages and unsustainable deficits, and indeed one of the report's recommendations was to cut back on investments requiring substantial foreign exchange components. Left unmentioned were steady increases in Morocco's military budget, hostage to an arms race with wealthier Algeria. In constant 2005 dollars, estimated by the Swedish International Peace Research Institute, Morocco increased its budget by $309 million in 2006-08 from over $2 billion, but could not keep up Algeria's 38 percent increase to over $4 billion during the same two-year period (http://milexdata.sipri.org/). Further increases were expected.

Morocco's apparently healthy macroeconomy appeared vulnerable as the Great Recession wore on. And despite the World Bank's good report card, Morocco still ranked low in most business polls. The World Economic Forum placed it in 76th place (out of 117 countries), behind Egypt among countries at the lowest "factor-driven" level of development, and the World Bank's *Doing Business 2009* placed it in 128th place (out of 177 countries). Despite good marks from the IMF concerning its financial reforms, two concerns about the banking system still remained. First, its high concentration led to inefficient allocation of capital by excluding many entrepreneurs who did not enjoy some special relationship. Morocco was not a business-friendly climate for small and medium-sized enterprises, yet these were key to multiplying jobs (Comité 2006: chapter 4, 27-31). Bank al-Maghrib was encouraging the commercial banks to offer them better access to credit (IMF 2008: 19).

Secondly and more seriously, the entire system might be at risk. Leading banks could not refuse working capital and other credits to enterprises like those connected to the ONA, which was in turn controlled by the makhzan. Although Morocco seemed to be doing a better job than its neighbors of controlling its nonperforming loan portfolio, the system of royal patronage seemed at greater risk than during the reign of King Hassan. The new king had mandated his private secretary, an American-trained MBA, to rationalize Siger (*regis*, "of the king" in Latin, spelled backwards), the holding company of other holdings such as ONA, to which the Société Nationale d'Investissment was now merged. Consequently, Siger became staffed with high-powered analysts and administrators, effectively controlling much of the economy, including some two-thirds of the capital exchanged on the stock market. The ONA, hitherto the preserve of royal family members, experienced three CEOs within a seven-year period. One of them, the dynamic young architect of the merger between BCM and Wafabank, apparently resigned rather than toe the line with the rationalized Siger (*L'Economiste*, May 23, 2007). Siger struck again one morning in June 2009, when the CEO of the Caisse de Dépôt et de Gestion (CDG) discovered that he had been replaced. Under royal encouragement he had transformed the Caisse from a sleepy public enterprise attached to the Ministry of Finance into a relatively autonomous investment bank, funded by postal savings and various retirement funds, but its 2008 income statement, published just after he was fired, indicated a two-thirds drop in income due to a higher cost of funds, hence declining margins, and provisions for depreciating property and stock market assets (*L'Economiste*, July 17, 2009). Then, as mentioned above, it was required in 2010 to fund the undercapitalized BMCE. Could Siger's holding company of other holdings also collapse one day like a house of cards, now that it was rationalized?

Conflicts of interest were inevitable under such a highly centralized system, and the connections between money and power, opaque in Hassan's day, were becoming public knowledge. Some corrupted financial units, such as the Crédit Immobilier et Hôtelier, "a cash-cow for decades" for well-connected speculators, accumulated much of Morocco's nonperforming loan portfolio until 2004 but was subsequently exposed (Transparency International 2007: 232–5). So also were the government's broad-based efforts to fight corruption, not only by official initiatives, such as laws against money laundering and terrorism, public procurement, and various judicial reforms, but also by enabling civil society initiatives such as corporate codes of governance promoted by the CGEM and a well-publicized National Observatory of Corruption established by the Moroccan branch of Transparency International (TI).

Indeed, Morocco, although hardly a democracy, was for many years the only country apart from democratic Lebanon to permit a fully operational chapter of the international NGO. But TI's *2009 Global Corruption Barometer*, which included public opinion surveys of Morocco and Lebanon, also revealed the growing cynicism of Morocco's urban public concerning the country's many initiatives. Sixty-four percent of the 500 Moroccans considered the government's measures to be ineffective (TI 2009: 33), and 58 percent admitted that someone in their household had bribed the police in the past year (*L'Economiste*, June 4, 2009). The national sample of the Lebanese was just as skeptical about government cleanup campaigns as the Moroccans, but there were interesting differences: although each group surprisingly had almost identical, negative assessments of their overall situations, the Moroccans focused more blame on their public officials and legal system, whereas the Lebanese spread it more equally on the politicians, parliament, businesses, and the public media as well, not that these were so much better viewed in Morocco (TI 2009: 29, 31).

Morocco, however, retains a civil society at least on a par with Lebanon's and certainly better articulated than those of its praetorian neighbors and more effective in absorbing Islamist organizations. Many more Moroccan than Algerian or Tunisian NGOs were represented at the Beijing Women's Congress in 1995, for instance, although Ben Ali also carefully cultivated women's organizations for his political purposes. Although the opposition parties have weakened in Morocco, the palace simultaneously tolerated if not actively encouraged networks of NGOs, orchestrated and sustained by policies of political decentralization. Some Islamist cultural associations emerged, and the Party for Justice and Development (PJD) was supposed to supplant the stronger but more radical, banned party of Sheikh Abdeslam Yassine, who was released from house arrest in 2000 on condition that he no longer engage in politics. The Moroccan monarchy seemed better able to divide and dominate the Islamists than Husni Mubarak, Ben Ali, or the faceless Algerian "deciders." As "Commander of the Faithful," King Hassan had actively dominated the field of religious discourse ever since his rise to power in the 1960s. One measure of his success was the virtual elimination of alternative discourses, but his son has reopened the option of Islamic finance, a tool that might strengthen an Islamist alternative to Sheikh Yassine's (and his daughter's) antimonarchical discourse.

Until 2007 the kingdom rejected Islamic finance apparently because it carries the implication that existing banks, including Siger's Attijariwafa Bank, are not in compliance with Islam and therefore that the Commander of the Faithful is neglecting his duty. But in 2007 the Bank al-Maghrib bowed to regional trends. In Saudi Arabia, conventional banks had been responding to local demand by opening Islamic windows for their customers. Just as the Saudi Arabian Monetary Authority vetted these practices, the Bank al-Maghrib (BAM) decided legally to define certain Islamic instruments for usage in Morocco's commercial banking community. Amounting to only $25 million in 2009, these assets represented a tiny fraction of the total, and they were taxed heavily, but the central bank Governor, although staunchly secular, a leader in his student days of the prosocialist Union Nationale des Etudiants Marocains, was responsive to the PJD members of parliament requesting more favorable treatment of the new Islamic products, demands that were progressively met in 2008 and 2009. BAM was intent on building a business-friendly environment for potential Gulf investors but was not yet ready to respond favorably to requests for licenses for exclusively Islamic banks, demanded by the PJD. And the slowing of investments from the Gulf in 2009 also delayed any Moroccan initiatives.

Were Islamists to become more involved in the country's economic reforms, they could conceivably help to bridge the growing gap between young, largely unemployed generations and ageing political leaderships. They could support economic liberalization as an Islamic initiative, operating in a more favorable political terrain than Algeria had offered in

1989–91. As of 2010, however, the Moroccan establishment remained distrustful of the efforts of the PJD to develop any Islamist economic constituency. As the late Rémy Leveau once observed, King Hassan had consistently opposed "a coalition bringing together young unemployed graduates, ideologists producing a discourse on Islamic modernity, and new currents of the liberal bourgeoisie, [for] it could offer a credible alternative if the present [governing] coalition experiences difficulties" (Leveau 1999: 14–15). Much earlier in Hassan's reign, in 1965, Moroccan agents had kidnapped Mehdi Ben Barka in Paris – in effect eliminating the "third moment" of Morocco's colonial dialectic. Perhaps the late king had feared that the new dialectic of globalization could complete Ben Barka's revolutionary project, were Islamist moralizers to develop a practical synthesis. His son might try instead to stay in power by reigning over (and reining in) such a practical synthesis. As Morocco in 2009 spent a week celebrating the tenth anniversary of his accession to the throne, Mohammed VI seemed to be recycling his father's checkerboard with new players. A year later the reorganization of his conglomerates was inaugurating a new game further blurring distinctions between the private sector and royal patronage.

Saudi Arabia – "developmental monarchy" for the GCC?

With 16.5 million Saudis counted in the 2004 census, hence an indigenous population of about 19 million in 2010, the Kingdom has less than two-thirds of Morocco's indigenous population for an economy more than five times its size. Saudi Arabia has neither the elaborate infrastructure of parties and associations nor even the degree of ethnic and regional pluralism that favors the role of patrimonial arbitrator in Morocco. Saudi politics are less transparent than Morocco's, where big business oligopolies still veil royal influence in the private sector. Although less tightly controlling other business holdings than the Moroccan makhzan, the Saudi monarchy probably exercises more direct influence on the economy, not only grappling with such issues as privatization and other economic reforms, but also deciding on oil prices and OPEC quotas and, most of all, allocating its gigantic resources to ambitiously planned development. Unlike Morocco, Saudi Arabia has the resources to be a developmental state and has learned after experiencing the boom and bust cycles of 1973–98 how to react to the volatility of the oil cycle by steering a steady course. After incurring successive annual budget deficits from 1984 to 1993 averaging over 17 percent of GDP, the government reduced them to 3 percent by 1997. Many subsidies, including those to the agricultural sector, were trimmed back. Setting the tone for sustainable development, Crown Prince Abdullah established the Higher Economic Council in 1999 under his chairmanship and including a consultative committee of private-sector representatives as well as the key economic ministers and the governor of the central bank. Finally succeeding his comatose older half-brother Fahd in 2005, King Abdullah continued to lay the foundations of an industrialization program far surpassing Algeria's stillborn program of "industrializing industries" in the 1970s.

By the beginning of the third great oil boom, after slightly less than thirty years of huge investments of petrodollars, the rulers of Saudi Arabia had welded together a substantial political base, developed a state administrative capacity – albeit one characterized by islands of efficiency in seas of torpor – and vastly upgraded the country's human and physical resources, all three elements being vital to the development strategy. In retrospect these foundations laid during the first two oil booms for a potential "developmental monarchy" were reinforcing. The first imperative was political support, commencing within the core of the ruling family/tribe of Saud, spreading out to include tribal allies from their home Najd province, still further to the small but important class of merchants and businessmen that had in some cases, such as in Jeddah, predated and in others were the product of oil wealth, finally reaching the population at large through transfers and entitlements that comprised the "social contract." Each of these constituencies received its specially tailored patronage, with leading Saudi princes being provided top government positions and specific allocations of oil exports, with lesser ones being given stipends, titles to public land, and preferred access to government contracts. Najdi allies were provided a wide range of government-supported business opportunities, including liberal access to credit, as were prominent business families elsewhere in the Kingdom. Chaudhry, for example, notes that the loans from specialized state banks went disproportionately to prominent Najdi families in the 1970s, but became more inclusive in the 1990s (1997: 161–2, 170–2, 298–9). The monarch clearly retains vast patronage at his disposal, but he has to distribute much of it to his siblings, their children, and various other relatives – many thousands of greedy rentiers – to maintain royal family harmony. The *Economist* reported that $4 billion of the $7 billion windfall of unexpected oil revenues in 1999 disappeared in a "bonanza of unbudgeted expenditure" (April 22, 2000: 47). King Abdullah, however, has tried to rationalize these family allocations (Hertog 2010).

Paralleling and to some extent underpinning the purchase of political loyalty has been the construction of a larger, more diversified state administrative structure. The near-guarantee of public employment for citizens has resulted in a majority of the Saudi workforce being on the public payroll (SAMA 2009: 244–6). Although size and capacity are not directly or probably even closely related, by the beginning of the twenty-first century increasing functional differentiation of the Saudi state did make at least segments of it much more capable of overseeing the development effort (Niblock 2007; Hertog 2010). The recruitment of foreigners into the Saudi and other GCC public services has been a key factor in that capacity building (Lippman 2009a). So, too, was the conceptualization of state-society relations by the ruling family and its merchant allies, an understanding shared by other GCC rulers. Virtually from the beginning of the rapid expansion of their states and markets, they were willing to grant greater autonomy to private economic actors than were their counterparts in Arab republics, especially those in the bunker praetorian states. First and foremost, Saudi Aramco, the consortium of U.S. oil companies that was gradually nationalized between 1972 and 1990 (when Aramco-Delaware finally stopped running the company), was permitted to continue to operate on strictly commercial lines, even keeping substantial numbers of American technical advisors. So also with SABIC, now the world's largest petrochemical company, which is 70 percent government owned but, like Saudi Aramco, is permitted to operate autonomously.

Such outcomes, leaving these major state players far more autonomous than big ostensibly private-sector Moroccan enterprises, were by no means guaranteed as Saudi production expanded and wealth accumulated in the 1970s. Some elements within the Saudi elite sought to implement a more nationalist, state-centric model of ownership and operation of the oil industry, creating Petromin as their preferred vehicle with which to integrate and control upstream and downstream operations. For several years Aramco and Petromin competed, but the former ultimately triumphed and the latter was disbanded (Hertog 2008). Other GCC national oil companies, such as Abu Dhabi National Oil Company (ADNOC) and Qatar Petroleum, more closely resemble Aramco than they do other national oil companies that enjoy little autonomy from the state, such as Algeria's Sonatrach, Egypt's GUPCO, Iraq's Iraqi National Oil Company, the National Iranian Oil Company, or Mexico's Petromex for that matter (Marcel 2006). The Saudi government, unlike those in the Arab republics, has thus managed to perform both patronage and development functions. Limits were imposed by ruling elites on the reach of state-owned enterprises, which were further constrained by exposure to global competition. Central bank management was also viewed as a strategic sector like hydrocarbon extraction, processing, and transport and related petrochemical downstream development. The Saudi Arabian

Monetary Authority (SAMA), protected from royal meddling on behalf of their friends, was for instance not about in 2009 to buy up the $15 billion debt of Ahmad Hamad Algosaibi & Bros. and Maan Al-Sanea's Saad Group, whatever the latter's credentials as a dashing ex-fighter pilot married to Gosaibi's daughter, a member of one of the most prestigious merchant families linked to the Saudi rulers (*Saudi Gazette*, September 6, 2009).

As already observed in Chapters 2 and 3, Saudi Arabia made impressive strides on the World Bank's Government Effectiveness and other indicators, in 2009 reaching thirteenth place (out of 183 countries including the United States and other OECD economies), ahead of Japan, in the Bank's overall assessments of business climates, and of course well ahead of the rest of MENA, including Israel. But narrow measures of administrative competence or doing business should not be confused with an evaluation of the broader responsibilities of government, a key one of which is mediating sociopolitical conflicts. Indeed, theorists of the developmental state in East Asia argue that it is the successful performance of this function that enabled those states to guide economic development, precisely because they minimized or averted the debilitating consequences of sociopolitical conflict. The major question surrounding the future of Chinese economic development turns on exactly this matter, for the Chinese government, under the control of the Chinese Communist Party, has chosen to suppress conflict rather than to seek to minimize or resolve it by mediating between contesting forces. In this regard Saudi Arabia more closely resembles China than East Asia's democratic developmental states, although the Saudi approach is based more on the carrot of patronage than on the stick of repression, inverting the ratio that obtains in the bunker and bully praetorian states. So although the house of Saud has not created a state with capacities equivalent to those of, say, Japan, Taiwan, or Korea, which are effective in managing governmental functions, providing incentives to private actors, and mediating between sociopolitical forces, it does feature islands of administrative competence, primarily because of its wealth and interconnections with the West, and it has restrained the temptation to subordinate all major economic actors, private and public. Rather than mediate effectively between sociopolitical forces, however, the Saudi state seeks to maintain sociopolitical stability through patronage, thus suggesting it to be a rentier developmental monarchy – a possible contradiction in terms, as will be discussed later.

The third foundation for subsequent development that Saudi Arabia began to lay during the boom period of the mid-1970s through early 1980s and continued to expand subsequently was that of improved human and physical infrastructure. Education and health data for Saudi

Arabia indicate the degree of commitment to human resource development in both that and other GCC countries. Public expenditure on education rose rapidly in the late 1970s and early 1980s, then stabilized at a high level, such that by 2006 almost 28 percent of total governmental expenditures were for that purpose, with only Costa Rica, Lesotho, and Oman devoting higher percentages of their budgets to public education. The Saudi percentage was exactly double that of upper-middle-income countries as a whole, and more than double the European area commitment of 11 percent. Saudi Arabia was in 2006 spending 6.8 percent of its GDP on public education, whereas upper-middle-income countries averaged 4.1 percent and high-income countries 5.4 percent. Only a handful of countries, including Denmark, Norway, Israel, and Tunisia, committed more of their national resources to education.

These expenditures resulted in significant improvements in educational performance. Whereas in 1991, 87 and 39 percent of the relevant age groups were in primary and secondary education, respectively, by 2006 the percentages had risen to 93 for the primary and 60 for the secondary level. The completion rate for primary students jumped from 55 percent to 85 percent over that fifteen-year period. Female youth literacy rose from 81 to 95 percent, while male literacy reached 97 percent. As the government began to trumpet its aspirations to build a "knowledge economy," it increased its already substantial investment in higher education expenditure by committing some $12 billion to the construction of an all-new King Abdullah University of Science and Technology, which opened in October 2009. Governmental commitment to health improvement and the consequences of that commitment are similar, although less dramatic. The Saudi government was in 2005 spending 8.7 percent of its budget on health, compared to 8.2 percent for MENA governments as a whole and 10.9 percent in high-income countries. Life expectancy at birth rose from 68 to 73 years over the years from 1990 to 2006, while infant mortality dropped from 35 to 21 per 1,000 live births.

Physical infrastructure and its capacities were transformed throughout the GCC over the thirty-some years following the first oil boom. Again Saudi Arabian figures reflect the general trend. Its ports handled a greater tonnage of container traffic than those of Russia, South Africa, or Turkey in 2006, although less than half that of the UAE, but by that year this neighbor of Saudi Arabia was one of the world's leading entrepôts, its ports handling a greater container tonnage than those of the United Kingdom. Saudi telephone services had reached developed-world standards in the 1990s, and by 2006 the average per capita utilization of international phone calls, at 216 minutes per person per year, was higher than the 204-minute average for high-income countries and more than six times the average MENA utilization rate. Its expenditures on information and communication technologies were $308 per capita in 2006, just behind the average for upper-middle-income countries of $339. Saudi ground transportation is dominated by the automobile, with almost one vehicle for every two persons, a figure only slightly less than in high-income countries and almost three times that for upper-middle-income ones. Energy consumption soared between 1990 and 2005, going from some 371 million metric tons of oil equivalent to 577, compared to 75 and 100, 186 and 134, and 886 and 1641 for Japan, Germany and China, respectively. Only China expanded its energy production over this period faster than Saudi Arabia, but its production on a per capita basis remained a fraction of Saudi Arabia's. In a fashion reminiscent of the East Asian tigers, Saudi Arabia had provided the bases for export-led growth in which the private sector could play the leading role. But this begged the question as to whether the royal-family regime would grant any aspiring capitalist class sufficient latitude and whether they in turn could be weaned off the rents that the state had distributed over three decades to weld together political and administrative systems.

The evidence reveals an absolute increase of private-sector activity and private capital accumulation during the third oil boom, but also suggests the continued predominance of government in the economy and that the new capitalists do not play a role equivalent to that in fully developed market systems, in East Asia, or even in some other MENA countries, such as Turkey and Israel. In Saudi Arabia the percentage of domestic credit to the private sector of GDP reached some 50 percent by 2006, up from less than 10 percent in the early 1970s, although still well behind averages of almost 100 percent of GDP in East Asia. What one Western bank refers to as "robust growth of the non-oil private sector" is reflected in the comparison between growth of the real GDP and that of the non-oil sector, with the latter growing more rapidly than overall GDP every year except one since 2001. In 2006, for example, when real GDP grew by 3 percent, the non-oil private sector's contribution to GDP grew by 6 percent (Sfakianakis et al. 2009: 2) The surge of the Saudi stock market after 2000 also reflects rapid private capital accumulation. In nine years it rose from 29 to 135 percent of GDP, while the value of shares traded as a percent of GDP skyrocketed from 8 to 186 percent. But the limits of capitalist growth are also suggested by the fact that the number of listed companies, rising from 75 in 2000, was still only 127 in 2008 (Table 3.3), compared for example to 1,771 companies listed on the Serbian exchange in 2007. However, although the Saudi companies lost half their value in 2008, they were still worth $246 billion, which was twenty times the capital accumulated by the Serbs and, as Table 3.4

indicates, the largest accumulation of equity capital in the MENA and slightly ahead of comparator Mexico. Giacomo Luciani, in his systematic investigation of capital accumulation and the relationship between it and an emerging bourgeoisie, finds that there are several thousand Saudi families whose net worth exceeds $100 million and that the "bourgeoisie as a class may now be estimated at well over 500,000, or 3–4 percent of the population at the very least" (Luciani 2005: 165). The very fact that some of the names of businesspersons in GCC countries have become known throughout the region and even around the world, such as Prince al Walid bin Talal, Khalid bin Mahfouz, Abd al Rahman al Zamil and, among women, Lubna Ulayan in Saudi Arabia and Lubna al Qassimi in the UAE, or even that of the bin Laden family, whose patriarch was a successful Saudi contractor who got his start in the 1930s, is indicative of this business elite's growing economic importance. The process of decoupling this elite from the state was further hastened by accession to the WTO, which Saudi Arabia completed in 2005, for among other things that required the termination of agency agreements as a prerequisite for foreign companies to do business within the respective country. The termination of these rents, a major source of income to both royals and commoners, created an incentive for more entrepreneurial behavior, an incentive that appears to have had a positive impact (Hertog 2006).

Yet, the umbilical cord that once tied most GCC capitalists tightly to the state has not been completely severed, as suggested by the names of ruling families amid the leading businesspersons in all of the countries, as well as names of long-established merchant families, such as the al Gosaibi, whose wealth has been accumulated largely as a result of close relationships with ruling dynasties. Nor has the state moved completely aside to make way for the private sector, as indicated not only by its domination of upstream hydrocarbon extraction and processing, which is of course standard in emerging markets, but by its heavy involvement downstream as well, as evidenced by Saudi Arabia's SABIC, which remains 70 percent government owned. Private investment as a share of GDP remained basically unchanged at around 10 percent between 1995 and 2006, a level below that of other GCC states and even less than that in Algeria, Egypt, or Tunisia (World Bank 2009a: 53).

In effect the development strategy offers a foreign exchange base that enables a Saudi capitalist class to engage in import substitution industrialization without the constraints that had doomed Nasser's public-sector experiment in the 1960s. The presence of a nascent capitalist class also offers Saudi Arabia some capacity to implement the general strategy that emerged during the third oil boom. This strategy is on the one hand to develop downstream petroleum and related industries, from refineries in China to petrochemical complexes in the ten big Saudi industrial cities that are in various stages of development. The other prong of the strategy is to encourage Saudi capitalists to invest in local enterprises depending especially on the ten geographic poles of development. The grand global export strategy that accumulates the foreign exchange is of course highly capital intensive and therefore does not meet the other Saudi need for employment of its burgeoning youth. These needs may be met by import substitution that is more labor intensive, coupled with services ranging from banking and insurance to tourism. Saudi Arabia's ambitious educational and social programs are also a means of generating more employment for the private sector, as long as requirements for hiring Saudis do not dry up private investment. The protectionism that is usually associated with import substitution may be alleviated by joint ventures with foreign manufacturers, attracted by the country's business-friendly environment despite various restrictions on foreign staffing. But, as is discussed in Appendix A, the Saudi hydrocarbon value-added development strategy also confronts several economic obstacles.

Governance challenges

Four political challenges are associated with forging a developmental state out of a rentier monarchy while simultaneously implementing an export-led growth strategy unique in its dependence on vertical integration of hydrocarbon extraction and processing industries. First, despite receiving relatively favorable evaluations from the World Bank on "government effectiveness" and creating business environments seen as being reasonably conducive, governance remains deficient outside such islands of efficiency as Saudi Aramco, SABIC, and SAMA. Public administration is not yet up to the task of guiding and regulating a relatively complex and demanding development strategy. Governmental bureaucracies are segmented, with parallel structures dominated by different members of the royal family (Hertog 2010; Al-Rasheed, 2008 and 2009). Devoted to serving the purpose of maintaining royal family cohesion by providing administrative fiefdoms and their associated spoils to constituent elements and to the purpose of absorbing the otherwise unemployed, the task of upgrading public bureaucracies would necessarily involve reconfiguring power relationships within ruling families and between ruling families and their subjects, not just upgrading the skills of bureaucrats. King Abdullah seemed to signal his awareness of the need to centralize authority over the country's bureaucracy in February 2009, when he instigated a wide-ranging reshuffle of key ministries, replacing a host of conservatives with liberals apparently loyal to himself. But if the octogenarian king's intent was to harness the state's administration to his will, overcome its internal divisions, and then utilize it to implement a reform agenda, his age and apparent ill health did not augur well for those prospects. The steadily expanding size of the Saudi and other GCC ruling families, combined with increasing needs and demands for improved governance, suggests that centralizing reforms of the sort implied by King Abdullah's 2009 reshuffle are vital to both political stability and governance, but also that the challenges of overcoming internal divisions within ruling families and the administrative appendages extending from them are possibly too great to overcome.

A second challenge of any aspiring "developmental monarchy" is that of mediating between sociopolitical forces. This task becomes steadily more challenging in Saudi Arabia as political competition intensifies between Sunni and Shi`a, Islamists and secularists, rich and much less rich, inhabitants of different regions, royals and nonroyals, and citizens and expatriates. Permitting more open, structured political competition between sociopolitical forces would be the most effective way of integrating them and achieving appropriate balances. Always cautious, the Saudis have watched other GCC rulers experiment with political liberalizations that included drafting constitutions and establishing or upgrading representative bodies (Khalaf and Luciani 2008 Ehteshami and Wright 2008; Kapiszewski 2005). But as the third oil boom gathered momentum, allocation appeared once again to displace reforms that would enhance participation. Qatar and Bahrain reduced the pace of promised legislative empowerment, while Saudi Arabia's Consultative Council, although enlarged, remained an appointed body. Elections to Saudi municipal councils, pioneered for half of the members of some of them in 2005, were in 2009 postponed until 2011. Kuwait's recent experiences, of greatest interest as an experimental laboratory in partial democracy, surely did not inspire further reform efforts in Saudi Arabia. The ruling Sabah family simply reappointed as prime minister in 2009 Sheikh Nasser al Sabah, a nephew of the Emir whose behavior in that position had been a cause of conflict between parliament and the ruling family that had caused it to be suspended and new elections to be held. Parliamentary democracy in Kuwait seemed to lead to paralysis, not development. In fact, Michael Herb (2009), comparing Kuwait with the United Arab Emirates, where electoral participation is almost as restricted as in Saudi Arabia, shows how the Kuwaiti parliament played on resource nationalism and desires for instant gratification to limit any developmental efforts. Nowhere in the GCC are political parties legal.

Despite the flagging pace of political reform, some close observers remain confident that Saudi Arabia, cautiously following the other GCC states, is on a trajectory that ultimately will result in quasiconstitutional monarchy in which sociopolitical forces would openly compete over the making of "low policy," while royals would continue to make "high policy" in the key areas of internal and external security, foreign affairs more generally, and the overall strategic direction of economic development, especially for the vital hydrocarbon sector (Luciani, 2007b). One mechanism by which this modus vivendi would be achieved is by the withdrawal of royals from all but the most vital of cabinet portfolios, thereby opening up low-policy domains to contestation. Evidence for such change at high political levels is not strong, but at the underlying level of civil society there is evidence to suggest somewhat greater incorporation of interests, a precondition for their representation in policy-making institutions (Hertog 2005b). Newly created professional syndicates and business associations have in some cases become active and have also provided forums within which women contest office.

So although it is possible to envision a gradual transition to constitutionalism that legitimates monarchy while circumscribing its authority as it broadens and institutionalizes competition over at least matters of low public policy, this benign outcome is by no means guaranteed, either in Saudi Arabia or elsewhere in the GCC. Economic pressure is simulating demands, revealing royal transgressions, and reducing available patronage, thereby creating a dynamic that could lead to compromises on which a new constitutionalism would be built, or to stronger repression, or conceivably even to system breakdown. The expanding size of ruling families creates growing potential for intra-elite conflict, as internal feuding within the ruling al Sabah family of Kuwait attests. Such conflict could serve either to impede historic compromises resulting in constitutionalism, as it seems to have done in Kuwait where the al Sabah have dug in against parliament, or to facilitate them. Whatever the outcomes, the present capacities of GCC governments to ameliorate conflicts by mediating between social forces are almost exclusively informal and based on allocation, and hence probably not sufficiently sophisticated to cope with the political side effects their ever more globalizing development strategies will generate. If indeed that is the case and fundamental political uncertainty spreads, capital flight from the GCC countries, among the most liquid of emerging economies, would accelerate, thereby rendering implementation of the capital-intensive development plan yet more problematical.

A further political challenge is the most basic one of survival. As noted earlier, the GCC was founded in 1981, while Iran and Iraq were at war, to provide security. In effect the treaty enables Saudi Arabia to take any appropriate measures to protect its neighbors against security threats, whether arising locally, from Iraq, Iran, or Yemen, or from further afield. The subregion's energy reserves are a potentially fatal attraction, as actors including Egypt's Nasser, Iraq's Saddam, Iran's ayatollahs, and Saudi Arabia's very own Usama bin Laden have sought to bring them under their control. Since the end of the British "moment" in the Gulf, the United States and, to a much lesser extent, Britain and now France have, at the invitation of GCC rulers, provided the overall security umbrella. For rendering their protection, these three powers have been rewarded through the purchase of their weapons systems, as reflected by the fact noted in Chapter 2 that four of the six GCC countries rank in the world's top fifteen spenders on the military by population size ("Arming Up," 2009). Although effective in deterring external state-led challenges to Gulf security, the very presence of Western and especially U.S. forces has stimulated terrorism, however, and requires careful management by ruling elites. Caught between their own country's inability to defend itself against security threats, and the political cost of having outside protectors, ruling families have chosen various ways to resolve the dilemma. The Saudis were able to outsource their embarrassing American presence to Qatar, where there were relatively vast spaces – the peninsula being about the size of Connecticut – with a very small public of potential critics. As part of its counterbalancing "branding efforts" (Sakr 2001) Qatar burnished its Arab nationalist credentials by hosting Al-Jazeera, the satellite television broadcaster enjoying some 50 percent of the market across the entire Arab region for its forthright discussions of public affairs, excluding only those of its indigenous 180,000 Qataris. But continued military weakness and dependence on the West undermines the legitimacy of ruling families, as was manifested most clearly in Kuwait in reaction to the al Sabah taking flight in the face of the 1990 Iraqi invasion. Creating an indigenous military capacity appropriate to the threat level, however, exceeds both the demographic and organizational capacities of the GCC states. So, the security dilemma will persist and intensify, adding to the political challenges that GCC rulers have to confront.

A final political challenge affecting Saudi Arabia as much as the surrounding microstates of the GCC is that of forging a national identity sufficiently coherent to support the development strategy, while reducing conflicts arising from it. Tahsin Bashir, one of President Sadat's diplomatic advisors, may have been too dismissive in describing the GCC countries in the early 1970s, when Qatar, Bahrain, and the UAE achieved independence, as "tribes with flags" (Glass 1990), but his expression does point to both the origins of these states in the tribal domains of their ruling families and continuing problems of "branding" their national identities, as distinct from tribal, religious, or local ones. Recognizing the need for nationhood, all GCC rulers have expended impressive amounts to engender and display it (Alsharekh and Springborg, 2008). The Sultan of Oman, being the sole GCC ruler without a solid family and tribal base and faced with a more numerous and ethnically and religiously heterogeneous population than the other GCC microstates, has been the most assiduous in seeking to build an identity that simultaneously glorifies the Sultan himself (Valeri 2009). But identity conflicts persist in Oman and elsewhere in the GCC, including in Saudi Arabia, where regional and sectarian loyalties, separating Hijazis from Najdis and Sunnis from Shi'a, remain strong and divisive. In Dubai, the most globalized of the GCC city-states, manifestations of conflicts between cultural preferences and practices of citizens, on the one hand, and expatriates on the other, are most pronounced, as jailings of British tourists for cavorting on local beaches or kissing in public indicate. But all GCC states face the task of reconciling contradictions between globalized aspirations and local manifestations of that globalism on the one hand, and indigenous cultures on the other. The potential for anti-globalist backlash is growing (Davidson 2008 and 2009). Although a common GCC identity analogous to that of an emerging EU one shows some signs of appearing, presumably it is at least a generation away, like its European counterpart. In sum, GCC national identities are stronger than the "tribes with flags" caricature suggests, in part because ruling elites have spared no effort to cultivate them. But these identities continue to have a new, manufactured, artificial, and fragile feel to them, again suggesting that they will be put to the test as globalizing development proceeds.

More governance challenges: transparency and accountability

Although GCC leaders were in good company in their failure to foresee the severity of the 2008–9 economic crisis, they were singular in their persistent denial that it was affecting their countries when evidence to the contrary began to mount. Dubai, the most highly leveraged economy in the Gulf, with its $75 to $90 billion of public debt (the range of estimates by published and informed sources) exceeding 100 percent of its GDP, was the most vehement in its denials. Amidst rumors of falling real estate prices in late 2008, the government stated they had dropped by less than 10 percent, a vast underestimate as subsequent events revealed (Woertz 2009). The second most important indicator of economic activity in that city-state – the movement in and out of expatriates – was also caught up in rumor and denial. With reports of expatriates fleeing the Emirate, even abandoning their cars at the airport, the government announced that 1,000 new expatriate employees were arriving daily. Dramatically falling rents and rising vacancy rates suggested otherwise. Early in 2009 the leading Swiss Bank, UBS, released a forecast that Dubai's population of 1.5 to 1.7 million would decline 8 percent by the end of the year.

That reality could no longer be ignored was signaled in February 2009, when Dubai's rulers had to request their wealthier neighboring emirate, Abu Dhabi, to purchase $10 billion worth of bonds. Three months later the government announced that fully half that amount had been given to Nakheel, the leading real estate company within the Dubai World holding company that the *Financial Times* discreetly characterized as "government linked" (Kerr 2009c: 17). That Nakheel was a black hole in Dubai's economy and balance sheet did not augur well for the company's or the Emirate's immediate financial future, for Nakheel had a *sakk*, (singular of *sukuk*, or Islamic bonds) of $3.5 billion maturing in December and had plenty of competition from other failing Dubai companies for further financial infusions from the government. Emaar, for example, another real estate giant in which the government holds 30 percent of the shares and which is led by Muhammad al Abbar, a "close confidant" of ruler Sheikh Muhammad bin Rashid al Maktum, saw its shares collapse by 80 percent from 2008 to mid-2009, prompting it to suspend its dividend for that year amidst howls of protest at its annual general meeting (Kerr 2009a: 7). That the deepening crisis was causing conflicts within Dubai's ruling circles over the degree of transparency to be permitted was made clear by the abrupt removal in May 2009 of Nasser al Shaikh as director general of the department of finance. A highly regarded young technocrat, he had been charged by Shaikh Muhammad with steering Dubai through the perilous times and had tried to pursue a course of increasing transparency, overseeing publication of the Emirate's first truly detailed budget in January 2009 and pushing for a sovereign rating for the country's government debt (Kerr, 2009b:7). Possibly these and other manifestations of demands for transparency in Dubai and elsewhere in the GCC, especially Kuwait, were the cause of the Emir of Qatar transferring authority over the Qatar Investment Authority (QIA) in 2009 from the Ministry of Economy to a newly created higher council, over which he and other members of the al Thani family preside. Had he not done so, the management of the QIA could in future have been subjected to questioning by the legislature, whose power the Emir previously committed to expand.

The lack of transparency reflects limitations on political participation. Dubai is possibly the most extreme example of the general GCC model, in which citizens have limited political rights, but extensive material entitlements. The term "Dubai Incorporated" used in reference to that city-state suggests overlap, indeed, merger, between state and market. The ruling al Maktoum perceive no contradiction in their roles as prime movers in both business and government, and hence no need to clearly delineate between their personal assets and those of the state. In this conception citizens are analogous to employees, in that they receive wages, but do not determine who their bosses are or how the company (country) is run. The majority of the population is excluded both from effective political participation and from the productive labor force, which is composed overwhelmingly of expatriates. The economic strategy of value-added hydrocarbon processing, combined with financial coupon clipping and globalized services, is inherently capital and skill intensive, thereby ensuring low labor participation rates by nationals into the indefinite future. Even in Dubai, however, the lack of transparency and accountability, reflecting constraints on participation, is an increasingly politically sensitive issue. As the Great Recession's effects washed through the Gulf in 2009, leaving exposed numerous leading businesses and the prominent, frequently royal families associated with them, so did demands for transparency and accountability increase. The unusual sight of boisterous shareholder meetings, with attendees demanding facts and figures and even the resignations of management, was witnessed from Dubai to Kuwait. Demands for economic and political accountability are particularly closely linked in the GCC context precisely because of the lack of clear separation between the private purses of ruling families and their governments.

The financial tumult that began in 2008 also revealed deficiencies in the globally oriented governance structures that GCC countries had erected during the boom. Such institutions as the Dubai International Financial Center (DIFC), with its in-house court, simply could not cope with the rush of litigation and, more importantly, with the interface between expatriates and multinational corporations, on the one hand, and local citizens and businesses, on the other. Potential litigants found that their cases, frequently involving claims for unfulfilled contractual obligations in the real estate sector, fell under the jurisdiction of local courts, which had neither the capacities nor impartiality effectively to adjudicate. The thin layer of international institutional respectability erected during the boom was punctured by its first major test. In November 2009, Omar bin Sulaiman, the DIFC's high-profile American-educated governor, was summarily dismissed, his replacement being the Emir's confidant, Ahmad al Tayir. Within days, the director of the Dubai Finance Department announced a "standstill" on repayment of debt by Dubai's flagship holding company, Dubai World, which sent shockwaves throughout the GCC and beyond, as reflected by sudden, dramatic drops in equity markets in the Gulf and elsewhere. Holders of the $3.5 billion Islamic bond issued by Nakheel, the high-flying property company within Dubai World, were confronted with the unpleasant reality of the government of Dubai disclaiming any responsibility for Nakheel's debt, the assets of which are primarily in Dubai, apparently beyond the reach of bondholders, in part because the Emirate's courts are essentially controlled by the ruler himself.

GCC wealth generated by hydrocarbon exports is held in several forms along a public-private continuum, the categories of which shade into one another. At the pure governmental end, central banks and sovereign wealth funds (SWFs) are the main repositories, with the balance of holdings between the two typically determined by the overall size of reserves in proportion to budgets and population size. In Saudi Arabia, for example, the Saudi Arabia Monetary Authority (SAMA), which serves as the country's central bank, holds the vast bulk of public reserves, with the country's relatively small SWF only being created in the spring of 2008. As is typically the case for central banks as opposed to SWFs, SAMA has invested conservatively, largely in government debt and especially that of the United States, with some 80 percent of its holdings in dollar-denominated assets (Setser and Ziembar, 2009: 10). SWFs, by contrast, especially those in Kuwait, Qatar, and Abu Dhabi, are intended to serve as more aggressive, risk-taking investment vehicles to add further to the wealth of these diminutive entities with huge hydrocarbon revenues. The world's fifty-three SWFs in 2007 held assets of some $3.8 trillion, of which as much as 40 percent was ascribed to those in the GCC. Taken together, the assets of GCC central banks and SWFs at the peak of the boom in 2008 reached at least $1.5 trillion. Whereas central bank holdings and especially those of SAMA were not profoundly affected by the Great Recession, assets of GCC SWFs fell by about one third (Setser and Ziembar, 2009: 11; Behrendt, 2008: 5).

Prior to the onset of the Great Recession, the wealthiest of the GCC states had begun to proliferate their SWFs, in part to specialize and to spread risk, but also because of competition among members of ruling families for control of assets. The cloning of ADIA, the oldest of the GCC SWFs, headed by Shaikh Khalifa bin Zayid al Nahyan, the ruler of Abu Dhabi and President of the UAE, illustrates the process more generally. In 1984 the government established the International Petroleum Investment Company (IPIC). Shaikh Mansour bin Zayid al Nahyan, brother of the crown prince and one of the six sons of UAE founding President Shaikh Zayid by his favorite wife Fatima, was awarded control of this $17 billion investment fund in 1994 when he was twenty-four years of age. His fame spread when IPIC purchased Manchester City football club, followed in late 2008 by its acquisition of shares worth 3.5 billion pounds sterling in the beleaguered Barclays Bank, a portion of which was sold seven months later for a profit of some $2.5 billion. It was not revealed whether the investment was made on behalf of the government of Abu Dhabi or Shaikh Mansour (England and Kerr, 2009: 7). Shaikh Mansour also sits on the board of ADIA and is head of the Abu Dhabi Department of Justice. In 2002 the powerful Shaikh Muhammad bin Zayid, the crown prince, established Mubadala, a SWF with some $15 billion in assets, a significant portion of which is in a joint venture with the U.S. multinational GE. At the height of the boom in 2007 the ruler himself, Shaikh Khalifa bin Zayid al Nahyan, already the head of ADIA, set up under his control the Abu Dhabi Investment Council, which had under management two years later some $100 billion. Several other, smaller SWFs, managed by clients of key members of the ruling family, including Taqa, the Advanced Technology Investment Company and the Abu Dhabi Investment Company, were also established during the 2002–8 boom (Behrendt 2008).

The complexity of ownership and control of Abu Dhabi's SWFs and the investment companies that are virtually indistinguishable from them is similarly illustrated in Dubai, where Dubai International Capital (DIC), established in 2004 with $13 billion in capital, is in turn owned by Dubai Holding, which is in turn owned by the ruler of Dubai, Sheikh Muhammad bin Rashid al Maktum. Istithmar World, established a year before DIC, is Dubai's principal SWF, but governmental ownership is exercised "only through a layer of several holdings" (Behrendt 2008: 11). The Qatar Investment Authority is headed by Shaikh Hamid bin Jassim al Thani, who also serves as Prime Minister and Foreign Minister. Like Shaikh Mansour of Dubai, Shaikh Hamid purchased Barclay's Bank shares in late 2008, and hence was in a position to reap a profit in excess of $1.5 billion a few months later. Whether that profit would be credited to his or the Qatari government's account was impossible to determine, as was the case with his Dubai equivalent. In Kuwait, the Kuwait Investment Organization (KIO) was created alongside the long-established Kuwait Investment Authority (KIA), with the only clear difference between the two seeming to be that the new SWF was managed entirely by Kuwaiti nationals, unusual for GCC SWFs. Possibly this move reflects the fact that the Kuwaiti parliament has been much the most vigorous legislative body in the GCC in pushing for greater transparency and oversight of the nation's SWFs.

The blurring of the distinction between the private purse of rulers and the public purse of their governments, as evidenced by SWFs, also characterizes many leading GCC companies. The prominent Dubai-based holding companies, Dubai World, Investment Corporation of Dubai, and

Dubai Holding, are conglomerates whose assets are held in an opaque mix of ownership by the government, leading members of the ruling family, and private investors. At the private end of the public-private continuum of GCC ownership of assets, especially foreign ones, are individuals, who consist of a mix of members of royal families and commoners, the precise ratio varying from country to country, with royals being most prominent in the UAE, Qatar, and Saudi Arabia. Saudi Prince al Walid bin Talal, for example, whose Kingdom Holdings is a key investment and takeover vehicle, is one of the world's richest men. However, by family background as well as economic behavior, this Saudi prince may be more accurately categorized as member of an emerging entrepreneurial bourgeoisie than a coupon-clipping royal parasite. Son of a "red prince," known in his day for Saudi radicalism associated with Abdullah Tariki and oil resource nationalism, and raised in Lebanon where the prince had married into a local family dynasty, Prince Walid graduated from Menlo College in California and Syracuse University before getting into the investment business.

Financial pressure resulting from the Great Recession revealed some examples of the complexity of business ownership in the GCC, where 90 percent of enterprises are family owned. In May 2009, for example, the International Banking Corporation of Bahrain, wholly owned by Ahmad Hamad Algosaibi and Brothers Company, one of the leading business families in the country, defaulted on its debt. A group "that could borrow on its reputation alone," with a family member on the Forbes world rich list, had clearly overextended thanks to easy credit from Saudi banks, which had lent it more than $2.5 billion (England and Allam 2009b: 8). Less than a month later SAMA suddenly announced it had frozen the assets of Maan al Sania and his family. Al Sania, who was listed by Forbes in 2008 as having a personal net worth of $7 billion and whose Saad Group was a major conglomerate in Saudi Arabia with assets of some $30 billion in 2009 and which at one stage owned 3 percent of HSBC, is linked to the al Gosaibi through the marriage of Maan al Sania to a sister of the founder of the Algossaibi and Brothers Company. Although both the al Gosaibi and Maan al Sania denied any linkages between their various companies, there was much "market speculation" about such relationships (England and Allam 2009a: 13).

Almost simultaneously, in Abu Dhabi, the ruling al Nahyan family was embarrassed by the apparent collapse of Hydra, a major real estate firm run by Shaikh Suliman al Fahim, the flamboyant thirty-two-year-old owner of the Portsmouth English football club and a protégé of another of Shaikh Zayid's thirteen sons, Shaikh Tahnun al Nahyan. Precisely because of the lack of transparency the rumor mills in both countries began to churn out explanations of the demise of these high flyers. In the case of Maan al Sania, one story was that the son of former King Fahd and governor of the Eastern Province, Prince Muhammad bin Fahd, like other members of the Saudi ruling family, resented the rise of commoners and used his authority to derail al Sania, who, a former fighter pilot from relatively humble origins, had miscalculated by thinking that his connection to the al Gosaibi would provide protection from Prince Muhammad and other Saudi royals. Whatever the truth in this and other cases of business collapse in the GCC, the reality is that a triumvirate of actors, including governments, royals, and members of leading merchant/ business families, typically own conglomerates in some mix, with royals playing the key role as they have direct access to governmental resources.

GCC royals and commoners – an emerging, interconnected Islamic bourgeoisie?

Closer examination of the interconnections of wealthy families in the GCC states reveals it may be not a "Saudi" or "Kuwaiti" bourgeoisie so much as an Arabian Gulf one that is increasingly accumulating capital and projecting an Islamic identity. From their rise to international prominence out of the oil shocks of the 1970s, many of these families enjoyed more than one GCC affiliation (Field 1986). Many "royal" (ruling) family members as well as other merchant families enjoy business connections across state lines. As these princes and merchants move into the businesses of expanding private sectors, they appear to be taking an increasing Islamic shape, with interesting political implications. As Rodney Wilson observes, "what is starting to emanate from the GCC states is a new form of Islamic capitalism" (Wilson 2009b: 3).

The contours of a new Islamic bourgeoisie are being shaped by Islamic finance, which has a particularly curious history in Saudi Arabia. SAMA always avoided any official mention in its encyclopedic annual reports of Islamic banks, despite the existence in Jeddah of the Islamic Development Bank, a consortium development bank established by the Conference of Islamic States in 1974, and the subsequent emergence of two major privately owned transnational groups of Islamic banks established by two Saudi citizens, Prince Muhammad al-Faisal and Sheikh Salah Kamel, the latter a self-made businessman. The first privately owned self-styled "Islamic bank" opened for business in Dubai in 1974, but SAMA did not permit one to be established in Saudi Arabia, perhaps because the consensus within the ruling family and their allied religious regulators and legitimators, the Sheikh family, was that no bank could be deemed un-Islamic in this most Islamic of monarchies – similar to the reasoning that prevailed in Morocco. But like the Banque al Maghrib, SAMA had to compromise with financial and political realities. First, in 1988 SAMA gave a normal banking license to a large money-changing agency that was too big to be permitted to fail when the bankruptcy of a sister agency had led to the abolition of these unregulated nonbank entities. The new bank, Al Rajhi, promptly declared itself to be Islamic, hence opposed to granting interest to its depositors in any form, even as "commissions," the transparent artifice employed by the kingdom's conventional banks. The new bank flourished, being more profitable with its cost-free funds than the competitors. In the following decade, however, as Islamic finance expanded in Kuwait, Bahrain, and then the Emirates and Qatar, demand grew among those several hundred thousand wealthy Saudis counted by Luciani (as noted earlier) to emulate their practices.

Pressures from other commercial banks, as well as the legal concerns of religious scholars and worries in the family about the Kingdom's legitimacy, probably also explained the paradox of discouraging Islamic financial institutions in an avowedly Islamic state. Certainly more Islamic banking would cut into the markets and profits of prominent families with stakes in interest-based banking. Other Islamic banks might also take deposits away from Al-Rajhi by offering depositors a share of their profits. Conventional banks also benefited from the cost-free funds of depositors who refuse to take interest. Possibly the interests that would be most adversely affected were those of Prince Walid bin Talal, who had propelled a major Saudi bank merger and had a substantial interest in the Saudi American Bank (SAMBA). He instead seems to have successfully met the rising demand for Islamic financing by partially converting this dynamic bank to Islamic practices while still keeping it under a technical management agreement with Citigroup, which has also developed shari'ah-compliant operations.

SAMBA actively developed Islamic finance windows in efforts to capture Saudi deposits without going through the pain of converting to a full-fledged Islamic bank, restricted in its action by a religious advisory council. It coopted a shari'ah board, however, to legitimate the activities of its Islamic windows and branches. As evidenced by its annual reports, around 13 percent of the bank's total assets and a third of its lending took Islamic forms in 2008. Other major Saudi banks reveal similar patterns. National Commerce Bank, Saudi Arabia's largest and oldest bank, had been mismanaged until SAMA restructured and privatized it. The new management claims to be converting it into an Islamic bank;

annual reports intimated some 44 percent of its deposits were shari'ah compliant in 2006 and 2007, but the financial statements were couched in the general format required by SAMA that translated any Islamic instruments into conventional ones, the term "commission" always substituting for "interest." SAMA's website presents no official definitions of Islamic finance's distinctive instruments, such as *murabaha* (sale with fixed markup) or *ijara* (leasing). These are left to the deliberations of the shari'ah board that a bank's management is free to coopt to legitimate its practices in the eyes of the public. Because Islamic finance essentially mimics conventional finance, bankers can convert any Islamic statements into conventional ones. SAMA also sponsors seminars advocating shari'ah-compliant practices without officially recognizing "Islamic banks" as such lest they delegitimate other financial institutions. Opinion among Muslims committed to "Islamizing" contemporary political economies is in fact divided. Tariq Ramadan, for instance, argues that Islamic finance has delayed social and economic transformation by integrating Muslims into a global financial order that violates Islamic principles (Ramadan 2000: 174), and one veteran Muslim banker has labeled Islamic finance a charade (Saleem 2006).

"Offshore" in Bahrain (attached to Saudi Arabia by a causeway since 1986), however, official Islamic banking is publicly promoted. Just as the island's Monetary Agency once encouraged Bahrain to become an important international hub for offshore banking, it subsequently projected it to be the headquarters of Islamic Finance. The Accounting and Auditing Organization for Islamic Financial Institutions (AAOIFI) was established in Bahrain in 1991 to establish generally accepted accounting standards, and the Bahrain Monetary Agency introduced the first Islamic T-bill, a nontradable set of certificates, *sukuk al-salam*, in 2000. The following year Bahrain pioneered a way of bundling Islamically acceptable leases into the first tradable Islamic debt security, *sukuk al-ijara*. These sukuk were a major boost in meeting the global needs of international Islamic finance, thereby positioning the new industry to benefit from the third oil boom. Local Islamic banks, some of which were affiliated with the major Islamic transnational groups, also flourished. By 1999 at least sixteen Islamic banks and other financial institutions had operating licenses in Bahrain (*MEED* August 20, 1999: 4). The oldest, the Bahrain Islamic Bank, had served the local market for three decades and was joined in the mid-1980s by Masraf Faisal al-Islami, established as the regional headquarters for the Faisal group but renamed the Shamil Bank of Bahrain E.C. (Islamic Bankers) in 2000, and by Albaraka Islamic Investment Bank, representing Islamic finance's other major transnational. Recent

Table 6.1 *GCC Sharia compliant assets as per cent of commercial bank assets, 2005–2008*

	2005	2006	2007	2008
Bahrain	8.6%	10.1%	11.5%	
Kuwait	22.6%	23.7%	24.4%	
Qatar	14.5%	14.9%	13.2%	
including conventional banks				30.0%
Saudi Arabia	14.0%	14.1%	13.7%	
including conventional banks				38.4%
United Arab Emirates	14.4%	16.3%	16.1%	

Sources: Kuwait Institute of Banking Studies, GCC Banks: Financial Report 2005–2007
http://www.kibs.edu.kw/publications/for/GCCBanks/toc.htm
Top 500 Islamic Financial Institutions, The Banker, Nov. 2009
Qatar National Bank, *Annual Report* 2008

arrivals include investment banks and Islamic subsidiaries of large conventional banks. The Bahrain Monetary Agency introduced Al-Salam (Islamic) bonds to serve as treasury bills, backed by commodities such as oil or aluminum, to help Islamic banks resolve their chronic liquidity problems (*MEED* February 9, 2001: 9). Through such initiatives and other private ones, Islamic finance was acquiring the necessary scale to be able to compete more effectively with conventional banks in the region. Table 6.1 offers some indication of the progress of Islamic finance among five of the six GCC countries. Saudi Arabia clearly leads the way when the Islamic windows of its conventional banks are taken into account, although other major banks not included in *The Banker*'s November 2009 Supplement on Islamic financial institutions may also have Islamic windows, like those at Egypt's Bank Misr, that are not recorded.

Confined to Islamic banks and comparing their share of assets with those of other GCC commercial banks, Table 6.1 offers only a partial picture of a phenomenon that has taken off in the first decade of the twenty-first century. According to *The Banker* (2009), shari'ah-compliant assets, over 80 percent of which are based in the MENA and more than 40 percent concentrated in the GCC countries, have been increasing at annual rates of close to 30 percent from 2006 to 2009 (albeit in current, depreciating dollars); in the GCC countries these assets grew by 34.5 percent in the year of 2008–9, as the world entered the Great Recession, and the Islamic bond market was reviving despite the embarrassment in 2009 surrounding Dubai's $3.5 billion sukuk of Nakheel. On the day before Thanksgiving and the Muslim Eid Al-Adha, investors believing in implicit government guarantees as a result of Abu Dhabi banks releasing $5 billion to Dubai's Economic Support Fund lost more than

30 percent of their investment in the space of two hours when Dubai World then announced its six-month moratorium on debt repayments (Woertz 2009: 5).

Shari'ah-compliant financial assets nevertheless exceeded the $822 billion counted by *The Banker* in 2009, and the Great Recession, far from impeding its growth, enhanced its standing in the world of global finance. Medieval and often inconsistent rules regulating and constraining its growth did after all present a viable alternative to the excesses of deregulated conventional finance that had almost destroyed the global economy. As Ibrahim Warde explains, "at a time when conventional finance was unable to be self-critical or resist the lure of easy profits, Shariah Boards, by scrutinizing every innovation on the basis of criteria other than profitability, provided badly needed checks and balances – always the best way of reining in excesses" (2010: 249–50).

More significant for the development of an Islamic bourgeoisie may be the public support Islamic banking and finance receives, notably in Kuwait (Smith 2004). Technically, the Kuwait Finance House (KFH) is not a bank at all; until 2003 it was regulated by the commerce ministry, not the Central Bank of Kuwait. However, it is in fact among the largest and oldest of Islamic commercial banks in the region, second only to Saudi Arabia's Al-Rajhi in total assets, and it performs retail as well as other functions, serving notably as the repository for the salaries of employees of various government agencies. It is Kuwait's third largest bank in total deposits, and it enjoys strong political support among Islamists. In 2003 the Central Bank of Kuwait was finally able to integrate KFH into Kuwait's commercial banking system. A new law, under discussion since 1998, definitively broke the KFH monopoly over Islamic finance, which had enjoyed the support of Islamist members of parliament (*MEED* March 5, 1999: 10), by enabling other banks to open subsidiaries engaging in Islamic financial services. As a result, by 2007 there were three Islamic banks attracting over 20 percent of Kuwait's deposits and financing 30 percent of the system's advances to clients. Supplementing the commercial banking system, some 48 "shari'ah-compliant" investment companies slightly outnumbered conventional ones by July 2008, although their total assets of 7.9 billion Kuwaiti dinars ($29.7 billion) were still only 43 percent of the total. No longer is it true, as in the previous edition of this book, that Islamic finance, like its conventional equivalents, is principally a vehicle for investing private fortunes abroad in "Islamic" mutual funds, although Dow Jones maintains an Islamic index (excluding firms dealing with pork or alcohol or being excessively leveraged by interest-based debt) as a benchmark for Islamic investors. Substantial proportions of the sums being mobilized by Islamic finance are being reinvested in the region. In Kuwait, the Islamic investment companies were reported in July 2008 to have exported only 24 percent of their assets, compared to their conventional counterparts, which had parked 43 percent of theirs abroad (*Thaindian News* 2008).

Additional economic reforms are still needed, however, if much of the private wealth of GCC nationals held abroad, estimated at not less than $2 trillion, is to be repatriated. Islamic banks are in fact in greater need than conventional banks of such reform if they are to invest in the region. They are currently at a disadvantage because they are not permitted to invest their funds in many ways open to conventional commercial banks, although they may enjoy a competitive edge in their ability to attract deposits. At present the bulk of Islamic financing takes the form of leasing, installment sales, or simple deferred payment sales. Expansion of Islam's distinctive equity-like financing presupposes more transparency, accountability, and regulatory authority than any Middle Eastern business environment yet promises. As two leading authorities on Islamic banking explain, "If, in addition to risks of the investment projects, the investor has to be concerned with the credibility of government policies, or arbitrary government decisions or distortions that threaten long-term price stability in the economy, he/she would be reluctant to invest in contracts that do not provide fixed nominal payoffs" (Iqbal and Mirakhor 1999: 402). In other words, in unreformed business environments, investors may prefer interest-bearing bonds or notes over any Islamic profit-sharing instrument, despite the advent of sukuk pioneered by the Bahrain Central Bank. These were growing at annual rates of 25 to 35 percent until 2008, when, before the major global crisis erupted, a meeting of Islamic jurists in Bahrain convened by AAOIFI ruled that over half of the extant sukuk were not shari'ah compliant.

Islamic finance, accompanied, especially in Saudi Arabia, by an active stock market, is already implementing many of the guidelines of the Washington Consensus and notably the Tenth Commandment – property rights guaranteed by accountable institutions and transparent practices. Although the enforcement of contracts lags, the Kingdom has made progress in cultivating the "business friendly" environment that may specially benefit shari'ah-compliant financiers. Saudi Arabia presents a style of capitalism that already resembles the Anglo-American variety in important respects. An articulate Islamist business community reflected in leading Islamic banks could further promote a more competitive and transparent economy. Offshore, too, gaining strength in Kuwait, Bahrain, Qatar, and the United Arab Emirates, Islamic financial institutions also continue to attract Saudi capital.

Saudi Arabia, however, faces a major dilemma. Saudi Arabia needs rapid economic growth to mop up unemployment, but continued reform may have political costs. A larger and more competitive private sector could sweep away the Najdi bureaucratic and merchant support on which the regime has relied since the 1970s, without generating any new sources of support. Were the big Saudi public sector to be further privatized in ways that transferred real control from the bureaucrats to new core managers, the likeliest victors would be princes such as Walid al-Talal, perhaps in association with foreign investors, whose entry is facilitated by new legislation. The royals would dominate the stock market and the commercial banking system, but without the same implications for political control as in Morocco. Economic liberalization could exacerbate competition within the royal family while dissipating any lingering myth of a tacit division of political and economic labor between the royals and other merchant families. The division of labor has gradually unraveled, amid much talk of corruption (Aburish 1995) since the early 1980s. Full-scale economic liberalization might further upset any tacit understandings and possibly consolidate the holdings of royal-family factions in the stock market. Dissension in the family could also provoke more intense Islamist opposition. The hope is that Islamic finance, which carries wealth and prestige for a new coalition of learned scholars who serve on the religious committees appointed by the banks, might serve as a counterweight to more conservative scholars who try to dominate the kingdom's religious establishment and oppose reform. Alliances between the Islamic capitalists, their religious advisors, and progressive members of the royal family conceivably could then offer stability as a new generation comes to power, but instilling an Islamic work ethic in support of capitalism would be a major further challenge (see Appendix A).

Jordan and Kuwait: bellwether monarchies?

Most of the monarchies permit a greater degree of political and economic competition than do the praetorian republics. Their long-term prospects may depend, however, on an ability to absorb Islamist opposition movements into their political mainstreams. They survived the colonial dialectic, which overturned the most powerful of the region's monarchies, in part because they were so peripheral to the Arab world, where the rising tides of nationalism were centered in Cairo and the Levant. Globalization, however, is less escapable, and it incites moralizing oppositions to reform. Countries having never experienced a revolutionary third moment may be more vulnerable to new forms of political radicalism than countries where old ruling classes were displaced. But monarchies are not necessarily fated to be overthrown. They may be better able than praetorian republics to develop institutions within which to absorb political oppositions. Praetorian republics, by contrast, currently display tendencies to destroy institutions and keep dictatorship in the family, like the Asads of Syria.

The process of absorbing Islamist oppositions has proceeded further in Jordan and Kuwait than in Morocco or Saudi Arabia. The two smaller countries display a wide spectrum of Islamists with varying degrees of loyalty to their respective monarchies. Jordan was already very exposed to nationalist and Islamist backlashes by virtue of its treaty with Israel in 1994. King Hussein stepped ahead of Yasser Arafat and Hafez al-Asad in the peace process and then found himself isolated. He still carefully nurtured domestic support and survived a variety of economic and political crises. His response to the bread riots of 1989 had been to open the country up to more democracy. Initial successes were due in part to the close ties established with the Muslim Brotherhood, which Hussein had used in the 1950s and 1960s as a counterweight to Gamal Abdel Nasser. Elections in 1989 brought it substantial representation in the Jordanian parliament, and some Islamists were even admitted into the government. The government rearranged the electoral law in 1993, however, so as to reduce their representation (by increasing tribal representation at the expense of more organized urban constituencies). In response to more IMF reforms and bread riots in 1996, the government cracked down on the demonstrators rather than further liberalize the regime. King Hussein visibly backed his prime minister and the IMF reforms (Ryan 1998: 58). Subsequent elections in 1997 appeared so rigged, in fact, that the National Islamic Front officially called for a boycott, although in the end a reduced number of Islamists were elected anyway. In February 1999, King Abdullah inherited a deliberalizing monarchy (Wiktorowicz 1999).

Advised by his military friends, he continued to crack down on potential centers of opposition. Not only were the leaders of Hamas expelled, but the security forces also conducted a widespread dragnet – perhaps for American consumption (Andoni 2000: 87) – for Islamist terrorists reputed to be followers of Usama Bin Laden. Despite this atmosphere of intimidation, however, some dialogue with the Muslim Brotherhood continues. Its political arm, the Islamic Action Front (IAF), boycotted the 1997 elections but was persuaded to participate in the 2003 elections, as it did in 1993 despite changes in the electoral law discriminating against its urban constituents (Lukas 2005: 78–9), and again in 2007, when the IAF suffered a major defeat, losing 11 of its 17 seats in the popularly elected House of (104) Representatives. Islamists connected with business and financial circles may still provide the young king with some cover as he persists in efforts to globalize Jordan's economy and consolidate the peace process with Israel. The reforms have been enacted, however, without their participation except on the fringes of the banking sector. In Jordan's far from transparent atmosphere, the old families of the traditional power structure seem more likely to benefit from the reforms than do new entrepreneurs, whether Islamist or not.

Jordan and Kuwait, in addition to their guarded inclusions of Islamists, have also tried to move on the economic front, pursuing market reforms while tolerating opposition in their respective parliaments. Their very size, of course, differentiates them from the larger monarchies. They are more heavily dependent on outside powers, for aid as well as trade. Kuwait, for instance, is so much in need of the protection of the international community that its government tried to invite all of the permanent members of the Security Council, including China, to take positions in the development of its petroleum resources. The Saudis, by contrast, reject any foreign upstream investment and refused in 1999 even to renew a Japanese offshore concession, just when Kuwait was positively soliciting foreign involvement upstream. The Kuwaiti government was determined for strategic reasons to include an American company in the development of its northern oil fields bordering Iraq, but its parliamentary democracy has blocked the project for more than a decade. During the war between Iran and Iraq (1980–8), Kuwait had persuaded both the Soviets and the Americans (catalyzed by Soviet competition) to reflag its oil tanker fleet.

Jordan, sandwiched between Syria, Iraq, and Israel, is almost as vulnerable as Kuwait but enjoys strategic rents based on geographic location. Being dependent on economic assistance and international loans, it needs to stay in the good graces of the international financial community. Like many small countries, it has been quicker than bigger ones to adapt to international circumstances. It has undertaken reforms to globalize its economy more easily than bigger countries have, because its domestic opposition has been as aware as the government of the country's inherent vulnerability. Perceptions of external threats may dull the moralizing zeal of opponents of economic reform, rendering comparisons with bigger states problematic. In Jordan, the principal obstacles to reform came more from within the regime than from its Islamist opposition. The experiences of both Jordan and Kuwait suggest that economic reform may run in parallel with political reform that partially opens the door to Islamist oppositions. Islamists have offered these globalizing monarchies useful political cover. They have been involved as official parties in politics for many years, with leaders even serving as ministers and cabinet members in both Jordan and Kuwait and sharing in some of the patronage. It may also not be coincidental that Jordan, like Kuwait, has been in the forefront of Arab states hosting Islamic banking.

Even before Kuwait, Jordan integrated Islamic banks into a single system under the control of the Central Bank of Jordan. The Jordan Islamic Bank for Finance and Investment, partly owned by the Dallah Al-Baraka Holding Company, attracts around 8 percent of the deposits of Jordan's private sector. To capture some of this market and expand it, the Arab Bank established a separate Arab International Islamic Bank in 1998. Founded in Palestine in 1930, the Arab Bank is the most respected and one of the largest of banks in the Arab world, and its new venture was testimony to the rising tide of Islamic banking in Kuwait, Bahrain, and Qatar. Unlike among the Kuwaiti Islamists (Ghabra 1997: 60), Jordan's Islamic banks keep their distance from Islamist politicians, but Jordan seems, like Kuwait, to offer sufficient political and economic space for coalitions to develop (Malley 2004). Like Morocco and Kuwait, its conventional commercial banking system is relatively concentrated. Its spreads between deposit and lending rates, however, were low, suggesting, as in Kuwait, a reasonably competitive market place (Figure 3.6).

Jordan's relatively well capitalized local stock market, however, has much less turnover than Kuwait's. The somnolent market in Amman reflects the economic activities of royalty and family retainers brought to Amman by Emir Abdullah, the great-grandfather of King Abdullah II, in the 1920s. Many of the listed companies are run, in effect, by the government. The royal family and leading political families of ministers and higher civil servants have buttressed their political power with economic holdings in land, commerce, and industry (Piro 1998: 81–3, 96–7). In Kuwait the Sabah family is also engaged in commerce, and some of its leading members lost millions in the crash of Kuwait's informal Souk al-Manakh in 1982. Indeed, it took the central bank until 1993 finally to clear the rickety Kuwaiti banking structure of bad debts because some of the princes were so recalcitrant to any settlement that might diminish their fortunes. Again in 2010 parliament passed a law requiring the government to buy up some $21.6 billion of private citizens' debt, but the government refused to obey (APF 2010). Competition in Kuwait seems more open and freewheeling than in Jordan, and big declines in 1998 and in 2006 only slightly dampened its hyperactive stock market. Kuwait is among the first, along with Egypt, Israel, and Turkey, to have opened up its stock exchange to foreign investors.

Jordan has moved ahead with economic reform, but it illustrates, better than wealthier and less populated Kuwait, some of the dilemmas that the other bigger monarchies will face. Inheriting a stagnant economy in the summer of 1999 in which one-third of the population was estimated to live below the poverty line (*MEED* June 9, 2000: 21), King Abdullah concentrated almost exclusively on economic reform during the first years of his reign. He appointed Abdel Raouf Rawabdeh, a hard-line member of Jordan's ruling club, as prime minister, but also, perhaps taking a leaf out of the book of his royal namesake in Saudi Arabia (see earlier discussion), he established a Higher National Economic Consultative Council under his personal chairmanship and including private-sector figures alongside ministers. Jordan entered the WTO before Saudi Arabia, and the new king followed up a U.S. Agency for International Development report on the promising job and export earnings potential of the private sector by meeting with world business leaders at the World Economic Forum in Davos, Switzerland, in February 2000. Subsequently he invited Bill Gates and others to develop Jordan's information technology sector. He has vigorously marketed Qualifying Industrial Zones (which qualify goods partly made in Israel and Jordan to enter the United States duty- and quota-free) to potential foreign investors while pushing further packages of reforms on privatization, landlord-tenant relations, and taxation. Evidently his priority was to improve Jordan's anemic economic growth rates by finding new sources of capital to supplement the dwindling supplies of Palestinian capital repatriated from Kuwait that kept Jordan going until the mid-1990s. However, he antagonized some of Jordan's most ardent globalizers by governing with a traditional unreformed power structure, needed to keep nationalist and Islamist opposition to the reforms at bay. Prime Minister Rawabdeh did not hesitate to expel the Jordanian Palestinian leadership of Hamas to Qatar in January 2000, and there have been many subsequent crackdowns on the press. Academic institutions were not spared. Mustafa Hamarneh, an outspoken Georgetown University PhD, lost the directorship of Jordan University's Center for Strategic Studies for organizing and reporting on polls indicating declines in the government's popularity (Andoni 2000: 86). The irony is evident: not crackdowns but greater transparency lies at the heart of any effective reform program, especially one stressing information technology as part of the solution to Jordan's economic needs.

Conclusion

Like the praetorian republics, the monarchies, too, need to open their economies and confront the challenges of globalization, yet they may be more vulnerable than the praetorians to backlashes by radical nationalist or Islamist oppositions because they never experienced the full play of the colonial dialectic. Kuwait has progressed furthest in defending itself from backlashes by admitting political Islamists into ruling coalitions and deriving some legitimacy from them for their reforms. But the reforms have been more limited and gradual than poorer monarchies such as Jordan, Morocco, and even wealthy Saudi Arabia ultimately require. Jordan's young king pushed ahead with reforms without the Islamists. Were he to seek more political cover, however, to be insulated from his military coalition and to give himself greater autonomy as an indispensable arbitrator, he might have to turn again, like his father in 1989, to the Muslim Brotherhood. In Amman and elsewhere, coalitions between the Islamic financiers and Islamist political oppositions could be useful safety valves for incumbent regimes. They offer kings and governments greater strategic depth and margins for maneuver. Not only can Islamic finance moderate Islamist political oppositions, by giving them stakes in the economic system, but it can also legitimate government efforts to reform their respective economies. In Kuwait, Islamists joined other deputies in parliament to adopt government laws for regulating the stock market to make its operations more transparent and to encourage foreign investment. Islamic finance has the potential to transform the ostrich-like second moment, comprising those rejecting globalization, into an Islamization of the Washington Consensus. The political cost to the monarchies, however, may be new Islamic institutions that render their political economies more transparent and their governments more accountable than the old generation of monarchs could ever have accepted.

The monarchies, like praetorian republics, still tend to be information averse. The exceptions are Kuwait, Bahrain, and even tinier Qatar, whose relatively progressive ruler, Hamad bin Khalifa al-Thani, enabled a controversial satellite TV station, Al-Jazeera, to broadcast throughout the Arab world, as mentioned earlier. Little Qatar stood firm despite the decision of three information-averse praetorians, Tunisia, Libya, and Iraq, to withdraw their ambassadors in May 2000. The new generation of monarchs may be readier to accept greater transparency and accountability, although both King Mohammed VI of Morocco and King Abdullah II of Jordan deferred to their military hardliners and cracked down periodically on the press during the first decade of their respective reigns.

Suggestions for further reading

Hammoudi (1997), Sater (2010) – and Howe (2005) from a more journalistic perspective – update the picture of the Moroccan monarchy depicted by Waterbury (1970) that is still worth reading. On Saudi Arabia, see the excellent collections of essays collected by Aarts and Nonneman

(2005), along with Aburish (1995), Chaudhry (1997), Hertog (2010) Lacey (2009), Lippman (2009b), Niblock (2007), Vitalis (2007), and a special issue of the Middle East Institute (2009) presenting a variety of perspectives. Gause (1994; 2010) deals with the other GCC monarchies, as do Crystal (1990), Davidson (2008; 2009), Herb (1999), and Kostiner (2000). Piro (1998) discusses Jordan's political economy, and Lucas (2005) analyzes some of the political strategies behind it. Henry and Wilson (2004) present some possible political implications of Islamic finance in various MENA countries, and Wilson's essay available online (2009a) offers a timely and authoritative update of Islamic banking in the GCC countries, while Warde (2010) offers an excellent introductory text on the general subject; for the fine points, see El-Gamal (2006).

APPENDIX A: Economic challenges to the hydrocarbon value-added development strategy

The Saudi drive for global petrochemical markets, complemented by those of its smaller neighbors, is based on the comparative advantage of hydrocarbon reserves, accumulated capital, and strategic location astride three continents. Its most important component is generating value added from hydrocarbons by moving steadily downstream from extraction into refining, shipping, wholesaling and retailing, and increasingly, into processes utilizing comparatively inexpensive oil and gas to produce petrochemicals and related feedstocks for downstream industries such as plastics, paints, rubber, chemicals, and pharmaceuticals, as well to support energy-intensive manufacturing processes, such as metals, fertilizer, and cement. Qatar and Kuwait have led the move downstream into external marketing, the former with regard to liquefied natural gas and the latter with refined oil, entering directly into European markets by virtue of having constructed the required infrastructure of processing plants, shipping facilities, and outlets. Saudi Arabia, while acquiring shares of refineries and other downstream operations in large export markets such as the United States and China, has also led the GCC downstream move into hydrocarbon processing and energy-intensive industries. SABIC has become the world's largest petrochemical company. By 2006 Saudi Arabia produced 10 percent of the world's petrochemicals, with its global share of ethylene, the standard measure of petrochemical capacity, scheduled to reach one-fifth between 2010 and 2015 (Alsheikh 2007; Luciani 2007a). Saudi Arabia, followed by Abu Dhabi and Qatar, went on a spending spree during the third great oil boom, purchasing petrochemical companies in Europe, the United States, and elsewhere, while entering business relationships with multinational companies for the local production and processing of petrochemicals. In the final two years of the great oil boom, GCC countries invested some $125 billion in their petrochemical industries, of which Saudi expenditures accounted for more than 60 percent. In the final year of the third great oil boom, GCC counties had energy-intensive industrial projects underway worth some $115 billion, significant portions of which were being constructed in new industrial cities, such as the Industrial City of Abu Dhabi and Dubai Industrial City as well as in the ten Saudi industrial cities. The GCC's comparative advantage in manufacturing processes dependent on oil and gas and the speed with which it intensified its capacities reverberated globally, with European, North American and even Asian competitors realizing that in the face of such competition, their futures were bleak. Many sought to sell their facilities to GCC interests, or to invest in capacity in the GCC. The WTO agreement reached by Saudi Arabia and agreed in 2005 did not limit its access to world petrochemical markets, so the anticipated speed with which its market share would expand was accelerated (Sfakianakis 2006). The vital, hydrocarbon-based component of the GCC development strategy, in other words, if judged by expanding world market shares and the behavior of competitors, was a success.

There are, however, challenges to the long-term economic viability of a development strategy based heavily on the vertical integration of oil and gas industries. They result from the wasting nature of the resource; the price volatility of hydrocarbons and their derivative products; the correlation between energy prices and world economic cycles; and the capital-intensive nature of extraction and processing.

Reserve-to-production ratios for both oil and gas in the MENA are extremely favorable by world standards. As a result, life expectancies of proven MENA reserves at current rates of production in 2008 were 76 years for oil and 188 years for gas at current rates of production (Aissaoui 2008). Despite this apparent abundance, the GCC in fact faces energy shortfalls. Its share of the world oil market has stagnated over the past three decades as local consumption has grown at the world's fastest rate, eating up an ever larger share of production, which itself has not been substantially increased. Failure to invest adequately in production and distribution facilities, other than in Qatar, has resulted in chronic gas shortages, such that by 2015 it is anticipated that annual demand will exceed supply in the GCC by 7,000 billion cubic feet. At present the UAE, which holds some 3.4 percent of the world's gas reserves, imports 2 billion cubic feet a day from Qatar and, in the summer months, imports coal from Australia to generate electricity. Bahrain was in talks in 2009 to import gas from Iran, despite the fact that its GCC neighbors hold more than one-fifth of the world's total reserves. Whereas most OECD countries now generate the bulk of their electricity from gas, Kuwait, having failed to develop its gas reserves, burns comparatively expensive and environmentally unsound oil to produce power. The UAE is considering construction of nuclear power plants as it anticipates that even with full development of known volumes of natural gas by 2020, electricity demand of 40,000 MW will outstrip supply, which will be only about half that (England 2009:3). Given construction already underway or planned of petrochemical plants that depend on gas feedstocks, especially in Saudi Arabia, it is apparent that gas shortages will become yet more chronic in the years ahead.

Although some of the failure to gear up oil and gas production to meet demand can be explained by the calculation to keep reserves in the ground where their value may appreciate faster than petrodollars – a preference sometimes reinforced by nationalist-inspired demands, such as in Kuwait – or by failures to project and prepare for rapid increases in demand, especially of gas, there are underlying structural factors that call into question the economic rationale for ever-expanding exploitation of GCC energy reserves. First is the challenge of calculating returns on investments, especially when those costs are high and price volatility of energy is so great. The magnitude of the financial stakes involved is suggested by the fact that expenditures on energy development in the MENA were anticipated to total $180 billion for the period 2004–8, but then to escalate to $395 billion in 2007–11. The increase was due much more to rising costs than to a greater number of projects (APICORP 2006). Of this latter amount, $345 billion was required for the Arab world alone, much the largest share of that being in the GCC countries, with Saudi Arabia and Qatar accounting for almost half the total amount. Yet investments even of this magnitude do not guarantee returns, even when prices are at the top of cycles. Saudi Arabia, for example, completed in 2008 a five-year program to expand its oil production capacity from 10 million barrels per day (b/d) to 12.5 million b/d, at a cost of $70 billion. At that time it had 4.5 million b/d of idle capacity, suggesting negative net return on that substantial investment. And this occurred during a period of intense demand for hydrocarbons, a demand that declined precipitously in 2009 and that, in the eyes of some, will decline in the future as a result of alternative energy sources and new technologies, whose development will be driven both by competitive cost and by environmental concerns. In the meantime, energy price cycles and those of the increasingly globalized economy have, since the 1970s, become virtually identical, thereby accentuating cyclical impacts on countries heavily reliant on energy exports and earnings from petrodollars. The classic problem for mono-crop economies, price volatility, is if anything magnified for GCC countries, where direct oil and gas industries alone typically account for some 35 to 40 percent of GDP (APICORP 2008). Their petrodollar investments, which provided at least some counter-cyclical balance when they were placed conservatively, have become more subject to cyclical effects as sovereign wealth funds and GCC private investors have increasingly favored riskier, more volatile assets. As the GCC invests steadily more in downstream hydrocarbon processing, so, too, does that segment of the economy become captive to oil price volatility, for petrochemical prices are highly correlated with those for gas and oil.

The problems of high costs and volatile prices are illustrated in the refining and petrochemical industries. Although GCC countries enjoy comparative advantage because of cheap oil and gas, this does not necessarily ensure that their products are competitive. The cost of construction and operation of facilities tends to be higher there than elsewhere. As a result, a considerable amount of older, less expensive plant in North America and Europe remains competitive. During the bust that followed the third boom, the decline in demand for petrochemicals resulted in idle capacity in recently constructed GCC plants. A similar problem confronted Qatar's LNG industry in 2009, with declining demand for gas and falling prices rendering its comparatively expensive product less competitive than gas delivered through pipelines.

A second challenge is that of competing uses for oil and gas. Governments derive proportionately the greatest revenue benefits from their export. Indeed, as much as 90 percent of government revenue in the key GCC producing countries is derived from hydrocarbon exports. In the absence of those revenues, they would need to extract more resources from their populations, thereby likely simulating greater demands for accountability. So ruling families have political incentives to maintain exports while retaining domestic energy subsidies, the latter of which are consuming an ever-greater share of production as populations increase, per capita energy demand rises, and production fails to keep pace. Governments derive the least direct benefits from value-added hydrocarbon industries, for the private sector is more prevalent downstream, where it collects rents generated from the difference in local as opposed to international oil and gas prices. Although the private actors who are able to capture those rents typically are crony capitalists, many of them members of ruling families, the capacity to service these three competing markets is declining, especially in Saudi Arabia with its large and rapidly expanding population. So governments are caught up in ever more difficult balancing acts as they seek to mobilize capital to increase production without allowing the providers of that capital to capture control or disproportionate rewards, or to create political backlashes. They also have to balance off immediate governmental needs for revenues and broad political support against longer term, downstream development.

A third economic challenge resulting from the hydrocarbon value-added strategy is that of employment. The capital-intensive upstream and downstream hydrocarbon industries do not create enough jobs for rapidly expanding GCC populations, nor do they create the types of jobs that most citizens have the skills to fill. In Saudi Arabia, for example, the oil industry generates almost 40 percent of GDP, but provides less than 3 percent of employment. This ratio may be even less favorable for yet more capital-intensive downstream hydrocarbon processing enterprises. And as GCC energy economies move downstream into ever more sophisticated processing, the educational and training requirements for employment become steadily more demanding. So, whereas the traditional upstream oil industries in the GCC have absorbed relatively large numbers of citizens, the newer, more technologically complex petrochemical industries remain heavily dependent on foreign engineers and technicians. GCC educational institutions have not excelled at preparing students for careers in these hydrocarbon industries. The incentive structure for youths in the GCC, which favors governmental or non-technical employment in the private sector, has not been brought into alignment with the hydrocarbon-based development strategy. The East Asian tigers articulated their educational systems to their newly emerging manufacturing industries, thereby generating employment and reducing the need for expatriate labor. By contrast, the GCC states have developed neither appropriate educational systems nor incentive structures to underpin their industrializing hydrocarbon sectors, as reflected by their failure to reduce the percentage of expatriates in their labor forces since the first oil boom.

Thus, GCC labor forces have too few citizens and too many expatriates, with problems arising from both conditions. GCC labor force participation rates are among the lowest in the world, with Saudi Arabia, for example, having an employment-to-population ratio (the proportion of working-age population that is employed) of less than 34 percent, compared to a world average of over 61 percent and a MENA average of some 46 percent (APICORP 2008). That almost two-thirds of working-age Saudis are not gainfully employed, despite the fact that the government, which employs 900,000 nationals out of a total national population of some 19 million, acts as a labor sponge, suggests how vital (and expensive) the elaborate system of subsidies and entitlements is, what a drag it imposes on the economy, and how low is its probability of being substantially reduced.

In sum, the GCC's hydrocarbon value-added development strategy is not guaranteed a successful outcome, not only because of governance challenges faced by these countries, but because of economic factors inherent in their application of the strategy.

7 Precarious democracies

The MENA is the world's least democratized region, so it is not surprising that even its democracies have substantial flaws. Indeed, it is only by adopting an undemanding definition of democracy, which is change of government through free and fair elections, that one can even speak of democracies in the region. If one were to add slightly more restrictive criteria, such as provision of political rights and civil liberties to all citizens, to say nothing of yet more stringent ones such as a political culture supportive of democratic norms and processes, then the region could be deemed to be entirely without established democracies. Israel, the only country in the region that has consistently managed to change its government through free and fair elections, denies equal rights to its Arab citizens and any rights whatsoever to those living under its occupation in the West Bank and its imposed isolation of Gaza. Turkey's military removed elected governments in 1960, 1971, 1980, and 1997. Since 2002, it has intermittently sought to undermine the authority of the moderate Islamist AKP (Justice and Development Party) government elected in that year and reelected by a historic margin five years later. In Lebanon, which essentially lost its sovereignty to Syria in the late 1970s and did not regain it until 2005, sectarian divisions that have always cleaved the country have increasingly taken geographic form, so that the country has been "ethnically cleansed" into virtual self-governing cantons, which are themselves not democratic. But most deficient of all is Iran, which made it into the democratic category for our previous edition by virtue of President Muhammad Khatami's election in 1997. Alas, that election ultimately did not truly change the government, for Supreme Leader Ayatollah Ali Khamenei, backed by elements of the clerical establishment and the Islamic Revolutionary Guard Corps, first curtailed the exercise of President Khatami's power and then, in 2005 and again in 2009, ensured that their fellow hardliner, Mahmud Ahmadinejad, won the presidential election, in the later case with a preposterous margin. So Iran has slid down to the status of being a bully (Islamic) republic, thereby suggesting the fragility of MENA democracies more generally.

Kuwait, the most liberal of the GCC monarchies, does hold free and fair elections, but their outcomes determine not who governs, but who sits in a parliament that has tried but thus far failed to truly circumscribe monarchial rule.

The heterogeneity of MENA democracies conceals a shared element in their political traditions. Israel is a Jewish settler state in which political institutions were imported from Europe. Turkey is the rump portion of the once expansive Ottoman Empire, its political institutions also based on European models having been erected under the tutelage of Mustafa Kemal (Atatürk) and the military. Lebanon, once a small fragment of that Empire, also owes the inspiration for its political institutions to European and especially French, at least quasi-"orientalist" views of how Levantines could best be made to live together under one political roof. And Iran, along with Egypt and China one of the world's few modern states based on an ancient empire, is currently ruled under a constitution modeled on its 1906 forerunner, which is in turn beholden to a continental European prototype. Thus in all of these cases, nationalist elites consolidated power within political frameworks influenced by Western democratic experience, but not directly shaped by European colonialists, if in the case of Israel one can distinguish between Zionist settlers and European powers. But this lineage alone cannot account for these countries' contemporary claims to democratic status, for other states in the region are also inheritors in greater or lesser measure of European constitutional traditions, with the bully republics of Egypt and Tunisia having the longest such legacies.

But, although also propping up the bullies, contemporary Western and especially U.S. support for Israel, Turkey, and Lebanon may indeed be germane. All three have been long-standing, primary beneficiaries of public foreign assistance, with Israel capturing a greater per capita share than any other nation on earth. Israel's path to structural adjustment in the 1980s and 1990s was paved in large part by additional U.S. financial support. With U.S. urging, the IMF has repeatedly bailed Turkey out of economic distress, the last such agreement ending in 2007 amid reports of negotiations being underway for follow on assistance. And like Israel, Turkey's path to stabilization and then structural adjustment was also paved by outside support, in this case, more the IMF than the United States directly. The Lebanese, also perennial Western favorites for foreign assistance, were rescued from economic disaster due to civil war and borrowing beyond their means, and from the effects of the Israeli invasion in 2006, in the international conferences of donors of 1989, 2002, and 2007, dubbed as Paris I, II and III, respectively. By contrast, the U.S.-led and UN-endorsed embargo of Iran has steadily tightened.

That public foreign assistance provided to the three MENA democracies by the United States or by international financial institutions influenced by it has been driven in significant measure by political rather than economic calculations is suggested by their relative wealth. The GDPs per capita of Israel, Turkey, and Lebanon in purchasing power parity were in 2006 some $24,000, $8,400, and $9,700, respectively. This comparative wealth gave them the best of both worlds, placing them above the $6,000 threshold that Adam Przeworski sees as being essential to sustain democracy (Przeworski et al. 2006), while not depriving them of external assistance, presumably having less to do with their democratic status than their influence or attractiveness to Washington for geostrategic reasons. A further element in sustaining democracy in Israel and Turkey is that they have been under the American security umbrella continuously since the onset of the Cold War. Lebanon, whose democracy is weaker, has had more intermittent Western protection, suggesting that democracy may benefit substantially from durable, external security guarantees in the rough-and-tumble MENA.

But although security guarantees may provide the confidence and stability necessary for democratic and even national survival, it cannot be claimed that MENA democracies have experienced less internal and cross-border violence or fewer security guarantees than their nondemocratic neighbors. After its creation during a state of war in 1948, Israel fought major wars with Arab states in 1956, 1967, and 1973 and since the 1970s has been in a state of protracted, frequently violent conflict with Lebanon, as it has been with Palestinians in the Occupied Territories since 1967, the latter violence frequently spilling over into Israel itself. Turkey, less affected by violent conflict than either Israel or Lebanon, has nevertheless been battling a Kurdish insurrection for three decades, a battle that has since 2007 intermittently lapped over into Kurdish areas in northern Iraq. Turkey maintains the largest standing army in NATO. Lebanon was invaded and occupied by Israel in 1982 and then, following the withdrawal of 2000, was re-invaded in 2006. It was convulsed by civil war for almost fifteen years from 1975 and has confronted domestic political violence intermittently since that time. By comparison, the level of internal and cross-border violence in all of the monarchies and bully republics has been less, whereas that in many of the bunker states, such as Algeria, Yemen, Syria and Iraq, has been of similar magnitude.

Violence has been economically and politically costly for the MENA democracies. It is associated with high, although declining, levels of military expenditures. As a percentage of GDP in 2006 Israel, Turkey, Lebanon and Iran spent on their militaries 8, 4, 3, and 5 percent, respectively, a substantial decline for Israel, because fifteen years previously it had committed 12 percent of its GDP to the military. The average for lower and upper-middle-income countries globally in 2006 was 2 percent and for all MENA countries 3.5 percent, suggesting that the MENA democracies as a whole were outspending their comparators globally and regionally. Central government expenditures on the military also remained substantial, amounting to almost 20 percent of Israel's budget, 10 percent of Turkey's, and 19 percent of Iran's. As noted in Chapter 2, Israel, Turkey, and Iran were among SIPRI's top twenty arms importers in the period 2000–8 (Figure 2.6). Military personnel constituted 7 percent of Israel's labor force in 2006, down from 12 percent in 1990, whereas in Turkey they were 2 percent and in Lebanon 5 percent. In the MENA as a whole they constituted 3.1 percent of labor forces and in lower and upper middle-income countries, less than 1 percent. The MENA democracies, in sum, are devoting more of their resources to the military than their global comparators and even than most MENA states.

Not surprisingly, armed forces are politically influential in the MENA democracies. The Turkish military, through its holding company, OYAK, operates an autonomous economic empire that has helped to underpin its political standing. It has actually brushed aside civilian governments, and although the Turkish military's role has much diminished since the last, "postmodern" coup of 1997, it is not yet fully subordinate to civilian authority. A "deep state" of murky connections and intrigue dating back to the early Cold War era and tying the military and security services together, along with some fellow travelers, is argued by many observers to pose a threat to Turkish democracy (Ünver 2009). This threat appeared to intensify from 2007 when an arms cache allegedly controlled by elements in the deep state was discovered in an Istanbul suburb. Less than a year later the government launched what became known as the "Ergenekon Trial," a series of over 200 hearings held by the spring of 2010 in which evidence implicating the military and intelligence services was adduced. In February 2010 the government intensified pressure on the military, arresting more than fifty high ranking officers, including the former commanders of the navy and air force and the deputy chief of staff, on charges of plotting in so-called "operation sledgehammer" to overthrow the government in 2003. Although most detainees were subsequently released, a new round of arrests was commenced in April just as the government announced a package of proposed constitutional reforms that would subject the military to greater civilian control. The Turkish judiciary, itself a target of the package of constitutional reforms, then split, with senior prosecutors unsympathetic to the government ordering the release of officers for whom other judges had issued arrest warrants. Whether this was the moment of truth or simply another episode in the drawn out struggle between the AK Party government and the military was not clear.

By contrast to the Turkish military, the manifest political power of Israel's military is undeniably on an upward trajectory. The increasing militarization of the seeming endless struggle against the Palestinians is probably the major contributing factor to this trend, which is evidenced among other things by military domination of an all-encompassing security policy that extends into such politically vital areas as settlements in the West Bank. And as in Turkey, there is in Israel a military-industrial complex, although Israel's is more integrated into the civilian economy than is Turkey's. Lebanon's military traditionally has been too weak to be a dominant political actor in its own right, but its commander in chief has occasionally been looked to as a savior of the nation, most recently with the election of Michel Sulaiman as president in 2008. The country's security intelligence services played a vital political role during the long Syrian occupation, and they continue to assert substantial behind-the-scenes influence (Salloukh 2007). In Iran the Islamic Revolutionary Guard Corps, combined with its paramilitary offshoot, the Basij, provided the coercive power that enabled the Supreme Leader and his conservative allies to derail President Khatami's reform efforts and then to impose his successor on an unwilling population. The tentacles of these coercive forces extend into the economy through bonyads, or charity enterprises. By the standards of established democracies, where armed forces are subject to effective civilian oversight and control and do not operate independent business empires, the MENA democracies clearly fall short.

But by the standards of the MENA, where the bulk of the population lives in states run more or less directly by the armed forces, or where, as in most of the monarchies, militaries are virtual extensions of ruling families, the democracies have managed to restrain the exercise of political power by the institutional means of coercion. Civilians do occupy top political positions; military expenditures are subject to some oversight and control; national security policy is a matter for public debate and democratic decision making; and citizens are provided at least limited protection from arbitrary actions by security forces.

In each of the MENA democracies there are countervailing civilian political forces strong enough to contest with and constrain armed forces, and hence to defend constitutionalism and the rule of law. In Israel that role has traditionally been played by well-organized, deeply rooted political parties acting through the Knesset, supported by an independent judiciary. The gradual weakening of mainstream parties, such as Labour and Likud, the fragmentation of the party system generally, and the rise of ultrareligious and ultranationalist movements and their associated parties have, however, steadily although not fatally weakened civilian oversight of the armed forces. Civil-military relations in Turkey are on the opposite trajectory. The traditional Kemalist civilian elite did not have a fundamental objection to the military viewing itself as the guardian of the nation and stood aside as the military intervened in politics. But moderate Islamists, led by the AKP since 2001, having experienced unwanted tutelage from the military, are profoundly suspicious of it. Paradoxically, inspired by the prospect of membership in the European Union, which necessarily implies civilian control of the military, Turkish Islamists have sought with considerable success to subordinate the military since coming to power in 2002. Constitutional reforms introduced in the spring of 2010, bolstered as they were by an apparent purge of the officer corps, could prove to be the turning point in the history of civil-military relations in republican Turkey. Historically, in Lebanon armed forces were controlled by the very weakness of the state, the military included, and the comparative strength of traditional political notables who, as leaders of their respective confessions, could speak on their behalf. The counterbalancing role of these elites has been augmented since the early 1970s by the emergence of new leaders whose power rests on popular mobilization, including the formation of confession-based militias. Although the size and power of the military has expanded in the wake of the Ta'if Agreement that ended the civil war in 1989, the military can only operate effectively with the consensus of leading political forces (Sayigh 2009). So in both Turkey and Lebanon, where constitutionalism, the rule of law, parliaments, and courts are weaker than in Israel, civilian control of the armed forces rests more on political balances of power than on institutional, legal restraints. In Iran, by contrast, virtually all restraints have been swept aside as conservative mullahs have steadily anchored more of their power in the IRGC and the Basij.

Just as autonomous political actors constrain armed forces in the MENA democracies, so do independent economic ones provide capacity for these states to benefit from globalization. But as the divergent histories of these democracies attest, economic outcomes are determined by the interaction between state policy and civil society capacities. In Israel and Turkey, for example, the state was assigned a dominant role in the economy from the time of its foundation, a role associated with import substitution industrialization that ran its course in both countries in the 1970s, as attested by mounting budget and current account deficits, coupled with high inflation. Both countries then underwent stabilization and structural adjustment measures that, combined with export-led growth strategies, began to produce favorable results in the 1980s, although in

Turkey's case a much too rapid opening of its capital accounts, combined with profligate domestic lending, led to a major crisis in 2000–1. In both cases private sectors responded rapidly and effectively to opportunities provided by retreating states and relaxations of restrictions on trade, thereby raising the question of whence this capitalist capacity arose.

In both countries its sources were twofold. First, Israel and Turkey had well-established business families that had kept one foot in the public and another in the private sector during the long era of state capitalism (Nitzan and Bichler 2002; Henry 1996: 106–109). It was a relatively easy matter for them to shift weight from the former to the latter in lock-step with implementation of the Washington Consensus in their respective countries. But the comparative economic success of both countries would not have been so robust had it depended entirely on these long-established economic elites who prevailed over the commanding heights of their economies, especially in finance and manufacturing. In both countries a nascent capitalist subclass based on small and medium enterprises (SMEs) emerged fully once appropriate macroeconomic incentives were in place. In Israel, these entrepreneurs were concentrated in high-tech industries, which in turn depended on the capacities of Israeli universities, its military, its global linkages – especially to the United States – and its established, if then much more primitive, industrial sector. The midwife facilitating the birth of this subclass was venture capital, again made possible by the liberalized economic policy environment and the country's global links.

In Turkey the SME sector, which had long existed in the shadow of the public sector and the major, state-protected or -affiliated private sector, quickly blossomed when provided with export opportunities and capital. The former resulted from the opening up of niche markets and global production chains as world manufacturing moved from concentrated "Fordism" to integrated but decentralized, globalized manufacturing systems. As noted in Chapter 2, Turkey's Intra-Industry Trade Index, although not reaching Israeli levels, was substantially higher than those of the Arab countries or Iran. The "Anatolian Tigers" as Turkey's new entrepreneurs were nicknamed, were able to capitalize on this opportunity because, as was the case in Israel, they fortuitously also had access to a new source of finance, which in Turkey was made available by the emerging and diversified Islamic financial sector that included both small- and medium-scale financial cooperatives as well as larger Islamic banks. In both Israel and Turkey, then, latent entrepreneurial capacities, combined with technical know-how and finance, made it possible for economies to rapidly adjust to global opportunities opened up by macroeconomic policy changes.

The state's role in this process, in addition to "getting the policy right," was to facilitate the growth of the required human and physical infrastructures. This is not to suggest, however, that these states were laissez faire or that implementing the Washington Consensus was their sole policy priority. In both Israel and Turkey, the governments consciously sought to foster key sectors to drive export-led growth. In the latter this went so far as the theoreticians of the AKP and its predecessors looking east rather than west, in the sense that they were more enamored of the success and model of East Asia's developmental states than they were of neoliberal orthodoxy. This preference was based in part on observed comparative performance; in part on the fact that Turkey's moderate Islamists and their primary constituency among small and medium, typically provincial capitalists, were reacting against the pro-Western, secularist dogma of the capitalist elite associated with the governing elite; and in part on the alleged positive role of indigenous culture in the Asian developmental state model. This last factor had particular resonance within the ranks of Islamists, who wanted to demonstrate that their culture and religion were every bit as supportive of economic growth and development as Western cultures and religions. Israel and Turkey, in sum, although Western allies and model students of the Washington Consensus, relied heavily, and in the case of the latter, explicitly, on East Asian style state-guided, export-led development.

But that all MENA democracies are so comparatively nimble is belied by the cases of Lebanon and Iran, even prior to the latter's slide into bully praetorianism. As with Israel and Turkey, both of these countries also had established capitalists. Lebanon's business elite, concentrated in trade and services, was virtually coterminous with its confession-based political leadership, whereas Iran's was bifurcated between traditional bazaaris working in commerce, and the state-associated elite that had grown up under the regimes of the Pahlavi shahs. Although the latter were displaced by the revolutionary regime, the former might have served as the nucleus for capitalist-led development. Instead, however, that regime chose to impose the state it controlled on the economy, thus extending its political control, but undermining the country's capacities for economic growth by subordinating or removing its capitalists and by elevating political over economic calculations.

In Lebanon the overlap of political and economic interest is rather different, but with similar, negative consequences. The political/mercantile elite that dominated the "merchant republic," as Lebanon was referred to prior to the civil war, was content with a laissez faire state that allowed the merchants to wheel and deal and awarded the private sector primary responsibility for developing human infrastructure. Public physical infrastructure served as a source of political patronage and so was geared to petty politics rather than to a development strategy. For its economic success, the model had depended on Lebanon's role as middleman between the West and the MENA, especially the oil states including Iran and Iraq, a role that became increasingly irrelevant as the Gulf developed its own physical and human capacities. The residual of that role is the presence of large numbers of Lebanese expatriates in the GCC countries, whose remittances, along with those repatriated by the global Lebanese diaspora, accounted for about 21 percent of Lebanon's GDP in 2008, higher than Jordan's and one of the highest in the world. Far from providing a motor force for development, remittance income simply reinforces the rentier-style economy that emerged after the civil war, much as if the Gulf has come to Lebanon.

As for Lebanon's dynamic capitalists, the civil war thinned out the ranks of the mercantile elites, but replenished them with militia leaders and others with political backing. Facing shrinking opportunities for business, as the basic model of middleman or entrepôt was no longer appropriate and the country had in any case been largely destroyed by fifteen years of war, established and aspiring capitalists focused their attention on gaining a share of governmental largesse, which was doled out in proportion to political influence. The system was fully entrenched under Prime Minister Hariri, who in the 1990s remade the country in the image of the Saudi Arabia in which he had made his fortune, oil being the only lacking ingredient. But Hariri and his team, most of whom had backgrounds in finance, including his former accountant Fuad Siniora who succeeded him as Prime Minister, created a system that has continued to produce petrodollar equivalents without the petroleum. Based on a spread in interest rates and willingness to accumulate public debt, the system guaranteed Lebanese banks, which hold more than three quarters of the country's domestic debt and are owned by the much decayed capitalist class and various foreign, especially Gulf partners, a guaranteed 8 to 10 percent annual return on their holdings. It was virtually a Ponzi scheme on a national scale. As a result, credit to the private sector evaporated and the public debt has skyrocketed, becoming as a proportion of GDP one of the largest in the world. The system, depending on a stable Lebanese currency, has been sustained by external support in the form of promises and actual deliveries of financial assistance from the Gulf and from the West. In 2006, for example, Lebanon received $174 per capita in foreign assistance, compared to $54 for the MENA as a whole in that year. Although that amount exceeded recent average annual inflows because of the Israeli invasion in that year, Lebanon typically receives three to four times the MENA per capita average, which was in 2006 the world's highest. Lebanon, in sum, has been drawn into the network of Gulf petrodollar economies, which is in turn reinforced by Western strategic interests. But also as in the Gulf, the rentier economy generates comparatively few jobs, so Lebanon, despite pervasive migration including one of the proportionately largest brain drains in the world, suffers from chronic unemployment, poverty, and stagnating incomes, especially for workers, while itself hosting several hundred thousand expatriate laborers from Syria (Chalcraft 2009). This economic system has in turn exacerbated tensions between those with access to rents and those without, thereby reinforcing vertical, patronage-based confessional politics and tensions between the confessions. Largely excluded from this system, roughly half of the country's Shi'a population turned to Hizbollah, which collects its rents primarily from Iran and Syria, combined with some support from wealthy Shi'a who have made their money abroad. Dubbed the "precarious republic" by Michael Hudson (1968) in the 1960s, Lebanon remains thus.

The divergent cases of Israel and Turkey, on the one hand, and Iran and Lebanon, on the other, suggest that competent capitalists do not guarantee national economic success, although they are a precondition for it. Successful capitalism requires an appropriate macroeconomic framework, adequate human and physical resources, access to capital, and engagement with global markets. All four of these requirements have been met in greater or lesser measure in Israel and Turkey, whereas none has been met in Iran and Lebanon. Governments in these two economically failed democracies have created counterproductive macroeconomic systems; have failed to adequately develop infrastructure (including in Iran's case its vital oil and gas production facilities); have deprived entrepreneurs of capital; and have deglobalized. Iran has retreated from the global economy only partly out of choice, but that deglobalization is consonant with and supportive of the survival strategy of its regime. Lebanon's disengagement with the world results from its failure to develop a new, productive model for its economy and its subordination to the Gulf petroleum-based economy. Neither Lebanon nor Iran is a member of the WTO or any significant multilateral or bilateral trading bloc.

But one should not conclude that democracy, even of the distorted and "precarious" MENA variety, has little if any relationship to national economic success. Israel has developed what is in essence an OECD economy, highly engaged with the world and capable of competing with market leaders in several vital and growing industrial subsectors. Turkey, with its 75 million people, has created the world's seventeenth largest economy. Its exports more than tripled to some $116 billion in the decade

ending in 2006, whereas its GDP grew from $150 billion in 1990 to
$402 billion in 2006, surpassing growth rates in the MENA praetorian
states and even in Europe, thereby narrowing the economic gap between
it and its hoped-for European partners. Revolutionary Iran was a very
marginal, flawed democracy even prior to its lapse into praetorianism,
whereas Lebanon's democracy has also always been conditional, further
weakened by external forces meddling in the country. So, within the category of MENA democracies, there is a correlation between the degree
of democracy and economic growth, suggesting that there may be something about democracies, at least in the MENA, that predisposes them
to outperform their authoritarian neighbors.

A key factor is their ability to cope with sociopolitical conflict. As
the existence of free and fair elections resulting in governmental change
suggests, the MENA democracies have managed to institutionalize more
effectively than praetorian republics or monarchies peaceful means for
political competition over incumbency and formulation of public policy.
This is not because social forces in these countries are fundamentally any
less antagonistic than they are elsewhere in the region, including in the
bunker states. The examples of Arabs and Jews in Israel, Christians and
Muslims in Lebanon, Kurds and Turks in Turkey, and multiple minority
ethnic groups in Iran, including Arabs, Kurds, Azeris, and Baluchis,
suggest that the level of primordial hostility may be just as great between
social forces in these democracies as it is in Iraq or Yemen. Indeed, when
political order has broken down in the democracies, the bloodletting has
been of a magnitude that, by this measure, would qualify them as bunker
states. But what differentiates the democracies from the other states is that
at least intermittently they have managed to integrate those social forces
into national political institutions, where they have contested for power
peacefully, if not equally. The democracies, in other words, may appear
at a cursory glance to have weaker states than republics or monarchies,
but in fact are stronger – better able to integrate social forces into the
body politic and give them the experience, at least once, of changing their
rulers through the ballot box.

But political inclusion is not cost free. It creates a problem that is
virtually the mirror image of the fundamental defect of state-society relations in praetorian republics. In those republics, the state is either overly
autonomous from society (i.e., the bully republics), or the prisoner of one
or more social forces within it (i.e., the bunker republics). In the democracies, by contrast, the state has too little autonomy from society to make
optimal economic policies. So whereas in the praetorian republics ruling
elites have to utilize the state to subdue society, and thus cannot grant
sufficient autonomy for effective capitalist development, incumbent elites

in the democracies have to make expensive side payments to constituencies in order to retain their support. Such side payments include benefits of various sorts, as well as purposeful market distortions and privileged access to state structures. As a consequence, imposing the fiscal and monetary discipline necessary for sustained capitalist development is difficult, as the economic histories of Israel and Turkey attested into the 1990s. Although substantial improvements have been made since that time, Israel continues to make extensive side payments to politically vital constituencies, such as the ultraorthodox, and Turkey has since 2007 witnessed substantial backsliding in its public finances, probably reflecting the AKP government's effort to buy political support in the face of various challenges. Whereas political elites in praetorian republics are in a sense enemies of their societies, in the democracies they are prisoners of them, having to bribe social forces to construct and maintain ruling coalitions.

Although the need to build coalitions among social forces is not unusual in national politics, the excessive fragmentation of political communities and a concomitant fracturing of political institutions inflate the costs of coalition formation in the MENA democracies, none of which was able prior to 2002 to host a majoritarian political party, when Turkey's AKP with about a third of the votes won a parliamentary majority, a majority that it then increased in both raw votes and parliamentary seats in the 2007 election. In Israel, Lebanon, and Turkey, the formation of government has traditionally been a laborious process of gluing together minority parties, with the adhesive being side payments to those parties and the social forces they represent. So in Israel, for example, the dominant Labour Party from 1948 to 1977 made a side payment to the National Religious Party to induce it to join the governing coalition dominated by Labour secularists. That payoff took various forms, including the portfolio of education, which in turn provided the means for subsidies to be channeled to religious educational institutions. In the Islamic Republic of Iran, where political parties are illegal, virtually the entire governmental apparatus was, prior to consolidation of power under Supreme Leader Ali Khamenei, an elaborate coalition of competitive factions to whom various sinecures and fiefdoms were parceled out.

All forms of government, including democracy, have both costs and benefits. The primary benefit of democracy in these countries is that it has been comparatively successful in facilitating peaceful resolution of conflicts between competitive social forces. Only in Lebanon has a sustained bloodletting occurred, but that was when the Palestinian-Israeli conflict spilled over and drowned the state. In Turkey, the counterinsurgency campaign against Kurds was run by a military that was not under effective civilian control, a deficiency partially rectified with the AKP's ascent to power, as reflected in a substantial reduction in violence and Kurdish electoral support for the AKP. These partial exceptions, when compared with much more devastating and protracted violence in Algeria, Iraq, Sudan, Syria, and Yemen, for example, suggest what a benefit societal peace truly is. On the other hand, that benefit comes at the cost of being able to maintain optimal macroeconomic policies, including appropriate levels of public expenditure and employment. In Israel, for example, size of government is the only indicator of the ten that comprise the Heritage Foundation's Index of Economic Freedom on which it scores below 50. Its score of 35 in 2009, although slightly better than its 30 in 1995, still is only slightly above half the average of its scores on the other nine indicators and places it among the world's most poorly performing economies. Compensation of employees accounted in 2006 for one-third of central government expenses in Lebanon and a prodigious 40 percent in Iran, as compared to an average in low- and middle-income countries of 26 percent. Overgrown state structures, including large public sectors, are retained precisely because those structures help to alleviate conflicts between competitive social forces. These social forces hinder economic performance by penetrating the state, but the economic damage seems less than that caused by the bunker or bully states that repress or even war against them.

Interaction between economies and polities in the democracies, despite the drag effects of side payments to maintain sociopolitical cohesion, is more mutually beneficial than in most other MENA systems, as reflected by information flow, economic freedom, and relative trust in financial systems. Vital to both political democracy and economic performance, information flow is freer in the democracies than elsewhere in the MENA, as indicated in Figure 3.3. In its 2008 Freedom of Press World Ranking, Freedom House had ranked Israel, Turkey, and Lebanon above all the other MENA countries except Kuwait, which performed just slightly better than Lebanon, but Israel dropped from "free" to "partly free" in 2009.

According to the 2009 Heritage Foundation's Index of Economic Freedom, which is based on ten factors, nine of which (excluding "fiscal freedom") are essentially surrogates for the Washington Consensus and are displayed in Table 7.1, the most economically "free" states are the small GCC states, which marginally outperform the democracies, which in turn on average are slightly freer than the non-GCC monarchies, somewhat more free than the bully republics, and substantially more free than the bunker states. Among these states, Israel stands out as having improved

Table 7.1 *Index of Economic Freedom, MENA countries, 2009*

Name	Overall average	Business freedom	Trade freedom	Government size	Monetary freedom	Investment freedom	Financial freedom	Property rights	Freedom from corruption	Labor freedom
Bahrain	72	79.6	80	79.4	74	60	80	60	50	85.1
Israel	68.7	67.8	86	35.1	83.7	80	70	70	61	64.9
Oman	63.5	63.3	83.6	61.1	71.4	60	60	50	47	75
Jordan	63.4	68.9	78.8	56.9	80.2	50	60	55	47	74.1
Qatar	62	75.7	81.6	69.1	67.3	40	50	50	60	64.7
Kuwait	61.8	67.4	81	63.7	71.7	50	50	50	43	79.3
United Arab Emirates	60.8	57.4	80.8	86.3	69.8	30	50	40	57	76.2
Saudi Arabia	60.4	79.6	81.8	73.4	68.4	40	50	40	34	76.4
Turkey	60.3	69.9	86.6	83.4	71.1	50	50	50	41	40.3
Morocco	56.9	76.2	68	76.5	80.5	60	50	35	35	30.8
Tunisia	55.9	81.6	53	78.3	78.4	30	30	50	42	60
Egypt	54.5	64.7	63.4	66.1	65.9	50	50	40	29	61.3
Lebanon	54.4	60	80.8	64.1	77.3	30	60	30	30	57.4
Algeria	54.4	72.5	68.6	74.1	78.6	50	30	30	30	55.5
Yemen	53.9	74.9	76.2	57.1	66.5	50	30	30	30	75.8
Syria	47.4	61.4	54	74.9	67.2	40	20	30	24	54.8
Iran	40.6	60.6	57.4	79.7	60.1	10	10	10	25	52.4
Libya	39.3	20	90	68.1	70.2	30	20	10	25	20

Source: Heritage Foundation 2009a

its performance most since 1995, with Turkey having only marginally improved its own and Lebanon's having fallen. As regards the most direct measure of globalization, which is trade freedom, Israel, Lebanon, and Turkey score 86, 80, and 86, respectively, essentially European performance levels, which the GCC states also achieve and the other MENA states trail. The data thus suggest that economic freedom can exist without democracy, as attested to by the GCC countries, but that overall there is a correlation between political and economic freedom. It may also be the case that the comparative wealth of the GCC states enables them to provide rents while simultaneously sustaining relatively free economies with favorable business environments. MENA democracies, by contrast, have a tougher job in that they have to generate resources for side payments to potentially fractious social forces, without having oil rents to draw on. But necessity is the mother of invention, as demonstrated by Israel and Turkey, which have both utilized strategies of globalization to enhance national wealth, which has in turn facilitated domestic conflict resolution and inclusion of potentially antagonistic social forces. By contrast, the praetorian states have allowed insufficient economic freedom for their capitalists, nascent or otherwise, to engage sufficiently successfully with global markets to in turn make possible political openings.

That there is a relationship between the strength and autonomy of political institutions on the one hand and economic ones on the other is suggested by the indicator of institutional credibility presented in Table 3.2, which is the ratio of contract-intensive money to total money supply. The highest performers on this measure in 1997, in descending order, had been Israel, Lebanon, Turkey, Kuwait, Turkey, Bahrain, Qatar, the UAE, and Iran. In 2008 this rank ordering remained essentially unchanged, being Lebanon, Israel, Kuwait, Qatar, Bahrain, UAE, Iran, and Turkey. In fact, citizens in the democracies trust their financial institutions more than they do even in the oil-rich GCC monarchies, for Saudi Arabia's uninspiring score of 90, if weighted by size of population or economy, drags the GCC average down well below that of the democracies. As for the bully and bunker praetorian republics, their low CIM scores suggest a lack of both economic and political trust on the part of their citizens. Good politics seems to make for good finance, and vice versa.

The grouping of the democracies on the CIM index cannot be a by-product of similar historical development of their financial systems. Israeli and Iranian banking was historically run according to the French model, with ubiquitous governmental involvement in the allocation of credit. Turkey's system evolved from the German model, with concentrated but relatively autonomous banking, whereas Lebanon's freewheeling financial sector has always been both deconcentrated and autonomous, more or less along American lines despite French ancestry. But regardless of their different origins, these banking systems, except Iran's, underwent substantial expansion in recent years. And even the Iranian government under reformist President Khatami in 2000 introduced legislation authorizing private banks to operate, but that legislation essentially remained a dead letter as the state, primarily under the control of Khatami's conservative opponents, continued to direct the financial sector. Lebanon's banks grew and became increasingly profitable in the twenty-first century, reflecting their status as conduits for governmental patronage and safe havens for Gulf money, especially that fleeing increasingly unsafe GCC banks once the Great Recession hit. Banks in both Israel and Turkey responded more effectively to the threats and challenges of globalization. In 2003 Israel, seeking to develop Tel Aviv as a financial hub and to connect it more directly to its successful high-tech export businesses, enacted a batch of reforms modeled on American practices. Turkey reduced the number of its state banks and their share of the financial sector, with private banks, like those in Israel, assuming an increasingly important role in support of exports.

As far as stock markets are concerned, Israel's and, to a lesser extent Turkey's feature the greatest numbers of listed companies, the highest turnovers, and the largest proportions of foreign investment in the MENA. Their combination of size and diversity of economy, access to external investors, amount and reliability of relevant information, rate of return, and general confidence in the political system apparently attracts investors. As shown in Table 3.3, Israel's market capitalization as a percentage of GDP quadrupled from 36 percent in 1998 to 144 percent in 2007, roughly that of the United States. Not quite as capitalized as Tel Aviv's stock exchange, the Istanbul exchange was exceptionally active, with its turnover ratio reaching 155 percent by 2008. The Beirut exchange, by contrast, listed only eleven companies in 2008, and their turnover ratio was an anemic 7 percent. Despite slightly higher turnover ratios, Tehran's exchange was less capitalized, the value of its listed companies amounting to only 16 percent of GDP in 2007. The value of its traded shares (the product of turnover and market capitalization) amounted like Lebanon's in 2007 to about 3.1 percent of GDP, much lower than most of the other countries and regions included in Table 3.1.

In sum, two of the MENA's democracies, Israel and Turkey, have been able to capitalize on opportunities provided by globalization. The former, drawing on its extraordinary human resources and global connections, a temporarily favorable regional environment resulting from the signing of the Oslo Accords in 1993, and from neoliberal economic reforms under the 1996–9 Likud Government, substantially increased its rates of growth, national wealth, and global economic integration. Turkey, also supported by the West, successfully managed a synthesis of globalism and Islamism, which underpinned economic reforms that accelerated economic growth. In both cases democracy made possible reconciliation of competitive sociopolitical forces, as well as the emergence of new capitalist forces capable of taking advantage of more favorable business environments. Lebanon, by contrast, continued to be buffeted by the Arab-Israeli conflict and the related intensification of domestic sociopolitical conflict. As a consequence, its weakened government and broader political economy were sucked into the rent-seeking, Gulf-oriented oil economy, which neutralized possibilities for a more independent, effective development strategy. Iran's democracy, instead of rising to the challenges of globalization and management of increasingly polarized domestic sociopolitical forces, collapsed into praetorianism, the economic consequences of which were to exacerbate its relative isolation from the global economy and to stimulate the further growth of patronage and systemic corruption. Because Turkey is as yet the region's sole case of an effective synthesis between globalism and localism – an accomplishment for which its democratic system was key – it is the MENA democracy to be reviewed in greatest detail.

Turkey

Patronage to dampen social conflicts has traditionally accompanied democratic politics in Turkey. As a recent report on the country sponsored by the Commission of the European Union reports, "the distinguishing character of the Turkish polity is the predominance of distributive politics, or what has been called 'populism' in Turkey, whereby the use of public resources to generate political support has become the main instrument through which a political party tries to gain advantage over its competitors" (*The Road Ahead for Turkey* 2005: 5). In the early years of democratic politics, the primary political divide was between the urban-based elite whose power stemmed from the state, and rural social forces that felt and indeed were disadvantaged by the workings of that state. This divide continues to be a central one, but the political expression of the interests of those rural social forces, which were first mobilized into politics against the then-ruling Republican People's Party by the Democratic and then Justice parties, has changed. Most notably, that expression is now primarily within an Islamist framework. The thesis of a secular, state-based civilian elite backed ultimately by an ardently secular military establishment has over the past forty years stimulated an Islamist antithesis that at its core appeals to those who resent what they see as the privileges of that elite and its apparent belief in its own right to rule. But Turkish Islamism has managed to expand from that core of marginalized, provincial supporters and become the dominant political force in the country, precisely because Turkey is a democracy in which political competition induced Islamists to moderate in search of material support, legitimacy, and votes.

As the 1990s progressed, the Kemalists lost popularity primarily as a result of economic mismanagement and political ineptitude. Islamists, by contrast, steadily gained support, culminating in the Islamist Welfare Party taking the largest share of votes, although only 21.6 percent of the total, in the December 1995 elections. After months of tension during which the Welfare Party–led government adopted policies that challenged the established republican order, the military, acting through the National Security Council, forced it from government in February 1997 in what was dubbed a "postmodern coup" because no actual force was used. In January 1998 the Constitutional Court dissolved the Welfare Party and banned its veteran leader, Necmettin Erbakan, from participating in politics for five years. Yet constraints on arbitrary rule were already then much greater in Turkey than in the Arab praetorian republics. The military could not eradicate Islamists as was done in Syria in 1982, for example.

Steps taken against the Welfare Party ultimately proved to be counter-productive for the military, for they resulted in replacement of radical by more moderate leadership and a general softening of the Islamist line that broadened the movement's appeal. A successor Islamist party, the Party of Virtue, was permitted to form and contest the April 1999 elections, in which, despite harassment by the authorities, it managed to finish third in the balloting and to attract younger, urban, higher-status voters into its ranks. A key policy change that appealed to this more sophisticated constituency was to endorse, rather than oppose membership in the EU, with which an accession agreement was reached in Helsinki in December, 1999. But the full evolution of the Islamist movement into the country's dominant political force did not occur until after the Virtue Party was also closed down, in this case by the Constitutional Court, which ruled in 2001 that it was an illegal "center of anti-secular activities." The movement then split into the Felicity Party, in which Erbakan's hard line, traditional faction prevailed, and the Justice and Development Party (AKP), led by the reformer Recep Tayyip Erdogan. The comparatively radical Islamists were thus marginalized within the Islamist movement and in Turkey as a whole, as the Felicity Party did not win more than 3 percent of the votes in either the 2002 or 2007 elections, whereas the AKP won 34 percent in the former and almost 47 percent in the latter.

Further suggesting the AKP's success in broadening its appeal was the fact that it won majorities not only in its Anatolian heartland in such cities as Konya and Kayseri, but also in Ankara and Istanbul, and that many of its deputies were former leading social democrat politicians who were attracted to the AKP banner (Onis 2009: 26). Prime Minister Erdogan and his close AKP colleague, Abdullah Gül, who served as Foreign Minister in the first AKP government and then as president from 2007 in the face of the military's objection – because his wife wears a head-scarf – were clearly better at reading public opinion. Had they remained die-hard Islamists, their party would have foundered, as suggested by the fact that even within the ranks of AKP members, 70 percent oppose the implementation of the *shari'ah*, with a yet higher percentage in the general population being against it (Duzgit and Cakir 2009: 87–107).

That Islamism withstood the state's heavy blows attests to the political skills it developed and the financial resources it tapped. Its leadership, already comparatively sophisticated by the mid-1990s, had to become even more adroit if it was to add to its political appeal without providing the military an excuse to pounce on it yet again. Necmettin Erbakan, the leader of the Welfare Party, had honed his political skills while serving as a cabinet minister in the 1970s. A host of the party's members, including Recep Tayyib Erdogan, subsequently cut their political teeth as mayors of Turkish towns and cities, including Istanbul itself. The leadership could draw on a dense network of Islamist social organizations that provided both human and material resources for political contestation. That Turkish Islamism eschewed violence also reinforced its position, for that rendered attempts by elements of the Kemalist elite to portray it as a mortal threat to the state scarcely credible.

But political talent, Islamist voluntarism, moderation, and a democratic system would, by themselves, be insufficient to sustain Islamism as the country's largest and most effective political movement, were it not for the material resources on which it draws. Those resources include the large-scale, formal financial system, a more informal adjunct of it, and the plethora of small and medium business enterprises owned and operated by provincial capitalists, especially those in the country's heartland of Anatolia, and whose businesses constitute at least a quarter of the country's export capacity (Osmanoglu 2009: 9). Their cultural roots are Islamic, and they resented the secularism and governmental privileges bestowed on the big capitalist cronies of the Kemalist military-political elite. "Special Finance Houses," Turkey's equivalent of Islamic banks without advertising the fact in the secular state, date to the early 1980s, when the then prime minister, Turgut Özal, was seeking to develop economic linkages to the oil-producing Arab states and a domestic political counterbalance to the secular left, which he was seeking to weaken to help pave the way for structural adjustment. The Islamic banks prospered and provided a source of capital to a steadily growing small to medium Islamist business sector. Joining these banks have been numerous investment companies specialized in serving the needs of Turkish workers abroad, especially those in Europe. The Association of Independent Industrialists and Businessmen (MÜSIAD), founded in 1990, reflects the growing material and organizational capacities of "Islamist capitalists" and has come to aggregate their interests and speak on their behalf. Several MÜSIAD members were elected as AKP deputies in both the 2002 and 2007 elections. Underpinning MÜSIAD and reflecting the outward orientation of its Islamist-inclined members was the increasing integration of its Anatolian heartland into the global economy. Konya, which has the greatest number of MÜSIAD members after Istanbul, and whose MÜSIAD members comprise nine of eleven board members of the local 20,000-member Chamber of Industry, increased its exports from some $100 million in 2001 to almost $500 million in 2006. Sixty-four percent of Konya industrialists in 2007 reported they exported their products, double the number of exporters in 2001, with 60 percent of exports destined for Europe (Baskan 2009: 1).

The globalization dialectic in Turkey has thus proceeded further than elsewhere in the region, a consequence of the country's more open polity and developed economy. Globalization spawned a first generation of state-linked capitalists, who, had they not been outflanked by a second generation of moralizers and hemmed in by them on one side and by the state on the other, might have been able to engineer a more thoroughgoing liberalization of the polity and economy. But their economic links to the state and fears of the Islamist challenge led them to backpedal on earlier demands for reform (Bugra 1998: 521–39). This in turn cleared the way for an Islamist antithesis, which has forged a synthesis between the globalist challenge and Islam, a pivotal element of which was Islamic finance (Jang 2005). It is worth highlighting some of its key elements, including the fact that President Abdullah Gül was steeped in these traditions, having earlier served in Jeddah as an economist in the research department of the Islamic Development Bank, which had pioneered Islamic finance. Turkey is developing a model that other countries in the region might emulate – just as Nasser, for example, apparently was much influenced by Atatürk and his state-centered approach.

The economic response is an effort to reconcile globalism and Islam, not use the latter in an attempt to combat the former. That reconciliation, or synthesis, includes several dimensions. One is an embrace of the world capitalist economy and even instruments of the Washington

Consensus. The Welfare Party, for example, nurtured strong ties to the IMF and World Bank. A second element is an embrace of elements of the Washington Consensus itself. Indeed, having been less favored by the state than their secularist competitors, Islamist capitalists in Turkey are free marketers, wanting the state to be downsized. The Welfare Party, for example, privatized at a faster pace than any other government in Turkish history. But the embrace of globalism is not uncritical or without qualifications. For one thing, it requires recognition and utilization of Islamic methods of finance. For another, it seeks implementation of some elements of an Islamic moral economy, in which competition is tempered by ethical and moral concerns. This particular element of the synthesis appears to grow out of the very nature of Islamist capitalist enterprise in Turkey, which tends to be small and medium scale and family based. It is, therefore, stridently anti–labor union, arguing that commonality of interests of owners and workers, with recognition of their mutual and shared objectives, should provide the guidelines for any model of labor-management relations. Finally, the Islamist synthesis prioritizes the Islamic world as a source for capital and markets and general economic interaction.

But synthesizing imperatives of globalization and local political culture does not necessarily guarantee economic success. Although Turkey's economic performance under the AKP has exceeded that under preceding, secular governments, it still suffers from considerable unevenness and since 2006 has shown signs of backsliding into greater dependence on patronage at the expense of production. A brief review of the country's recent economic performance illustrates these trends.

In the early 1980s, Turkey became a prize pupil of the IMF and World Bank, and hence the recipient of massive infusions of public foreign assistance in support of stabilization and structural adjustment programs. Despite some recalcitrance to reform and unevenness in performance, GNP growth per capita accelerated after 1985, averaging an annual 2.8 percent 1986–2008, just 0.5 percent less than Tunisia's top performance in the region. Manufactured exports as a percentage of GDP rose appreciably in the decade after 1987, resulting in Turkey ranking fourth in the MENA on this measure by 1998, after Israel, Jordan, and Tunisia, but second in absolute amount, just behind Israel. Its growing integration into global commodity production chains is reflected in its score on the intra-industry trade index, which jumped from 0.159 to 0.284 between 1984–6 and 1992–4, placing it behind only Israel, Oman, and Tunisia, and at about the same level achieved by the Andean Pact countries. Despite shaky financial management and turbulent politics, Turkey during the 1990s continued to attract large amounts of foreign private capital, receiving more FDI than any other country in the region in the decade 1998–2007 (Figure 2.11). Among these countries, Turkey was then second only to Israel in attracting private-equity investment to its stock market. Contributing to Turkey's appeal to investors was its financial system, which boasted a relatively unconcentrated, private-sector-led, competitive banking system and a comparatively large and active stock market in which value traded as a percentage of GDP and turnover ratios, highest in the region in 1998, were exceeded only by Saudi Arabia's in 2008.

Uneven economic performance, however, is suggested in the first instance by measures of financial stability, which reveal extremely weak governmental discipline over the budget, given Turkey's level of overall economic development. Turkey's inflation rate, which vexed the serious economists throughout the 1980s, in fact increased in the 1990s, reaching the region's highest level of almost 85 percent per annum in 1998, as compared with an average of 51 percent in the 1985–9 period. Driving this almost runaway inflation were large budget deficits, which grew from 3.5 percent to 8.4 percent of GDP during the same period. Its debt service ratio in the 1990s remained within the range of the region's worst offenders, Algeria, Iran, and Morocco (Figure 2.12). Fiscal laxity was due in considerable measure to the public sector's drag on the economy. Despite extensive privatization in the 1990s that dropped its share of employment from 3.7 percent in the late 1980s to 2.9 percent in the 1990s, the public sector sucked up substantially more capital from the government in this latter period. Its deficit almost doubled as a percentage of GDP over those years. Reflecting the surprising persistence of the public sector in this "prize pupil" economy was the fact that in the mid-1990s its private sector received less credit, as a percentage of GDP, than any others in the MENA countries except Algeria, Iran, Sudan, Syria, and Yemen.

Thus, twenty years after the 1980 coup that paved the way for neoliberal reforms, the Turkish economy was still plagued by structural weaknesses, key of which was persisting inability to impose macroeconomic discipline, a problem that in turn resulted from increasingly intense political competition and the propensity of weak coalition governments to "buy votes." The state's governance capacities, especially those of regulation, had been upgraded on paper, but this "rhetorical transition... failed to be translated into effective implementation" (Onis and Bakir 2007: 147–64). This poorly regulated economy, characterized by persisting fiscal deficits and high inflation, was unprepared to cope with the forces of financial globalization, to which it was exposed from 1989 by a premature opening of capital accounts with full currency convertibility, as prescribed by the Washington Consensus and urged by the IMF and World Bank. In February 2001, following financial crises in 1994 and again in 2000, a third and much more profound financial crisis resulting from overly expansive credit, much of which was directed at favored political constituencies by state-owned banks, reverberated throughout the economy, resulting quickly in rapidly rising unemployment and a precipitous 7 percent drop in GDP.

The magnitude of the collapse paved the way for the appointment as Treasury Minister of Kemal Dervis, a World Bank vice president who stood above politics and who, with his team of advisers from the Bank and the IMF, immediately commenced implementation of the "Strong Economy Program." By November 2002, when the AKP won the election and formed a government, many needed reforms, especially to the financial regulatory system, had already been enacted. The AKP endorsed and expanded those reforms, which in turn paved the way for a dramatic decrease in inflation and rapid increase in growth that reached a record 9.9 percent of real GDP in 2004. GDP expanded at an average of 7 percent annually from 2002 to 2007. By 2006, exports amounted to $116 billion, up from $36.5 billion in 1995. FDI mushroomed, from an average of $1 billion annually between 1992 and 2002, to $22 billion in 2007. As a percentage of GDP, FDI was 5 percent in 2006, compared to 3.5 percent for upper-middle-income countries globally and 4.2 percent in the MENA as a whole. Reforms in the financial sector were manifested by a rapid drop to the low level of 3.2 percent of nonperforming loans, compared, for example, to Egypt's MENA-leading rate of 24.7 percent or Tunisia's 19 percent. The capital-to-asset ratio of banks rose to 11.3 percent in 2006, compared to 10.5 percent in the United States. By 2008, 51 percent of total equity in Turkish banks was owned by foreign investors, including HSBC, Citigroup, BNP Paribas, Fortis, and other prominent global banks. Foreigners also held 70 percent of shares listed on the Istanbul stock market (Skinner 2008: 4). So when the global financial crisis hit in 2008, the Turkish financial sector was well provisioned against rising defaults and remained profitable, despite the near collapse of FDI, which dropped from $8 billion in the first two months of 2007 to $1.6 billion in the same period in 2008. The lira remained relatively stable, and inflation rates actually dropped to levels comparable with those of OECD countries.

Intensification of conflict between the ruling AKP and its Kemalist opponents entrenched in the military and at least the normal, if not the "deep state," commenced in the lead up to the 2007 elections. As the government became increasingly embroiled in that sometimes subterranean conflict, it postponed planned constitutional and other reforms and began to succumb to the time-tested temptation of issuing side payments to maintain political allegiances. But even prior to this relapse, there were signs of persisting economic weakness. The current account deficit increased by a factor of more than ten times in the decade ending in 2006, when it reached $32.7 billion. Total external debt tripled in that period, reaching $207 billion in 2006. By 2009 Turkey, with the world's seventeenth largest economy, had the world's sixth largest balance of payments deficit and the sixth highest debt service ratio (*The Economist Pocket World in Figures* 2009: 36, 43). Turkey was not growing its economy in pace with the expansion of its foreign borrowings, which in light of the Great Recession began to assume worrying proportions.

Underlying growing indebtedness was the failure to move up global production chains fast enough, which in turn resulted from inadequate investment, especially in the private sector, comparatively poor labor force training and utilization, and a government that remained too obtrusive and expensive. Turkey's performance on the Intra Industry Trade Index (IIT) is suggestive. Although in 2006 at .217 it was second only to Israel's (.430) in the MENA, by a more appropriate comparison, such as to Argentina, a country of similar size and factor endowments and to which Turkey is frequently compared, the performance was less impressive (Onis 2006: 239–63). Despite ranking well below Turkey in its percentage of world trade (44 as compared to 30), Argentina's IIT Index scores of .156 and .313 on the three- and five-digit measures, respectively, exceed Turkey's. To place these scores on the IIT index in perspective, the EU's was .886 in 1992–4 (Brülhart 2008). Domestic credit to the private sector remained relatively low by 2006, when it was 34.1 percent, as compared to the upper-middle-income country average of 41.4 percent. The Heritage Foundation/Dow Jones rankings of economic freedom suggest continued governmental restraints on the private sector. In 2008 Turkey ranked a rather low 74th in the world on that index, with MENA comparators Kuwait, Israel, Lebanon and Egypt ranking 39th, 46th, 73rd, and 85th, respectively. Turkey was assessed by Freedom House as having more economic freedom in 1995 (61.3) than in 2009 (60.3). The three indicators on the ten-indicator index that continue to drag down Turkey's score are those for financial freedom, presumably because of the comparatively small share of the private sector in overall credit; freedom from corruption; and labor freedom. That corruption continues to be a major liability is also suggested by the World Bank's ranking of Turkey about even with India on its measure of corruption, with surveys in both countries reporting that almost half of businessmen queried report making "unofficial payments" to public officials (World Development Indicators 2008). Expenditure on research

and development is not commensurate with Turkey's level of industrialization, being 0.67 percent of GDP in 2006, as opposed to 1.03 percent
in Tunisia and upper-middle-income countries generally. Turkey's labor
participation rate, which declined from 57 percent at the beginning of the
1990s to less than 49 percent in 2004 (*The Road Ahead for Turkey* 2005:
2), is the ninth lowest in the world, while its unemployment rate, which
was some 8.5 percent in the early 1990s, has remained stubbornly high
in the twenty-first century, exceeding 10 percent in the period 2002–6
before the onset of the Great Recession drove it up to 14 percent in
2009 (Strauss 2009: 1). Turkey has extremely high levels of informal
employment, some 60 percent according to one report (*The Road Ahead
for Turkey* 2005: 6), and more than half of the workforce is outside the
social security system. A 2001 survey revealed that "the population's
trust in public institutions is very low," which its authors concluded was
a primary cause of resort to informal economic activity and tax evasion
(Davutyan 2008: 2).

The Turkish economy is thus not sufficiently developed to play the
"lead goose" role of Japan in the "flying geese" pattern of East Asian
development, despite some similarities. As Turkey has slowly moved up
production chains, such as into automobile manufacturing and nonelec-
trical machinery, it has offshored some labor-intensive, low-technology
processing operations to other MENA countries, especially Egypt and
particularly in foodstuffs, textiles, and ready-made garment manufacturing. FDI outflow from Turkey grew after 2002, reaching almost $1
billion annually (Onis and Bakir 2007: 157). Medium technology industries have been the most rapidly growing manufacturing subsector, their
products rising from 16.5 percent of manufactured exports in 1993 to
almost 37 percent in 2004 (*The Road Ahead for Turkey* 2005: 71). But
Turkey's high-technology exports remained in 2006 at around $250 mil-
lion, less than 10 percent of exports and a very small fraction of the
average for upper-middle-income countries. Despite a favorable external
setting, including access to European markets and receipt of substantial
FDI from both Europe and the Gulf, the domestic political economy has
not been strong enough to climb up production chains within multinational corporations. Its human resource capacities remain insufficiently
developed, as suggested by the fact that in 2007 its real GDP per capita
rank minus its HDI rank, as reported in Chapter 2 (Table 2.1), was still –
16 (a slight improvement over the –22 recorded in 1997), indicating that
the country continues to fail to develop the potential of its citizens to a
level commensurate with their incomes. Its Education Index ranked 49
places below GDP. The female illiteracy rate in 2006 was 20 percent,
which is not high by MENA standards, where it is 37 percent overall, but

far higher than among Turkey's upper-middle-income global comparators, where it is only 8 percent. The government continues to absorb too
high a proportion of available credit, some two-thirds of that available,
compared to slightly over half in MENA and upper-middle-income countries. And Turkey's commercial banks in turn are too oriented to their
government client, holding some 85 percent of its domestic debt (Bilgin
and Ozkan 2009: 2). Turkey's three state-owned banks also continue to
hold a substantial market share, having in 2007 some 35 percent of total
assets, 42 percent of total deposits, and more than 21 percent of total
loans (Ozcan and Kafali 2007: 6). Macroeconomic management continues to be plagued by overborrowing, with interest payments accounting
in 2006 for 29 percent of central government expenditures, compared to
an average of 5 percent in upper-middle-income countries.

The mixed economic picture reflects a similarly mixed political one.
The external context offers advantages, but it also poses threats. Turkey
has for more than half a century been a "poster child" for the West and
especially the United States, which first supported it less because it was a
democracy than because it was a bulwark against the USSR, then because
it seemed to be a bulwark against radical Islam and a model for its conversion into a more moderate, benign form. Europe has also thrown its substantial weight behind Turkey, for similar reasons, including committing
itself in 1999 to explore full EU membership. In addition to the financial
largesse that has flowed into Turkey from Western countries and international financial institutions, the country has served as a laboratory for
economic experimentation by them, not always with beneficial results, as
the 2001 financial crisis attested. Although on the whole Turkey has benefited from the Western embrace, its geopolitical setting, relatively remote
from Europe although bordering it and with potential or real enemies on
its borders, has been less favorable. Commitments to the military have
declined in relative terms as the economy and population have grown,
but they remain substantial and above levels in comparator countries.
The percentage of GDP allocated to the military is almost 50 percent
higher than in upper-middle-income countries as a whole, as is the percentage of the labor force in the military, although on both measures
Turkey is below MENA averages. But when compared to its potential
EU sister state Germany, which has a slightly higher population but only
246,000 armed-forces personnel in 2006 compared to Turkey's 612,000,
the implied cost of being in the MENA, albeit on the periphery, is evident.

External support, both economic and political, has been generous and
does compensate in considerable measure for the economic drag effect
of military expenditures, but Turkey's dramatic economic recovery after
2001 is due more to domestic than external factors. The policies that

have made for modern Turkey's longest and most substantial period of economic growth have been underpinned by what Ziya Onis has termed "conservative globalism." The AKP strategy combined a progressive outlook with concern for traditional and especially Islamic values, or, in Onis's words, "a global strategy embedded in the local" (Onis 2009: 26). Turkey's fragmented democracy made this synthesis possible by providing Islamists both the space and the means with which to develop the strategy and then put it into practice, while simultaneously preventing opponents from blocking that experiment. But democracy has also enabled Kemalism to persist, with the ongoing political contest between these two political forces intensifying, posing increasing risks to both the polity and the economy. A recent survey pointed to the depth of division of public opinion. Whereas 44.6 percent of respondents identified themselves primarily as Muslims, thereby implying support for Islamism, one-third of respondents expressed concern about the erosion of secularism (cited in Duzgit and Cakir 2009: 91). Turkey's is not a consolidated democracy, so by definition backsliding into authoritarianism remains possible. Although direct military intervention still seemed unlikely even as the spring 2010 crisis in civil-military relations intensified, continued political sparring between these profoundly antagonistic political forces could undermine governmental performance to the point that support for democracy is eroded and calls for authoritarianism, whether under a secularist or Islamist banner, are heeded. Resat Kasaba has observed that in its modern history, Turkey has oscillated between "democratization, sustainable economic development and social justice," on the one hand, and "retreat to political closure, economic instability, and societal polarization," on the other (Kasaba 2008: 1). So as this history suggests, Turkey's regionally innovative and largely successful experiment in reaction to globalization remains precarious. It nevertheless has already demonstrated the utility of democracy in mediating between global threats and opportunities, on the one hand, and local political and economic forces, on the other.

Israel

Israel's endowment of factors of production suggested that it was the MENA country best equipped to deal with the challenges of the new wave of globalization that began at the end of the Cold War. Its human resources were the envy of the region. Life expectancy, at 80.7 years, was the highest in the MENA in 2007. It was one of the few MENA countries that then, as now outperformed its level of income on the Human Development Index, as presented in Table 2.1. Perhaps most relevant to globalization was the fact that Israel already had the highest percentage of scientists in its population of any country in the world, with 135 for every 10,000 citizens, compared, for example, with 85 in the United States (Dunn 1998: 11). Israel, although having no oil, was almost as well endowed with capital as the MENA's wealthiest oil exporters. On a per capita basis, its GDP was higher than that of all but the minuscule GCC oil producers – Kuwait, the UAE, Bahrain, and Qatar. Including foreign public and private capital transfers, financial resources available per capita in Israel were the most in the MENA.

Several indicators suggest that Israel was beginning to use these assets to cash in on the new opportunities provided by globalization. Its manu-factured exports rose from $7.2 billion in 1987 to $20.7 billion a decade later, making them the region's most valuable, just ahead of Turkey's at $19.7 billion. Of these exports, high-tech goods and services accounted in 1997 for almost one-third, or some $6.2 billion, which were far and away the highest proportional and absolute amounts in the MENA (Dunn 1998: 11). Its intra-industry trade index rating, the highest in the MENA, suggested that Israel was the most integrated into global commodity pro-duction chains. That Israel succeeded in bringing its import duties down from 4.9 percent of total tax revenues in 1987 to only 2.1 percent five years later and 0.8 percent by 2007, the lowest in the MENA, indicated a commitment to becoming globally competitive, as did the fact that its effective duty of 2.7 percent in 2006 was the lowest in the MENA (Table 3.4).

A more detailed examination reveals that it was not until the very end of the twentieth century that Israel successfully overcame various aspects of its state- and nation-building legacies that impeded its drive to globalize its economy. Among the first MENA countries to undergo economic stabilization, which it did in the mid-1980s, for more than a decade thereafter Israel was unable to bring its inflation rate down even to the level of such MENA competitors as Jordan, Morocco, and Tunisia, to say nothing of the GCC countries, which had the lowest inflation rate in the region until it accelerated midway through the third great oil boom. Israel's average per capita GDP growth rate, instead of tracing a steady upward trajectory, continued to gyrate, sinking from 4.5 percent for the period 1965–75, the highest in the MENA, to 1.2 percent in the following decade, among the lowest in the region. It recovered in the decade after 1985 to again become one of the region's leaders, but after 1995 fell off rapidly, dropping by 1997 to a negative 0.8 percent. As was the case virtually since the state's foundation, Israel continued to run a balance-of-trade deficit, which deepened sharply from 1989 until beginning an upward climb in 1997.

The explanation for Israel's hesitancy in seizing on opportunities provided by globalization lies primarily with legacies of its unique state- and nation-building processes. Civil society in Israel has from the outset been closely tied to the state, the Zionist enterprise being a centrally organized one with capital provided through the organizations that ultimately became integrated into the state itself. Capital in Israel was traditionally concentrated and lacking autonomy from the government. The close association with different elements of the Zionist movement of three of the four largest commercial banks illustrated the nexus between state and capital. Bank Leumi was founded shortly after the turn of the century by the Zionist movement, which continued to own it until, like the other big banks, it came under direct government ownership in 1983. Bank Ha'Poalim was controlled by the Histadrut, the Federation (of Israeli workers), and Bank Ha'Mizrahi was owned by a movement of Orthodox Jews that constituted one of the country's important political parties. Although not directly owned by the government, "the banking system was an agent for the government, both in raising money from the public and in issuing credit... Most credit extended by the banking system was steered by the government to its preferred objectives. The government set the price of this credit... and took responsibility for the risk" (Paroush 2007: 131). What amounted to the nationalization of these banks in 1983 resulted from a financial crisis brought on by their use of their depositors' funds to speculate in their own shares. The ensuing crash caused the stock exchange to be closed for two weeks as the government put together a rescue package that transferred to it controlling interest in the banks, where it remained until Ha'Poalim was privatized in 1997–2000. Having structured much of Israeli manufacturing and commerce into cartels, the government utilized the banks to ration credit to them, something which the banks preferred as "it provided a guarantee in the sense of diminution of the risk incurred by the lending bank" (Plessner 1994: 170).

Mirroring the French-style, statist, concentrated banking system, the Israeli economy was under tight governmental control. The cartels just referred to, which were founded during the 1930s and strongly supported by the chief business lobby, the Manufacturers' Association, dominated the large-scale private sector until the late 1980s. These cartels were supported not only by the allocation of credit through the banks, but by high tariffs and extensive export subsidies. The companies within the cartels were and, in some cases, still are owned by the leading banks. The legal framework within which they operated typically established monopolies, such as those regarding the importation, shipping, and sale of oil (Plessner 1994: 146). Alongside the nominally private cartels, the public sector provided for direct governmental involvement in the economy. As late as the mid-1980s, it accounted for about a quarter of the ownership of the country's largest fifty enterprises, and very much more if the Histadrut-controlled companies are thought of as being in the public sector, which for all intents and purposes they were. Histadrut-controlled companies accounted in the 1980s for about one-fifth of all employment and an equal share of the GNP, bringing the public sector's total share of ownership of large companies to more than half, its employment to more than one-third of the country's total, and its contribution to GNP to just less than one-half (Plessner 1994: 115).

Civil society's search for material resources thus had led it to the state, with the politicians acting as doorkeepers. For the secular left, the dominant role of the state, manifested especially as it was for them in the Histadrut, was ideologically acceptable while being sound tactically, for the left controlled that state without interruption from its formation until 1977. What is harder to understand is why the right, as represented by the Likud Party and its allies, accepted more or less the same formula of quasisocialism, ostensibly committed as they were – or at least as election sloganeering claimed – to a free-market economy.

That paradox is resolved with reference to two considerations – the primary objective and the political base of the right. Its objective was to maximize the size of the country, not economic growth. Committed to Greater Israel, Likud and its allies needed the state to fulfill their Zionist dream. Business, if left to its own devices, might well decide that a smaller Israel and peace with its neighbors would be better for business than an aggressive, expansionist state. Likud, in other words, did not trust the large-scale, cosmopolitan private sector, nor was it trusted by it. So a natural alliance between business and the political right had not eventuated, leaving the Labour Party to compete effectively for ties with the private sector and for it to be the architect of Israel's original stabilization program. The political base of the right also impeded its embrace of capitalism, for from the Begin era of the late 1970s it increasingly rested on Sephardim, the poorest, most marginal component of Jewish society. Constituents of the right were thus yet more demanding of social transfers and services than those of the nominal left, whose ideology and long-established expectations also supported such expenditures. For coalitions of the right or left, therefore, reining in governmental expenditures was politically difficult to the point of being impossible, so deficits, inflation, and pervasive governmental involvement in the economy hobbled Israel's growth.

In the mid to late 1990s, several factors began to converge that within several years had resulted in major changes in the Israeli political economy. Israel's strong linkages to the West, including those of its economists, ensured awareness of and support for the then-emerging Washington Consensus. Rapid globalization, including the rise of East Asia and especially China, provided opportunities from which Israel, and especially its emerging high-tech economy, could benefit. That portion of the economy in particular received a shot in the arm from the arrival in the early 1990s of immigrants from Russia, tens of thousands of whom were engineers and scientists who had worked in Soviet electronics, weapons, and other sophisticated industries. The regional context, which from Israel's perspective had improved substantially as a result of its 1979 peace treaty with Egypt, became dramatically more favorable as a result of the 1993 Oslo Accord, quickly followed by the signing of a peace treaty with Jordan. The way was thus cleared for Israel finally to establish political and economic relations with numerous states that previously had shunned it on account of its unresolved conflict with the Palestinians. For the first time in its history, Israel could envision operating within relatively benign regional and global environments. The economy, which from the outset had been harnessed to the Zionist political effort, as reflected in the tight linkage between its political components and the financial sector, especially banks, could be allowed to become more "normal." This relaxation was also evident in the Israeli party system, with the grip of Labour and Likud being loosened as their members and voters drifted away into other parties, an increasing number of which were strictly sectarian or issue focused, such as the Pensioner's Party. So the neoliberal reforms that began in the 1990s, especially in 1996–9 under Prime Minister Benjamin Netanyahu's Likud government, fell on fertile economic and political grounds, taking root and becoming so well established that within a decade even Labour embraced neoliberalism. In the 2009 parliamentary elections conducted during the Great Recession, it and the Likud offshoot, the Kadima Party, both embraced tax cuts, emphasized the need for economic growth over redistribution, and called for reduced government intervention in the economy and fewer government expenditures. As Meir Javedanfar, an Israeli political analyst commented at the time, "We are turning into a little America" (Javedanfar 2009).

The key that finally unlocked Israel's economic potential was the overhaul of its financial sector. As noted in Chapter 3, the leading banks were privatized between 2000 and 2005, with Bank Leumi and the Israel Discount Bank attracting foreign purchasers. Other reforms underpinned the overhaul of the banking sector. In 1985, foreign exchange controls had been partially lifted, followed by their complete removal in 2001. Pension funds and equity markets were overhauled in 2003 and 2004, whereas the Bachar Committee reforms of 2005 targeted the banks' overall control of the financial sector. This last step was long overdue, as not only was the banking market highly concentrated, with the two largest banks, Ha'Poalim and Leumi, controlling more than two-thirds of deposits, but as universal banks they also controlled the country's provident and mutual funds, credit card issuance and mortgage banking. Operating the most concentrated universal banking system in the world, Israel's leading banks averaged net annual returns on capital of 9 percent in the 1990s and into the first few years of the twenty-first century (Paroush 2007: 139). Not only did concentration guarantee these profits, but it increased risk, resulting in intermittent crises and reduced efficiency, as manifested in the relatively high cost of capital and a comparatively large percentage of nonperforming loans. Mutual and provident funds also underperformed because, owned by the banks, they invested heavily in those banks and the companies they controlled (Goldwasser, Zaks, and Shlush 2007: 5; Paroush 2007: 131). Bank credit to the business sector also retarded the growth of the equities market, total capitalization of which was 6 percent of GDP in 1990 and still only 53 percent in 1996, about half the average level in high-income economies.

The combination of concentration, inefficiency, and conflicts of interest drove the reform process, which by 2007 had succeeded in increasing competition in the broader financial market, although not in deconcentrating it. The Bechar Reforms actually increased the market share of the three largest banks from 78 to 81 percent in the following two years, but their control of provident funds dropped from 73 to 25 percent of the market and of mutual funds from 80 to less than 1 percent. Paralleling this diminution of banks' control over the broader financial market was the banks' declining share of credit to private businesses, which fell steadily from 72 percent in 2003 to 55 percent in 2008 as nonbank domestic credit, including that from stocks and bonds, rose from 11 to 27 percent in that period. While total bank credit to business rose from 362 billion NIS in 2003 to 408 billion NIS in 2008, that provided by nonbank sources expanded from 56 billion NIS to almost 200 billion NIS, to which the Tel Aviv stock exchange contributed 14 billion NIS (Bank of Israel 2009: 171, 198). By 2007 that exchange's capitalization had reached 144 percent of GDP, 24 percent more than the average for high-income economies (Table 3.3). The lure of returns on investments in Israel's high-tech industries had by 2008 stimulated the growth of the venture capital component of the financial sector, with some fifteen hedge funds operating in that year that, along with other investment funds, were attracting Israelis back from their posts on Wall Street and the City of London (Buck 2008: 7). In 2008 Israel attracted as much venture capital as France and Germany combined. It had in that year 3,850 startups and more companies listed on the technology-heavy NASDAQ exchange than both China and India (Senor and Singer, 2009). Reflecting the steady if uneven process of financial-sector reform, credit to the private sector, as reported in Table 3.4, commenced an ascent from 73 percent of GDP in 1998 (and 60 percent the early 1990s) to 90 percent by 2007.

The more efficient mobilization of capital helped to propel Israel's globalization, including its attractiveness to international investors. Figure 7.1 reveals that exports of goods and services and of high-tech manufactures, coupled with the inflow of FDI, commenced their ascent more or less jointly in the mid-1990s. By the early years of the twenty-first century, Israel's economy had become as globalized as those of high-income countries, with its merchandise trade as a percentage of GDP reaching 69 percent in 2006, compared to 65 percent in the Euro area (World Development Indicators, 2008). Its weighted mean tariff had by then dropped to 2.7 percent, compared to an OECD average of 2.1 percent. Globalization in turn helped to stimulate Israel's competitiveness, with total factor productivity growing at a very respectable average annual rate of 1.1 percent from the mid-1990s (Bank of Israel 2008: 66). Underlying productivity growth were the products of research and development, expenditure on which at 4.7 percent of GDP in 2008 led the world (*The Economist Pocket World in Figures* 2009: 63) Governance further ensured Israel's global competitiveness, as its MENA-leading scores placed it at OECD levels, especially on the vital measure of Governmental Effectiveness, on which in 2008 it was in the 88th percentile.

As in the Turkish case, successful engagement with the global economy has enabled Israel to progress to a higher level of development. Decoupling the financial sector from the state, which has also occurred in Turkey, both improved the efficiency of capital allocation and reduced side payments to political constituencies. Economic growth in Turkey and Israel has gradually replaced access to state patronage as the central measure of successful political performance and basis for political loyalties, at least among many constituencies. This in turn loosens the bonds linking voters to parties, undermining the strength of the latter, but stimulating overall political competition. Democracy in both provided the structure of incentives for political elites to appeal to voters through strategies of economic globalization, which in turn required and reinforced domestic reforms.

But as is the case in Turkey, problems remain in Israel. The most important have to do paradoxically with the very success of its globalization strategy. Driven to globalize in part because of its regional isolation, Israel's success militates against the perceived need to reach an accommodation with its Arab and Muslim neighbors, key among which are the Palestinians. Before the Oslo process commenced, Israeli business elites

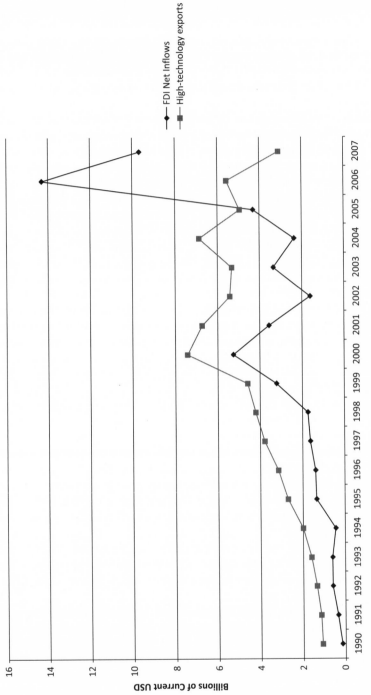

Figure 7.1 Israel's Foreign Direct Investment Inflows and High-Technology Exports, 1990–2007

acted in some measure as a dovish pressure group on Israeli political elites out of the calculation that business interests would be served by peace, not the least payoff being cessation of the Arab boycott. Oslo provided that and other benefits to Israel, but ultimately did not deliver the promised peace. Having essentially leapt over regional barriers to engage with the world, Israelis now have fewer incentives to make sacrifices for peace, preferring to isolate and contain Palestinians while dealing with Jordan and Egypt and their business communities relatively openly and with other Arab economies and business communities, especially those in the Gulf, surreptitiously.

The Israelis are having their cake and eating it, too, or at least so it seems to the majority of them. But the cake would be still larger were Israel to resolve its conflict with the Palestinians. The direct cost of occupation, according to an Israeli think tank, was some $11 billion over the two decades ending in 2008. Its rate of growth of 43 percent between 1997 and 2006 was hobbled by the conflict, hence lagged behind world economic growth of 67 percent and U.S. and EU growth of 68 percent during that period. "The truth is that the conflict with the Palestinians is like a millstone around the neck of Israel: it undermines economic growth, burdens the budget . . . and threatens the future of its existence as a Jewish nation-state" (Adva Centre cited in McCarthy 2008: 16). Opportunity costs of the conflict may be still higher. Continued high military expenditures constitute part of those costs. Less apparent but still important is the cost of the lack of financial market integration in the Middle East. According to a careful comparative study, the magnitude of potential gains from risk sharing among Middle East financial markets would exceed those obtained in the OECD. Even if that risk sharing were among subgroups of Middle Eastern countries, such as Egypt, Israel, and Jordan, there would still be "very high potential gains" (Sorensen and Yosha 2003: 1–19). The lure of profits from integration into regional financial markets may, therefore, assume greater importance in Israeli decision making toward the Palestinian issue as the centrality of the financial market to the Israeli political economy increases.

But identity politics in the MENA democracies can easily trump economic rationality. Turkey's success since 2001 could ultimately be undermined by increasing polarization between Islamists and secularists. The steady growth of ultraorthodox and ultranationalist political movements within Israel and their extension via settlements into the Occupied Territories militate against compromise with the Palestinians. Even the United States has, under President Obama, begun to express concern over Israeli recalcitrance. Israel may have to choose between indulging its diehard Zionists, and thereby forgoing further integration into the MENA and possibly jeopardizing existing regional and global ties, or reining in the zealots and achieving deeper regional and global integration. Although democracy may provide the framework that prevents these conflicting forces from fracturing the body politic, it may do so through compromises and accommodations that are economically and politically costly to both Israel and its Arab, especially Palestinian, neighbors.

Lebanon

Lebanon has a fraught relationship with globalization. The most globalized of Arab countries until the mid-1970s, when civil war essentially removed it from the global and even regional economy for fifteen years, Lebanon embarked on a reconstruction program in the early 1990s that led to a segmented, partial reglobalization that favored its banking sector while undermining much of the broader economy. The political economy of Lebanon has thus traced a path that is the obverse of that followed by the praetorian Arab republics. When they were pursuing policies of import substitution industrialization and essentially isolating their economies, Lebanon was their window on the world, a cosmopolitan, essentially free-trade area governed with the light hand of laissez-faire. All that was really required was to stabilize the currency, as Lebanon's vigorous mercantile capitalism did the rest. But when the praetorians commenced their cautious, controlled openings to the global economy in the late 1980s and 1990s, Lebanon emerged from its civil war to embrace not global capitalism, but external patrons whose support would sustain the critical banking sector and the domestic political elite heavily dependent on it. Whereas Lebanon's MENA neighbors were more reluctant to open their financial than other sectors of their economies, Lebanon became a profitable regionalized, if not fully globalized, banking safe haven, but one with little other residue of its former, broader entrepôt economy that had included merchandise trade and a broad range of services.

The paradox of Lebanon, the putative inheritor of the Phoenician mercantile tradition, becoming a petrodollar-dependent economy importing capital and tourists while exporting its skilled manpower, just as most other MENA economies were beginning to broaden their economic interactions with the world, resulted from regional and domestic political factors. Chief among the former was increasing Syrian control of the country, especially after 1990. Although Syria may have wanted its own Hong Kong, it exerted too much control over both the polity and the economy for Lebanon to play that outward-oriented role. But following Syria's expulsion in April 2005, the Lebanese did not reorient their economy. By this stage the symbiotic relationship with GCC states, whereby they and their citizens banked petrodollars in Beirut and vacationed there, while Lebanese worked in the Gulf and sent remittances home, was too firmly established. It was further reinforced by other sources of external support, including FDI, public foreign assistance, and remittances from Lebanese working elsewhere, such as in West Africa or North America. Domestic political factors, shaped first by Syria's presence and throughout by the pattern of political reconstruction, can be summed up as the restoration of an elitist consociational democracy in which power and privilege were distributed among those traditional elites who survived the civil war period, joined by newer ones who emerged during it. The revised "national pact" between them all was to ensure preservation of their respective domestic patronage networks, based on externally provided resources parceled out through the banking sector. The financial mechanism by which these system-sustaining rents are generated was created by Prime Minister Rafiq Hariri and has outlived him. Its key components are central bank pegging of the local currency to the U.S. dollar, made possible by sustained external financial support, and the issuance of short-term, high-yielding government debt in Lebanese pounds and even Euros, debt that is absorbed almost entirely by Lebanese banks, whose guaranteed and healthy profits feed the political machines that further augment their resources by direct state patronage and, frequently, external subventions. This last source results from Lebanon having managed to convert the Iranian-Arab and Syrian-Saudi regional competitions to its advantage, with Iran bolstering Hizbollah among Shi'a while its Gulf competitors and especially Saudi Arabia finance Sunnis and the broader alliance that Rafiq Hariri cobbled together and his son Saad inherited.

Hariri, the country's merchant prince who had made his fortune in Saudi Arabia, seduced his countrymen with a dream of an entirely new steel, glass, and concrete Beirut that would be the financial center of the MENA region. The Faustian bargain he was offering was that in return for promises of petro- and other dollars flowing into the country, thereby stabilizing the Lebanese pound, they would award him the right to run the country's affairs. The residual state was placed at the disposal of the warlords who had been recycled as politicians, giving them governmental resources to be doled out to their followers. Having struck this bargain on coming to power in late 1992, Hariri immediately set about building his own state alongside the decrepit, confessionalized, patronage-based one that he had inherited and which he essentially turned over to the other politicians.

Hariri's state consisted of an opaque mix of public and private institutions. He imposed his confidants on the commanding heights, which were those that channeled the flow of public monies. His former stockbroker at Merrill Lynch became the head of the central bank, for example, whereas the Ministry of Finance was given to the chief financial officer for Hariri's business conglomerate. Solidere, a private company founded and controlled by Hariri, was ceded ownership of central Beirut, whereas the Council for the Development and Reconstruction of Lebanon, nominally a governmental agency but in fact under the direct control of Hariri's team, was awarded a virtual monopoly over governmental construction. The monopoly could be used, among other things, to provide a vast network of infrastructure for Solidere's city center. From this public/private base, Hariri reached out to bring the media and banking sectors under his control, buying up the most prestigious newspapers and television stations and taking controlling interests in the country's most profitable banks, yet further enriched by the T-bills that Hariri's central bank auctioned off.

Hariri, in sum, created a business enterprise-cum-state alongside the rickety old confessionalized state that he had inherited. Ultimately, however, Hariri overplayed his hand vis-à-vis both the Syrians and his domestic political competitors. Although Syria supported his return to the role of prime minister in 2002, within two years his efforts to pry Lebanon loose from Syria's grasp resulted in his dismissal and then, in 2005, his death. During this protracted behind-the-scenes struggle, the Hariri machine's power ebbed away both to Hizbollah and to the components of the more traditional consociational state. Although Saad Hariri's March 14 movement won the majority of parliamentary seats in the June 2009 election and he became prime minister, his personal power was much weakened by internal divisions within his coalition, by the strategic agreement that gave Hizbollah veto power over critical governmental decisions, and by the continuing presence of confession-based machines and their leaders who flew the flag of convenience of 14 March but could just as easily fly others' flags. Symbolic of the new prime minister's weakness was the fact that a month after the election, his cabinet was yet to be formed, primarily because Syria and Saudi Arabia were still dickering over who would be in it.

Lebanon thus remains the "precarious republic" described by Michael Hudson in the 1960s. But it is now more precarious politically, because the rickety confessional system has not been reformed as promised by the Ta'if Accords, as well as economically. Instead of reaching a national consensus on modernization of the political economy that would create a more effective, more representative government while drawing on the country's entrepreneurial talents to propel a globalizing economy, Lebanon's political leaders have focused on securing their share of rents generated by an economy whose only globally competitive sectors are banking and tourism. These shortcomings are evidenced by the coexistence of external rents with internal indebtedness; by flagging globalization and economic reform efforts; by low standards of governance; by poor utilization of human resources, the quality of which is also not keeping pace with regional and global comparators; and by growing inequity.

The principal sources of capital inflows into Lebanon are bank deposits, aid, FDI, remittances, tourism, and portfolio investments. Despite growing indebtedness and intermittent instability, Lebanese expatriates and Gulf depositors have continued to be attracted by the high rates of return and the secrecy provided by Lebanese banks, thus helping to propel the steadily rising ratio of commercial bank deposits to GDP that reached 324 percent in 2009, the highest in the MENA and one of the highest in emerging markets generally. Since 1990, annual deposit growth has never fallen below 4 percent and in fact accelerated to 15.6 percent in December 2008 as a result of the global financial crisis stimulating searches by GCC citizens and residents for banking safe havens (IMF April 2009b: 9). As the IMF notes, "deposit growth appears . . . to be increasingly correlated to the economic cycle in the GCC" (IMF April 2009b: 12). In the face of intermittent crises, including the assassination of Rafiq Hariri in February 2005 and the Israeli invasion in the summer of 2006, Lebanon's main GCC backers, led by Saudi Arabia, have acted swiftly to stem possible runs on the Lebanese currency and banks by putting at their disposal significant sums – in excess of $1 billion in those particular cases. The U.S., EU, and international financial institutions led by the IMF have added their muscle to these crisis-related efforts as well as to more sustained, general budgetary support. As a consequence, foreign aid per capita has also climbed steadily, from $65 in 1998 to $174 in 2006, compared to a MENA average in these two years of $16 and $54, respectively. FDI has risen at a much more dramatic rate, going from $35 million in 1995 to $2.8 billion in 2006, which in that latter year amounted to 12.3 percent of GDP, compared to a regional average of 4.2 percent. The bulk of that FDI also came from GCC countries, some 60 percent in the period 2002–7 according to the IMF, with more than half of that invested in real estate. Lebanon receives about one-third of all GCC FDI in the MENA (IMF Country Report No. 09/131 2009: 11). By contrast, the Lebanese stock market remains anemic, its total capitalization growing from 9.4 percent of GDP in 2000 to only 36.4 percent in 2007 as the number of listed companies dropped from twelve to eleven. The value of shares traded as a percentage of GDP rose from 0.7 percent to a still meager 9 percent. Solidere continues to account for almost two-thirds of the market's total capitalization. Clearly the guaranteed, healthy returns provided by the banking sector, combined with the attractions of building second homes and tourist facilities in the "Switzerland of the Mediterranean," are much more compelling to GCC and Lebanese investors than are shares in Lebanese companies, excepting Solidere. Substantial as these various sources of capital inflow are, they are all outpaced by remittances, which exceeded $5 billion in 2006 and hovered between one-fifth and one-quarter of GDP through-out the first nine years of the twenty-first century, a ratio exceeded in the world only by Tajikistan, Tonga, and Guyana. Tourism has added another healthy dollop of funds, amounting to about 40 percent of total exports, more than double the MENA average, which is itself the highest ratio of any of the world's regions. Half of those tourists are from GCC countries. Lebanon, in sum, attracts extraordinary amounts of capital, especially from the Gulf and its own citizens living abroad.

All the more surprising, then, is the mountain of public debt that has been accumulated since the end of the civil war, of which reconstruction expenses, including those following the 2006 Israeli invasion, account for only a portion. The World Bank, for example, estimated the destruction in 2006 to have cost Lebanon $3.5 billion, whereas assistance pledged by the bank and donor countries in 2007 to repair that damage amounted to $8.6 billion (Jane's Sentinel Security Assessment, Country Report, Lebanon, 2009). The total "external" debt, virtually all of which is held in Lebanon as even Eurobond issues are purchased principally by Lebanese banks, was almost $50 billion in 2009, more than 160 percent of GDP, one of the world's highest proportions. Of the country's total debt in 2008, the banking sector held $47 billion while $13.7 billion was held outside the banking sector. More than 60 percent of bank credit is sucked up by the government as a result of high interest rates, which reached almost 30 percent in the 1990s, and which were still in the 8 to 10 percent range in 2009 at a time when Federal Reserve rates in the United States were 0.5 percent and international interest rates hovered around 5 percent. Given this extraordinary rate of return on T-bills and even Eurobond issues, banks have little interest in lending to the private sector, which is starved of credit. In 2008 the government of Lebanon paid some $5 billion interest on its debt, which amounted to almost 80 percent of total government revenues and almost half of its expenditures (Jane's Sentinel Security Assessment, Country Report, Lebanon 2009: 27–9). A former minister of finance, when asked what the reason was behind the policy of profound indebtedness and high interest rates, responded that it was to "provide high and continuous banking profits" (Corm 2009: 42–3).

The nexus of sustained international capital flows, which in turn under-write banking profitability that in turn provides the patronage necessary to service the networks which underpin the country's consociational democracy, has prevented reform efforts from succeeding. Lebanon has accumulated capital but has not developed. Repeated attempts to privatize the largest state-owned enterprises, of which the key ones are in the electricity and mobile-phone sectors, have failed, for the jobs they provide and the income they generate are sources of patronage. Whatever losses state-owned enterprises incur are also converted into patronage through further government borrowings that in turn generate interest payments. The commitments made at Ta'if, to overhaul the public administration and improve governance generally, have not been fulfilled, as suggested by the World Bank's assessments. On the four governance measures that directly address the administrative capacity of government – government effectiveness, regulatory quality, rule of law, and control of corruption – Lebanon's performance over the decade ending in 2008 declined on all but regulatory quality. On control of corruption and rule of law the declines were precipitous, from almost the 50th percentile to the 20th in the case of the former and from almost the 50th to the 26th in the latter. On the key measure of government effectiveness, Lebanon in 2008 was outperformed by some 70 percent of the world's countries and, in the MENA, by all countries except Syria, Iran, Libya, Yemen, and Iraq. On all these four governance measures, except regulatory quality, Lebanon in 2008 was below the MENA average. Like the World Bank, the IMF is not impressed by governance in Lebanon. In its assessment of the adequacy of the government's data for IMF surveillance according to the terms of the most recent standby agreement, "data provision has serious shortcomings . . . There are serious issues in the compilation of the national accounts, employment, general government and the rest of the nonfinancial public sector, and balance of payments," in sum, all but one of the data categories monitored by the IMF (IMF April 2009b: 7).

Declining quality of governance has been associated with stagnating globalization. Once the most outward-looking of the Arab economies, Lebanon, unlike most of its Arab neighbors, has yet to join the WTO because it has been unable to meet various of that organization's requirements. Lebanon's trade as a percentage of GDP, which prior to the civil war was the envy of the region's non-oil exporters, slumped to the 52 to 64 percent range in the period 2002–6, about the MENA average. The much vaunted Lebanese system of laissez faire capitalism is now hobbled by an inefficient state, as various measures of ease of doing business suggest. Opening a business requires 46 days, compared to a regional average of 39, and collecting a debt costs 27 percent of the total, against a MENA average of 18 percent. The shortcomings of the judicial system are reflected in the 721 days it requires on average to enforce a contract, compared to 437 for the MENA as a whole (*Profil Pay Liban* 2005: 146). The 2008 World Bank's report on doing business ranked Lebanon 132nd on ease of starting a business, 113th on dealing with licenses, and 121st in enforcing contracts. Lebanon, which used to be a transportation and communication gateway to the Arab east and the Gulf, now has fewer mobile phones per 100 population than all MENA countries except Sudan and Yemen.

Lebanon is hardly the only Arab country not "refocusing the development agenda firmly on people's well being" as the *Arab Human Development Report 2009* prescribes (United Nations Development Programme, 2009: v), but it exports a higher percentage of its labor force than any other. Because those "exports" tend to be Lebanese with the most education and training, the economy suffers from a brain drain. In 2000, for example, college-educated emigrants equaled nearly 40 percent of the country's total college-educated population, twice the rate in Morocco and Iran, the two countries ranking second and third, respectively, in the MENA on this measure (Gonzalez et al. 2008: 227). Push factors behind emigration are strong, as suggested by an unemployment rate that has hovered around 8 percent even during the third great oil boom, rising to 27 percent for those aged 15 to 19 and 17 percent for those 20 to 24. The unemployment rate for university graduates exceeds that for those who have less than secondary educations, suggesting that the economy is not generating demand for those with high skill levels (Gonzalez et al. 2008: 228). Other push factors for emigration include a declining labor force participation rate, especially for males; stagnating per capita income, which was still one-third below the 1975 level in 2005 (Gonzalez et al. 2008: 207, 219); and a government-imposed nominal wage freeze in 1996 that was still in effect in 2008 (Dibeh 2009: 8). Wages as a percentage of national income dropped from the 50 to 55 percent range in the prewar years to about a third in the late 1990s (Dibeh 2009: 12). Further downward pressure on wages has been exerted as a result of large-scale inward labor migration, with estimates ranging upwards from 300,000 foreign workers being in the country at any given time (Chalcraft 2009). During the period 1993 to 2003, the annual average growth rate for industry was −0.4 percent and for the manufacturing subsector, −1.8 percent (Dibeh 2009: 13), so that sector theoretically most capable of creating high-quality employment has stagnated. There is also evidence to suggest that human resource development is in decline, which would be natural given the lack of emphasis on it in the overall development model. The UNDP reported in 2002 that "the system of primary and secondary education is widely perceived as failing to produce sufficient numbers of graduates with the skills required for direct entry into the labor market or continued study at the post-secondary level" (cited in Gonzalez et al. 2008: 221). Lebanon participated in international assessments of its school system in 2003 and 2007. Its eighth-graders placed 31st of 45 countries in mathematics, 30 points below the average, whereas in science they were 41st out of the 45 countries, 80 points below the average of 473. On the science test Lebanese school children underperformed those in all MENA countries who also took the test, including Jordan, Iran, Tunisia, Egypt, Bahrain, the Palestinian National Authority, Morocco, and Saudi Arabia (cited in Gonzalez et al. 2008: 222). Not surprising, given these signs of disdain for human well-being, "poverty in Lebanon is high," as the IMF concludes, and adult illiteracy exceeded that of neighboring Jordan (Table 2.2). Its real GDP per capita rank minus its HDI rank, as reported in Chapter 2 (Table 2.1), was still –7, and despite a tradition of good private schools, its Education Index rank was 22 places below its GDP rank.

The Lebanese political economy, in sum, illustrates in a perverse way the structural power of capital in a fragmented democracy. The banking sector, largely controlled by those who command their confessions, supplemented by externally provided patronage as well as by that generated through the state's "service ministries" and public-sector companies, provide the means to sustain consociationalism. Sociopolitical conflict is managed by confession-based elites, who contain it through side payments to their respective constituencies. Challenges to the system inevitably confront cross-confession elite coalitions that form to defend the status quo that benefits those elites. But the failures to reform the state and the economy and make them more responsive to the broad population inevitably also exacerbate sociopolitical tension, thereby contributing to the further separation, indeed virtual cantonization, of the various sects, including in once-cosmopolitan Beirut. The safety valve of migration is of utmost importance in maintaining internal peace, but like the system as a whole, it depends on external factors that, by definition, are beyond Lebanon's control. The country remains, as it has long been, a precarious, dependent republic.

Iran

The Islamic Republic of Iran has contributed much less to a viable synthesis between globalization and Islam than has nominally secular Turkey. This paradox results from the fact that in postrevolutionary Iran there has been no sustained dialogue between globalizers and moralizers. The revolution swept away the secular, pro-Western elite and delivered the state to Islamists, thus removing the thesis against which an Islamist antithesis could react. Instead of becoming a tool with which to forge a synthesis with globalization, the Islamic state turned in on itself, both because of the imposition of sanctions by the United States and because of the perceived need to consolidate and defend the revolution. Thus it became the exercise of state power, rather than a reaction against it, and the use of that power in the international economy that have preoccupied Iran's moralizers. And as in other MENA democracies, but to an even greater extent, the state has been used as a distributive tool to alleviate sociopolitical conflicts, thus impairing its ability to propel more rapid economic development.

To be fair, the regional and global contexts have hardly been propitious. Since the revolution of 1979, the Iranian government has had to contend with an eight-year war with Iraq, an economic embargo imposed by the United States, a massive influx of refugees from Iraq and Afghanistan, and three oil price collapses. But the instinctive impulse of Iran's Islamist revolutionaries, once in power, was in any case inimical to economic growth or formulating a productive response to the challenges of globalization. That impulse included, as is typically the case in the wake of revolutions, taking direct control of capital allocation and nationalizing the means of production.

In 1983–4, 28 of the country's 36 banks, 13 of which had foreign partners, were nationalized, followed by forced mergers that reduced the number of banks to 6 commercial and 3 specialized ones and the number of total branches from some 8,300 to less than 6,600 (Zangeneh 1998: 123). The financial sector has remained tightly controlled since that time and so has failed to deepen, diversify, or improve its efficiency. As Figure 3.5 indicated, 69 percent of total deposits are held by only three of Iran's six big commercial banks. Government ownership of some 89 percent of total bank assets is exceeded in the MENA only by Algeria and Syria. Interest margins have been highly variable and determined more by political than economic criteria. On coming to office in 2005, President Mahmoud Ahmadinejad launched an attack on high interest rates, with spreads at that time being in the 4 to 6 percent range in real terms. He required both private and government banks to lower their lending rates, to 17 and 14 percent, respectively, taking them into negative territory in real terms. Private banks responded by ceasing lending, whereas government banks' capital positions began to erode. Private borrowers were forced to turn to the bazaar, where prevailing interest rates were 30 to 40 percent (Looney 2007b: 417–27). In January 2010 the central bank ordered commercial banks to limit daily cash withdrawals to 150 million rials, thereby stimulating a run on the banks and further displacement of banks' credit function by informal savings funds that had proliferated since 2005 (Bozorgmehr 2010). Underlying rumors of banks' insolvency was the government's own admission that nonperforming loans had reached $45 billion, a two-thirds increase on 2009 and a ninefold increase since Ahmadinejad had become president. Independent reports indicated nonperforming loans by spring 2010 exceeded a quarter of all loans, rivaling those of the bunker states depicted in Figure 3.8 (Bozorgmehr 2010; Amuzegar 2010a). The Milken Institute's Capital Access Index in 2009 ranked Iran 81st out of 120 countries on its measure of "level of involvement of deposit-taking institutions in financing businesses." Only Syria and Yemen among MENA countries ranked lower (Angkinand et al. 2009).

Given the degree of concentration and governmental control of the banking sector, it is not surprising that it is both inefficient and opaque. Indeed, it is the least transparent in the MENA region, with Iran scoring a region low of 28 on the World Bank's Bank Disclosure Index in 2006, with only Libya being even close at 29 (Table 3.4). This low score does indeed appear to reflect reality, for in 2009 it was revealed by the Iranian State Audit Agency that there were discrepancies over the preceding four years in governmental accounts in the amount of $66 billion, the equivalent of annual average oil revenues, with explanations of the missing billions by pundits ranging from corruption, to political infighting, to attempts to hide expenditures on weapons development and clandestine foreign adventures ("Ahmadinejad's Administration" 2009). On the Heritage Foundation's Index of Economic Freedom, Iran in 2009 had the MENA's lowest scores on monetary freedom, investment freedom, and financial freedom, with its overall average on the nine measures being only marginally better than last-place Libya. Not surprising, given the lack of transparency surrounding the financial sector, the Tehran stock exchange has failed to keep pace with growth rates of equity markets elsewhere in the region. In 2006 its capitalization was only some 17 percent of GDP, while the value of shares traded in that year was a paltry 2 percent of GDP. On the Milken Institute's measure of equity market development, which "reflects the importance of equity markets for business financing," Iran in 2008 ranked 89th out of 113 countries, again with only Syria and Yemen within the MENA scoring lower. In the critical area of providing access to foreign capital, the Iranian financial sector performed still worse, ranking 110th out of 122 countries on the Milken Institute's measure.

Coupled with seizure of control of the financial sector by the Islamic revolutionaries was nationalization of the means of production. In order to control private enterprises, including those formerly owned by the shah's Pahlavi Foundation, the mullahs established bonyads, or what a former Iranian minister of finance has referred to as "independent and monopolistic . . . mafia-type religious conglomerates" (Amuzegar 1998: 90). Bonyads coexist uneasily alongside a directly state-controlled public sector comprising yet other nationalized enterprises, as well as those that the Islamic revolutionaries inherited directly from the shah's large public sector. The oldest and biggest bonyad, the Foundation for the Oppressed and War Veterans, originally formed to take control of the assets of the Pahlavi Foundation, "is second in size only to the central government." It is claimed by its president to be the largest economic enterprise in the Middle East (Akhavi-Pour and Azodanloo 1998: 80). It accounts for a fifth of all textiles and apparel produced in Iran, a quarter of the sugar, and about half the beverages, plus dominant shares of construction materials markets. The U.S. Congressional Research Service reported in 2009 that it contributed more than 10 percent of the total GDP, had more than 200,000 employees and 350 subsidiaries, and an estimated value of $3 billion (Ilias 2009: 8). The share of *bonyads* within the larger public sector is impossible to determine precisely, for, according to one expert, "perhaps not surprisingly there are little reliable/detailed data on the activities of *bonyads* . . . and official statistics do not separate the activities of *bonyads* from the rest of the private/public economic activities." This expert notes that "their general influence in the economy . . . goes well beyond their economic operations due to their links to the supreme leader and the *sepah*" (i.e., IRGC) (Pesaran 2009).

Conservatives, especially those entrenched in the bonyads, bitterly and successfully opposed a home-grown structural adjustment program that President Ali Akbar Hashemi Rafsanjani had launched shortly after the death of Ayatollah Khomeini. The privatization program ground to a halt by 1994, leaving the state and the bonyads in control of four-fifths of the economy, producing some 5,000 different goods and services, employing about a fifth of the labor force, handling about three-quarters of all imports, and achieving total annual sales of $3.5 billion (Amuzegar 1998: 90). The contribution of *bonyads* to GDP apparently increased in tandem with the power of conservatives, possibly reaching as much as 40 per cent of GDP under Ahmadinejad (Looney 2006: 29–37). In 2005 Ayatollah Ali Khamenei agreed that 80 percent of banks and big industries, including downstream oil, gas, and petrochemicals, could be privatized. What ownership change that has in fact occurred has been the transfer of companies from one state sector to another as government-affiliated funds, state-owned banks, ministry retirement funds, and more recently the IRGC have bought majority stakes. By 2009, the private sector still constituted only about one fifth of the total economy (Bozorgmehr, 2009).

Despite intermittent efforts from 1989 to 2005 by Presidents Hashemi Rafsanjani and President Mohammed Khatami to roll back some of the more excessive governmental controls while adopting more rational macroeconomic policies and reconnecting the economy to the world, it has remained relatively unproductive, dependent on oil, and deglobalized. Total factor productivity as measured by the IMF averaged between –1.8 percent and 1.0 percent from 1988 to 2000, compared to the 1 to 3 percent average range for developing countries (Looney 2007b: 421). Oil, which provided 55 percent of government revenues in 1997, supplied almost 70 percent in 2007 (Table 2.3). In that year FDI inflow was $754 million, down from $917 million two years earlier and a small fraction of the $24.3 billion FDI to Saudi Arabia, $22 billion to Turkey, and $11.6 billion to Egypt (Ilias 2009: 28). Associated with deglobalization has been a deterioration in quality of governance, which scored on most indicators below all other MENA states except Iraq, Libya, Sudan and Yemen (Table 3.2). Because of profound economic inefficiencies combined with "petro-populism," as Robert Looney has characterized its political economy, inflation has been a continuing problem, running at about 30 percent in 2008.

The election of Muhammad Khatami as president in 1997 resulted in part from a widespread desire for improved economic performance, a desire to which his new government attempted to respond by fusing "development with social justice" as part of a strategy to satisfy both the champions of continued welfare subsidies and reformist technocrats (Amuzegar 1998: 86). But the combination of plummeting oil prices in 1998–9, division within Khatami's own camp, and, most of all, staunch opposition by the leadership of the conservative faction – entrenched in the bonyads and various parts of the state apparatus, key of which was the 120,000-strong Islamic Revolutionary Guard Corps (IRGC) and the some 3-million-member Basij militia – caused the mild reform to be stillborn. Even lukewarm attempts to render more transparent the state's accounts, which include large but unknown transfers and subsidies to the bonyads from the public treasury, ended in failure. In the first year of Khatami's presidency, no more than one-quarter of the some 1,200 state enterprises even bothered to submit their annual financial reports. Although the finance minister promised closer supervision of public finances, some of the public-sector companies financed by the state transferred money out of Iran and invested abroad without the control authorities' knowledge of the nature and magnitude of these outlays (Amuzegar 1998: 90).

The opacity of the Iranian political economy was purposeful, as competitive factions entrenched in the state used its resources to vie for power. As these struggles deepened following Khatami's election and then became yet more intense following the reformers' victory in the

2000 parliamentary elections and Khatami's reelection in 2001, they polarized the factions, which coalesced into two basic camps. "Conservatives" – in the sense that they want to conserve what they see as the gains of the revolution – claim the mantle of Ayatollah Khomeini. They seek to maintain the rule of the mullahs, most especially through the supremacy of the post of velayat-e faqih, or religious jurist, which is occupied by their leading figure, Ayatollah Ali Khamenei, a mullah with lackluster religious credentials whom Khomeini had charged with establishing the IRGC. The moderates, also known as liberals, reformers, or technocrats, found their first champion in President Khatami. They advocate greater respect for the rule of law, a commensurate reduction in revolutionary zeal, and more democracy, including an expanded political role for nonclerics. They clearly attract the support of Iran's youth, a frightening prospect for the Conservatives given than half of Iran's population is under 25 years of age and hence has no firsthand experience of the shah's regime or the revolution.

The steadily intensifying struggle between these two factions resulted in the state being carved up between them, with the reformers having the smaller slice. The constitutional/legal structure of the Islamic Republic, which is extraordinarily elaborate, was both the result and a cause of political competition and fragmentation. The executive and legislative branches consist not just of a single executive and legislature, but of numerous institutions assigned roles in both domains. The supreme leader, or faqih, was for many years counterbalanced by the president, and both have to deal with the Assembly of Experts, the Council of Guardians, and the Council for Discernment of Expediency, to say nothing of the parliament and the various components of the executive branch, almost all of which share numerous executive and legislative functions in Byzantine fashion. Roughly speaking, the Conservatives, whose champion is the faqih, became entrenched in what might be thought of as those institutions that parallel the normal state structure, within which the Moderates, first led by President Khatami, were entrenched. So, for example, the Moderates under Rafsanjani and Khatami tended to control the Council of Ministers, the central bank, and mayors, whereas the Conservatives held sway in the judicial branch and the assembly and councils identified earlier, most important for elections of which was the Guardian Council, composed of six clerics and six jurists closely associated with Ali Khamenei. Its power to approve potential electoral candidates, including for parliament, subsequently proved to be decisive (Akhavi-Pour and Azodanloo 1998: 70–2). In the economic domain, the major bases for the Conservatives were the bonyads and networks of religious institutions that generate revenues. Of vital importance in determining the outcome of the increasingly intense struggle between conservatives and moderates was the fact that the former controlled the principal means of coercion, at the core of which was the IRGC, which Ayatollah Khomeini had charged Ali Khamenei with bolstering as a counterforce to the regular military immediately after the revolution and which had subsequently acquired a vast network of business enterprises, thereby providing yet more patronage resources to the Conservatives.

Threatened by the popularity of reformers, as evidenced by their winning 65 percent of the vote in the 2000 parliamentary election, as opposed to 20 percent taken by hardliners, and by Khatami's 78 percent of the vote in the 2001 presidential election, as compared to 70 percent in 1997, the Conservatives became committed to ousting Moderates from their positions of power. Drawing on the constitutional authority of the Council of Guardians to approve candidates, they rejected more than 2,000 reformers who sought to contest the 2004 parliamentary election. A year later, by which time reformers had become dispirited, Ali Khamenei engineered the election of the obscure Mahmoud Ahmadinejad, the son of a blacksmith and former IRGC member, as president. The powers of the presidency were now at the at least indirect disposal of Khamenei, powers that were greatly enhanced by virtue of Ahmadinejad's connections with the IRGC, through which he had risen and from which he systematically recruited into the cabinet and other key political posts, while acting to further broaden the IRGC's ample patronage resources by ensuring that various companies under its control won increasingly lucrative contracts. Khatam al Anbya, for example, its main construction firm, in 2006 alone was awarded contracts worth some $7 billion, including those to build a gas pipeline eastward from the Persian Gulf and a new line for the Tehran subway. By the end of his first presidential term, Ahmadinejad's cabinet had a majority of members with backgrounds in the IRGC, which also supplied a third of the members of the new parliament. The IRGC's capacity to control the street was in 2007 upgraded by placing under its command the nationally organized Basij militia, itself commanded by Khamenei's son Mojtaba, and by the mission of the combined force being officially stated by its new commander, Mohammad Ali Jafari, to be "internal unrest" (Smyth 2009).

The stage was thus set for the showdown between Conservatives and Moderates that signaled the final slide of Iran's quasi democracy into bully praetorian status. The June 2009 presidential election sparked the confrontation by unleashing a "green wave" of popular dissatisfaction with President Ahmadinejad, coupled with an outpouring of support for the candidate who by default became the champion of the reformers, Mir Hossein Mousavi, who formerly had served as Prime Minister and Foreign Minister but had been politically marginal for more than a decade. That his political past could be traced back to participation both in the revolution itself and then in the government it gave rise to indicates how profoundly split the Iranian polity had become. Ahmadinejad, apparently acting with the support of Khamenei, preempted Mousavi's possible win by having the Electoral Commission announce on June 12 – very shortly after the polls closed and after mobile phone texting had been switched off nationwide, the Ministry of Interior surrounded by troops, and security forces deployed onto the streets – a record turnout of 85 percent, with Ahmadinejad taking 62 percent and Mousavi 34 percent of the vote. The popular reaction was immediate and took the form of both widespread demonstrations and criticism by a broad array of moderates, including former presidents Rafsanjani and Khatami, of the election and those responsible for rigging it. Khamenei and Ahmadinejad drew on their base of power in the IRGC, the Basij, the regular police and the courts and struck back. They instituted a veritable reign of terror, including widespread imprisonment and torture, culminating in show trials in August-September of scores of reformers, some of them closely connected to the movement's leaders. The revolution seemed to have followed the trajectory of its Russian and Chinese predecessors, with moderates being purged by hardliners entrenched in the coercive apparatus, who forced their humiliated opponents to "confess" their political sins.

What remained obscure were the exact relationships between key actors among hardliners, including the IRGC commander Mohammed Ali Jafari, the Basij, Khamenei, his son Mojtaba, and Ahmadinejad, to say nothing of the role of some of the more shadowy actors, including intelligence forces. So whether the dramatic moves in the summer of 2009 constituted final consolidation of power by Ayatollah Khamenei, the usurpation of his power by President Ahmadinejad, or a military coup was unclear. But what was obvious was that Iran's quasidemocratic status, in which competing factions shared power within the state with reasonably free and fair elections contributing substantially to that balance of power, and in which civil society was afforded considerable freedom, had come to an end. Iran by the fall of 2009 resembled the Arab praetorian republics much more closely than it did the MENA's democracies. As if to confirm its slide from relative grace, the Reporters Without Borders Press Freedom Index ranked Iran in 2009 172nd out of 175 countries, the lowest in the MENA and one in which the profession of journalist was among the most dangerous. That the deterioration of press freedom is unlikely soon to be reversed is suggested by the IRGC's increasing control over the media and the Internet. In October 2009 a firm under its control, Etemad Mobin Development Company, bought 51 percent of the shares of the government-owned telecommunications company that owns all land lines, two mobile phone companies, and all Internet providers in the country. The only rival bidder was from the private sector, but the bid was thrown out on grounds of national security. The IRGC has also come to dominate the country's leading news agency Fars, which is housed in premises owned by the IRGC that was formerly the headquarters of its intelligence unit. All members of its editorial board are former IRCG commanders. The IRGC announced in late 2009 its intention to launch a news agency modeled on the BBC, as part of its plan, in the words of a dissident Iranian journalist, to "dominate the flow of information and be the ones telling the world what's going on in Iran" (Fassihi, 2009).

The only real questions that remained were whether Iran's leaders were going to try to follow the comparatively soft authoritarian path of the bully praetorians or the harder, more draconian one of the bunker-based praetorians, and whether or not the comparatively broadly based, energized Iranian civil society could be subordinated as required by either model. President Ahmadinejad's nominations to his first new cabinet in August-September 2009 seemed to suggest that the regime might be leaning more toward bunker status because key portfolios, including petroleum and interior, were allocated to former IRGC members. This interpretation was reinforced by a simultaneous purge of high-ranking staff in the intelligence ministry, who were deemed to be too moderate, and by calls by IRGC commander Jafairi and others for political parties to be banned and their leaders arrested.

The broader lesson of the apparent demise of Iran's fragmented democracy may be that democracy is comparatively fragile throughout the MENA. The steady encroachment by the IRGC and Basij on civilian political authority and the progressive expansion of their political roles contributed substantially to the dramatic events of 2009. The MENA's other democracies, including Israel, have yet to establish unequivocal subordination of coercive forces to constitutionally based civil control. In Lebanon, the reconstruction of the army since the 1989 Ta'if Accord, accompanied by the invigoration of security forces under Syrian tutelage, has occurred without parallel strengthening of political institutions, thus possibly paving the way to the subordination of those institutions to these coercive forces. Alternatively, conflicting confessional interests within the army and security forces could result in their fragmentation, with those fragments then assuming power within their respective confessions, as had happened in 1976. That the two viable candidates for the presidency once Syrian influence had abated were generals – Aoun and Suleiman – is suggestive of the drift of political power away from civilians. In Turkey, competition between the AKP government and Kemalists is intensifying as trials of alleged conspirators in a "deep state" nicknamed *Ergenekon* and in the purported 2003 "sledgehammer" coup attempt grind on. In Israel, the ongoing struggle to subordinate Palestinians has steadily elevated the role of the military in the political system, as indicated by its enhanced importance in the making of national security policies and by the role of former officers in the political elite.

That coercive forces, acting in some relationship with hardline politicians, could terminate Iran's democracy results not just from their power, but also from the enervation and delegitimation of the political system, due primarily to its poor economic performance. Iran's comparative failure to benefit economically from globalization and the crude utilization of its economic resources to support political actors caused opposition, especially among the young, to steadily grow. Although the Iranian economy has significantly underperformed those of the MENA's other democracies, they, too, with the apparent exception of Israel, are vulnerable to economic deterioration. Lebanon's precarious, high-wire economic balancing act could tip over, whereas Turkey's steady growth has been paralleled by rising external debt. Major economic crises are thus still possible in both, and neither has so institutionalized democracy that it could without any doubt withstand such a crisis. At this stage, however, an Iranian-style descent into praetorianism for the region's other democracies appears unlikely. In none of them is the concentration of capital resources and their allocation so tightly within the hands of the state and a single faction within it, as increasingly became the case in Iran from the outset of the twenty-first century. The more diffuse structure of capital in Israel, Turkey, and Lebanon suggests more competitive pluralism and greater capacity of their polities to withstand economic or other shocks.

Conclusion

The MENA democracies govern societies that are sharply fragmented and threatened by the ever-present danger of violent political conflict. For the most part they have done a better job in managing this conflict than have the bunker states, where the solution to societal conflict is for one social force to seize the state and seek to impose its will on the others. The democrats probably spend less on side payments to those social forces than either the bunker or bully praetorians spend on control and coercion. And the indirect costs to economic development of side payments are probably on balance less than the costs of obtrusive state control, which in the most dramatic cases has pulverized capitalists and civil society, leaving the state without societal mechanisms to respond to whatever opportunities public policy might provide. Thus the democrats are rather more capable of meeting the challenges of globalization than the praetorians, but, because they govern more fractious societies, are not appreciably better placed than at least some of the monarchies. By and large, however, the democrats are less frightened of information flow; have stronger civil societies, more developed and competitive economic institutions, lower transaction costs, and better established external linkages; and, in general, are more cosmopolitan than either the praetorians or the monarchies. But in all MENA democracies, political systems continue to impede more rapid growth because questions of identity and security take precedence and drain resources.

Suggestions for further reading

Turkey's politics and economy are analyzed by Aydin (2005), Altug and Filiztekin (2006), Tugal (2009) and Yavuz (2009). For analyses of the Israeli political economy, see Nitzan and Bichler (2002 and 2009), Barkai and Liviatan (2007), and Senor and Singer (2009). The unique nature of the Lebanese political economy is the subject of both Gaspard (2004) and Makdisi (2004), whereas Dibeh (2005) focuses on economic reconstruction. On Iranian politics, see Buchta (2000), Takeyh (2006), and Abrahamian (2008); an analysis of the IRGC and its role in the political economy is provided by Wehrey et al. (2009). The Iranian economy is analyzed by Amuzegar (1993), Nuomani and Behad (2006), and Gheissari (2009).

8   Conclusion

Countries of the Middle East and North Africa (MENA) were well placed economically to take advantage of the surge of globalization that commenced some twenty years before the Cold War's end further accelerated its pace. World merchandise exports as a percentage of global GDP rose from 7 percent in 1950 (as compared to 8.7 percent at the end of the last great wave of globalization in 1913) to 11 percent in the early 1970s, 17 percent in 1995, and 26 percent in 2008. In the 1960s the MENA was the most rapidly developing region of the then "third world," appearing poised to ride the gathering wave of globalization destined to transform that "third world" into the much wealthier "emerging economies" of the twenty-first century.

Alas, in the event most MENA countries failed to take adequate advantage of opportunities afforded by accelerating international movements of capital, goods, and people. Hesitant to transform their inward-looking, state-dominated economies into outward-oriented ones in which private sectors would serve as the engines of growth, MENA countries began to fall behind more rapidly growing competitors elsewhere in the developing world. As the 1970s progressed, downward pressure on per capita growth rates in the MENA, temporarily revitalized by the first oil boom in the wake of the 1973 Arab-Israeli war, was intensified by rapidly growing populations. The second oil boom that accompanied the 1979 Iranian revolution similarly temporarily slowed but failed to halt the downward economic trajectory, which for most countries of the region began to reach crisis proportions by the latter half of the 1980s. In a quarter of a century, during which time the Middle East became the epicenter of the new global energy economy, many MENA countries had slid from the cutting to the trailing edge of third world development.

Faced with mountainous foreign debts, devaluing currencies, unsustainable fiscal and current account deficits, and increasingly restive populations, incumbent MENA political elites began cautiously to reform their political economies. The neoliberal "Washington Consensus," which was coming into vogue as the Cold War ended, provided the road map that they followed in varying degrees as they began the shift from public- to private-sector dominance of economies, which were opened to more external trade and capital flows. Accompanying political reforms addressed both "quality of administration" and "public accountability," the labels given by the World Bank to the two key components of the broader concept of "governance," a term which the Bank finds more politic to use than "democracy." (World Bank 2003). But for most purposes "public accountability" is democracy, and indeed in the late 1980s many of the MENA authoritarian regimes appeared to be commencing democratization in earnest as they were simultaneously seeking to improve the quality of governmental administration, especially as regards economic management.

This double-barreled reform process did not persist far into the 1990s, however, for those incumbent elites who tried it quickly realized that "public accountability" would undermine their power, possibly fatally. Moreover, they increasingly perceived that they could have their cake and eat it, too – that is, open up their economies but not their polities. Government administrations could be made equal to the task of managing increasingly complex, privatized economies generating regime-sustaining resources, without being embedded in broader "public accountability," meaning democracy. The Chinese example, which burst onto the world stage in the late 1990s, did not give rise to this strategy, but reinforced it. So, by the beginning of the new millennium, the trauma of the 1980s economic crisis had been replaced by a new self-confidence on the part of regimes that their authoritarianism was compatible with a reasonably successful, if cautious, economic globalization. Their reform efforts could, therefore, be concentrated on creating improved environments for business without fear of failure or inadvertently stimulating a more threatening reform of the broader political system. This rejection of democratization in turn necessitated an intensification of authoritarianism in order to contain the inevitable dislocations and backlashes resulting from economic liberalization and globalization and the inequities they intensified. Thus, administrative and economic reforms were taking place alongside intensification of repression by security and intelligence services, thereby raising the question of whether inadequate "public accountability" might in fact limit the extent and effectiveness of administrative and economic reforms. Indeed, the failure of economic growth to truly accelerate suggested there might well be a linkage in that a truly business-friendly environment required at least some measure of democratization.

But the need to answer this question definitively was postponed if not obviated by the third great oil boom that commenced in 2003. The surge in revenues resultant from rapidly rising oil and gas prices once again washed through the MENA region, stimulating trade, investment, employment, and growth. Moreover, the economic and administrative reforms that had been put in place since the previous two oil booms, combined with the development of human and physical infrastructure in the meantime, made it possible for this boom's petrodollars to be invested more directly in productive enterprises. The wealthy oil and gas export-ing countries greatly intensified value-added processing of hydrocarbons and the building of energy-intensive industries. Neighboring countries turned their attention to delivering services and labor to the wealthy exporting countries while utilizing capital sent by the oil exporters to build their domestic economies. As a result, growth rates, which had stagnated throughout the 1990s and into the twenty-first century, finally began to accelerate, reaching a respectable regional national average of around 6 percent by 2007.

This flurry of economic activity stimulated by the oil boom did not, however, fundamentally transform regional economies, as began to become apparent even before the boom ended in late 2008. Per capita growth rates, averaging around 2 percent, although high by the region's recent standards, lagged behind competitors, especially those in East Asia, where they were at least double that. As a destination for foreign direct and portfolio investment, the MENA became more attractive, surg-ing in 2006 to over 10 percent of such investment to low- and middle-income countries (Figure 2.10) when its population size would merit a 5.7 percent share. Much of that investment was intraregional, however, rather than being composed of funds flowing from Europe, North Amer-ica, Asia, or elsewhere. And as had been the case previously, most of the extraregional investment was in hydrocarbon extraction, processing, and delivery, not in manufacturing (World Bank 2009b: 55). MENA finan-cial sectors were upgraded, but remained comparatively ineffective in delivering credit to private sectors, especially the vital small and medium enterprises that account in many countries of the region for as much as 90 percent of total private-sector employment. Economic diversification did not proceed very far, as more than two-thirds of the region's exports remained those of raw materials. The Arab countries' contribution to manufactured goods in global trade, although rising slightly, still hov-ered around 1 percent, in gross terms the equivalent of such exports from Hungary, or about half of those from Finland.

Most importantly, the MENA's key challenge, which is to make effec-tive economic use of the biggest demographic gift (the difference between the growth of the working-age and total population) in modern world history, resulting from the region's rapid population growth, was not being met. Unemployment rates declined somewhat and labor force participation rates increased, but not dramatically. The latter remained the lowest in the world and the former higher than any other region except Sub-Saharan Africa. Despite much talk of "knowledge economies," especially in the rich Gulf states, MENA human resources proved unable to meet this challenge. The social contract through which MENA regimes traditionally distributed public benefits, including health services and education, in exchange for political quiescence failed in most MENA countries to generate scores on basic human development indicators consistent with their income levels (Table 2.1). Evidently a "lowest common denominator" approach to delivering health services and education, more or less without accountability to consumers or in competition with other service providers, has resulted in human resource capacities attuned to the needs not of expanding private sectors, but to civil services and public sectors, which were the implicit markets they were designed to serve. Globally competitive private sectors, especially those in industry, required graduates with more skills than local institutions produced, so where possible, private firms hired expatriates and contributed not to local employment, but to unemployment. On key measures of educational competitiveness and achievements, such as reputations of educational institutions, publication rates of faculty, registration of patents, or engagement in research and development, MENA institutions and individuals failed to make up ground, remaining at or near the bottom of global league tables (except in Israel).

Human resource shortcomings, combined with lack of integration of cutting-edge technologies into productive processes, largely because multinational corporations remain hesitant to invest outside the hydrocarbon sector in the MENA, resulted in an inability of MENA economies to increase productivity. Thus, although total output was increased during the third oil boom as a result of more investment and employment, the failure to reap gains through improvement in productivity both limited per capita income gains and rendered the MENA economy vulnerable to downturns in gross inputs, especially investment. Having failed to move up production chains and relying heavily on investments in low-tech areas, such as construction, to generate employment and income, the MENA was more vulnerable to the Great Recession that began in late 2008 than its degree of globalization would suggest. Indeed, while incumbent elites in 2009 were informing their peoples that they would not be heavily impacted by the Great Recession precisely because national economies were reasonably insulated from the global economy, they simultaneously were falling back on the time-tested social contract components of consumer subsidies, civil service employment, and wage raises in efforts to ride out the storm that was bearing down on them. The third oil boom had come and gone, and the MENA, if not back exactly to where it had started, had not progressed much in terms of its global economic competitiveness or the basic strategy of its governments to retain incumbency and maintain order through allocations of entitlements, rather than through "public accountability."

Although MENA national political economies are sufficiently similar to be recognized as constituting parts of a regional whole, there are both national and subregional differences that globalization has accentuated. Within the Arab world, the six states that constitute the Gulf Cooperation Council – Saudi Arabia, Kuwait, Qatar, Bahrain, the United Arab Emirates, and Oman – have, as a result of the three oil booms since 1973, become a distinctive subregion, substantially wealthier and more integrated and globalized than the Arab states of North Africa or the Levant. The most recent oil boom accelerated the momentum of their downstream move into hydrocarbon processing and energy-intensive manufacturing, while stimulating the growth of their service industries and financial sectors. Indeed, alone among the subregions of the MENA, the GCC states have developed reasonably coherent strategies for long-term growth based on these three pillars of hydrocarbon extraction, processing, and utilization; expansion into global service provision; and worldwide investment of petrodollars. In the view of one close observer, the leading GCC state, Saudi Arabia, has become a "developmental monarchy," with its "embedded" state performing the strategic planning and coordinating roles equivalent to those discharged by the East Asian developmental states (Niblock 2007). Another close observer of GCC politics notes that the rise of an entrepreneurial bourgeoisie, on the one hand, and the gradual expansion of constitutionalism and political rights, on the other, signals that sustainable political reform is underway that is likely ultimately to result in quasiconstitutional monarchies in which ruling families directly dominate only "high politics," with public policies in areas other than defense, national security, and foreign affairs being openly and publicly contested (Luciani 2007b).

Whether sustained economic development and political liberalization are indeed in store for the GCC states is debatable, but what is certain is that those states have steadily opened performance gaps between themselves and other Arab states. Per capita GDPs have grown faster than those elsewhere in the Arab world, as has the quality of public administration, which has in turn rendered GCC countries substantially more "business friendly" than other Arab states. But on measures of "public accountability," GCC states have failed to open up gaps with the Arab republics, Jordan, or Morocco, suggesting that if indeed democratization is coming to the GCC, it may not be coming any faster than in North Africa or the Levant. And in those subregions, public accountability remains notable by its absence. Algeria, Libya, Yemen, Syria, and Sudan, for example, despite gaining substantial revenues from hydrocarbon exports, not only made little headway in developing their economies and enhancing individual incomes during the third oil boom, but the quality of their public administrations continued to languish while their governments showed no signs of becoming more accountable to citizens. By the end of the boom, Iraq was also earning substantial revenues from its export of some 2 million barrels of oil per day, but its government remained one of the most corrupt in the world, if not the most corrupt, while being accountable more to outside powers than to its own people. Morocco, Tunisia, and Jordan, despite their lack of hydrocarbon exports, as well as Egypt with its expanding exports of gas, all managed small but steady increases in national income while making substantial improvements in economic policies, if rather less impressive ones with the actual management of their economies. But like both the GCC states and the other Arab energy exporters, these four Arab states also made no discernible move to democratize. Indeed, if anything, their security and intelligence agencies became more repressive as the oil boom progressed, thereby belying any hope that rising incomes might be accompanied by political liberalization, or that improvements in public administration might unleash parallel moves at the broader political level. The political economies of the Arab states, in sum, have become more diverse as the energy exporters have prospered disproportionately, but the political substructures on which they all rest remain fundamentally unchanged.

Paradoxically, the two MENA states that enjoyed greatest success in improving economic productivity and competitiveness, Israel and Turkey, were entirely without hydrocarbon exports. Instead of relying on windfalls from rising oil and gas prices, these two democracies drew on the comparatively high quality of their public administrations, business sectors, and human resources to grow their economies. Israel in particular became much more integrated into the global economy, with its more than 4,000 high-tech companies, 100 venture-capital funds, and some 70 listed firms on America's NASDAQ exchange leading the way. Underpinning the emergence of globally competitive companies in electronics, communications, computing, and health-care industries are Israeli human resources, which include the world's highest ratio of PhDs, engineers, and scientists per person. Privatization and upgrading of the historically cumbersome Israeli financial sector, combined with substantial increases in foreign direct and portfolio investment, ensured that the country's enterprises were fueled with adequate financial resources. But while Israel enjoyed remarkable success in integrating its economy into the commanding heights of global high-tech industries, it simultaneously was disengaging yet further from the MENA region as its unresolved conflict with the Palestinians rendered relations with Arabs and Muslims ever more problematical. Economic relations with Jordan and Egypt, brokered by the United States in the 1990s, proved to be small bridgeheads that did not expand much in those countries and not at all into the region. So despite its economic success, Israel remained a political anomaly in the region.

Turkey's further entry into the global economy was not at such rarified technological levels, but was reasonably impressive nevertheless. One measure of that success was rising real wages, which drove many of Turkey's textile and manufacturing firms to offshore low-value production to neighboring countries, such as Egypt, while moving up production chains in their home-based plants. But as has historically been the case with Turkey's democratic populism (and which was also the case in Israel prior to major reforms in the 1990s), the urge to simultaneously invest and to consume, the latter beyond the country's means, resulted in a burgeoning foreign debt leading the country in 2010 to consider entering into negotiations with the IMF for a standby facility. Simultaneously increasing political tension between the ruling AK Party and the military threatened to undermine the political stability upon which continued economic growth depends.

These two cases suggest that democracy may favor but certainly does not guarantee successful economic globalization. The performance of the region's other two democracies underscores that point. Iran, a democracy prior to 2005 only in the highly qualified sense that its head of state was elected in a relatively free and fair election – which in turn suggests just how low the bar is set in the authoritarian MENA – despite possessing vast hydrocarbon reserves, failed to leverage its growth during the third great oil boom. Caught between sanctions and the populism of President Mahmoud Ahmadinejad, the Iranian economy, even including the production and export of oil and gas, languished as the government focused on distributive measures at home and the projection of political power throughout the region. The highly contentious presidential election in June 2009 confirmed the country's slide into praetorianism. The third surviving MENA democracy, Lebanon, benefited from the oil boom primarily by exporting its people. By 2004 fully one-quarter of the Lebanese

GDP was derived from worker remittances, the highest proportion in the world, and they stayed above 20 percent, supplementing a real estate boom and a growing wave of tourists. Meanwhile, the Lebanese public debt continued to climb, making it one of the world's highest as a percentage of GDP. So Turkey, Iran, and Lebanon all abundantly illustrated one of the economic perils associated with democracy: fiscal irresponsibility resulting from political competition driving distribution at the expense of production. But despite that frailty – which still plagues Israel, but in lesser measure because of reforms in economic management and the higher level of per capita income – the non-oil-exporting democracies managed to keep pace with per capita growth rates achieved by the large oil exporters.

The MENA, then, is becoming more economically diverse, but as a whole is still playing catchup in many vital areas with the rest of the world. The oil boom did not resolve its endemic problems. Key among them is the failure adequately to educate, train, employ, and provide services for the rapidly expanding, youthful population. The region's unemployment rate, which declined gradually during the boom, started to climb as soon as oil prices commenced their fall. Even during the boom, expanding employment was disproportionately "informal," meaning without contract or registration in national pension and insurance programs. Although the middle class, almost however it is defined, expanded in most MENA countries during the boom, it did not grow nearly as fast as in the more successful countries of East and South Asia, Eastern Europe, or Latin America. In some MENA countries, the share of population still living on less than $2 per day did not drop below the same two-fifths proportion that obtained when the boom commenced.

Underlying the failure to lift large proportions of their populations through employment into secure middle-class status were continuing deficiencies in economic performance resulting primarily from poor governance. Public-sector employment in the MENA region, and its attendant wage bill, remained the highest in the world as a percentage of total employment and of governmental expenditure, respectively. So although the MENA did improve the quality of governmental management of the economy, as measured on various indicators by the World Bank and other organizations, it did so more at the easier policy level than at the more difficult institutional level. Its governmental structures remained too large, too inefficient, and too disconnected from global economic threats and opportunities to effectively guide economic development, however consistent new policies were with neoliberal best practice. The economic technocrats managed to introduce policy changes that at least nominally improved business climates, but they could not force their political leaders to take the risks inherent in downsizing and overhauling governmental institutions, on which much regime power rests. Wanting economic growth without taking major political risks to obtain it, political elites ruled out fundamental changes. As a result, real economic transformation, including rapid growth of industry, moving up production chains, and achieving higher rates of productivity, could not be achieved.

Political constraints on economic growth had additional, negative consequences. On the input side, political caution combined with preoccupation of ruling elites with conflict management at national and regional levels militated against adoption of a coherent model on which strategic planning might be based. Globalized neoliberals in other regions continued to celebrate their Washington Consensus despite an increasing number of skeptics, some of whom began to extol the virtues of the Beijing Consensus, but leaders of MENA political economies were both too busy and too worried either to systematically and universally apply the tenets of such a model to their national economy, or to work on developing an indigenous one. The very identification of other regions of the emerging world with specific development models is suggestive of their more coherent, self-conscious strategizing. East Asia's "developmental states," China's "Beijing Consensus," Latin America's populism, and the embrace by much of Eastern Europe of state-guided capitalism under the auspices of the EU all speak of some level of commitment to and consensus on a national development strategy informed by a view of the economic future. Islamic economics is claimed by some to be the homegrown equivalent in the MENA, but its comparatively minor role in much of the region's financial surfaces indicates that it is still more aspiration than reality. Islamic capitalists do not yet play a significant role in guiding formulation of national economic policies, but their control over strategic banking sectors in the GCC countries is increasing, with overall annual growth rates 2003-9 averaging 26 percent (Warde 2010: 247). The Great Recession offered the Islamic finance movement new legitimacy "by default" against the excesses of conventional finance, even though its image was also tarnished in the Dubai meltdown (Warde 210: 247).

Other than the GCC states, whose reasonably coherent development strategies are driven by the imperative of hydrocarbon wealth, and Israel, which has predicated its growth on high-tech industries associated with its knowledge economy, the states of the region have failed to articulate clear strategies for their economies. As a result, to the extent that their present economic policies reflect a development model, it is that of the globally dominant neoliberal Washington Consensus. But because that model has not been wholeheartedly embraced, and because policies are in every case contingent on political calculations, development strategy remains more ad hoc than planned and coherent, characterized by stop-start, partial changes. The discrediting of the Washington Consensus by the global financial crisis of 2008 and ensuing Great Recession renders even its comparatively limited guidance still less compelling, short of it being effectively synthesized with a regionally buoyant Islamic finance.

On the output side of these polities, the consequences of inadequate development reinforce the status quo. Incomes have not risen broadly or quickly enough to lift a sufficiently large percentage of the MENA population into a middle class that could provide the basis for a new, more liberal political order. Outside the high-performing GCC states and Israel, the majority of citizens lack the security and predictability that is implied by arrival in the middle class. Indeed, even during the third oil boom the greatest component of employment growth was in informal private sectors, so that even though their new incomes might have lifted considerable numbers of Middle Easterners into the lower rungs of local if not global middle-class status, they are there only precariously. The Great Recession, which by early 2009 had already driven unemployment of those under twenty-five in even Turkey's comparatively high-performing economy to over 25 percent, is particularly threatening to those on that lower rung, who earn between $2 and $9 daily ("Burgeoning Bourgeoisie" 2009). In the MENA the majority of those employed work in secure but poorly rewarded government jobs, or in agriculture or micro or small enterprises, where jobs are typically precarious. In many MENA countries, even employment in medium-sized and large firms is increasingly informal, without security of contract, social insurance, or provision of pensions. Such employment is not supportive of the emergence of a politically engaged middle class sufficiently secure and confident to contemplate and possibly engage in politics on a sustained basis. The currency of politics thus remains distribution, with incumbent elites dispensing patronage to buy support rather than earning it through performance, for which they would be held to account by politically engaged publics. The threshold per capita annual income level of some $6,000 to $7,000, beyond which countries are much more likely to be democracies and those that rarely, if ever, backslide into authoritarianism, is a level only the wealthier MENA oil exporters along with Israel and Tunisia achieve. The rentier nature of the former militates against democracy (Ross 2009). In sum, then, virtually all MENA states are too poor or too oil-rich to cross what seems globally to be a key economic threshold for democratization. Underlying that numerical threshold presumably is the fact that it is the level at which a middle class becomes sufficiently large to transform politics from being patronage based to being competitive and accountable. The MENA's economic underperformance thus exerts a drag effect on its political development, which in turn impedes improved economic performance. The region, in other words, is locked into a stagnating spiral, from which the vast earnings of the third great oil boom did not liberate it.

References

Aarts, Paul, and Gerd Nonneman, 2005, *Saudi Arabia in the Balance: Political Economy, Society, Foreign Affairs*, London, Hurst

Abdel-Kader, Khaled, July 2006, *Private Sector Access to Credit in Egypt: Evidence from Survey Data*, Cairo, Egyptian Center for Economic Studies, Working Paper 111

Abdesselam, Belaid, blog, available at www.belaidabdesselam.com

Abrahamian, Ervand, 2008, *A History of Modern Iran*, New York, Cambridge University Press

Aburish, Saïd K., 1995, *The Rise, Corruption and Coming Fall of the House of Saud*, London, Bloomsbury

Addi, Lahouari, 1991, "Les réformes économiques et leurs limites," *Les cahiers de l'Orient*, v. 23, no. 3, pp. 115–22

Addi, Lahouari, March 1999, "L'armée algérienne se divise," *Le monde diplomatique*

Adva Centre, cited in Rory McCarthy, June 4, 2008, "Occupation has cost Israel dear, says report," *The Guardian*, p. 16

Agence France Presse (APF), January 6, 2010, "Kuwait parliament approves debt relief law"

"Ahmadinejad's administration accused of stealing billions," available at http://www.inquisitr.com/44858/ahm,adinejads-administration-accused-of-stealing-billions/

Aissaoui, Ali, January–February 2008, "Diversifying MENA petroleum-dependent economies – where does Saudi Arabia stand?" *Economic Commentary*, v. 3, no. 1–2

Akhavi-Pour, Hossein, and Heidar Azodanloo, Fall 1998, "Economic bases of political factions in Iran," *Critique: Journal for Critical Studies of the Middle East*, v. 13

Al-Ahnaf, M., Bernard Botiveau, and Frank Frégosi, 1991, *L'Algérie par ses islamistes*, Paris, Karthala

Al-Atrash, Hasan, and Tarik Yousef, January 2000, *Intra-Arab Trade: Is It Too Little?* IMF Working Paper 00/10

Al-Awadi, Hesham, 2004, *In Pursuit of Legitimacy: The Muslim Brothers and Mubarak, 1982–2000*, London, I. B. Tauris

Alexander, Christopher, 2010, *Tunisia: Stability and Reform in the Modern Maghreb*, Abingdon, Oxon, and New York, Routledge

Al-Hashimi, Muhammad, 1998, *The Politicization of Islam: A Case Study of Tunisia*, Boulder, Colorado, Westview

Al-Kikhia, Mansour O., 1997, *Libya's Qaddafi: The Politics of Contradiction*, Gainesville, University Press of Florida

Al Masri Al Yawm, December 2, 2008, available at www.almasry-alyoum.com

Almounsor, Abdullah, 2008, "Capital flight accounting and welfare implications in the MENA region," *Review of Middle East Economics and Finance*, v. 4, no. 2, Article 1, available at http://www.bepress.com/rmeef/vol4/iss2/art1

Al-Rasheed, Madawi, 2008, *Kingdom without Borders: Saudi Arabia's Political, Religious and Media Frontiers*, London, Hurst

Al-Rasheed, Madawi, 2009, Money Replaces Ideas as Petitioner's Silence Leaves Saudi Reform at an Impasse, and Princely Power to Test Succession Plans, in Joshua Craze and Mark Huband, eds., *The Kingdom: Saudi Arabia and the Challenge of the 21st Century*, pp. 19–24, 30–4, London, Hurst

Alsharekh, Alanoud, and Robert Springborg, eds., 2008, *Popular Culture and Political Identity in the Arab Gulf States*, London, Saqi Books

Alsheikh, Hend M., March 21–25, 2007, Prospect of Future Energy Investment in Saudi Arabia, paper delivered to the Eighth Mediterranean Social and Political Research Meeting, European University Institute, Florence

Altug, S., and A. Filiztekin, eds., 2006, *The Turkish Economy*, London, Routledge

Amin, Galal, 2004, *Whatever Else Happened to the Egyptians*, Cairo, AUC Press

Amin, Galal, 2006, *The Illusion of Progress in the Arab World: A Critique of Western Misconstructions*, Cairo, AUC Press

Amuzegar, Jahangir, 1993, *Iran's Economy under the Islamic Republic*, London, I. B. Tauris

Amuzegar, Jahangir, February 11, 2010a, "The Rial Problem," *Foreign Policy*, available at http://www.foreignpolicy.com/articles/2010/02/11/the_rial_problem

Amuzegar, Jahangir, March 2010b, "Iran's Economy in Turmoil," *International Economic Bulletin*, Carnegie Endowment, Washington, DC, available at http://www.carnegieendowment.org/publications/index.cfm?fa=view&id=40354

Andoni, Lamis, Spring 2000, "King Abdullah: In His Father's Footsteps?" *Journal of Palestine Studies*, v. 29, no. 3, pp. 77–89

Angkinand, Apanard, James R. Barth, Tong Li, Wenling Lu, and Glenn Yago, April 2009, *Capital Access Index 2008: Best Markets for Business Access to Capital*, Milken Institute

APICORP Research, October 1, 2006, *Review of Energy Capital Investment Requirements in the MENA Region and the Arab World for the Period 2007–2011*, Arab Petroleum Investments Corporation

APICORP, 2008, *Economic Commentary*, 3: 1–2 (January–February)

Arab Trade Financing Program, July 2009, dataset retrieved from www.atfp.org. ae

"Arming up: The world's biggest military spenders by population," June 9, 2009, *The Economist*, available at www.economist.com/daily/news

Assaad, Ragui, 2009, Labor supply, employment, and unemployment in the Egyptian economy, 1988–2006, in Ragui Assaad, ed., *The Egyptian Labor Market Revisited*, pp. 1–52, Cairo, The American University in Cairo Press

Assaad, Ragui, and Fatma El Hamidi, 2009, Women in the Egyptian labor market: An analysis of developments, 1988–2006, in Ragui Assaad, ed., *The*

Egyptian Labor Market Revisited, pp. 219–57, Cairo, The American University in Cairo Press

Aydin, Zulkuf, 2005, *The Political Economy of Turkey*, London, Pluto Press

Ayubi, Nazih N., 1995, *Over-stating the Arab State: Politics and Society in the Middle East*, London, I. B. Tauris

Bagehot, Walter, 1904, *Lombard Street: A Description of the Money Market*, London

Bank Al-Maghrib, August 2009, *Revue Mensuelle de la Conjoncture Économique, Monétaire et Financière*

The Banker, November 2009, Supplement: Top 500 Islamic Financial Institutions

Bank of Israel, April 2009, *Annual Report 2008*, v. 66, no. 171, p. 198, available at http://www.thebanker.com/news/fullstory.php/aid/6128/Global_sharia_market_chalks_up_27_25_growth.html

Banque du Liban (BDL), March 1999, *Quarterly Bulletin*, v. 80

Barkai, Haim, and Nissan Liviatan, 2007, v. 1, *The Bank of Israel: A Monetary History*, and v. 2, *Selected Topics in Israel's Monetary Policy*, New York, Oxford University Press

Basha, Hasan Abu, 1990, *Mudhakkirat Hasan Abu Basha fi al amn wa al siyasah (Memoirs of Hasan Abu Basha in Security and Politics)*, Cairo, Dar al Hilal

Baskan, Filiz, March 2009, Political Involvement of the Rising Islamist Business Elite in Turkey, paper delivered to the Tenth Mediterranean Research Meeting, European University Institute, Florence

Batatu, Hanna, 1999, *Syria's Peasantry, the Descendants of its Lesser Rural Notables, and their Politics*, Princeton, New Jersey, Princeton University Press

Beattie, Kirk J., 1988, Egypt: Thirty-five years of praetorian politics, in Constantine Danopoulos, ed., *Military Disengagement from Politics*, pp. 201–30, New York, Routledge

Beau, Nicolas, and Catherine Graciet, 2009, *La régente de Carthage: Main basse sur la Tunisie*, Paris, La Découverte

Beau, Nicolas, and Jean-Pierre Tuquoi, 1999, *Notre ami Ben Ali: l'envers du "miracle tunisien,"* Paris, Editions La Découverte

Beck, Thorsten, Asli Demirguc-Kunt, and Ross Eric Levine, 2009, *A New Database on Financial Development and Structure* (updated May), World Bank, available at http://econ.worldbank.org/WBSITE/EXTERNAL/EXTDEC/EXTRESEARCH/0,contentMDK:20696167~pagePK:64214825~piPK:64214943~theSitePK:469382,00.html

Behrendt, Sven, October 2008, *When Money Talks: Arab Sovereign Wealth Funds in the Global Public Policy Discourse*, Washington, DC, Carnegie Papers, v. 12

Belkhodja, Tahar, 1998, *Les trois décennies Bourguiba*, Paris, Publisud

Bellin, Eva, January 2000, "Contingent democrats: Industrialists, labor and democratization in late-developing countries," *World Politics*, v. 52, pp. 175–205

Benfodil, Mustapha, February 28, 2010, "L'architecture de l'appareil de sécurité à l'épreuve de l'hémorragie des ses cerveaux," *El Watan*, p. 2

Bennoune, Mahfoud, and Ali El-Kenz, 1990, *Le hasard et l'histoire: entretiens avec Belaid Abdesselam*, 2 vols., Algiers, ENAG

Berger, Sharon, June 6, 2000, "Gov't to raise up to NIS 2.6b. from sale of Bank Hapoalim today," *Jerusalem Post*, p. 11

Berger, Suzanne, and Ronald Dore, eds., 1996, *National Diversity and Global Capitalism*, Ithaca, New York, Cornell University Press

Bergsten, C. Fred, November–December 2009, "The dollar and the deficits," *Foreign Affairs*, v. 88, no. 6, pp. 20–38

Bilgin, Berkso, and F. Gulcin Ozkan, March 2009, The Banking Sector and Macroeconomic Performance – Is There a Role: The Case of Turkey, paper delivered to the Tenth Mediterranean Research Meeting, European University Institute, Florence

Bill, James A., and Robert Springborg, 2000, *Politics in the Middle East*, 5th edn., New York, Addison-Wesley

Bolbol, Ali A., February 1999, "Arab Trade and Free Trade: A Preliminary Analysis," *International Journal of Middle East Studies*, v. 31, no. 1, pp. 3–17

Boogaerde, Pierre Van Den, September 1991, *Financial Assistance from Arab Countries and Arab Regional Institutions*, Washington, DC, IMF

Bowker, Robert, 2010, *Egypt and the Politics of Change in the Arab Middle East*, Cheltenham, UK, Edward Elgar

Bozorgmehr, Najmeh, November 5, 2009, "Revolutionary Guards march roughshod over private sector," *Financial Times*, p. 7

Bozorgmehr, Najmeh, March 13–14, 2010, "Iranians switch to informal savings funds as loans dry up," *Financial Times*, p. 7

Bradley, John R., 2008, *Inside Egypt: The Land of the Pharaohs on the Brink of a Revolution*, London, Palgrave Macmillan

Brahimi, Abdelhamid, 1991, *L'économie algérienne: défis et enjeux*, 2nd edn., Algiers, Dahlab

Brand, Laurie A., 1998, *Women, the State and Political Liberalization: Middle Eastern and North African Experiences*, New York, Columbia University Press

British Petroleum (BP), 2009, *Statistical Review of World Energy 2009*, available at http://www.bp.com/productlanding.do?categoryId=6929&contentId=7044622

Brown, L. Carl, 1984, *International Politics and the Middle East: Old Rules, Dangerous Game*, Princeton, New Jersey, Princeton University Press

Brown, Nathan, 1997, *The Rule of Law in the Arab World*, Cambridge, Cambridge University Press

Brownlee, Jason, 2007, *Authoritarianism in an Age of Democratization*, New York, Cambridge University Press

Bruck, Tilman, Christine Binzel, and Lars Handrich, December 2007, Evaluating economic reforms in Syria, DIW Berlin, Politikberatung Kompakt, for the Deutsche Gesellschaft fur Technische Zuesammenarbeit (GTZ)

Brülhart, Marius, February 2008, *An Account of Global Intraindustry Trade, 1962–2006*, Background paper, World Development Report, Washington, DC, World Bank

Brülhart, Marius, 2009, "An account of global intra-industry trade, 1962–2006," *World Economy*, v. 32, no. 3, pp. 401–59

Buchta, Wilfried, 2000, *Who Rules Iran: The Structure of Power in the Islamic Republic*, Washington, DC, Washington Institute for Near East Policy

Buck, Tobias, April 21, 2008, "Israel seeks to reinvent itself as finance hub," *Financial Times*, p. 7

Bugra, Ayse, November 1998, "Class culture and state: An analysis of interest representation by two Turkish business associations," *International Journal of Middle East Studies*, v. 30, no. 4, pp. 521–39

Burgat, François, 2008, *Islamism in the Shadow of al-Qaeda*, Austin, University of Texas Press

"Burgeoning Bourgeoisie," February 12, 2009, *The Economist* Special Report available at http://www.lexisnexis.com/us/Inacademic/results/docview/docview. do?risb=21_T9346321105&treeMax=false&sort=&docNo=1&format= GNBFULL&startDocNo=0&treeWidth=0&nodeDisplayName=&cisb= &reloadPage=false

Camau, Michel, and Vincent Geisser, 2003, *Le syndrome autoritaire: Politique en Tunisie de Bourguiba a Ben Ali*, Paris, FNEP

Cammett, Melani Claire, 2007, *Globalization and Business Politics in Arab North Africa: A Comparative Perspective*, New York, Cambridge University Press

Caprio, Gerard, Ross Eric Levine, and James R. Barth, 2008, *Bank Regulation and Supervision* (updated June), World Bank, available at http://econ. worldbank.org/WBSITE/EXTERNAL/EXTDEC/EXTRESEARCH/0, contentMDK:20345037~pagePK:64214825~piPK:64214943~theSitePK: 469382,00.html#Survey_III

Carapico, Sheila, 1998, *Civil Society in Yemen: The Political Economy of Activism in Modern Arabia*, Cambridge, Cambridge University Press

Carothers, Thomas, October 2009, *Revitalizing Democracy Assistance: The Challenge of USAID*, Carnegie Report, available at www.carnegieendowment.org/ publications/index.cfm?fa=view&id=24047

Cassarino, Jean-Pierre, Winter 1999, "The EU-Tunisian ASSOCIATION Agreement and Tunisia's structural reform program," *Middle East Journal*, v. 53, no. 1, pp. 69–72

"CDG-BMCE Bank: Les enjeux du rapprochement," 2010, *L'Economiste* (Casablanca), March 24

Chalcraft, John, 2009, *The Invisible Cage: Syrian Migrant Workers in Lebanon*, Stanford, Stanford University Press

Chandrasekaran, Rajiv, 2006, *Imperial Life in the Emerald City: Inside Iraq's Green Zone*, New York, Knopf

Chaudhry, Kiren Aziz, 1992, Economic liberalization in oil-exporting countries, in Ilya Harik and Denis J. Sullivan, eds., *Privatization and Liberalization in the Middle East*, pp. 145–66, Bloomington, Indiana University Press

Chaudhry, Kiren Aziz, 1997, *The Price of Wealth: Economies and Institutions in the Middle East*, Ithaca, New York, Cornell University Press

Chon, Gina, March 18, 2009, "Iran's cheap goods stifle Iraq economy," *The Wall Street Journal*, p. 1.

Clague, Christopher, Philip Keefer, Stephen Knack, and Mancur Olson, October 1997, *Contract Intensive Money*, IRIS Working Paper 151, College Park, University of Maryland

Comité Directeur du Rapport, 2006, 50 ans de Développement Humain & Perspectives 2025, Cinquantenaire de l'Indépendance du Royaume du Maroc, available at http://www.arab-hdr.org/publications/other/undp/hdr/ 2005/morocco-f.pdf

Committee to Protect Journalists (CPJ), April 10, 2009, 10 worst countries to be a blogger, available at www.cpj.org/reports/2009/04/10-worst-countries-to-be-a-blogger.php

Cook, Steven A., 2007, *Ruling but Not Governing: The Military and Political Development in Egypt, Algeria, and Turkey*, Baltimore, The Johns Hopkins University Press

Cooper, Mark, May 1982, The demilitarization of the Egyptian cabinet, *International Journal of Middle East Studies*, v. 14, no. 2, pp. 201–19

Copley, Gregory R., 1995, *Defense and Foreign Affairs Handbook on Egypt*, v. 67, p. 132, London, International Media Corporation

Cordesman, Anthony H., March 17, 2009, Economic Challenges in Post-conflict Iraq, Washington, DC, Center for Strategic and International Studies

Corm, Georges, January–March 1993, "La réforme économique algérienne: une réforme mal aimée?" *Maghreb-Machrek*, v. 139, pp. 9–27

Corm, Georges, 1998, Reconstructing Lebanon's Economy, in Nemat Shafik, ed., *Economic Challenges Facing Middle Eastern and North African Countries*, New York, St. Martin's Press

Corm, Georges, February 2009, "*The Monthly* meets former Minister of Finance Georges Corm," *The Monthly*, no. 79, pp. 42–3

Crumley, Bruce, September 23, 2003, "Crash and burn," *Time*, available at www.time.com/time/magazine/article/0,9171,485713,00.html

Crystal, Jill, 1990, *Oil and Politics in the Gulf: Rulers and Merchants in Kuwait and Qatar*, Cambridge, Cambridge University Press

Dagge, John, March 2008, "Syria Moves to Accelerate Pace of Islamic Banking," *The Middle East*, pp. 25–8

Davidson, Christopher M., 2005, *The United Arab Emirates: A Study in Survival*, Boulder, Colorado, Westview

Davidson, Christopher M., 2008, *Dubai: The Vulnerability of Success*, London, Hurst

Davidson, Christopher M., 2009, *Abu Dhabi: Oil and Beyond*, London, Hurst

Davidson, Christopher M., and Peter Mackenzie-Smith, 2008, *Higher Education in the Gulf States: Shaping Economies, Politics and Culture*, London, Saqi Books

Davis, Eric, 2010, The Political Economy of Modern Iraq, in David S. Sorenson, ed., *Interpreting the Middle East*, pp. 337–62 Boulder, Colorado, Westview

Davutyan, Nurhan, May 2008, *Estimating the Size of Turkey's Informal Sector: An Expenditure Based Approach*, Cairo, Economic Research Forum, Working Paper 403, p. 2

Dekmejian, H. Hrair, 1971, *Egypt under Nasir: A Study in Political Dynamics*, Albany, State University of New York Press

Dhillon, Navtej, and Tarik Yousef, eds., 2009, *Generation in Waiting: The Unfulfilled Promise of Young People in the Middle East*, Washington, DC, Brookings Institution Press

Dibeh, Ghassan, July 2005, *The Political Economy of Postwar Reconstruction in Lebanon*, Tokyo, United Nations University, Research Paper no. 2005/44

Dibeh, Ghassan, March 25–28, 2009, The Political Economy of Stabilization in Lebanon, paper delivered to the Tenth Mediterranean Research Meeting, Florence

Dillman, Bradford, 1997, "Reassessing the Algerian economy: Development and reform through the eyes of five policy-makers," *Journal of Modern African Studies*, v. 35, no. 1, pp. 153–74

Dillman, Bradford, 2000, *State and Private Sector in Algeria: The Politics of Rent-Seeking and Failed Development*, Boulder, Colorado, Westview

Dillman, Bradford, Spring 2001, "Facing the market in North Africa," *Middle East Journal*, v. 55, no. 2, pp. 198–215

Doron, Gideon, 1996, Two civil societies and one state, in Augustus Richard Norton, ed., *Civil Society in the Middle East*, v. II, pp. 193–220, Leiden, Brill

Dreher, Axel, 2006, "Does globalization affect growth? Evidence from a new index of globalization," *Applied Economics*, v. 38, no. 10, pp. 1091–110

Dreher, Axel, Noel Gaston, and Pim Martens, 2008, *Measuring Globalization – Gauging its Consequence*, New York, Springer

Drummond, James, December 2007, "Once off limits, and now seen on YouTube," *Financial Times*, p. 8

Dunn, Michael Collins, 1986, Egypt: From domestic needs to export market, in James Everett Katz, ed., *The Implications of Third World Military Industrialization*, pp. 119–34, Lexington, Massachusetts, Lexington Books

Dunn, Ross, April 29, 1998, "High-tech success beats toil in the soil," *Sydney Morning Herald*, p. 11

Dunne, Michele, January 2006, *Evaluating Egyptian Reform*, Washington, DC, Carnegie Endowment, Carnegie Paper no. 66

Duzgit, Senem Aydin, and Rusen Cakir, 2009, Turkey: A sustainable case of de-radicalisaton? in Michael Emerson, Kristina Kausch, and Richard Youngs, eds., *Islamist Radicalisation: The Challenge for Euro-Mediterranean Relations*, pp. 87–107, Brussels, Centre for European Policy Studies

Economic Research Forum Annual Report 2003–2004, 2004, Cairo, Economic Research Forum

The Economist Pocket World in Figures, 2009, London, The Economist

Egypt, Ministry of Finance, 2010, website http://www.mof.gov.eg/english/pages/home.aspx

Egypt: Economic Performance Assessment, April 2008, produced by Nathan Associates for USAID/Cairo

Egypt and the Global Economic Crisis: A Preliminary Assessment of Macroeconomic Impact and Response, August 16, 2009, v. 1, Washington, DC, World Bank

Ehteshami, Anoushiravan, 2009, *Globalization and Geopolitics in the Middle East: Old Games, New Rules*, London, Routledge

Ehteshami, Anoushiravan, and Steven M. Wright, eds., 2008, *Reform in the Middle East Oil Monarchies*, London, Ithaca Press

El-Erian, Mohammed A., March 1996, "Middle Eastern Economies' External Environment: What Lies Ahead?" *Middle East Policy*, v. 53, pp. 137–46

El-Gamal, Mahmoud A., 2006, *Islamic Finance: Law, Economics, and Practice*, New York, Cambridge University Press

El-Gamal, Mahmoud A., and Amy M. Jaffe, 2009, *Oil, Dollars, Debt, and Crises: The Global Curse of Black Gold*, New York, Routledge

El-Ghonemy, M. Riad, 1998, *Affluence and Poverty in the Middle East*, London, Routledge

El-Gibali, Abdel-Fattah, 2009, "More work needed," *Al Ahram Weekly*, available at http://weekly.ahram.org.eg/print/2009/952/ec4.htm

El Kadi, Ihsan, 1998, "L'administration, éternel butin de guerre," *Pouvoirs: Revue francaise d'etudes constitutionelles et politiques*, v. 86, pp. 57–66

El-Kenz, Ali, ed., 1991, *Algeria: The Challenge of Modernity*, East Lansing, Michigan State University Press

El Mahdi, Alia, and Ali Rashed, 2009, The changing economic environment and the development of micro- and small enterprises in Egypt, 2006, in Ragui Assaad, ed., *The Egyptian Labor Market Revisited*, pp. 87–116, Cairo, The American University in Cairo Press

El-Mahdi, Rabab, and Philip Marfleet, eds., 2009, *Egypt: The Moment of Change*, London, Zed Books

El-Mikawy, Noha, and Ramy Mohsen, 2006, Civil Society Participation in the Law-Making Process in Egypt, in Noha El-Mikawy, ed., *Governance of Economic Reform: Studies in Legislation, Participation and Information, Egypt, Morocco and Jordan*, pp. 445–64, Cairo, Economic Research Forum

Elmussa, Sharif, and Jeannie Sowers, October 21, 2009, "Damietta mobilizes for its environment," *Middle East Report Online*, available at www.merip.org/mero/mero102109.html

El-Nahhas, Mona, December 3–9, 2008, "A matter of security," *Al Ahram Weekly*

El Watan, Algiers, Algeria, http://www.elwatan.com/

England, Andrew, May 26, 2009, "Oil-rich region faces gas shortfall," *Financial Times*, p. 3

England, Andrew, and Abeer Allam, June 2, 2009a, "Saudi group admits to debt squeeze," *Financial Times*, p. 13

England, Andrew, and Abeer Allam, May 28, 2009b, "Saudi family groups feel the pain," *Financial Times*

England, Andrew, and Simon Kerr, June 6–7, 2009, "Shrewd Sheikh on a roll," *Financial Times*, p. 8

Entelis, John P., 1986, *Algeria: The Revolution Institutionalized*, Boulder, Colorado, Westview

Entelis, John P., and Lisa J. Arone, 2nd quarter 1992, "Algeria in turmoil: Islam, democracy and the state," *Middle East Policy*, v. 40, pp. 23–35

Etling, Bruce, John Kelly, Robert Faris, and John Palfrey, June 2009, *Mapping the Arabic Blogosphere: Politics, Culture, and Dissent*, Berkman Center, Harvard University, http://cyber.law.harvard.edu/sites/cyber.law.harvard.edu/files/Mapping_the_Arabic_Blogosphere_0.pdf

European Commission, May 25–26, 2000, *Reinvigorating the Barcelona Process*, working document of the European Commission services for the "think tank" meeting of Euro-Mediterranean Foreign Ministers, Lisbon, p. 5

European Union (EU), January 15, 2007, MEDA I and II Commitments and Payment, available at http://ec.europa.eu/external_relations/euromed/docs/meda_figures_en.pdf

Farrell, Diana, and Susan Lund, Winter 2008, "The new role of oil wealth in the world economy," *McKinsey on Finance*, v. 26, pp. 14–19, available at http://corporatefinance.mckinsey.com/_downloads/knowledge/mckinsey_on_finance/MoF_Issue_26.pdf

Faruq, Abd al Khalaq, April 1, 2009, *al Araby al Nassery*, available at www.al-araby.com/docs/article5110.html

Fassihi, Farnaz, November 4, 2009, "Revolutionary Guard Corps pushing into a new domain: The media," *Wall Street Journal*, available at http://online.wsj.com/article/SB125730352972127145.html

Field, Michael, 1986, *The Merchants: The Big Business Families of Saudi Arabia and the Gulf States*, New York, Penguin

Freely, Maureen, February 2007, "Why they killed Hrant Dink," *Index on Censorship*, available at www.eurozine.com/articles/2007-06-06-freely-en.html

From Privilege to Competition: Unlocking Private-Led Growth in the Middle East and North Africa, 2009, Washington, DC, World Bank

Fuller, Graham E., 2004, *The Youth Crisis in Middle Eastern Society*, Clinton, Michigan, The Institute for Social Policy and Understanding, available at http://ispu.org/reports/articledetailpb-62.html

Galal, Ahmed, ed., 2008, *Rethinking the Role of the State: Industrial Policy in the Middle East and North Africa*, Cairo, The American University in Cairo Press

Galal, Ahmed, and Nihal El Megharbel, 2009, Do governments pick winners or losers? An assessment of industrial policy in Egypt, in Ahmed Galal, ed., *Rethinking the Role of the State: Industrial Policy in the Middle East and North Africa*, Cairo, The American University in Cairo Press

Galloux, Michel, July–October 1999, "The State's responses to private Islamic finance experiments in Egypt," *Thunderbird International Business Review*, v. 41, no. 4–5, pp. 494–6

Gaspard, Toufic K., 2004, *A Political Economy of Lebanon 1948–2002: The Limits of Laissez-Faire*, Leiden, Brill Academic Publishers

Gause, Gregory, 1994, *Oil Monarchies: Domestic and Security Challenges in the Arab Gulf States*, New York, Council on Foreign Relations Press

Gause, Gregory, 2010, *The International Relations of the Persian Gulf*, Cambridge, UK, Cambridge University Press

Gerges, Fawaz A., 2005, *The Far Enemy: Why Jihad Went Global*, Cambridge, UK, Cambridge University Press

Gerstenfeld, Dan, May 31, 2000, "Arison Seeks to Sell Holdings in Housing & Construction," *Jerusalem Post*, p. 12

Ghabra, Shafeeq N., May 1997, "The Islamic Movement in Kuwait," *Middle East Policy*, v. 5, no. 2, pp. 58–72

Gheissari, Ali, 2009, *Contemporary Iran: Economy, society, politics*, New York, Oxford University Press

Ghilès, Francis, 1998, "L'armée a-t-elle une politique économique?" *Pouvoirs: Revue française d'études constitutionelles et politiques*, v. 86, pp. 85–106

Ghoneim, Ahmed F., and Miria Pigato, 2006, *Egypt after the End of the Multiple-Fiber Agreement: A Comparative Regional Analysis*, ECES Working Paper No. 114, Cairo, Egyptian Center for Economic Studies

Glain, Stephen J., May 23, 2000, "Stronghold can backfire: Iraqi tribes are key source of loyalty, rebellion," *Wall Street Journal*, p. 2

Glass, Charles, 1990, *Tribes with Flags: A Journey Curtailed*, London, Secker and Warburg

Goldwasser, Amit, Diana Zaks, and Shahr Shlush, July 25, 2007, *Beyond Bachar: Next Steps for Financial Reform*, Los Angeles, Milken Institute

Gonzalez, Gabriella, Lynn A. Karoly, Louay Constant, Hanine Salem, and Charles A. Goldman, 2008, *Facing Human Capital Challenges in the 21st Century*, RAND–Qatar Policy Institute, Santa Monica, California

Gray, John, 1998, *False Dawn: The Delusions of Global Capitalism*, New York, The New Press

Guazzone, Laura, and Daniela Pioppi, eds., 2009, *The Arab State and Neo-Liberal Globalization: The Restructuring of State Power in the Middle East*, Reading, Ithaca Press

Hachemaoui, Mohammed, 2009a, "Qui gouverne? Les règles du jeu politique algérien," *Politique étrangère*, summer, pp. 309–321

Hachemaoui, Mohammed, 2009b, *La corruption politique en Algérie. Dynamiques, structures et acteurs d'un système de gouvernement*, book manuscript to be published by Paris, Presses Universitaires de France, 2011

Hadj-Nacer, Abderrahmane Roustoumi, ed., 1989, *Les cahiers de la réforme*, Algiers, ENAG

Haggard, Stephan, and Chung H. Lee, 1993, The Political Dimension of Finance in Economic Development, in Stephan Haggard, Chung H. Lee, and Sylvia Maxfield, eds., *The Politics of Finance in Developing Countries*, pp. 3–20, Ithaca, New York, Cornell University Press

Hamidi, Muhammad al-Hashimi, 1998, *The Politicization of Islam: A Case Study of Tunisia*, Boulder, CO, Westview Press

Hammoudi, Abdellah, 1997, *Master and Disciple: The Cultural Foundations of Moroccan Authoritarianism*, Chicago, University of Chicago Press

Handoussa, Heba, et al., 2008, *Egypt's Social Contract: The Role of Civil Society*, Cairo, Egypt Human Development Report, United Nations Development Program

Havrylyshyn, Oleh, and Peter Kunzel, 1997, *Intra-industry Trade of Arab Countries: An Indicator of Potential Competitiveness*, IMF Working Paper WP/97/47

Henry, Clement M., 1996, *The Mediterranean Debt Crescent: Money and Power in Algeria, Egypt, Morocco, Tunisia, and Turkey*, Gainesville, University Press of Florida

Henry, Clement M., 2007, Tunisia's "sweet little" regime, in Robert Rotberg, ed., *Worst of the Worst: Dealing with Repressive and Rogue Nations*, pp. 300–723, Washington, DC, Brookings Institution Press

Henry, Clement M., and Rodney Wilson, eds., 2004, *The Politics of Islamic Finance*, Edinburgh, Scotland, Edinburgh University Press

Henry, Pierre, and Bénédict de Saint Laurent, May 2007, *Les investissements directs étrangers dans la région MEDA en 2006*, Notes et Documents No. 23, Agence Française pour les Investissements Internationaux

Herb, Michael, 1999, *All in the Family: Absolutism, Revolution and Democracy in the Middle Easern Monarchies*, Albany, State University of New York Press

Herb, Michael, 2009, "A Nation of Bureaucrats: Political Participation and Economic Diversification in Kuwait and the United Arab Emirates," *International Journal of Middle East Studies*, v. 41, no. 3, pp. 375–95

Heritage Foundation, 2009a, *Index of Economic Freedom, The Link Between Economic Opportunity and Prosperity*, available at www.heritage.org/Index/Default.aspx

Heritage Foundation, 2009b, *Syria Information on Economic Freedom*, available at www.heritage.org/index.Country/Syria

Herring, Eric, and Glen Rangwala, 2006, *Iraq in Fragments: The Occupation and its Legacy*, London, Hurst

Hertog, Steffen, 2005a, Segmented clientelism: The political economy of Saudi reform efforts, in Paul Aarts and Gerd Nonneman, eds., *Saudi Arabia in the Balance: Political Economy, Society, Foreign Affairs*, pp. 111–43, London, Hurst

Hertog, Steffen, 2005b, "Building the body politic: the emerging corporatism in Saudi Arabia and the Gulf," *Chroniques du Yémen et de la Péninsule Arabe* 12(1).

Hertog, Steffen, March 22–26, 2006, Labour Policy in the Gulf: Unintended Consequences of Regulatory Ambition, paper delivered to the Seventh Mediterranean Social and Political Research Meeting, Robert Schuman Centre for Advanced Studies of the European University Institute, Florence

Hertog, Steffen, 2008, "Petromin: The slow death of statist oil development in Saudi Arabia." *Business History* v. 50, no. 5, pp. 645–67

Hertog, Steffen, 2010, *Princes, Brokers, and Bureaucrats: Oil and State in Saudi Arabia*, New York, Columbia University Press

Heydemann, Steven, ed., 2004, *Networks of Privilege in the Middle East: The Politics of Economic Reform Revisited*, London, Palgrave Macmillan

Hidouci, Ghazi, 1995, *Algérie: la libération inachevée*, Paris, Editions de la Découverte

Hilal, Rida, 1987, *The Construction of Dependency* (in Arabic), Cairo, Dar Al-Mustaqbal Al-Arabi

Hilferding, Rudolph, [1910] 1981, *Finance Capital: A Study of the Latest Phase of Capitalist Development*, London, Routledge

Hinnebusch, Raymond, and Soren Schmidt, 2008, *The State and the Political Economy of Reform in Syria*, St. Andrew's, St. Andrew's Papers on Contemporary Syria

Hirst, David, May 27, 1997, "Behind the Veil of Sudan's Theocracy," *The Guardian*, p. 8

Howe, Marvine, 2005, *Morocco: The Islamist Wakening and Other Challenges*, Oxford, UK, Oxford University Press

Hudson, Michael, 1968, *The Precarious Republic: Political Modernization in Lebanon*, New York, Random House

Hudson, Michael, 1977, *Arab Politics*, New Haven, Connecticut, Yale University Press

Human Rights Watch, June 2005, *Reading between the "Red Lines": The Repression of Academic Freedom in Egyptian Universities*, 17, 6, available at http://www.hrw.org/en/reports/2005/06/08/reading-between-red-lines-repression-academic-freedom-egyptian-universities-0

Human Rights Watch, December 4, 2007, *Political Opposition and Violence in Egypt*, available at http://hrw.org./reports/2007/eghypt1207/3.htm

Humphreys, Charles, Arup Banerji, and Mustapha Nabli, eds., 2003, *Better Governance for Development in the Middle East and North Africa: Enhancing Inclusiveness and Accountability*, Washington, DC, The International Bank for Reconstruction and Development, World Bank

Humphreys, Macartan, Jeffrey D. Sachs, and Joseph E. Stiglitz, 2007, *Escaping the Resource Curse*, New York, Columbia University Press

Ilias, Shayerah, June 15, 2009, "Iran's Economic Conditions: U.S. Policy Issues," *CRS Report for Congress*, Washington, DC, Congressional Research Service

International Institute for Strategic Studies (IISS), 1998, *The Military Balance 1998/1999*, London

International Monetary Fund (IMF), various dates, International Financial Statistics, available online http://www.imf.org/external/data/htm

International Monetary Fund (IMF), September 1998, *Algeria: Special Issues and Statistical Appendix*, Staff Country Report No. 98/87

International Monetary Fund (IMF), November 2007, *Turkey: 2007 Title IV Consultation*, Country Report No. 07/362

International Monetary Fund (IMF), October 2008, *Tunisia: 2008 Title IV Consultation*, Country Report No. 08/345

International Monetary Fund (IMF), May 2009a, *Regional Economic Outlook: Middle East and Central Asia*, Washington, DC

International Monetary Fund (IMF), April 2009b, *Lebanon: 2009 Article IV Consultation and Assessment of Performance under the Program Supported by Emergency Post-conflict Assistance*, Report 09/131

International Monetary Fund (IMF) Staff Report, February 2009, *Syrian Arab Republic: 2008 Article IV Consultation*, Country Report 09/55

International Monetary Fund (IMF), 2010, *Lebanon: Article IV Consultation Mission Concluding Statement*, June 9

Iqbal, Zamir, and Mirakhor, Abbas, July 1999, "Progress and Challenges of Islamic Banking," *Thunderbird International Business Review*, v. 41, pp. 4–5

Ismail, Salwa, 2009, Changing social structure, shifting alliances and authoritarianism in Syria, in Fred H. Lawson, ed., *Demystifying Syria*, 13–28, London, Saqi Books

Jabar, Faleh A., Summer 2000, "Shaykhs and ideologues: Detribalization and retribalization in Iraq, 1968–1998," *Middle East Report*, v. 215

Jane's Sentinel Security Assessment – Eastern Mediterranean, 2009, July 2, 2009, Country Report, Lebanon

Jang, Ji-Hyang, 2005, *Taming Political Islamists by Islamic Capital*, PhD dissertation, The University of Texas at Austin, available at http://repositories.lib.utexas.edu/handle/2152/1942

Javedanfar, Meir, February 9, 2009, quoted in Lionel Laurent, "Israel: Don't mention the economy," *Forbes*

Kabbani, Nader, and Noura Kamel, 2009, Tapping into the Economic Potential of Young Syrians During a Time of Transition, in T. Yousef and N. Dhillon, eds., *Generation in Waiting: The Unfulfilled Promise of Young People in the Middle East*, Washington, DC, Brookings Institution Press

Kapiszewski, Andrzej, March 16–20, 2005, Elections and Parliamentary Activity in the GCC States, paper delivered to the Sixth Mediterranean Social and Political Research Meeting of the Robert Schumann Centre of the European University Institute, Florence

Karawan, Ibrahim, 1996, Egypt, in Constantine P. Danopolous and Cynthia Watson, *The Political Role of the Military: An International Handbook*, pp. 107–22, Westport, Connecticut, Greenwood Press

Karl, Terry Lynn, 1997, *The Paradox of Plenty: Oil Booms and Petro-States*, Berkeley, University of California Press

Kasaba, Resat, 2008, Introduction, in Resat Kasaba, ed., *The Cambridge History of Turkey*, v. 4, pp. 1–12, Cambridge, UK, Cambridge University Press

Kelly, John, and Bruce Etling, February 12, 2009, *Mapping Change in the Iranian Blogosphere*, Berkman Center, Harvard University, available at http://blogs.law.harvard.edu/idblog/2009/02/12/mapping-change-in-the-iranian-blogosphere/

Kerr, Simeon, May 19, 2009a, "Dissenters upstage ruler's court for Dubai investors," *Financial Times*, p. 7

Kerr, Simeon, May 19, 2009b, "Concern rises as emirate demotes finance director," *Financial Times*, p. 7

Kerr, Simeon, May 12, 2009c, "Dubai developer resorts to state funds," *Financial Times*, p. 17

Khalaf, Abdulhadi, and Giacomo Luciani, 2008, *Constitutional Reform and Political Participation in the Gulf*, Dubai, Gulf Research Center

Kheir-El-Din, Hanaa, 2008, *The Egyptian Economy: Current Challenges and Future Prospects*, New York, The American University of Cairo Press

Kheir-El-Din, Hanaa, and Hoda El-Sayed, September 1997, *Potential Impact of a Free Trade Agreement with the EU on Egypt's Textile Industry*, Cairo, Egyptian Center for Economic Studies

Kingdom Holding, 2000, Annual Report

Kostiner, Joseph, ed., 2000, *Middle East Monarchies: The Challenge of Modernity*, Boulder, Colorado, Lynne Rienner

Kukis, Mark, May 23, 2009, "How the economy could crush Iraq's Hopes," *Time*, available at www.time.com/time/printout/0,8816,1899880,00.html

Kurtz, Marcus J., and Andrew Schrank, May 2007, "Growth and governance: Models, measures, and mechanisms," *Journal of Politics*, v. 69, no. 2, pp. 563–9

Lacey, Robert, 2009, *Inside the Kingdom: Kings, Clerics, Modernists, Terrorists, and the Struggle for Saudi Arabia*, New York, Viking

Lahlou, Kamal, March 27, 2010, "Un capitalism d'avenir," *Challenge* (Casablanca)

Lamloum, O., 2006, Tunisie : quelle transition démocratique? in Jean-Noël, Ferrié, Jean-Claude Santucci, eds., *Dispositifs de démocratisation et dispositifs autoritaires en Afrique du Nord*, Aix-en-Provence, Edition CNRS, 121–47

Lawson, Fred, 1992, Divergent modes of economic liberalization in Syria and Iraq, in Ilya Harik and Denis J. Sullivan, eds., *Privatization and Liberalization in the Middle East*, pp. 123–44, Bloomington, Indiana University Press

Lawson, Fred H., ed., 2009, *Demystifying Syria*, London, Saqi Books

Lesch, Ann Mosely, 1996, The destruction of civil society in the Sudan, in A. Richard Norton, ed., *Civil Society in the Middle East*, Leiden, E. J. Brill

Leveau, Rémy, 1985, *Le fellah marocain défenseur du trône*, 2nd edn., Paris, Fondation Nationale des Sciences Politiques

Lindsey, Ursula, August 5, 2009, "Morocco suppresses poll despite favorable results for king," *Christian Science Monitor*, available at http://www.csmonitor.com/World/Middle-East/2009/0805/p06s07-wome.html

Lippman, Thomas W., 2009a, Cooperation under the radar: The U.S.-Saudi Arabian Joint Commission for Economic Cooperation (JECOR), in *The*

Kingdom of Saudi Arabia, 1979–2009: Evolution of a Pivotal State, pp. 71–5, Washington, DC, The Middle East Institute

Lippman, Thomas W., 2009b, *Sand Trap inside the Mirage: America's Fragile Partnership with Saudi Arabia*, Boulder, Colorado, Westview

Liverani, Andrea, 2008, *Civil Society in Algeria: The Political Functions of Associational Life*, London, Routledge

Looney, Robert, First Quarter 2006, "The Iranian economy: Crony capitalism in Islamic garb," *Milken Institute Review*, pp. 29–37

Looney, Robert, March 2007a, "Beyond the Iraq Study Group: The elusive goal of sustained growth," *Strategic Insights*, v. 6, no. 2, available at www.ccc.nps.navy.mil/si/2007/Mar/looney/Mar07.asp

Looney, Robert, 2007b, "The re-emergence of Iranian petro-populism," *Gulf Yearbook 2006–2007*, pp. 417–27, Dubai, Gulf Research Center

Lopez-Claros, Augusto, Michael E. Porter, and Klaus Schwab, 2005, *The Global Competitiveness Report 2004–2005*, World Economic Forum

Lowi, Miriam R., 2009, *Oil Wealth and the Poverty of Politics*, New York, Cambridge University Press

Lucas, Russell E., 2005, *Institutions and the Politics of Survival in Jordan: Domestic Responses to External Challenges, 1988–2001*, Albany, The State University of New York Press

Luciani, Giacomo, 2005, From Private Sector to National Bourgeoisie: Saudi Arabian Business, in Paul Aarts and Gerd Nonneman, eds., *Saudi Arabia in the Balance: Political Economy, Society, Foreign Affairs*, pp. 144–81, New York, New York University Press

Luciani, Giacomo, 2007a, The GCC refining and petrochemical industries in global perspective, in Eckart Woertz, ed., *Gulf Geo-Economics*, pp. 165–98, Dubai, Gulf Research Center

Luciani, Giacomo, 2007b, Economic and political reform in the Middle East, in Oliver Schlumberger, ed., *Debating Arab Authoritarianism: Dynamics and Durability in Nondemocratic Regimes*, Stanford, Stanford University Press

Lustick, Ian S., 1999, Hegemony and the riddle of nationalism, in Leonard Binder, ed., *Ethnic Conflict and International Politics in the Middle East*, Gainesville, University Press of Florida

Mahdavy, Hussein, 1970, The patterns and problems of economic development in rentier states: The case of Iran, in M. Cook, ed., *Studies in Economic History of the Middle East*, London, Oxford University Press

Mahdi, Kamil A., 2009, *Oil and Oil Policy in Iraq*, London, Pluto Press

Mahdi, Kamil A., Anna Wurth, and Helen Lackner, 2007, *Yemen into the Twenty-first Century: Continuity and Change*, Reading, Ithaca Press

Mahroug, Moncef, July 1996, "Champions, menaces et condammés," *Jeune Afrique* v. 1853, p. 91

Makdisi, Samir, 2004, *The Lessons of Lebanon. The Economics of War and Development*, London, I. B. Tauris

Malley, Mohammed, 2004, Jordan: A case study of the relationship between Islamic finance and Islamist politics, in Clement M. Henry and Rodney Wilson, eds., *The Politics of Islamic Finance*, pp. 191–215, Edinburgh, Scotland, Edinburgh University Press

Marcel, Valerie, 2006, *Oil Titans: National Oil Companies in the Middle East* Washington, DC, Brookings Institution Press

Marshall, Shana, Summer 2009, "Syria and the Financial Crisis: Prospects for Reform?" *Middle East Policy*, v. 16, no. 2, pp. 106–15.

Mattina, Todd, and Aliona Cebotari, December 2007, "Focusing fiscal adjustment on relatively inefficient spending," in *Arab Republic of Egypt – Selected Issues*, Country Report 07/381, p. 38, available at http://www.imf.org/external/pubs/ft/scr/2007/cr07381.pdf

Meyer, Guenter, 2001, *Survival of Small-scale Manufacturing in Cairo during Structural Adjustment: Results from a Long-term Study*, Economic Research Forum for the Arab Countries, Iran and Turkey, Working Paper 2021

The Middle East Institute, 2009, *The Kingdom of Saudi Arabia, 1979–2009: Evolution of a Pivotal State*, Washington, DC

Monroe, Elizabeth, 1981, *Britain's Moment in the Middle East, 1914–1971*, rev. edn., Baltimore, The Johns Hopkins University Press

Montety, Henri de, [1940] 1973, Old families and new elites in Tunisia, in I. William Zartman, ed., *Man, State, and Society in the Contemporary Maghrib*, pp. 171–80, New York, Praeger

"The Monthly meets former Minister of Finance George Corm," February 2009, *The Monthly*, Beirut, issue 79, pp. 42–3, available at http://www.georgescorm.com/personal/download.php?file=the-monthly-english.pdf

Moore, Clement Henry, 1970, *Politics in North Africa*, Boston, Little, Brown

Moore, Clement Henry, 1994, *Images of Development: Egyptian Engineers in Search of Industry*, 2nd edn., Cairo, The American University in Cairo Press

Moore, Pete W., September 2009, "Making money on Iraq," *Middle East Report*, available at www.merip.org./mer/mer252/moore.html

Morocco, Institut Royal des Etudes Stratégiques (IRES), May 2009, *Le Maroc face à la crise économique et financière mondiale: Enjeux et orientations de politiques publiques*, available at www.ires.ma/spip.php?article634

Mostafa, Hadia, June 1997, "Pennies from heaven," *Business Today*, pp. 52–8

Moustafa, Tamir, 2007, *The Struggle for Constitutional Power: Law, Politics, and Economic Development in Egypt*, New York, Cambridge University Press

Murphy, Emma C., 1999, *Economic and Political Change in Tunisia: From Bourguiba to Ben Ali*, New York, St. Martin's Press

Myntti, Cynthia, 1999, *Paris along the Nile: Architecture in Cairo from the Belle Epoque*, Cairo, The American University in Cairo Press

Naim, Moises, Spring 2000, "Washington Consensus or Washington Confusion?" *Foreign Policy*, pp. 87–103

Nashashibi, Karim, Patricia Alonso-Gamo, Stefania Bazzoni, Alain Féler, Nicole Laframboise, and Sebastian Paris Horvitz, 1998, *Algeria: Stabilization and Transition to the Market*, IMF occasional paper 165, Washington, DC

Nasr, Sherine, July 2–8, 2009, "Big efforts for small industries," *Al Ahram Weekly*, no. 954, available at weekly.ahram.org.eg/2009/954/ec3.htm

Niblock, Tim, with Mona Malik, 2007, *The Political Economy of Saudi Arabia*, London, Routledge

Nitzan, Jonathan, and Shimshon Bichler, 2002, *The Global Political Economy of Israel*, London, Pluto Press

Nitzan, Jonathan, and Shimshon Bichler, 2009, *Capital as Power: A Study of Order and Creorder*, London, Routledge

Noland, Marcus, and Howard Pack, April 2007, *The Arab Economies in a Changing World*, Washington, DC, Peterson Institute

Nuomani, Farhad, and Sohrab Behad, 2006, *Class and Labor in Iran: Did the Revolution Matter?* Syracuse, New York, Syracuse University Press

O'Driscoll, Gerald P., Jr., Kim R. Holmes, and Melanie Kirkpatrick, 2000, *2000 Index of Economic Freedom*, Washington, DC, The Heritage Foundation

Onis, Ziya, 2006, "Varieties and crises of neoliberal globalisation: Argentina, Turkey and the IMF," *Third World Quarterly*, v. 27, no. 2, pp. 239–63

Onis, Ziya, March 2009, "Conservative globalism at the crossroads: the Justice and Development Party and the thorny path to democratic consolidation in Turkey," *Mediterranean Politics*, v. 14, no. 1, pp. 21–40

Onis, Ziya, and Caner Bakir, June 2007, "Turkey's political economy in the age of financial globalization: The significance of the EU Anchor," *South European Society and Politics*, v. 12, no. 2, pp. 147–64

OPEC (Organization of Petroleum Exporting Countries), 2008, *Statistical Bulletin*, available at www.opec.org/library/Annual%20Statistical%20Bulletin/interactive/2008/FileZ/Main.htm (retrieved November 6, 2009)

Owen, Roger, 2004, *State, Power, and Politics*, 3rd edn., London, Routledge

Owen, Roger, and Sevket Pamuk, 1998, *A History of Middle East Economics in the Twentieth Century*, London, I. B. Tauris

Osmanoglu, Berrin, March 2009, *The Political Character of Islamic Businessmen in Turkey*, paper delivered to the Tenth Mediterranean Research Meeting, European University Institute, Florence

Ozcan, Kivilcim Metin, and Nur Sevim Kafali, September 2007, *The Structure of the Turkish Banking Sector after the 2000–2001 Crisis: An Empirical Investigation*, Cairo, Economic Research Forum, Working Paper 709

Paroush, Jacob, 2007, Banking supervision in Israel, in Nissan Liviatan and Haim Barkai, eds., *The Bank of Israel: Selected Topics in Israel's Monetary Policy*, v. 2, pp. 130–9, Oxford, UK, Oxford University Press

Patton, Marcie J., January–June 1999, "Open for Business: Capitalists and Globalization in Turkey and Morocco," *CEMOTI (Cahiers d'études sur la Méditerranée Orientale et le monde Turco-Iranien)*, 27, pp. 195–212

Pavel, Tal, November 4, 2009, "On line social networks in Syria," *Tel Aviv Notes*, Tel Aviv University, Israel, Tel Aviv University Notes [TAUNOTES-L@LISTSERV.TAU.AC.IL]

Perthes, Volker, 1997, *The Political Economy of Syria under Asad*, London, I. B. Tauris

Pesaran, M. Hashem, October 19, 2009, private communication to authors

Phillips, Sarah, February 2007, *Evaluating Political Reform in Yemen*, Carnegie Papers, Number 80, Washington, DC

Piro, Timothy L. J., 1998, *The Political Economy of Market Reforms in Jordan*, London, Rowman and Littlefield

Plessner, Yakir, 1994, *The Political Economy of Israel: From Ideology to Stagnation*, Albany, State University of New York Press

Profil Pay Liban, January 2005, Institute de La Mediterranee, FEMISE, Marseille, and Cairo, Economic Research Forum, available at http://www.erf.org.eg/cms.php?id=NEW_publication_details_reports&publication_id=937

Przeworski, Adam, Michael Alvarez, José Antonio Cheibub, and Fernando Limongi, 1996, "What makes democracies endure?" *Journal of Democracy*, v. 7, no. 1, pp. 39–55

Qandil, Abdel Halim, 2008, *Al-Ayyam al-Akhira*, Cairo, Dar Ath-Thaqafa al-Jadida

Quandt, William B., 1998, *Between Ballots and Bullets: Algeria's Transition from Authoritarianism*, Washington, DC, Brookings Institution Press

Rady, Faiza, May 29–June 4, 2008, "A credible alternative," *Al Ahram Weekly*, no. 899

Ramadan, Tariq, 2000, *Islam, the West, and Challenges of Modernity*, Leicester, UK, Islamic Foundation

Raphaeli, Nimrod, June 2007, "Syria's fragile economy," *Middle East Review of International Affairs*, v. 11, no. 2, pp. 34–51

Raphaeli, Nimrod, and Bianca Gersten, May 28, 2008, "The economic dimensions of Syria's strategic relations with Iran," *The Middle East Media Research Institute, Inquiry and Analysis*, available at http://www.memri.org/report/en/0/0/0/0/0/0/2681.htm

"Réorganisation des holdings SNI et ONA," April 2, 2010, SNI-ONA Communiqué of March 25, *L'Economiste* (Casablanca)

Reporters without Borders (RSF), 2009, *Press Freedom Index 2009*, available at www.rsf.org/en-classement1003–2009.html (retrieved November 14, 2009)

Richards, Alan, and John Waterbury, 2008, *Political Economy of the Middle East*, 3rd edn., Boulder, Colorado, Westview

Rivlin, Paul, March 2000, "Trade potential in the Middle East: Some optimistic findings," *Middle East Review of International Affairs*, v. 4, no. 1, (July 26) available at www.biu.ac.il/SOC/besa/meria/journal/2000/issue1/jv4n1a6.html

Rivlin, Paul, 2009, *Arab Economies in the Twenty-First Century*, New York, Cambridge University Press

The Road Ahead for Turkey, August 2005, Cairo, Economic Research Forum, FEMISE Coordinators, available at http://www.erf.org.eg/cms.php?id=NEW_publication_details_report&publication_id=835

Roberts, Hugh, 1994, Doctrinaire Economics and Political Opportunism in the Strategy of Algerian Islamism, in John Ruedy, ed., *Islam and Secularism in North Africa*, pp. 123–47, New York, St. Martin's Press

Rocard, Michel, ed., 1999, *Strengthening Palestinian Institutions*, Washington, DC, Brookings Institution Press

Rodrik, Dani, July 2008, "Spence christens a new Washington Consensus," *Economists' Voice*, v. 5, no. 3, article 4, available at www.bepress.com/ev/vol5/iss3/art4/ (retrieved November 6, 2009)

Rogowski, Ronald, 1989, *Commerce and Coalitions: How Trade Affects Domestic Political Alignments*, Princeton, New Jersey, Princeton University Press

Ross, Michael L., January 1999, "The political economy of the resource curse," *World Politics*, v. 51, pp. 297–322

Ross, Michael L., February 2008, "Oil, Islam, and women," *American Political Science Review*, v. 102, no. 1, pp. 107–23

Ross, Michael L., March 2, 2009, Oil and Democracy Revisited, University of California at Los Angeles, online draft, available at http://www.sscnet.ucla.edu/polisci/faculty/ross/Oil%20and%20Democracy%20Revisited.pdf

Roy, Sara, Spring 1999, "De-development revisited: Palestinian economy and society since Oslo," *Journal of Palestine Studies*, v. 28, no. 3, pp. 64–82

Ruedy, John Douglas, 2005, *Modern Algeria: The Origins and Development of a Nation*, Bloomington, Indiana University Press

Rutherford, Bruce K., 2008, *Egypt after Mubarak: Liberalism, Islam, and Democracy in the Arab World*, Princeton, New Jersey, Princeton University Press

Ryan, Curtis R., October 1998, "Peace, Bread and Riots: Jordan and the IMF" *Middle East Policy*, 60, 54–66

Saaf, Abdallah, 2010, *La transition au Maroc: le purgatoire*, Rabat. Morocco, Editions du CERSS

Sachs, Jeffrey, Spring 1998, "International economics: Unlocking the mysteries of globalization," *Foreign Policy*, pp. 97–111

Sachs, Jeffrey, and Andrew Warner, 1995, Economic reform and the process of global integration, in William C. Brainard and George L. Perry, *Brookings Papers on Economic Activity*, v. I, pp. 1–117, Washington, DC, Brookings Institution Press

Said, Mona, 2009, The fall and rise of earnings and inequality in Egypt, in Ragui Assaad, ed., *The Egyptian Labor Market Revisited*, pp. 53–77, Cairo, The American University in Cairo Press

Sakr, Naomi, 2001, *Satellite Realms: Transnational Television, Globalization and the Middle East*, London, I. B. Tauris

Salamé, Ghassan, 1990, "Strong" and "Weak" States: A Qualified Return to the Muqaddimah, in Giacomo Luciani, ed., *The Arab State*, pp. 29–64, Berkeley, University of California Press

Saleem, Muhammad, 2006, *Islamic Banking: A Charade – Call for Enlightenment*, booksurge.com

Salehi-Isfahani, Djavid, Spring 1999, "Labor and the challenge of economic restructuring in Iran," *Middle East Report*, pp. 34–7

Salehi-Isfahani, Djavad, 2009, "Poverty, inequality, and populist politics in Iran," *Journal of Economic Inequality* v. 7, pp. 5–28

Salem, Eli, 1973, *Modernization without Revolution*, Bloomington, University of Indiana Press

Salloukh, Bassel, March 2007, *Opposition under Authoritarianism: The Case of Lebanon under Syria*, paper delivered to the Mediterranean Research Meeting, European University Institute

Sater, James N., 2010, *Morocco: Challenges to Tradition and Modernity*, Abingdon, Oxon, and New York, Routledge

Saudi American Bank (SAMBA), 2009, *Saudi Arabia: 2009 Mid-Year Economic Review and Forecast, June*, available at https://dxb.samba.com/GblDocs/SaudiArabia_2009_Midyear_Review_And_Forecast_Eng.pdf

Saudi Arabian Monetary Agency (SAMA), 1999, *Thirty-Fifth Annual Report 1420H (1999G)*, Riyadh, Research and Statistics Department

Saudi Arabian Monetary Agency (SAMA), 2009, *Forty-Fifth Annual Report 1430H (2009G)*, Riyadh, Research and Statistics Department

Saul, Samir, 1997, *La France et l'Egypte de 1882 à 1914 – intérêts économiques et implications politiques*, Paris, Ministère de l'Economie, des Finances, et de l'Industrie

Sayan, Serdar, ed., 2009, *Economic Performance in the Middle East and North Africa: Institutions, Corruption and Reform*, London, Routledge

Sayigh, Yezid, October 2009, *Fixing Broken Windows: Security Sector Reform in Palestine, Lebanon, and Yemen*, Washington, DC, Carnegie Endowment, Carnegie Papers, 17

Selim, Tarek H., December 2006, *On Efficient Use of Egypt's Energy Resources: Oil and Gas*, Cairo, Egyptian Center for Economic Studies, Working Paper 117

Senor, Dan, and Saul Singer, 2009, *Start-up Nation: The Story of Israel's Economic Miracle*, New York, Time Warner Paperbacks

Setser, Brad, and Rachael Ziembar, January 2009, *GCC Sovereign Funds: Reversal of Fortune*, Council on Foreign Relations, Center for Geoeconomic Studies, Working Paper

Sfakianakis, John, 2004, The whales of the Nile: Networks, businessmen and bureaucrats during the era of privatization in Egypt, in Stephen Heydemann, ed., *Networks of Privilege in the Middle East: The Politics of Economic Reform*, pp. 77–100, New York, Palgrave Macmillan

Sfakianakis, John, March 22–26, 2006, Saudi Arabia and the WTO, paper delivered to the Seventh Mediterranean Social and Political Research Meeting, Robert Schuman Centre for Advanced Studies of the European University Institute, Florence

Sfakianakis, John, Turki al Hugail, and Daliah Merzaban, October 15, 2009, *Prudent Overspending: Saudi State Spending and Signs of Recovery*, Riyadh, Banque Saudi Fransi

Shehata, Samer, March 2006, Campaigning with Munir: Voting Behavior in Egyptian Parliamentary Elections, paper delivered to the Seventh Mediterranean Social and Political Research Meeting, Robert Schuman Centre for Advanced Studies of the European University Institute, Florence

Siddiqa, Ayesha, 2007, *Military Inc.: Inside Pakistan's Military Economy*, London, Pluto Press

SIGIR, April 30, 2009, "Special Inspector General for Iraq Reconstruction," *Quarterly Report to the United States Congress*, pp. 101–3

Siino, François, 2004, *Science et pouvoir dans la Tunisie contemporaine*, Paris, Editions Karthala, and Aix-en-Provence, IREMAM

Skinner, Anthony, May 2008, "Turkey's darkest shadow," *The Middle East*, pp. 21–3

Skinner, Anthony, June 10, 2009, "In the premier division, but for how long?" *Financial Times*, p. 4

Smith, Kristin, 2004, The Kuwait Finance House and the Islamization of public life in Kuwait, in Clement M. Henry and Rodney Wilson, eds., *The Politics of Islamic Finance*, pp. 168–90, Edinburgh, Scotland, Edinburgh University Press

Smyth, Gareth, August 9, 2009, Why Iran's Revolutionary Guards Mercilessly Crack Down, available at http://abcnews.go.com/International/story?id=8275677&page=1

SNI-ONA, 2010, Official Communiqué, March 25 ("Mega-fusion SNI-ONA"), available at http://www.leconomiste.com/, Casablanca, Morocco

Snider, Lewis W., 1996, *Growth, Debt, and Politics: Economic Adjustment and the Political Performance of Developing Countries*, Boulder, Colorado, Westview

Soliman, Samer, 2005, *al nizam al qawi wal dawlat al da`ifa: Idarat al azmat al maliyya wal taghyir al siyasi fi `ahd Mubarak (The System of Power and the Weak State: Administration of the Financial Crisis and Political Change in the Mubarak Era)*, Cairo, Dar Merit

Sorensen, Bent E., and Oved Yosha, 2003, "Financial market integration in the Middle East: How big is the peace dividend?" *Israel Economic Review*, v. 2, pp. 1–19

Sorsa, Piritta, April 1999, Algeria – The Real Exchange Rate, Export Diversification, and Trade Protection, IMF Working Paper WP/99/49

Springborg, Robert, 1989, *Mubarak's Egypt: Fragmentation of Political Order*, Boulder and London, Westview

Springborg, Robert, ed., 2007, *Oil and Democracy in Iraq*, London, Saqi Books

Springborg, Robert, ed., 2009, *Development Models in Muslim Contexts: Chinese, "Islamic" and Neo-Liberal Alternatives*, Edinburgh, Scotland, Edinburgh University Press

Standard and Poor's, 2006, *Bank Industry Risk Analysis: Turkey, 31 October*, available at www2.standardandpoors.com/spf/pdf/media/turkey_bank_viewpoint.pdf, pp. 12s/15.

Stiglitz, Joseph E., 2006, *Making Globalization Work*, London, Allen Lane

Stockholm International Peace Research Institute (SIPRI), *Arms Transfer Database*, available at http://www.sipri.org/databases/armstransfers (retrieved June 2009)

Stockholm International Peace Research Institute (SIPRI), *Military Expenditure Database*, available at http://milexdata.sipri.org?result.php4

Stone, Martin, 1998, *The Agony of Algeria*, New York, Columbia University Press

Strauss, Delphine, June 9, 2009, "Policy inertia puts achievements at risk," *Financial Times*, Special Section, p. 1

"Students in Action," December 6–12, 2007, *Al Ahram Weekly*, v. 874, available at http://weekly.ahram.org.eg/2007/874/eg8.htm

Syria, 2009, *Reporters without Borders for Press Freedom*, available at www.rsf.org/en-rapport163-Syria.html

Syria Information on Economic Freedom, 2009, Heritage Foundation, available at http://www.heritage.org/index.Country/Syria.

Syrian Banker '09, 2009, Damascus, Forward Magazine Publications

Takeyh, Ray, 2006, *Hidden Iran: Paradox and Power in the Islamic Republic*, New York, Holt

Thaindian News, September 25, 2008, "More Islamic finance firms in Kuwait than conventional ones," available at www.thaindian.com/newsportal/world-news/more-islamic-finance-firms-in-kuwait-than-conventional-ones_10099654.html#ixzz0YsdKxbTw

Transparency International (TI), 2007, *Global Corruption Report 2007*, Cambridge, UK, Cambridge University Press

Transparency International (TI), 2009, *Global Corruption Report 2009*, Cambridge, UK, Cambridge University Press

Tripp, Charles, 2006, *Islam and the Moral Economy: The Challenge of Capitalism*, Cambridge, UK, Cambridge University Press.

Tripp, Charles, 2007, *A History of Iraq*, 3rd edn., Cambridge, Cambridge University Press

Tsalik, Svetlana, and Anya Schiffrin, 2005, *Covering Oil: A Reporter's Guide to Energy and Development*, Revenue Watch, Open Society Institute

Tugal, Cihan, 2009, *Passive Revolution: Absorbing the Islamic Challenge to Capitalism*, Stanford, Stanford University Press

United Nations Conference on Trade and Development (UNCTAD), 2008, *Handbook of Statistics*

United Nations Development Programme (UNDP), 2005, *Arab Human Development Report 2004: Toward Freedom in the Arab World*, New York, UNDP

United Nations Development Programme (UNDP), 2009a, *Human Development Report 2009*, New York, UNDP

United Nations Development Programme (UNDP), 2009b, *Arab Human Development Report 2009: Challenges to Human Security in the Arab countries*, New York, UNDP

Ünver, H. Akin, April 2009, *Turkey's "Deep-State" and the Ergenekon Conundrum*, The Middle East Institute, Policy Brief No. 23

U.S. Agency for International Development (USAID), July 1993a, *Assessment of the Legislative Sector*, II-47, Cairo, USAID

U.S. Agency for International Development (USAID), 1993b, *Assessment of the Potential for Liberalization and Privatization of the Egyptian Cotton Subsector*, II-3, Cairo, USAID

Utvik, Bjorn Olaf, 2006, *Islamist Economics in Egypt: The Pious Road to Development*, Boulder, Colorado, Lynne Rienner

Valeri, Marc, 2009, *Oman: Politics and Society in the Qaboos State*, New York, Columbia University Press

Vandewalle, Dirk, ed., 2008, *Libya since 1969: Qadhafi's Revolution Revisited*, New York, Palgrave Macmillan

Vayrnen, R., and T. Ohlson, 1986, Egypt: Arms production in the transnational context, in Michael Brzoska and Thomas Ohlson, eds., *Arms Production in the Third World*, pp. 105–24, London, Taylor and Francis

Vitalis, Robert, 1999, "Review of Chaudhry 1997," *International Journal of Middle East Studies*, v. 31, pp. 659–61

Vitalis, Robert, 2007, *America's Kingdom: Mythmaking on the Saudi Oil Frontier*, Stanford, Stanford University Press

Vogel, Frank, and Samuel L. Hayes III, 1998, *Islamic Law and Finance: Religion, Risk and Return*, Boston, Kluwer Law International

Wahish, Niveen, 2009, "A cup half full," *Al Ahram Weekly*, available at http://weekly.ahram.org.eg/print/2009/962/ec2.htm

Waldner, David, 1999, *State Building and Late Development*, Ithaca, New York, Cornell University Press

Warde, Ibrahim, February 1997, "Rating Agencies the New Superpowers?," *Le Monde Diplomatique*, available at http://mondediplo.com/1997/02/17ratingagencies

Warde, Ibrahim, 2010, *Islamic Finance in the Global Economy*, Edinburgh, Scotland, Edinburgh University Press

Waterbury, John, 1970, *Commander of the Faithful: The Moroccan Political Elite – A Study in Segmented Politics*, New York, Columbia University Press

Waterbury, John, 1997, From Social Contracts to Extraction Contracts: The Political Economy of Authoritarianism and Democracy, in John P. Entelis, ed., *Islam, Democracy, and the State in North Africa*, pp. 141–76, Bloomington, Indiana University Press

Wehrey, Frederick, Jerrold D. Green, Brian Nichiporuk, Alireza Nader, Lydia Hansell, Rasool Nafisi, and S. R. Bohandy, 2009, *The Rise of the Pasdaran: Assessing the Domestic Roles of Iran's Islamic Revolutionary Guard Corps*, Santa Monica, The Rand Corporation, National Defense Research Institute

Werenfels, Isabelle, 2007, *Managing Instability in Algeria: Elites and Political Change since 1995*, London, Routledge

Wigglesworth, Robin, Paul Taylor, and Joseph Menn, July 25, 2009, "BlackBerry rogue software leaves sour taste in UAE," *Financial Times*, p. 7

Wiktorowicz, Quintan, Autumn 1999, "The limits of democracy in the Middle East: The case of Jordan," *Middle East Journal*, v. 53, no. 4, pp. 606–20

Williams, Phil, June 2009a, *Criminals, Militias, and Insurgents: Organized Crime in Iraq*, Strategic Studies Institute, U.S. Army War College, available at http://www.strategicstudiesinstitute.army.mil/pubs/display.cfm?pubID=930

Williams, Timothy, August 4, 2009b, "Iraq seeks to keep a more watchful eye on Internet cafes, web sites and books," *New York Times*, p. A4

Williams, Timothy, October 14, 2009c, "Dueling demands in Iraq hinder bid for oil investors," *New York Times*, p. A12.

Williams, Timothy, August 15, 2009d, "Iraqi date farms show decline of economy," *New York Times*, p. A12.

Williamson, John, ed., 1994, *The Political Economy of Reform*, Washington, DC, Institute for International Economics

Wilson, Rodney, 2009a, *The Development of Islamic Finance in the GCC*, Working Paper, Kuwait Programme on Development, Governance and Globalisation in the Gulf States, available at www.lse.ac.uk/collections/LSEKP/documents/Wilson.pdf

Wilson, Rodney, September 14, 2009b, Shari'a Governance for Islamic Financial Institutions, paper presented to conference, Re-Imagining the Shari'a: Theory, Practice and Muslim Pluralism at Play, Warwick in Venice Palazzo

Winters, Jeffrey A., April 1994, "Power and the control of capital," *World Politics*, v. 46, no. 3, pp. 419–52

Woertz, Eckart, 2007, *Gulf Geo-Economics*, Dubai, Gulf Research Center

Woertz, Eckart, December 3, 2009, *Implications of Dubai's Debt Troubles*, Dubai, Gulf Research Center

World Bank, 1991, *Arab Republic of Egypt Cotton and Textile Sector Study*, Washington, DC, World Bank

World Bank, 1997, *World Development Report 1997: The State in a Changing World*, Washington, DC, Oxford University Press

World Bank, 2003, *Better Governance for Development in the Middle East and North Africa: Enhancing Inclusiveness and Accountability*, Washington, DC, World Bank

World Bank, August 13, 2007a, *Country Assistance Strategy Report for Tunisia*, Report No. 38572-TN

World Bank, November 13, 2007b, *Country Assistance Strategy Report for Morocco*, Report No. 41254-MA

World Bank, 2008a, *The Road Not Traveled: Education Reform in the Middle East and Africa*, Washington, DC, World Bank

World Bank, 2008b, *2008 MENA Economic Developments and Prospects: Regional Integration for Global Competitiveness*, Washington, DC, World Bank

World Bank, 2008c, *Doing Business 2009*, Washington, DC, World Bank, available at www.doingbusiness.org/Documents/FullReport/2009/DB_2009_English.pdf

World Bank, 2009a, *Doing Business 2010: Saudi Arabia*, Washington, DC, World Bank, available at www.doingbusiness.org/Documents/CountryProfiles/SAU.pdf

World Bank, 2009b, *From Privilege to Competition: Unlocking private-led growth in the Middle East and North Africa*, Washington, DC, World Bank

World Bank, 2009c, *2009 MENA Economic Development and Prospects: Navigating through the Global Recession*, Washington, DC, World Bank

World Bank, various years, *World Development Indicators*, CD-ROM and Internet database, Washington, DC

World Economic Forum, 2007, *Arab Competitiveness Report 2007*, Coligny (near Geneva), Switzerland, World Economic Forum, available at www.weforum.org/en/initiatives/gcp/Arab%20World%20Competitiveness%20Report/index.htm

World Factbook, Egypt, 2010, U.S. Central Intelligence Agency, available at https://www.cia.gov/library/publications/the-world-factbook/print/eg.html

World Trade Organization, 2005, *Report of the Working Party on the Accession of the Kingdom of Saudi Arabia*, WT/ACC/SAU/61/Add.2 (Nov. 1), available at http://www.wto.org/english/theWTO_e/acc_e/completeacc_e.htm

World Trade Organization, 2008, *Draft Report of the Working Party on the Accession of the Lebanese Republic to the World Trade Organization*, WT/ACC/SPEC/LBN/6 (Oct. 9), available at http://www.economy.gov.lb/NR/rdonlyres/51ED7F34-A5C3-449A-A323-56172C9CB127/0/DraftReportOct2008.pdf

Yavuz, M. Hakan, 2009, *Secularism and Muslim Democracy in Turkey*, Cambridge, UK, Cambridge University Press

Yeşilada, Birol, 1998, The Mediterranean challenge, in John Redmond and Glenda G. Rosenthal, eds., *The Expanding European Union Past, Present, and Future*, pp. 177–93, Boulder, Colorado, Lynne Rienner

Zangeneh, Hamid, October 1998, "The post-revolutionary Iranian Economy: A policy appraisal," *Middle East Policy*, v. 6, no. 2, pp. 120–3, available at http://www.mepc.org/journal_vol6/9810.asp

Zartman, W., ed., 1991, *Tunisia: The Political Economy of Reform*, Boulder, Colorado, Lynne Rienner

Zghal, Abdelkader, 1991, The new strategy of the movement of the Islamic Way: Manipulation or expression of political culture? in I. W. Zartman, ed., *Tunisia: The Political Economy of Reform*, pp. 205–17, Boulder, Colorado, Lynne Rienner

Zisser, Eyal, 2006, *Bashar al-Asad and the First Years in Power*, London, I. B. Tauris

Zoubir, Yahia, ed., 1999, *North Africa in Transition: State, Society, and Economic Transformation in the 1990s*, Gainesville, University Press of Florida

Zuhur, Sherifa, September 2007, *Egypt: Security, Political and Islamist Challenges*, Carlisle, Strategic Studies Institute, U.S. Army War College

Zybertowicz, Andrzej, 2007, Transformation of the Polish secret services: From authoritarian to informal power networks, in Hans Born and Marina Caparini, eds., *Democratic Control of Intelligence Services: Containing Rogue Elephants*, pp. 65–82, Ashgate Publishing

Zysman, John, 1983, *Governments, Markets, and Growth: Financial Systems and the Politics of Industrial Change*, Ithaca, New York, Cornell University Press

Index

AAOIF. *See* Accounting and Auditing
    Organization for Islamic Financial
    Institutions
'awlama, xiii, 12
al Abbar, Muhammad, 238
Abd al Monaim, Ayman, 200–201
Abd al Nur, Munir Fakri, 205
Abdesselam, Belaid, 118–126
Abdullah (king of Jordan), 252
Abdullah (king of Saudi Arabia), 227
Abu Dhabi Investment Council, 241
Abu Dhabi National Oil Company
    (ADNOC), 228
Abu Ghazala, Abd al Halim, 193
Abul Futuh, Abdal Monaim, 203–204
Abu Risha, Abdul Sattar, 153
Accounting and Auditing Organization for
    Islamic Financial Institutions
    (AAOIF), 245
Advanced Technology Investment
    Company, 241
Ahmadinejad, Mahmoud, 69, 261,
    309–310, 320
AKP. *See* Justice and Development Party
Alawi sect, 113, 140–142
al Aziz, Abd (king of Saudi Arabia
    1902–1953), 214
Albaraka Islamic Investment Bank, 245
Alexandria Quartet (Durrell), 1
Algeria
    Army of National Liberation, 117
    bunker state, 116–126
    CIM, 132
    colonialism impact, 117
    deindustrialization, 133
    Front of National Liberation, 117
    IMF economic stabilization, 129–131
    independence, 117–118
    military rule, 125–132
    oil rentier state, 44
    oil revenues, 123, 125
    pharmaceutical sector, 133–134

    private enterprise, 123
    public enterprise, restructuring,
        131–133
    reform and democracy (1989–1991),
        126–133
    reforms from bunker (1994–), 129–135
Algossaibi, Ahma Hamad, and Brothers
    Company, 242
Allegiance Council, Saudi Arabia, 214–215
Al Qaeda of the Islamic Maghrib (AQIM),
    132
Al-Salam (Islamic) bonds, 246
Amer, Abd al Hakim, 193
American-Egyptian Chamber of
    Commerce, 97, 205
AQIM. *See* Al Qaeda of the Islamic
    Maghrib
Arab Bank, 165
Arab Competitiveness Report (World
    Economic Forum), 23
Arab Contractors, 167
Arab Human Development (reports), 67, 73,
    84, 196, 302
Arab International Islamic Bank, 252
Arab-Israeli conflict, 32, 36, 165
Aramco, 4, 228
Arc of Crisis, 165
Arison-Danker Group, 99
arms transfers, 33–36
Army of National Liberation, 117
Aryan, Issamal, 199
al-Asad, Bashar (president of Syria), 141
al-Asad, Hafez, 8, 17, 113, 137, 140
Association of Independent Industrialists
    and Businessmen (MÜSIAD), 280
Association of Moroccan Journalists, 220
Atatürk, Mustafa Kemal, 16
Attijariwafa Bank, 217–218, 225

Baath regime, 137
Badr, Zaki, 195
Badr Brigade, 152